MW01502816

2153B: Implementing a Microsoft® Windows® 2000 Network Infrastructure

www. NHLI.com

ILM:

23BU - A627X - 4Q3E

CRAIG
VASQUEZ

Microsoft®

Course Number: 2153B
Part Number: X09-90430
Released: 03/2002

END-USER LICENSE AGREEMENT FOR MICROSOFT OFFICIAL CURRICULUM COURSEWARE –STUDENT EDITION

PLEASE READ THIS END-USER LICENSE AGREEMENT ("EULA") CAREFULLY. BY USING THE MATERIALS AND/OR USING OR INSTALLING THE SOFTWARE THAT ACCOMPANIES THIS EULA (COLLECTIVELY, THE "LICENSED CONTENT"), YOU AGREE TO THE TERMS OF THIS EULA. IF YOU DO NOT AGREE, DO NOT USE THE LICENSED CONTENT.

1.   **GENERAL.** This EULA is a legal agreement between you (either an individual or a single entity) and Microsoft Corporation ("Microsoft"). This EULA governs the Licensed Content, which includes computer software (including online and electronic documentation), training materials, and any other associated media and printed materials. This EULA applies to updates, supplements, add-on components, and Internet-based services components of the Licensed Content that Microsoft may provide or make available to you unless Microsoft provides other terms with the update, supplement, add-on component, or Internet-based services component. Microsoft reserves the right to discontinue any Internet-based services provided to you or made available to you through the use of the Licensed Content. This EULA also governs any product support services relating to the Licensed Content except as may be included in another agreement between you and Microsoft. An amendment or addendum to this EULA may accompany the Licensed Content.

2.   **GENERAL GRANT OF LICENSE.** Microsoft grants you the following rights, conditioned on your compliance with all the terms and conditions of this EULA. Microsoft grants you a limited, non-exclusive, royalty-free license to install and use the Licensed Content solely in conjunction with your participation as a student in an Authorized Training Session (as defined below). You may install and use one copy of the software on a single computer, device, workstation, terminal, or other digital electronic or analog device ("Device"). You may make a second copy of the software and install it on a portable Device for the exclusive use of the person who is the primary user of the first copy of the software. A license for the software may not be shared for use by multiple end users. An "Authorized Training Session" means a training session conducted at a Microsoft Certified Technical Education Center, an IT Academy, via a Microsoft Certified Partner, or such other entity as Microsoft may designate from time to time in writing, by a Microsoft Certified Trainer (for more information on these entities, please visit www.microsoft.com). WITHOUT LIMITING THE FOREGOING, COPYING OR REPRODUCTION OF THE LICENSED CONTENT TO ANY SERVER OR LOCATION FOR FURTHER REPRODUCTION OR REDISTRIBUTION IS EXPRESSLY PROHIBITED.

3.   **DESCRIPTION OF OTHER RIGHTS AND LICENSE LIMITATIONS**

        3.1   *Use of Documentation and Printed Training Materials.*

                3.1.1   The documents and related graphics included in the Licensed Content may include technical inaccuracies or typographical errors. Changes are periodically made to the content. Microsoft may make improvements and/or changes in any of the components of the Licensed Content at any time without notice. The names of companies, products, people, characters and/or data mentioned in the Licensed Content may be fictitious and are in no way intended to represent any real individual, company, product or event, unless otherwise noted.

                3.1.2   Microsoft grants you the right to reproduce portions of documents (such as student workbooks, white papers, press releases, datasheets and FAQs) (the "Documents") provided with the Licensed Content. You may not print any book (either electronic or print version) in its entirety. If you choose to reproduce Documents, you agree that: (a) use of such printed Documents will be solely in conjunction with your personal training use; (b) the Documents will not republished or posted on any network computer or broadcast in any media; (c) any reproduction will include either the Document's original copyright notice or a copyright notice to Microsoft's benefit substantially in the format provided below; and (d) to comply with all terms and conditions of this EULA. In addition, no modifications may made to any Document.

                Form of Notice:

                © 2000. Reprinted with permission by Microsoft Corporation. All rights reserved.

                Microsoft and Windows are either registered trademarks or trademarks of Microsoft Corporation in the US and/or other countries. Other product and company names mentioned herein may be the trademarks of their respective owners.

        3.2   *Use of Media Elements.* The Licensed Content may include certain photographs, clip art, animations, sounds, music, and video clips (together "Media Elements"). You may not modify these Media Elements.

        3.3   *Use of Sample Code.* In the event that the Licensed Content includes sample code in source or object format ("Sample Code"), Microsoft grants you a limited, non-exclusive, royalty-free license to use, copy and modify the Sample Code; if you elect to exercise the foregoing rights, you agree to comply with all other terms and conditions of this EULA, including without limitation Sections 3.4, 3.5, and 6.

        3.4   *Permitted Modifications.* In the event that you exercise any rights provided under this EULA to create modifications of the Licensed Content, you agree that any such modifications: (a) will not be used for providing training where a fee is charged in public or private classes; (b) indemnify, hold harmless, and defend Microsoft from and against any claims or lawsuits, including attorneys' fees, which arise from or result from your use of any modified version of the Licensed Content; and (c) not to transfer or assign any rights to any modified version of the Licensed Content to any third party without the express written permission of Microsoft.

3.5   *Reproduction/Redistribution Licensed Content.* Except as expressly provided in this EULA, you may not reproduce or distribute the Licensed Content or any portion thereof (including any permitted modifications) to any third parties without the express written permission of Microsoft.

4.   **RESERVATION OF RIGHTS AND OWNERSHIP.** Microsoft reserves all rights not expressly granted to you in this EULA. The Licensed Content is protected by copyright and other intellectual property laws and treaties. Microsoft or its suppliers own the title, copyright, and other intellectual property rights in the Licensed Content. You may not remove or obscure any copyright, trademark or patent notices that appear on the Licensed Content, or any components thereof, as delivered to you. **The Licensed Content is licensed, not sold.**

5.   **LIMITATIONS ON REVERSE ENGINEERING, DECOMPILATION, AND DISASSEMBLY.** You may not reverse engineer, decompile, or disassemble the Software or Media Elements, except and only to the extent that such activity is expressly permitted by applicable law notwithstanding this limitation.

6.   **LIMITATIONS ON SALE, RENTAL, ETC. AND CERTAIN ASSIGNMENTS.** You may not provide commercial hosting services with, sell, rent, lease, lend, sublicense, or assign copies of the Licensed Content, or any portion thereof (including any permitted modifications thereof) on a stand-alone basis or as part of any collection, product or service.

7.   **CONSENT TO USE OF DATA.** You agree that Microsoft and its affiliates may collect and use technical information gathered as part of the product support services provided to you, if any, related to the Licensed Content. Microsoft may use this information solely to improve our products or to provide customized services or technologies to you and will not disclose this information in a form that personally identifies you.

8.   **LINKS TO THIRD PARTY SITES.** You may link to third party sites through the use of the Licensed Content. The third party sites are not under the control of Microsoft, and Microsoft is not responsible for the contents of any third party sites, any links contained in third party sites, or any changes or updates to third party sites. Microsoft is not responsible for webcasting or any other form of transmission received from any third party sites. Microsoft is providing these links to third party sites to you only as a convenience, and the inclusion of any link does not imply an endorsement by Microsoft of the third party site.

9.   **ADDITIONAL LICENSED CONTENT/SERVICES.** This EULA applies to updates, supplements, add-on components, or Internet-based services components, of the Licensed Content that Microsoft may provide to you or make available to you after the date you obtain your initial copy of the Licensed Content, unless we provide other terms along with the update, supplement, add-on component, or Internet-based services component. Microsoft reserves the right to discontinue any Internet-based services provided to you or made available to you through the use of the Licensed Content.

10.   **U.S. GOVERNMENT LICENSE RIGHTS**. All software provided to the U.S. Government pursuant to solicitations issued on or after December 1, 1995 is provided with the commercial license rights and restrictions described elsewhere herein. All software provided to the U.S. Government pursuant to solicitations issued prior to December 1, 1995 is provided with "Restricted Rights" as provided for in FAR, 48 CFR 52.227-14 (JUNE 1987) or DFAR, 48 CFR 252.227-7013 (OCT 1988), as applicable.

11.   **EXPORT RESTRICTIONS**. You acknowledge that the Licensed Content is subject to U.S. export jurisdiction. You agree to comply with all applicable international and national laws that apply to the Licensed Content, including the U.S. Export Administration Regulations, as well as end-user, end-use, and destination restrictions issued by U.S. and other governments. For additional information see <http://www.microsoft.com/exporting/>.

12.   **TRANSFER.** The initial user of the Licensed Content may make a one-time permanent transfer of this EULA and Licensed Content to another end user, provided the initial user retains no copies of the Licensed Content. The transfer may not be an indirect transfer, such as a consignment. Prior to the transfer, the end user receiving the Licensed Content must agree to all the EULA terms.

13.   **"NOT FOR RESALE" LICENSED CONTENT.** Licensed Content identified as "Not For Resale" or "NFR," may not be sold or otherwise transferred for value, or used for any purpose other than demonstration, test or evaluation.

14.   **TERMINATION.** Without prejudice to any other rights, Microsoft may terminate this EULA if you fail to comply with the terms and conditions of this EULA. In such event, you must destroy all copies of the Licensed Content and all of its component parts.

15.   <u>**DISCLAIMER OF WARRANTIES.**</u> **TO THE MAXIMUM EXTENT PERMITTED BY APPLICABLE LAW, MICROSOFT AND ITS SUPPLIERS PROVIDE THE LICENSED CONTENT AND SUPPORT SERVICES (IF ANY) *AS IS AND WITH ALL FAULTS,* AND MICROSOFT AND ITS SUPPLIERS HEREBY DISCLAIM ALL OTHER WARRANTIES AND CONDITIONS, WHETHER EXPRESS, IMPLIED OR STATUTORY, INCLUDING, BUT NOT LIMITED TO, ANY (IF ANY) IMPLIED WARRANTIES, DUTIES OR CONDITIONS OF MERCHANTABILITY, OF FITNESS FOR A PARTICULAR PURPOSE, OF RELIABILITY OR AVAILABILITY, OF ACCURACY OR COMPLETENESS OF RESPONSES, OF RESULTS, OF WORKMANLIKE EFFORT, OF LACK OF VIRUSES, AND OF LACK OF NEGLIGENCE, ALL WITH REGARD TO THE LICENSED CONTENT, AND THE PROVISION OF OR FAILURE TO PROVIDE SUPPORT OR OTHER SERVICES, INFORMATION, SOFTWARE, AND RELATED CONTENT THROUGH THE LICENSED CONTENT, OR OTHERWISE ARISING OUT OF THE USE OF THE LICENSED CONTENT. ALSO, THERE IS NO WARRANTY OR CONDITION OF TITLE, QUIET ENJOYMENT, QUIET POSSESSION, CORRESPONDENCE TO DESCRIPTION OR NON-INFRINGEMENT WITH REGARD TO THE LICENSED CONTENT. THE ENTIRE RISK AS TO THE QUALITY, OR ARISING OUT OF THE USE OR PERFORMANCE OF THE LICENSED CONTENT, AND ANY SUPPORT SERVICES, REMAINS WITH YOU.**

16.   <u>**EXCLUSION OF INCIDENTAL, CONSEQUENTIAL AND CERTAIN OTHER DAMAGES.**</u> **TO THE MAXIMUM EXTENT PERMITTED BY APPLICABLE LAW, IN NO EVENT SHALL MICROSOFT OR ITS SUPPLIERS BE LIABLE FOR ANY SPECIAL, INCIDENTAL, PUNITIVE, INDIRECT, OR CONSEQUENTIAL DAMAGES WHATSOEVER (INCLUDING, BUT NOT**

LIMITED TO, DAMAGES FOR LOSS OF PROFITS OR CONFIDENTIAL OR OTHER INFORMATION, FOR BUSINESS INTERRUPTION, FOR PERSONAL INJURY, FOR LOSS OF PRIVACY, FOR FAILURE TO MEET ANY DUTY INCLUDING OF GOOD FAITH OR OF REASONABLE CARE, FOR NEGLIGENCE, AND FOR ANY OTHER PECUNIARY OR OTHER LOSS WHATSOEVER) ARISING OUT OF OR IN ANY WAY RELATED TO THE USE OF OR INABILITY TO USE THE LICENSED CONTENT, THE PROVISION OF OR FAILURE TO PROVIDE SUPPORT OR OTHER SERVICES, INFORMATION, SOFTWARE, AND RELATED CONTENT THROUGH THE LICENSED CONTENT, OR OTHERWISE ARISING OUT OF THE USE OF THE LICENSED CONTENT, OR OTHERWISE UNDER OR IN CONNECTION WITH ANY PROVISION OF THIS EULA, EVEN IN THE EVENT OF THE FAULT, TORT (INCLUDING NEGLIGENCE), MISREPRESENTATION, STRICT LIABILITY, BREACH OF CONTRACT OR BREACH OF WARRANTY OF MICROSOFT OR ANY SUPPLIER, AND EVEN IF MICROSOFT OR ANY SUPPLIER HAS BEEN ADVISED OF THE POSSIBILITY OF SUCH DAMAGES. BECAUSE SOME STATES/JURISDICTIONS DO NOT ALLOW THE EXCLUSION OR LIMITATION OF LIABILITY FOR CONSEQUENTIAL OR INCIDENTAL DAMAGES, THE ABOVE LIMITATION MAY NOT APPLY TO YOU.

17. **LIMITATION OF LIABILITY AND REMEDIES.** NOTWITHSTANDING ANY DAMAGES THAT YOU MIGHT INCUR FOR ANY REASON WHATSOEVER (INCLUDING, WITHOUT LIMITATION, ALL DAMAGES REFERENCED HEREIN AND ALL DIRECT OR GENERAL DAMAGES IN CONTRACT OR ANYTHING ELSE), THE ENTIRE LIABILITY OF MICROSOFT AND ANY OF ITS SUPPLIERS UNDER ANY PROVISION OF THIS EULA AND YOUR EXCLUSIVE REMEDY HEREUNDER SHALL BE LIMITED TO THE GREATER OF THE ACTUAL DAMAGES YOU INCUR IN REASONABLE RELIANCE ON THE LICENSED CONTENT UP TO THE AMOUNT ACTUALLY PAID BY YOU FOR THE LICENSED CONTENT OR US$5.00. THE FOREGOING LIMITATIONS, EXCLUSIONS AND DISCLAIMERS SHALL APPLY TO THE MAXIMUM EXTENT PERMITTED BY APPLICABLE LAW, EVEN IF ANY REMEDY FAILS ITS ESSENTIAL PURPOSE.

18. **APPLICABLE LAW.** If you acquired this Licensed Content in the United States, this EULA is governed by the laws of the State of Washington. If you acquired this Licensed Content in Canada, unless expressly prohibited by local law, this EULA is governed by the laws in force in the Province of Ontario, Canada; and, in respect of any dispute which may arise hereunder, you consent to the jurisdiction of the federal and provincial courts sitting in Toronto, Ontario. If you acquired this Licensed Content in the European Union, Iceland, Norway, or Switzerland, then local law applies. If you acquired this Licensed Content in any other country, then local law may apply.

19. **ENTIRE AGREEMENT; SEVERABILITY.** This EULA (including any addendum or amendment to this EULA which is included with the Licensed Content) are the entire agreement between you and Microsoft relating to the Licensed Content and the support services (if any) and they supersede all prior or contemporaneous oral or written communications, proposals and representations with respect to the Licensed Content or any other subject matter covered by this EULA. To the extent the terms of any Microsoft policies or programs for support services conflict with the terms of this EULA, the terms of this EULA shall control. If any provision of this EULA is held to be void, invalid, unenforceable or illegal, the other provisions shall continue in full force and effect.

Should you have any questions concerning this EULA, or if you desire to contact Microsoft for any reason, please use the address information enclosed in this Licensed Content to contact the Microsoft subsidiary serving your country or visit Microsoft on the World Wide Web at http://www.microsoft.com.

Si vous avez acquis votre Contenu Sous Licence Microsoft au CANADA :

DÉNI DE GARANTIES. Dans la mesure maximale permise par les lois applicables, le Contenu Sous Licence et les services de soutien technique (le cas échéant) sont fournis *TELS QUELS ET AVEC TOUS LES DÉFAUTS* par Microsoft et ses fournisseurs, lesquels par les présentes dénient toutes autres garanties et conditions expresses, implicites ou en vertu de la loi, notamment, mais sans limitation, (le cas échéant) les garanties, devoirs ou conditions implicites de qualité marchande, d'adaptation à une fin usage particulière, de fiabilité ou de disponibilité, d'exactitude ou d'exhaustivité des réponses, des résultats, des efforts déployés selon les règles de l'art, d'absence de virus et d'absence de négligence, le tout à l'égard du Contenu Sous Licence et de la prestation des services de soutien technique ou de l'omission de la 'une telle prestation des services de soutien technique ou à l'égard de la fourniture ou de l'omission de la fourniture de tous autres services, renseignements, Contenus Sous Licence, et contenu qui s'y rapporte grâce au Contenu Sous Licence ou provenant autrement de l'utilisation du Contenu Sous Licence. PAR AILLEURS, IL N'Y A AUCUNE GARANTIE OU CONDITION QUANT AU TITRE DE PROPRIÉTÉ, À LA JOUISSANCE OU LA POSSESSION PAISIBLE, À LA CONCORDANCE À UNE DESCRIPTION NI QUANT À UNE ABSENCE DE CONTREFAÇON CONCERNANT LE CONTENU SOUS LICENCE.

EXCLUSION DES DOMMAGES ACCESSOIRES, INDIRECTS ET DE CERTAINS AUTRES DOMMAGES. DANS LA MESURE MAXIMALE PERMISE PAR LES LOIS APPLICABLES, EN AUCUN CAS MICROSOFT OU SES FOURNISSEURS NE SERONT RESPONSABLES DES DOMMAGES SPÉCIAUX, CONSÉCUTIFS, ACCESSOIRES OU INDIRECTS DE QUELQUE NATURE QUE CE SOIT (NOTAMMENT, LES DOMMAGES À L'ÉGARD DU MANQUE À GAGNER OU DE LA DIVULGATION DE RENSEIGNEMENTS CONFIDENTIELS OU AUTRES, DE LA PERTE D'EXPLOITATION, DE BLESSURES CORPORELLES, DE LA VIOLATION DE LA VIE PRIVÉE, DE L'OMISSION DE REMPLIR TOUT DEVOIR, Y COMPRIS D'AGIR DE BONNE FOI OU D'EXERCER UN SOIN RAISONNABLE, DE LA NÉGLIGENCE ET DE TOUTE AUTRE PERTE PÉCUNIAIRE OU AUTRE PERTE

DE QUELQUE NATURE QUE CE SOIT) SE RAPPORTANT DE QUELQUE MANIÈRE QUE CE SOIT À L'UTILISATION DU CONTENU SOUS LICENCE OU À L'INCAPACITÉ DE S'EN SERVIR, À LA PRESTATION OU À L'OMISSION DE LA 'UNE TELLE PRESTATION DE SERVICES DE SOUTIEN TECHNIQUE OU À LA FOURNITURE OU À L'OMISSION DE LA FOURNITURE DE TOUS AUTRES SERVICES, RENSEIGNEMENTS, CONTENUS SOUS LICENCE, ET CONTENU QUI S'Y RAPPORTE GRÂCE AU CONTENU SOUS LICENCE OU PROVENANT AUTREMENT DE L'UTILISATION DU CONTENU SOUS LICENCE OU AUTREMENT AUX TERMES DE TOUTE DISPOSITION DE LA U PRÉSENTE CONVENTION EULA OU RELATIVEMENT À UNE TELLE DISPOSITION, MÊME EN CAS DE FAUTE, DE DÉLIT CIVIL (Y COMPRIS LA NÉGLIGENCE), DE RESPONSABILITÉ STRICTE, DE VIOLATION DE CONTRAT OU DE VIOLATION DE GARANTIE DE MICROSOFT OU DE TOUT FOURNISSEUR ET MÊME SI MICROSOFT OU TOUT FOURNISSEUR A ÉTÉ AVISÉ DE LA POSSIBILITÉ DE TELS DOMMAGES.

LIMITATION DE RESPONSABILITÉ ET RECOURS. MALGRÉ LES DOMMAGES QUE VOUS PUISSIEZ SUBIR POUR QUELQUE MOTIF QUE CE SOIT (NOTAMMENT, MAIS SANS LIMITATION, TOUS LES DOMMAGES SUSMENTIONNÉS ET TOUS LES DOMMAGES DIRECTS OU GÉNÉRAUX OU AUTRES), LA SEULE RESPONSABILITÉ 'OBLIGATION INTÉGRALE DE MICROSOFT ET DE L'UN OU L'AUTRE DE SES FOURNISSEURS AUX TERMES DE TOUTE DISPOSITION DEU LA PRÉSENTE CONVENTION EULA ET VOTRE RECOURS EXCLUSIF À L'ÉGARD DE TOUT CE QUI PRÉCÈDE SE LIMITE AU PLUS ÉLEVÉ ENTRE LES MONTANTS SUIVANTS : LE MONTANT QUE VOUS AVEZ RÉELLEMENT PAYÉ POUR LE CONTENU SOUS LICENCE OU 5,00 $US. LES LIMITES, EXCLUSIONS ET DÉNIS QUI PRÉCÈDENT (Y COMPRIS LES CLAUSES CI-DESSUS), S'APPLIQUENT DANS LA MESURE MAXIMALE PERMISE PAR LES LOIS APPLICABLES, MÊME SI TOUT RECOURS N'ATTEINT PAS SON BUT ESSENTIEL.

À moins que cela ne soit prohibé par le droit local applicable, la présente Convention est régie par les lois de la province d'Ontario, Canada. Vous consentez Chacune des parties à la présente reconnaît irrévocablement à la compétence des tribunaux fédéraux et provinciaux siégeant à Toronto, dans de la province d'Ontario et consent à instituer tout litige qui pourrait découler de la présente auprès des tribunaux situés dans le district judiciaire de York, province d'Ontario.

Au cas où vous auriez des questions concernant cette licence ou que vous désiriez vous mettre en rapport avec Microsoft pour quelque raison que ce soit, veuillez utiliser l'information contenue dans le Contenu Sous Licence pour contacter la filiale de succursale Microsoft desservant votre pays, dont l'adresse est fournie dans ce produit, ou visitez écrivez à : Microsoft sur le World Wide Web à http://www.microsoft.com

Contents

About This Course

This section provides you with a brief description of the course, audience, suggested prerequisites, and course objectives.

Description

This course is for new-to-product support professionals who will be responsible for installing, configuring, managing, and supporting a network infrastructure that uses the Microsoft® Windows® 2000 Server products. It also provides students with the prerequisite knowledge and skills required for course 2154, *Implementing and Administering Microsoft Windows 2000 Directory Services*. This course also supports those students who are on the Microsoft Certified Systems Engineer (MCSE) Windows 2000 certification track.

The content in this course applies to Windows 2000 Professional, Windows 2000 Server, and Windows 2000 Advanced Server, except as noted within the course.

Audience

This course is intended for new-to-product support professionals who will be responsible for performing the following tasks:

- Configuring the Dynamic Host Configuration Protocol (DHCP) Server service
- Configuring the Domain Name System (DNS) Server service
- Configuring Windows Internet Name Service (WINS)
- Configuring network security by using Public Key Infrastructure (PKI)
- Configuring network security by using Internet Protocol Security (IPSec)
- Configuring remote access to a network
- Supporting remote access to a network
- Integrating extended remote access capabilities by using Internet Authentication Service (IAS)
- Configuring Windows 2000 as a network router
- Configuring Internet access for a network
- Configuring a Web server
- Deploying Windows 2000 Professional by using Remote Installation Services (RIS)
- Managing a Windows 2000 network
- Identifying and resolving network connectivity problems by using Windows 2000 troubleshooting tools and utilities
- Enabling network connectivity among NetWare, Macintosh, and UNIX networks.

Student Prerequisites

This course requires that students meet the following prerequisites:

- Successful completion of course 2152, *Implementing Microsoft Windows 2000 Professional and Server*, or equivalent skills and knowledge, including the ability to:
  - Install or upgrade to Windows 2000
  - Configure the Windows 2000 environment
  - Connect Windows 2000–based client computers to networks
  - Create and manage user accounts
  - Manage access to resources by using groups
  - Manage data by configuring the NTFS file system
  - Provide network access to file resources
  - Configure disks and partitions
  - Monitor and optimize Windows 2000
  - Implement Windows 2000 security
  - Configure printing
  - Configure Windows 2000 for mobile computing
  - Configure and manage disks and partitions
  - Implement disaster protection
  - Install and configure Terminal Services
  - Implement Windows 2000–based client computers
  - Implement Windows 2000–based servers
- An understanding of Transmission Control Protocol/Internet Protocol (TCP/IP)

Course Objectives

At the end of the course, students will be able to:

- Configure the DHCP Server service.
- Configure the DNS Server service.
- Configure WINS; configure network security protocols.
- Configure network security by using PKI.
- Configure network security by using IPSec.
- Configure remote access to a network.
- Support remote access to a network.
- Extend remote access capabilities by using IAS.
- Configure Windows 2000 as a network router.
- Configure Internet access for a network.
- Configure a Web server.
- Deploy Windows 2000 Professional by using RIS.
- Manage a Windows 2000 network.
- Identify and resolve network connectivity problems by using Windows 2000 troubleshooting tools and utilities.
- Enable network connectivity among NetWare, Macintosh, and UNIX networks.

Student Materials Compact Disc Contents

The Student Materials compact disc contains the following files and folders:

- *Default.htm*. This file opens the Student Materials Web page. It provides students with resources pertaining to this course, including additional reading, review and lab answers, lab files, multimedia presentations, and course-related Web sites.

- *Readme.txt*. This file contains a description of the compact disc contents and setup instructions in ASCII format (non–Word document).

- *AddRead*. This folder contains additional reading pertaining to this course.

- *Answers*. This folder contains answers to the module review questions and hands-on labs.

- *Appendix*. This folder contains appendix files for this course.

- *Courses*. This folder contains the self-paced courses that are included with this course.

- *Fonts*. This folder contains fonts that are required to view the PowerPoint presentation and Web-based materials.

- *Labfiles*. This folder contains files that are used in the hands-on labs. These files may be used to prepare the student computers for the hands-on labs.

- *Simulation*. This folder contains files that are used for the simulated labs in this course.

- *Media*. This folder contains files that are used in multimedia presentations for this course. If this course does not include any multimedia presentations, this folder does not appear.

- *Webfiles*. This folder contains the files that are required to view the course Web page. To open the Web page, open Windows Explorer, and in the root directory of the compact disc, double-click **Default.htm**.

- *Wordview*. This folder contains the Word Viewer that is used to view any Word document (.doc) files that are included on the compact disc. If no Word documents are included, this folder does not appear.

Document Conventions

The following conventions are used in course materials to distinguish elements of the text.

Convention	Use
◆	Indicates an introductory page. This symbol appears next to a slide title when additional information on the topic is covered on the page or pages that follow it.
bold	Represents commands, command options, and portions of syntax that must be typed exactly as shown. It also indicates commands on menus and buttons, icons, dialog box titles and options, and icon and menu names.
italic	In syntax statements, indicates placeholders for variable information. Italic is also used for introducing new terms, for book titles, and for emphasis in the text.
Title Capitals	Indicate domain names, user names, computer names, directory names, folders, and file names, except when specifically referring to case-sensitive names. Unless otherwise indicated, you can use lowercase letters when you type a directory name or file name in a dialog box or at a command prompt.
ALL CAPITALS	Indicate the names of keys, key sequences, and key combinations—for example, ALT+SPACEBAR.
monospace	Represents code samples, examples of screen text, or entries that you type at a command prompt or in initialization files.
[ ]	In syntax statements, enclose optional items. For example, [*filename*] in command syntax indicates that you can choose to type a file name with the command. Type only the information within the brackets, not the brackets themselves.
{ }	In syntax statements, enclose required items. Type only the information within the braces, not the braces themselves.
|	In syntax statements, separates an either/or choice.
▶	Indicates a procedure with sequential steps.
...	In syntax statements, specifies that the preceding item may be repeated.
. . .	Represents an omitted portion of a code sample.

Microsoft®
Training &
Certification

Introduction

Introduction

- Name
- Company Affiliation
- Title/Function
- Job Responsibility
- Networking Experience
- Windows 2000 Experience
- Expectations for the Course

Course Materials

- **Name Card**
- **Student Workbook**
- **Student Materials Compact Disc**
- **Course Evaluation**

The following materials are included with your kit:

- *Name card.* Write your name on both sides of the name card.

- *Student workbook.* The student workbook contains the material covered in class, in addition to the hands-on lab exercises.

- *Student Materials compact disc.* The Student Materials compact disc contains the Web page that provides students with links to resources pertaining to this course, including additional readings, review and lab answers, lab files, multimedia presentations, and course-related Web sites.

The Student Materials compact disc also includes the following courses:

- Course 1279C, *Implementing Microsoft Windows Media Services*, is a self-paced course that provides the knowledge and skills necessary to install, configure, and maintain Microsoft® Windows Media™ Services.

- Course 1400A, *Deploying and Customizing Microsoft Internet Explorer 5 Using the Internet Explorer Administration Kit*, is a self-paced, online course that provides the knowledge and skills necessary to customize, deploy, and administer Microsoft Internet Explorer 5 by using the Internet Explorer Administration Kit (IEAK). The course describes product features, installation and configuration procedures, and how to manage the deployed software.

- Course 2000B, *Microsoft Windows 2000: First Look*, is a self-paced course that introduces the structure and features of the Microsoft Windows® 2000 operating systems. The goal of this course is to provide prospective customers with the knowledge necessary to evaluate the advantages and benefits of incorporating Windows 2000 into their business environments. Course content applies to all Windows 2000 operating systems.

Note   To open the Web page, insert the Student Materials compact disc into the CD-ROM drive, and then in the root directory of the compact disc, double-click **Default.htm**.

- *Course evaluation.* To provide feedback on the course, training facility, and instructor, you will have the opportunity to complete an online evaluation near the end of the course.

  To provide additional comments or inquire about the Microsoft Certified Professional program, send e-mail to mcphelp@microsoft.com.

Note   Evaluation copies of Windows 2000 Advanced Server and Windows 2000 Professional are included with this course. You can use these products for evaluation or for your training outside the classroom. Microsoft does not support these evaluation copies of the products.

Prerequisites

- **Complete Course 2152, *Implementing Windows 2000 Professional and Server*, or Equivalent Skills And Knowledge**

- **Understand Transmission Control Protocol/Internet Protocol (TCP/IP)**

This course requires that you meet the following prerequisites:

- Successful completion of course 2152, *Implementing Windows 2000 Professional and Server*, or equivalent skills and knowledge, including the ability to:

  - Install or upgrade to Windows 2000

  - Configure the Windows 2000 environment

  - Connect Windows 2000–based client computers to networks

  - Create and manage user accounts

  - Manage access to resources by using groups

  - Manage data by configuring the NTFS file system

  - Provide network access to file resources

  - Configure and manage disks and partitions

  - Monitor and optimize Windows 2000

  - Implement Windows 2000 security

  - Configure printing

  - Configure Windows 2000 for mobile computing

  - Implement disaster protection

  - Install and configure Terminal Services

  - Implement Windows 2000–based client computers

  - Implement Windows 2000–based servers

- An understanding of Transmission Control Protocol/Internet Protocol (TCP/IP)

Course Outline

- **Module 1: Introduction to the Microsoft Windows 2000 Networking Infrastructure**
- **Module 2: Automating IP Address Assignment by Using DHCP**
- **Module 3: Implementing Name Resolution by Using DNS**
- **Module 4: Implementing Name Resolution by Using WINS**
- **Module 5: Configuring Network Security by Using Public Key Infrastructure**
- **Module 6: Configuring Network Security by Using IPSec**

Module 1, "Introduction to the Microsoft Windows 2000 Networking Infrastructure," presents an overview of the Windows 2000 networking infrastructure and introduces key networking technologies. It starts with an overview of the networking infrastructure. It then describes how to establish Transmission Control Protocol/Internet Protocol (TCP/IP) connectivity and provide network security and support for remote users. It continues by explaining how to publish Web content. It then explains how to manage a Windows 2000 network. The module concludes by listing the non-Microsoft clients and servers that you can connect to a Windows 2000 network. At the end of this module, you will be able to describe the Microsoft Windows 2000 networking infrastructure.

Module 2, "Automating IP Address Assignment by Using DHCP," introduces the Dynamic Host Configuration Protocol (DHCP) and describes how it works on a network. The module begins with an explanation of DHCP. The module continues with an explanation of the requirements for DHCP servers and clients. Next, the module explains how to install the DHCP service. Finally, the module explains how to authorize the DHCP Server service. At the end of this module, you will be able to use DHCP to automate Internet Protocol (IP) address assignment on a network.

Module 3, "Implementing Name Resolution by Using DNS," introduces the Domain Name System (DNS) and describes how it is an integral part of client/server communications in an IP network. The module starts by identifying the two query types, iterative and recursive. It then explains how to install the DNS Server service. Next, it explains how to configure name resolution on client computers. The module then explains how to create and configure DNS zones and how to create a root zone. Finally, the module explains how to maintain and troubleshoot DNS servers. At the end of this module, you will be able to implement name resolution by using DNS.

Module 4, "Implementing Name Resolution by Using WINS," explains how to configure name resolution by using the Windows Internet Name Service (WINS) to support previous versions of Windows, such as Microsoft Windows NT® version 4.0 and Microsoft Windows 98. The module begins by explaining how to connect to network basic input/output system (NetBIOS)–based networks. It then provides an overview of WINS and explains how to configure WINS servers and clients. The module continues by explaining how to configure support for non-WINS clients. It also explains how to enable WINS database replication. Finally, the module concludes by describing maintenance activities on the WINS server database. At the end of this module, you will be able to implement name resolution by using WINS.

Module 5, "Configuring Network Security by Using Public Key Infrastructure," explains how to use the Public Key Infrastructure (PKI) in Windows 2000 to take full advantage of the Windows 2000 security architecture. The module begins by describing PKI. It then explains how to deploy Certificate Services. Next, it explains how to use and manage certificates to provide security. The module then explains how to configure the Active Directory™ directory service for certificates. Finally, the module explains how to troubleshoot Certificate Services. At the end of this module, you will be able to configure network security by using PKI.

Module 6, "Configuring Network Security by Using IPSec," explains how to use Internet Protocol Security (IPSec) to secure private communication over the Internet. The module starts by introducing IPSec. It then explains how to implement IPSec on a network. Next, the module explains how to configure TCP/IP for server functionality. Finally, the module explains how to troubleshoot network protocol security. At the end of this module, you will be able to configure network security by using IPSec.

Course Outline *(continued)*

- **Module 7: Configuring Remote Access**

- **Module 8: Supporting Remote Access to a Network**

- **Module 9: Extending Remote Access Capabilities by Using IAS**

- **Module 10: Configuring a Windows 2000-based Server As a Router**

- **Module 11: Configuring Internet Access for a Network**

- **Module 12: Configuring a Web Server**

Module 7, "Configuring Remote Access," explains how to configure remote access to a Windows 2000 network. The module begins by examining remote access in Windows 2000 and discusses the various remote access protocols that Windows 2000 supports. Next, the module describes multilink connections. Then, the module covers authentication and encryption protocols. Finally, the module covers hardware options for remote access. At the end of this module, you will be able to configure remote access in Windows 2000.

Module 8, "Supporting Remote Access to a Network," explains how to support remote access in Windows 2000. The module begins by explaining remote access policies and how to use them. Next, the module explains the remote access policy evaluation process. Then, the module explains how to create a remote access policy. Finally, the module explains how to troubleshoot remote access policies. At the end of this module, you will be able to support remote access connections to a network.

Module 9, "Extending Remote Access Capabilities by Using IAS," explains how you can use the Internet Authentication Service (IAS) to implement Remote Authentication Dial-In User Service (RADIUS) security on your network. The module first provides an overview of IAS and the functionality that IAS offers. Next, the module covers the installation and configuration of IAS on your network. At the end of this module, you will be able to use IAS to extend remote access to a Windows 2000 network.

Module 10, "Configuring a Windows 2000–based Server As a Router," explains the concept of routing in a network. The module begins with an overview of routers and router tables and describes what they do. Next, the module explains how to configure network connections. The module continues by explaining how to enable routing by using Routing and Remote Access. The module then explains how to configure static routes. The module concludes by explaining how to configure a routing interface. At the end of this module, you will be able to configure Windows 2000 as a network router.

Module 11, "Configuring Internet Access for a Network," explains how to configure Internet access for a network. The module starts by describing the options for connecting a network to the Internet. It then describes how to configure Internet access by using a router. Next, the module describes how to configure Internet access by using network address translation (NAT). At the end of this module, you will be able to configure Internet access for a network.

Module 12, "Configuring a Web Server," explains the process for configuring a Web server that is running Windows 2000. The module starts with an overview of Internet Information Services (IIS) and the features it offers. Next, the module explains how to prepare for an IIS installation. Then, the module describes the steps necessary to install IIS. Next, the module explains how to configure a Web site. Finally, the module explains how to administer and troubleshoot an IIS installation. At the end of this module, you will be able to configure a Web server.

Course Outline *(continued)*

- **Module 13: Deploying Windows 2000 Professional by Using RIS**

- **Module 14: Managing a Windows 2000 Network**

- **Module 15: Troubleshooting Windows 2000 Network Services**

- **Module 16: Configuring Network Connectivity Between Operating Systems**

Module 13, "Deploying Windows 2000 Professional by Using RIS," presents details on using Remote Installation Services (RIS), the basis of the Windows 2000 Remote OS Installation feature. The module starts with an overview of RIS. Next, the module explains how to install and configure RIS. Then, the module explains how to configure remote installation options, such as default options for client names and account locations. Next, the module explains how to deploy an image by using RIS. The module then describes how to create an RIPrep image for use in deployment. The module compares an RIPrep image with a CD-based image to identify the similarities and differences. The module concludes by examining solutions to potential RIS problems. At the end of this module, you will be able to deploy Windows 2000 Professional by using RIS.

Module 14, "Managing a Windows 2000 Network," begins by identifying several Windows 2000 management strategies. Next, the module explains how you can perform administrative tasks remotely. Then, the module provides an overview of the Simple Network Management Protocol (SNMP) service, and then it discusses how to install the service. Finally, the module explains how to configure SNMP security. At the end of this module, you will be able to manage a Windows 2000 network.

Module 15 "Troubleshooting Windows 2000 Network Services," explains the steps that you can use to troubleshoot a Windows 2000 network. The module starts with an overview of network troubleshooting. It then identifies the symptoms and causes of many common network problems. Next, the module explains how to resolve TCP/IP problems. The module then explains how to resolve name resolution problems. Finally, the module explains how to troubleshoot the network services and monitor network performance. At the end of this module, you will be able to troubleshoot a Windows 2000 network.

Module 16, "Configuring Network Connectivity Between Operating Systems," explains how to connect non-Microsoft operating systems to a Windows 2000 network. The module begins by explaining how to configure access to Novell NetWare resources. Next, the module explains how to configure connectivity for Macintosh users. The module then explains how to connect Systems Network Architecture (SNA) hosts by using Host Integration Server. Finally, the module explains how to configure access to UNIX resources. At the end of this module, you will be able to configure connectivity between Windows 2000 and other operating systems.

Microsoft Official Curriculum

- **Microsoft Windows Operating System**
- **Microsoft Office**
- **Microsoft BackOffice Small Business Server**
- **Microsoft SQL Server**
- **Microsoft Exchange 2000**

- **Microsoft BackOffice Server Infrastructure and Solutions**
- **Microsoft FrontPage**
- **Microsoft Systems Management Server**
- **Knowledge Management Solutions**

Microsoft® Official Curriculum (MOC) is hands-on facilitated classroom and Web-based training. Microsoft develops skills-based training courses to educate computer professionals who develop, support, and implement solutions by using Microsoft products, solutions, and technologies. MOC courses are available for the following products and solutions:

- Microsoft Windows® operating systems
- Microsoft Office
- Microsoft BackOffice® Small Business Server
- Microsoft SQL Server™
- Microsoft Exchange
- Microsoft BackOffice Server Infrastructure and Solutions
- Microsoft FrontPage®
- Microsoft Systems Management Server
- Knowledge Management Solutions

MOC provides a curriculum path for each product and solution. For more information on the curriculum paths, see the Microsoft Official Curriculum Web page at http://www.microsoft.com/traincert/.

The Microsoft Official Curriculum Web page provides information about MOC courses. In addition, you can find recommended curriculum paths for individuals who are entering the Information Technology (IT) industry, who are continuing their training on Microsoft products and solutions, or who currently support non-Microsoft products.

Microsoft Certified Professional Program

The Microsoft Certified Professional program is a leading certification program that validates your experience and skills to keep you competitive in today's changing business environment. The following table describes each certification in more detail.

Certification	Description
MCSA on Microsoft Windows 2000	The Microsoft Certified Systems Administrator (MCSA) certification is designed for professionals who implement, manage, and troubleshoot existing network and system environments based on Microsoft Windows 2000 platforms, including the Windows .NET Server family. Implementation responsibilities include installing and configuring parts of the systems. Management responsibilities include administering and supporting the systems.
MCSE on Microsoft Windows 2000	The Microsoft Certified Systems Engineer (MCSE) credential is the premier certification for professionals who analyze the business requirements and design and implement the infrastructure for business solutions based on the Microsoft Windows 2000 platform and Microsoft server software, including the Windows .NET Server family. Implementation responsibilities include installing, configuring, and troubleshooting network systems.
MCSD	The Microsoft Certified Solution Developer (MCSD) credential is the premier certification for professionals who design and develop leading-edge business solutions with Microsoft development tools, technologies, platforms, and the Microsoft Windows DNA architecture. The types of applications MCSDs can develop include desktop applications and multi-user, Web-based, N-tier, and transaction-based applications. The credential covers job tasks ranging from analyzing business requirements to maintaining solutions.
MCDBA on Microsoft SQL Server 2000	The Microsoft Certified Database Administrator (MCDBA) credential is the premier certification for professionals who implement and administer Microsoft SQL Server databases. The certification is appropriate for individuals who derive physical database designs, develop logical data models, create physical databases, create data services by using Transact-SQL, manage and maintain databases, configure and manage security, monitor and optimize databases, and install and configure SQL Server.

*(**continued**)*

Certification	Description
MCP	The Microsoft Certified Professional (MCP) credential is for individuals who have the skills to successfully implement a Microsoft product or technology as part of a business solution in an organization. Hands-on experience with the product is necessary to successfully achieve certification.
MCT	Microsoft Certified Trainers (MCTs) demonstrate the instructional and technical skills that qualify them to deliver Microsoft Official Curriculum through Microsoft Certified Technical Education Centers (Microsoft CTECs).

Certification Requirements

The certification requirements differ for each certification category and are specific to the products and job functions addressed by the certification. To become a Microsoft Certified Professional, you must pass rigorous certification exams that provide a valid and reliable measure of technical proficiency and expertise.

For More Information   See the Microsoft Training and Certification Web site at http://www.microsoft.com/traincert/.

You can also send e-mail to mcphelp@microsoft.com if you have specific certification questions.

Acquiring the Skills Tested by an MCP Exam

Microsoft Official Curriculum (MOC) and MSDN® Training Curriculum can help you develop the skills that you need to do your job. They also complement the experience that you gain while working with Microsoft products and technologies. However, no one-to-one correlation exists between MOC and MSDN Training courses and MCP exams. Microsoft does not expect or intend for the courses to be the sole preparation method for passing MCP exams. Practical product knowledge and experience is also necessary to pass the MCP exams.

To help prepare for the MCP exams, use the preparation guides that are available for each exam. Each Exam Preparation Guide contains exam-specific information, such as a list of the topics on which you will be tested. These guides are available on the Microsoft Training and Certification Web site at http://www.microsoft.com/traincert/.

Facilities

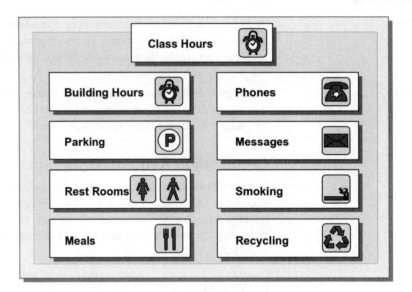

Classroom Configuration

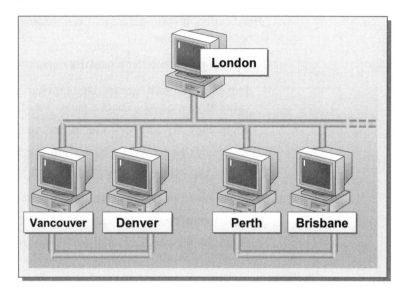

As you progress through this course, you will find it extremely useful to understand how the classroom computers are configured. All computers in the classroom:

- Are configured as domain controllers in a child domain of nwtraders.msft. Each child domain has two domain controllers.
- Are configured with two network adapters. Each adapter performs different functions:
  - One network adapter connects to a classroom network, which in turn connects all student computers and the instructor computer. Your instructor will lead you in an exercise to give this network connection the name *Classroom*.
  - The other network adapter connects to a private network that links each pair of student computers with each other. Your instructor will lead you in an exercise to give this network connection the name *PartnerNet*.

Note   Students with computers in the same domain will work in pairs to complete several labs in this course.

Renaming Network Connections

You can rename your computer's network connections to allow for easier identification. It is suggested that you rename the network connections on your computer at this time.

To rename your computer's network connections, perform the following steps:

1. Log on as administrator@*domain*.nwtraders.msft (where *domain* is the name of your domain) with a password of **password**.

2. Right-click **My Network Places**, and then click **Properties**.

3. Right-click **Local Area Connection**, and then click **Rename**.

4. Type **Classroom** and then press ENTER.

5. Right-click **Local Area Connection 2**, and then click **Rename**.

6. Type **PartnerNet**, and then press ENTER.

7. Close the Network and Dial-up Connections window.

Recording Computer Configuration Parameters

You will need to refer to the initial configuration of your computer throughout the labs. To record the configuration information, double-click the **Computer Configuration** file on your desktop and record the following information for your computer and your partner's computer:

Configuration Parameter	Your Computer	Partner's Computer
Computer Name:		
Domain:		

At a command prompt, type **ipconfig /all** and then record the following information for your computer and your partner's computer:

Configuration Parameter	Your Computer	Partner's Computer
Classroom network connection: IP Address		
Subnet mask		
Default gateway		
DNS servers		
WINS servers		
PartnerNet network connection: IP address		
Subnet mask		
Default gateway		
DNS servers		
WINS servers		
Student number (the last octet in the IP address for the Classroom network connection):		

Microsoft®
Training &
Certification

Module 1: Introduction to the Microsoft Windows 2000 Networking Infrastructure

Contents

Overview

- **Overview of the Windows 2000 Network Infrastructure**
- **Introduction to Intranets**
- **Identifying Remote Access Methods**
- **Communicating with Remote Offices**
- **Providing Internet Access**
- **Introduction to Extranets**

To maintain effective communication and connect remote locations, organizations need to set up and manage computer networks. Microsoft® Windows® 2000 offers a set of networking services that provide standards-based networking protocols and technologies that enable a reliable and interoperable network infrastructure.

At the end of this module, you will be able to:

- Define the components of a Windows 2000 network infrastructure.
- Describe the role of an intranet in a Windows 2000 network.
- Identify remote access methods.
- Describe how a remote office can be connected to an intranet.
- Identify the methods that are used to establish Internet access.
- Describe the purpose of an extranet.

Overview of the Windows 2000 Network Infrastructure

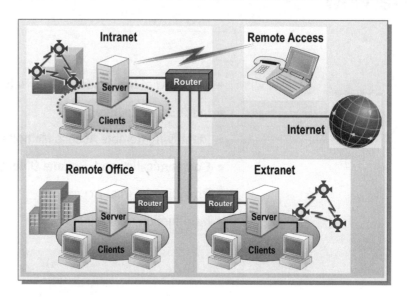

The Microsoft Windows 2000 server products offer several technologies and services that make installing, configuring, managing, and supporting your network infrastructure easier. A network infrastructure can contain any of the following elements:

- *Intranet*. A private network within an organization usually intended for the distribution of internal information. An intranet is also called a local area network (LAN). It includes services such as document distribution, software distribution, access to databases, and training. In addition to file and printer sharing services, an intranet usually employs applications associated with the Internet, such as Web pages, Web browsers, File Transfer Protocol (FTP) sites, e-mail, newsgroups, and mailing lists that only those within the organization can access.

- *Remote Access*. Provides remote networking for telecommuters, mobile workers, and system administrators who monitor and manage servers at multiple branch offices. All services that are typically available to a LAN-connected user, including file and printer sharing, Web server access, and messaging, can be accessed through a remote access connection.

- *Remote Office*. Part of an organization that is located in a geographically separate area. A LAN in a remote office can be connected to the general corporate network to create a wide area network (WAN).

The WAN connection is a shared remote access connection to the network that enables users in the remote office to communicate and share resources within the entire organization. WAN links are persistent, meaning that they are always available, whereas typical remote access connections must be connected and then disconnected when not in use.

- *Internet.* The worldwide collection of networks and gateways that use the Transmission Control Protocol/Internet Protocol (TCP/IP) suite of protocols to communicate with one another. The Internet comprises high-speed data communication lines between major nodes or host computers—consisting of thousands of commercial, government, educational, and other computer systems—that route data and messages.

- *Extranet.* A collaborative network that uses Internet technology to facilitate relationships between businesses and their suppliers, customers, or other businesses. An extranet may be a part of a company's intranet that other companies can access, or it may be a shared network for collaboration between companies. The shared information might be available only to the collaborating parties or, in some cases, might be public.

To set up your network infrastructure, you must properly configure all of the necessary network protocols, settings, and services that are used in each element of the network infrastructure.

Note For information about how to plan for and design a network infrastructure, see course 1562, *Designing a Microsoft Windows 2000 Networking Services Infrastructure.*

Introduction to Intranets

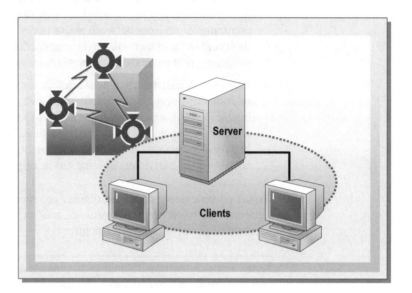

An intranet is a private network that links computers within an organization together to enable them to communicate with each other. The main function of an intranet is to enable users within the organization to share information and resources.

TCP/IP provides the basis for connectivity on your network. TCP/IP is a set of networking protocols that is an industry standard, and most of the networking services in Windows 2000 rely on it. The scalability of TCP/IP adapts to all network sizes, and the Windows 2000 implementation of TCP/IP includes all of the standard Internet Engineering Task Force (IETF) requirements for TCP/IP hosts and servers.

TCP/IP depends on name resolution to work properly. Name resolution is a process that provides users with easy-to-remember server names, instead of requiring them to use the numerical IP addresses by which servers identify themselves on the TCP/IP network.

Note TCP/IP is the default networking protocol that is installed during Windows 2000 setup.

Identifying Remote Access Methods

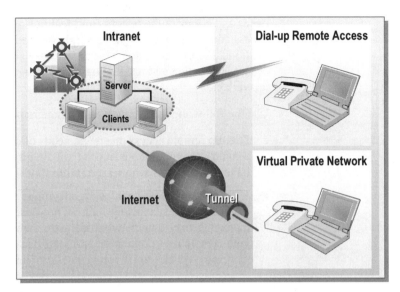

You can configure remote access to provide authorized users with connectivity to the corporate network. This enables remote access clients to access resources from remote locations as if they were physically attached to the network.

Remote Access Methods

Windows 2000 provides two different types of remote access connectivity:

- *Dial-up remote access*. To gain access to the network with dial-up remote access, a remote access client uses the public telephone network to create a physical connection to a port on a remote access server that resides in the private network. Typically, with dial-up remote access, you use a modem or Integrated Services Digital Network (ISDN) adapter to dial in to your remote access server.

- *VPN remote access*. A virtual private network (VPN) can provide secure remote access through the Internet, rather than through direct dial-up connections. The VPN client creates an encrypted, virtual, point-to-point connection with a VPN gateway that resides in the private network. Typically, with VPN remote access, you connect to the Internet first, and then create the VPN connection.

Evaluating Remote Access Methods

When deciding on a remote access solution, you identify your remote access needs and compare the benefits and features of direct-dial and VPN remote access. You can choose to use a single method for remote access or deploy both methods. For example, some organizations use a VPN as the primary remote access connection and use dial-up connections when Internet access is unavailable.

Use the following information to evaluate remote access methods:

- Dial-up remote access meets the needs of organizations that have small remote user populations, are satisfied with analog or ISDN performance, or have remote users who remain within local calling areas.

- VPN remote access enables organizations to reduce long-distance telephone expenses and use existing Internet network infrastructures instead of managing their own network infrastructures. Consider a VPN solution if your remote user population and long-distance telephone expenses are increasing quickly or if you need additional broadband support.

Communicating with Remote Offices

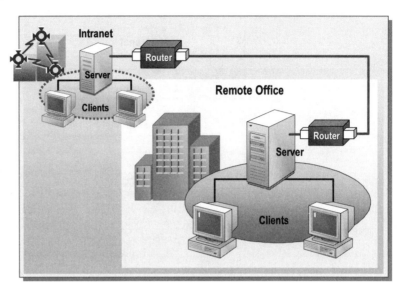

Organizations often extend to one or more remote office locations, with a LAN in each of them. By connecting those networks to each other, an organization can operate more effectively. For example, employees in remote offices can share information and communicate more easily with employees at corporate headquarters. In addition, employees who travel between offices can access their files and resources from any remote office location.

You can connect TCP/IP network segments together by using IP routers, which forward packets from one network segment to another. Routing is used in combination with other network protocol services to provide forwarding capabilities between hosts that are located on separate network segments within a larger TCP/IP-based network.

Providing Internet Access

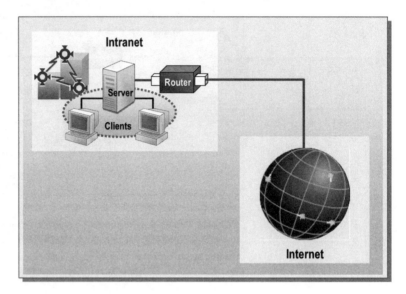

Many organizations require Internet access to establish a Web site, provide VPN remote access, and enable users to perform research and use e-mail. Windows 2000 provides services that enable an organization to connect to the Internet without compromising security, reliability, or performance.

Typically, Internet access is established by using the following methods:

- A dial-up connection to an Internet service provider (ISP). This method is used primarily in small organizations and by home-computer users.

- A dedicated line, such as a T1 carrier that is connected to a LAN. This method is used in large organizations that have their own node on the Internet or connect to an ISP that is a node.

Introduction to Extranets

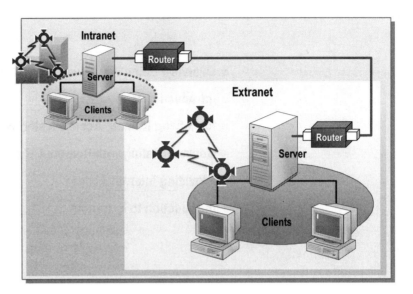

An extranet enables an organization to extend its network to customers, suppliers, and other business partners for information-sharing purposes. An extranet allows users who are outside of your network to have limited access to information on your intranet, based on the level of permissions that you assign to them.

Windows 2000 provides features that simplify the process of configuring an extranet, and that secure your intranet against unauthorized access. Typically, an extranet is provided through secured VPN connections, which you can configure to meet specific needs. For example, business partners may need extranet access, a department may need access to another department's intranet, or you may want to provide selective public access to your intranet.

Review

- **Overview of the Windows 2000 Network Infrastructure**
- **Introduction to Intranets**
- **Identifying Remote Access Methods**
- **Communicating with Remote Offices**
- **Providing Internet Access**
- **Introduction to Extranets**

1. What are the five elements that a Windows 2000 network infrastructure can contain?

2. What are the two types of remote access connectivity that Windows 2000 provides?

3. How can you connect remote offices to your intranet?

4. What are the two methods that are typically used to provide Internet access?

5. What is the purpose of an extranet?

Microsoft®
Training &
Certification

Module 2: Automating IP Address Assignment by Using DHCP

Contents

Overview

- **Overview of DHCP**
- **Installing the DHCP Service**
- **Authorizing the DHCP Service**
- **Creating and Configuring a Scope**
- **Customizing DHCP Functionality**
- **Configuring DHCP in a Routed Network**
- **Supporting DHCP**

Depending on the size of your network, the management and assignment of Internet Protocol (IP) addresses to client computers can require a significant amount of time and effort. But with a Microsoft® Windows® 2000 network, you can enable dynamic IP addressing by using the Dynamic Host Configuration Protocol (DHCP) on a DHCP server to automate the assignment and management of network IP addresses.

At the end of this module, you will be able to:

- Define DHCP and describe how to use it on a network.
- Install the DHCP service.
- Authorize the DHCP service.
- Create and configure a scope.
- Customize DHCP functionality.
- Configure DHCP in a routed network.
- Support DHCP on a network.

◆ Overview of DHCP

- Manual vs. Automatic TCP/IP Configuration
- DHCP Operation
- The DHCP Lease Generation Process
- The DHCP Lease Renewal Process
- Requirements for DHCP Servers and Clients

A DHCP Server uses a lease generation process to assign IP addresses to client computers for a specific period of time. IP address leases are normally temporary, so DHCP clients must periodically attempt to renew their leases with the DHCP server. Understanding the details of the DHCP lease generation and renewal process provides a foundation for effectively implementing dynamic IP addressing in your network environment.

Manual vs. Automatic TCP/IP Configuration

Manual TCP/IP Configuration	Automatic TCP/IP Configuration
Disadvantages	**Advantages**
IP addresses entered manually on each client computer	IP addresses are supplied automatically to client computers
Possibility of entering incorrect or invalid IP address	Ensures that clients always use correct configuration information
Incorrect configuration can lead to communication and network problems	Elimination of common source of network problems
Administrative overload on networks where computers are frequently moved	Client configuration updated automatically to reflect changes in network structure

To understand why DHCP is useful for configuring Transmission Control Protocol/Internet Protocol (TCP/IP) on client computers, it helps to compare manual TCP/IP configuration with automatic configuration by using DHCP.

Manual TCP/IP Configuration

When you configure TCP/IP manually on your network, you must enter an IP address on each client computer. This means that users can enter an incorrect or invalid IP address instead of using a valid IP address from the network administrator. Using an incorrect address can lead to network problems that can be very difficult to trace to the source.

Also, manually typing the IP address, subnet mask, or default gateway can lead to typographical errors, causing communication problems due to an incorrect default gateway or subnet mask, or problems associated with duplicate IP addresses. Moreover, there is administrative overhead on networks where computers frequently move from one subnet to another.

Automatic TCP/IP Configuration

Using DHCP to configure TCP/IP automatically means that users no longer need to acquire IP address from an administrator. Instead, the DHCP server automatically supplies all of the necessary configuration information to DHCP clients. It also ensures that network clients use correct configuration information, thereby eliminating a common source of network problems. Finally, DCHP automatically updates client configuration information to reflect changes in network structure and the relocation of users to other physical networks, without the need to manually reconfigure client IP addresses.

DHCP Operation

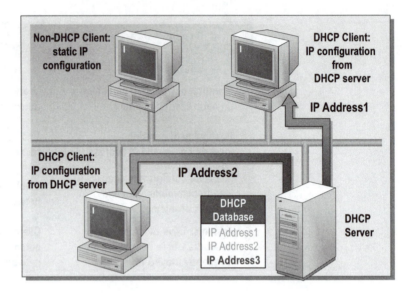

Each time that a DHCP client starts, it requests an IP address from a DHCP server. When the DHCP server receives the request, it selects an IP address from a range of addresses defined in its database. The DHCP server offers this address to the DHCP client.

If the client accepts the offer, the DHCP server leases the IP address to the client for a specified period of time. The default duration of an IP address lease is eight days, but this duration is configurable. The client then uses the IP address to access the network.

The IP addressing information sent by the DHCP server to the DHCP client can contain several elements, including:

- An IP address.
- A subnet mask.
- Optional values, such as:
    - A default gateway address.
    - The IP addresses of Domain Name System (DNS) servers.
    - The IP addresses of Windows Internet Name Service (WINS) servers.

Note For more information about DHCP, see RFCs 2131 and 2132 under **Additional Reading** on the Student Materials compact disc.

For more information about the Bootstrap Protocol (BOOTP) and how it interacts with DHCP, see RFCs 951, 1534, and 1542 under **Additional Reading** on the Student Materials compact disc.

The DHCP Lease Generation Process

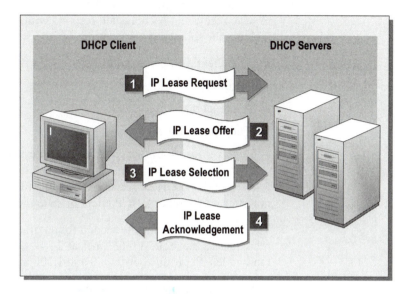

DHCP uses a four-step process to lease IP addressing information to DCHP clients:

1. IP lease request
2. IP lease offer
3. IP lease selection
4. IP lease acknowledgement

Note If a computer has multiple network adapters that are bound to TCP/IP, the DHCP process occurs separately over each adapter. The DHCP server assigns a unique IP address to each adapter that is bound to TCP/IP.

IP Lease Request

The lease generation process begins when a client computer either starts up or initializes TCP/IP for the first time. The lease process also begins when a client computer attempts to renew its lease and is denied (such as when you move a client computer to another subnet).

The process starts when the client initializes a limited version of TCP/IP and broadcasts a DHCPDISCOVER message for IP addressing information. The client does not yet have an IP address, so it uses 0.0.0.0 as the source address. And because the client does not know the IP address of a DHCP server, it uses 255.255.255.255 as the destination address. This broadcasts the message to the entire subnet.

The request message also contains the media access control (MAC) address, which is the hardware address of the client's network adapter. The message also contains the client's computer name so that DHCP servers can determine which client sent the request.

IP Lease Offer

All DHCP servers that have an IP address that is valid for the network segment to which the client is connected respond with a DHCPOFFER message, which includes the following information:

- The client's hardware address
- An offered IP address
- A subnet mask
- The length of the lease
- A server identifier, which is the IP address of the offering DHCP server

Each responding DHCP server reserves the offered IP address so that it does not offer it to another DHCP client prior to the requesting client's acceptance.

The DHCP client waits one second for an offer. If it does not receive an offer, it rebroadcasts the request four times at 2-, 4-, 8-, and 16-second intervals, plus a random length of time between 0 and 1,000 milliseconds.

If the client does not receive an offer after four requests, it uses an IP address in the reserved range from 169.254.0.1 to 169.254.255.254. The use of one of these autoconfigured IP addresses ensures that clients on a subnet without a DHCP server are able to communicate with each other. The DHCP client continues in an attempt to find a DHCP server every five minutes.

When a DHCP server becomes available, clients receive valid IP addresses, allowing them to communicate with hosts both on and off their subnet.

IP Lease Selection

The DHCP client responds to the first offer that it receives by broadcasting a DHCPREQUEST message to accept the offer. The DHCPREQUEST message includes the server identification of the server whose offer it accepted. All other DHCP servers then retract their offers and retain their IP addresses for other IP lease requests.

IP Lease Acknowledgement

The DHCP server issuing the accepted offer broadcasts a DHCP acknowledgement message (DHCPACK) to acknowledge the successful lease. This message contains a valid lease for the IP address and other configuration information.

When the DHCP client receives the acknowledgment, TCP/IP initializes by using the configuration information that the DHCP server provides. The client also binds the TCP/IP protocol to the network services and network adapter, permitting the client to communicate on the network.

Important All communication between a DHCP server and a DHCP client occurs using User Datagram Protocol (UDP) ports 67 and 68. Some switches do not properly forward DHCP broadcasts by default. For DHCP to function correctly, you may need to configure these switches to forward broadcasts over these ports.

The DHCP Lease Renewal Process

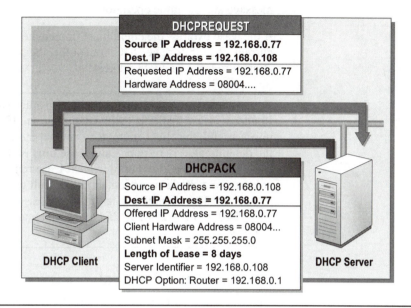

At specific intervals, a DHCP client attempts to renew its lease to ensure that it has up-to-date configuration information.

Automatic Lease Renewal

A DHCP client automatically attempts to renew its lease when 50 percent of the lease duration expires. To attempt a lease renewal, the DHCP client sends a DHCPREQUEST message directly to the DHCP server from which it obtained the lease.

If the DHCP server is available, it renews the lease and sends the client a DHCPACK message with the new lease duration and any updated configuration parameters. The client updates its configuration when it receives the acknowledgment. If the DHCP server is unavailable, the client continues to use its current configuration parameters.

If a DHCP client cannot renew its lease at the 50 percent interval, the client continues to use its current configuration parameters. It then broadcasts a DHCPDISCOVER message to update its address lease when 87.5 percent of the current lease duration expires. At this stage, the DHCP client accepts a lease that is issued by any DHCP server.

Note If a client requests an invalid or duplicate address for the network, a DHCP server can respond with a DHCP denial message (DHCPNAK). This forces the client to release its IP address and obtain a new, valid address.

If a DHCP server responds with a DHCPOFFER message to update the client's current lease, the client can renew its lease based on the server that offered the message and continue operation.

If the lease expires, the client must immediately discontinue its use of the current IP address. The DHCP client then begins the DHCP lease process in an attempt to lease a new IP address.

Note   When you restart a DCHP client, it automatically attempts to renew the IP address lease that it had when it shut down. If the lease request is unsuccessful, the client attempts to contact the configured default gateway. If the default gateway responds and lease time is still available, the DHCP client uses the same IP address until its next lease renewal attempt. If the DHCP client cannot renew the lease or contact the default gateway, it stops using the current IP address. The client then uses an IP address in the reserved range from 169.254.0.1 to 169.254.255.254 and tries to contact a DHCP server every five minutes.

Manual Lease Renewal

You can renew an IP lease manually if you need to update DHCP configuration information immediately. For example, if you want DHCP clients to immediately obtain the address of a newly installed router from a DHCP server, renew the lease from the client to change this configuration.

To renew the lease manually, use the **ipconfig** command with the **/renew** switch. This sends a DHCPREQUEST message to the DHCP server to update configuration options and to renew the lease time.

Note   You can use the **ipconfig** command with the **/release** switch to release a lease (for example, if you are relocating a client from one subnet to another). This sends a DHCPRELEASE message to the DHCP server to release a client lease. After you issue this command, the client can no longer communicate on the network by using TCP/IP.

Requirements for DHCP Servers and Clients

- **DHCP Server Requirements (Windows 2000 Server)**
  - The DHCP service
  - Static IP address, subnet mask, default gateway
  - Range of valid IP addresses
- **DHCP Clients**
  - Windows 2000 Professional or Windows 2000 Server
  - Windows NT Server or Workstation 3.51 or later
  - Windows 95 or Windows 98
  - Windows for Workgroups 3.11, running TCP/IP-32
  - Microsoft Network Client 3.0 for MS-DOS
  - LAN Manager 2.2c
  - Non-Microsoft operating systems

The Windows 2000 DHCP service has specific software requirements for the server and client computers.

DHCP Server Requirements

All products in the Windows 2000 Server family include the DHCP service. Consequently, a server running any of the Windows 2000 Server family of operating systems can serve as a DHCP server.

A computer running Windows 2000 Server and acting as a DHCP server requires:

- Installation of the DHCP service.

- A static IP address, subnet mask, and default gateway.

- A range of valid IP addresses for lease or assignment to clients.

DHCP Clients

You must configure client computers to automatically obtain IP addresses from a DHCP server. Client computers running any of the following operating systems can be DHCP clients:

- Windows 2000 Professional or Windows 2000 Server

- Microsoft Windows NT® Server version 3.51 or later, or Windows NT Workstation version 3.51 or later

- Microsoft Windows 95 or Microsoft Windows 98

- Microsoft Windows for Workgroups version 3.11 with TCP/IP-32 installed

- Microsoft MS-DOS® with the Microsoft Network Client version 3.0 for MS-DOS installed, and using the real-mode TCP/IP driver

- Microsoft LAN Manager version 2.2c (LAN Manager 2.2c for OS/2 is not supported)

- Many non-Microsoft operating systems

Enabling DHCP Clients

To enable DHCP support on a client computer that is running Windows 2000, you must configure the TCP/IP properties on that computer so that the computer obtains an IP address automatically.

To configure Windows 2000 clients to obtain IP addresses automatically:

1. Open the **Properties** dialog box for the network connection that you are configuring.

2. Click **Internet Protocol (TCP/IP)**, and then click **Properties**.

3. In the **Internet Protocol (TCP/IP) Properties** dialog box, on the **General** tab, click **Obtain an IP address automatically**.

4. If you assign DNS server addresses by using DHCP, click **Obtain DNS server address automatically**.

5. Click **OK** twice.

Installing the DHCP Service

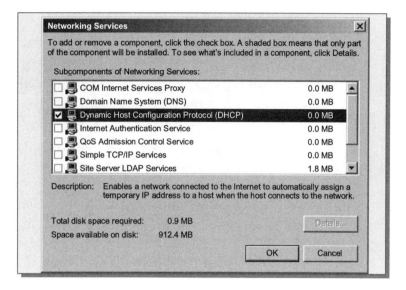

To create a DHCP server, you must install the DHCP service on a computer running Windows 2000 Server.

Important Before you can install the DHCP service on the computer that you want to designate as the DHCP server, you must specify a static IP address, subnet mask, and default gateway address for the network adapter that is bound to TCP/IP.

For more information about configuring these parameters, see "Configure TCP/IP for Static Addressing" in Windows 2000 Help.

To install the DHCP service:

1. In Control Panel, double-click **Add/Remove Programs**.

2. In **Add/Remove Programs**, click **Add/Remove Windows Components**.

3. In the Windows Components wizard, on the **Windows Components** page, under **Components**, click **Networking Services**, and then click **Details**.

4. In the **Networking Services** dialog box, under **Subcomponents of Networking Services**, select the **Dynamic Host Configuration Protocol (DHCP)** check box, and then click **OK**.

5. Click **Next**.

Authorizing the DHCP Service

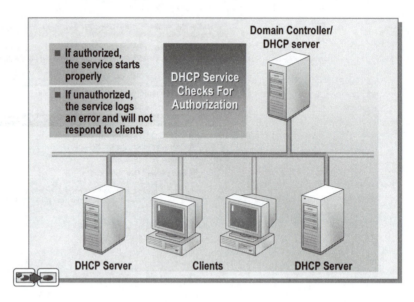

You must authorize a DHCP server before the server can issue leases to DHCP clients. Requiring authorization of the DHCP servers prevents unauthorized DHCP servers from offering potentially invalid IP addresses to clients. This requirement provides a network administrator with a great degree of control over IP lease assignments in a Windows 2000 network.

Note Only DHCP servers running Windows 2000 Server check for authorization. Other DHCP servers can still operate even though they are not authorized.

Detection of Unauthorized DHCP Servers

For DHCP authorization to work correctly, you must configure your network so that when the DHCP service starts, it sends out a DHCP informational message (DHCPINFORM) to the local broadcast address (255.255.255.255). When this occurs, other DHCP servers reply with DHCP acknowledgement messages (DHCPACK), which contain information about any Active Directory™ directory service root domain identified by each DHCP server.

The server that is attempting to initialize the DHCP service then contacts a domain controller in each of the domains that it identifies. It queries Active Directory for a list of DHCP servers that are currently authorized to operate on the network. If the DHCP server is authorized, the DHCP service on that computer starts properly. If the DHCP server is not authorized, the DHCP service logs an error in the system log and ignores all client requests.

Note A DHCP server broadcasts a DHCPINFORM message every five minutes in an attempt to detect other DHCP servers on the network. This allows it to determine changes in its authorization status and update its status accordingly.

Authorizing a DHCP Server

To authorize a DHCP server:

1. Open DHCP from the **Administrative Tools** menu.

2. In the console tree, right-click **DHCP**, and then click **Manage authorized servers**.

3. In the **Manage Authorized Servers** dialog box, click **Authorize**.

4. In the **Authorize DHCP Server** dialog box, type the name or IP address of the DHCP server to authorize, and then click **OK**.

5. In the **DHCP** message box, click **Yes** to confirm the authorization.

Important To authorize a DHCP server, you must be a member of the Enterprise Admins group. This group has network-wide administrative privileges. For more information about delegating the ability to authorize DHCP servers to a user who is not a member of the Enterprise Admins group, see "To Delegate Ability to Authorize DHCP Servers to a Non-Enterprise Administrator" in Windows 2000 Help.

Note Authorization problems can exist if there are multiple forests on the same network infrastructure. Authorization is not recognized between forests, and the DCHP server from the other forest will continue to issue IP addresses.

Lab A: Creating and Authorizing a DHCP Server

Objectives

After completing this lab, you will be able to:

- Install the DHCP Server service.
- Authorize a DHCP server.

Prerequisite

Before working on this lab, you must have knowledge of the concepts and function of DHCP.

Lab Setup

To complete this lab, you need the following:

- A computer running Windows 2000 Advanced Server that is configured as a domain controller in a child domain of the nwtraders.msft domain, has a static IP address, and uses the instructor computer for DNS name resolution.

- A partner with a similarly configured computer.

- The Eadmin user account in the nwtraders.msft domain. The instructor created this account for use in classroom labs, and the account is a member of the Enterprise Admins group in the domain nwtraders.msft. You will use this user account to authorize a DHCP server.

Important The lab does not reflect the real-world environment. It is recommended that you always use complex passwords for any administrator accounts, and never create accounts without a password.

Important Outside of the classroom environment, it is strongly advised that you use the most recent software updates that are necessary. Because this is a classroom environment, we may use software that does not include the latest updates.

Scenario

To simplify network administration, your organization has decided to implement automatic IP addressing by using DHCP. Before configuring client computers to obtain IP addresses automatically, you need to create a DHCP server by installing the DHCP Server service on a computer running Windows 2000 Server. You also need to authorize the server to assign IP addresses before clients can obtain IP addresses from it.

Estimated time to complete this lab: 15 minutes

Exercise 1
Installing and Authorizing the DHCP Server Service

Scenario

You want client computers to receive IP configuration information automatically from a DHCP server.

Goal

Install the DHCP Server service, and then add the DHCP server to the list of authorized servers for the network.

Tasks	Detailed Steps
1. Install the DHCP Server service.	a. Log on as administrator@*domain*.nwtraders.msft (where *domain* is the name of your domain) with a password of **password**.
	b. In Control Panel, double-click **Add/Remove Programs**.
	c. In Add/Remove Programs, click **Add/Remove Windows Components**.
ℹ **Note:** In the next detailed step, click the text **Networking Services** rather than the check box to avoid selecting all options under **Networking Services**.	
1. *(continued)*	d. In the Windows Components wizard, on the **Windows Components** page, click **Networking Services**, and then click **Details**.
	e. In the **Networking Services** dialog box, select the **Dynamic Host Configuration Protocol (DHCP)** check box, and then click **OK**.
	f. On the **Windows Components** page, click **Next**.
	g. If the **Files Needed** dialog box appears, type **London\Setup\Winsrc** and then click **OK**.
	h. When the configuration is complete, click **Finish**, and then close all open windows.

(continued)

Tasks	Detailed Steps
2. Add the DHCP server to the list of authorized servers for the network.	a. Click **Start**, point to **Programs**, point to **Administrative Tools**, right-click **DHCP**, and then click **Run as**. b. In the **Run As Other User** dialog box, in the **User name** box, type **eadmin@nwtraders.msft** c. In the **Password** box, type **password** d. Delete the contents of the **Domain** box, and then click **OK**.
❓ Why must you authorize the service by using an account other than the administrator account for your domain? _____ _____ _____ _____	
2. *(continued)*	e. In the console tree of DHCP, right-click **DHCP**, and then click **Manage authorized servers**. f. In the **Manage Authorized Servers** dialog box, click **Authorize**. g. In the **Authorize DHCP Server** dialog box, type the IP address of your Classroom network connection, and then click **OK**. h. In the **DHCP** message box, verify the name and address of the server that you want to add to the authorized list, and then click **Yes**. i. Click **Close** to close the **Manage Authorized Servers** dialog box.
❶ **Note:** The authorization may take a few minutes, depending on the speed at which information replicates across the network. When authorization is complete, the server icon in the console tree will appear with a green arrow when you click it. You do not need to wait for the authorization to complete this lab.	
2. *(continued)*	j. Close all windows, and then log off.

◆ Creating and Configuring a Scope

- **Overview of Scopes**

- **Using The New Scope Wizard**

- **Configuring a Scope with Options**

- **Customizing the Use of Scope Options**

- **Reserving IP Addresses for Client Computers**

To enable dynamic IP addressing, you must enter a range of valid IP addresses that the DHCP server can use to issue leases to clients. You perform this task after you install the DHCP service and authorize the DHCP server on the network.

Understanding how to create and configure this IP address pool allows you to configure DHCP clients automatically with IP addressing information and to minimize the administrative overhead associated with maintaining that information.

Note   You can use the **netsh** command to configure DHCP from a command prompt or to script DHCP commands for automatic DHCP configuration.

For more information about how to use the **netsh** command for DHCP administration, see "Use DHCP Command-line Tools" in Windows 2000 Help.

Overview of Scopes

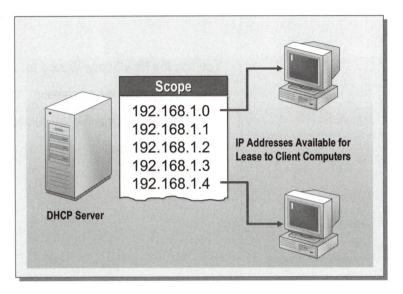

A *scope* is a range of valid IP addresses that are available for lease or assignment to client computers on a particular subnet. You configure a scope on the DHCP server to determine the pool of IP addresses that the server can assign to DHCP clients.

Scope Options

You also configure a scope with options so that the DHCP server can provide additional information with an IP address lease. For example, you can configure a scope to provide the default gateway to client computers. This variable information is called a *scope option*.

DHCP applies scope options to client computers in a specific order. As a result, you can define DHCP-assigned options with varying levels of authority so that certain options take precedence over other options.

Client Reservations

You can also configure a scope so that the DHCP server always provides the same IP address to a particular computer. For example, you can reserve an IP address for a computer that requires a permanent IP address, such as a DNS server, because other computers are configured to connect to it by using its IP address. These permanent IP address assignments are called *client reservations*.

Using the New Scope Wizard

You use the New Scope Wizard to:

- Configure scope parameters
- Change the default lease duration
- Activate a scope

In Windows 2000, you create a scope by using the New Scope wizard. To start the New Scope wizard, open DHCP from the **Administrative Tools** menu, right-click the name of the DHCP server on which you want to create the new scope, and then click **New Scope**.

Scope Parameters

The following table describes the parameters that you specify when creating a new scope by using the New Scope wizard.

Parameter	Description
Name	The name of the scope.
Description	An optional description of the scope to help you keep track of the purpose of the scope.
Start IP address and **End IP address**	Specify the range of addresses that the DHCP server can assign from this scope. To prevent problems with duplicate IP addressing, do not use the same IP addresses in more than one scope.
Length or Subnet mask	The subnet mask to assign to DHCP clients. To configure this parameter, enter the number of bits that make up the subnet mask, or type the four octets of the subnet mask.

(continued)

Parameter	Description
Exclusion address range (*optional*)	You can specify one or more ranges to exclude from the scope. Excluded addresses are not assigned to DHCP clients. To avoid duplicate IP addressing, exclude any statically assigned IP addresses on your network, such as computers acting as print servers.
Lease duration	The length of the IP address lease, in number of days, hours, and minutes. The default duration is eight days. To set the lease duration to unlimited, you must configure the scope properties after you create the scope. The wizard does not provide the option to configure an unlimited scope.

Important   After you create a scope, you cannot change the subnet mask that the scope assigns. To change this scope information, you must delete the scope and create a new scope with the correct information.

Changing The Default Lease Duration

There are benefits and drawbacks to changing the default lease duration.

Decreasing Lease Duration

When you decrease lease durations, clients obtain leases even if only a few IP addresses are available. In addition, leases expire shortly after computers are turned off or removed from the network, allowing their IP addresses to be assigned to other computers. Clients also obtain newly assigned settings quickly. However, this short lease duration generates more network traffic due to lease renewals, and leases can expire if a DHCP server is temporarily unavailable.

Increasing Lease Duration

Increasing lease durations reduces network traffic caused by lease renewals. In addition, clients tend to retain IP addresses even if a DHCP server is temporarily unavailable. However, if only a few IP addresses are available, client computers may not be able to obtain a lease. In addition, it can take longer for client computers to receive newly assigned settings.

Unlimited Lease Duration

With an unlimited lease duration, DHCP only generates network traffic when a computer is started. Clients retain IP addresses even if a DHCP server is unavailable for extended periods. However, if only a few IP addresses are available, client computers may not be able to obtain a lease. IP addresses used by computers that you have removed from the network do not become available to other clients unless you manually remove the lease. Finally, clients only receive newly assigned settings when you restart the client computers or manually renew the lease.

Activating A Scope

After you create a scope, you must activate it to make it available for lease assignments. To activate a scope, in DHCP, right-click the entry for the scope, and then click **Activate**.

Important   To ensure that all client computers receive complete configuration information, make sure that before you activate the scope, you set the scope options that you want.

Configuring a Scope with Options

Scope Options Supported by DHCP Include:

- IP Address of a Router

- IP Address of a DNS Server

- DNS Domain Name

- IP Address of a WINS Server

- Type of NetBIOS over TCP/IP Name Resolution

You can configure a scope to provide a variety of information along with a DHCP lease. For example, you can configure the DHCP server to issue the address of a router to allow clients to communicate across subnets.

Important   The networking software running on the client computer determines whether a client computer recognizes an option that a DHCP server supplies.

Common Scope Options

The New Scope wizard allows you to configure common scope options to provide additional IP addressing configuration information with the client lease. The following table describes the options that you can configure:

Option	Description
Router (Default Gateway)	The addresses of any default gateway, or router, for the scope
Domain name	The DNS domain to which the client computer belongs
DNS and WINS servers	The addresses of any DNS and WINS servers for clients to use for network communication

Scope Options Supported by DHCP

The following list describes the additional scope options supported by DHCP clients running Microsoft operating systems. You can use any of these options if clients require additional information for proper network operations.

- *The IP address of a router.* To issue this information, configure the **003 Router** option with the IP address of a default router. This router is commonly referred to as the default gateway.

- *The IP address of one or more DNS name servers available to clients.* To issue this information, configure the **006 DNS Servers** option with the IP address of one or more DNS servers.

- *The DNS domain name.* A DNS domain name defines the domain to which a client computer belongs. The client computer can use this information to update a DNS server so that other computers can locate the client. To issue this information, configure the **015 DNS Domain Name** option with the proper DNS domain name.

- *The IP address of one or more WINS servers available to clients.* The client uses a WINS server for network basic input/output system (NetBIOS) name resolution. To issue this parameter, configure the **044 WINS/NBNS Servers** option with the IP address of one or more WINS servers.

- *The type of NetBIOS over TCP/IP name resolution.* To issue this information, configure the **046 WINS/NBT node type** option with the appropriate NetBIOS node type. The type of name resolution determines the order in which a client uses NetBIOS name servers and broadcasts to resolve NetBIOS names to IP addresses.

Note   For information about NetBIOS node types, see RFCs 1001 and 1002 under **Additional Reading** on the Student Materials compact disc.

A complete list of the standard options that DHCP supports is currently defined in RFC 2132 on the Student Materials compact disc. However, most DHCP clients can accept only a few of the full set of standard, defined option types.

Configuring Additional Scope Options

To configure a scope with additional options:

1. Open DHCP from the **Administrative Tools** menu.

2. In the console tree, click the name of the DHCP server on which you want to configure additional scope options, and then wait for the server status to update.

3. In the console tree, expand the DHCP server, expand the scope entry, click **Scope Options**, right-click **Scope Options**, and then click **Configure Options**.

4. In the **Scope Options** dialog box, on the **General** tab, in the **Available Options** box, select the check box to the left of the option that you want.

5. In the **Data entry** box, specify the appropriate configuration information for the option.

Customizing the Use of Scope Options

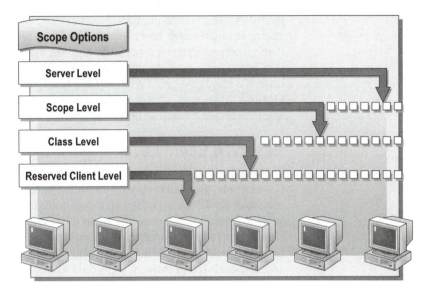

You can configure scope options so that they apply to all DHCP clients, to a group of clients, or to a single client. You can configure scope options at four levels: server, scope, class, and reserved client.

Note   TCP/IP properties that are specified on the client computer take precedence over any information that a DHCP server provides.

Server Level

Server-level options apply to all DHCP clients that lease an IP address from the DHCP server. You should configure options at the server level if all clients on all subnets require the same configuration information. For example, you might want to configure all clients to use the same DNS server or WINS server. To configure options at the server level, in DHCP, expand the server that you are configuring, right-click **Server Options**, and then click **Configure Options**.

Scope Level

Scope-level options are available only to clients that lease an address from that scope. For example, each subnet requires a different scope, and you can define a unique default gateway address for each scope. Options that you configure at the scope level take precedence over options that are configured at the server level. To configure options at the scope level, in DHCP, expand the scope that you are configuring, right-click **Scope Options**, and then click **Configure Options**.

Class Level

Options that you configure at the class level are available only to clients that identify themselves to the DHCP server as belonging to a particular class. For example, client computers running Windows 2000 can receive different options than all other clients on a network. Options that you configure at the class level take precedence over options that you configure at either the scope or server level. To configure options at the class level, in the **Server Options** or **Scope Options** dialog box, on the **Advanced** tab, select the vendor class or user class, and then under **Available Options**, configure the appropriate options.

Reserved Client Level

Options that you configure at the reserved client level apply to specific clients. For example, you can configure an option at the reserved client level so that a particular DHCP client uses a specific router to access resources outside its subnet. Options that you configure at the reserved client level take precedence over options that you configure at any other level. To configure options at the reserved client level, in DHCP, expand the scope that contains the client's address, click **Reservations**, right-click the entry for the client, and then click **Configure Options**.

Reserving IP Addresses for Client Computers

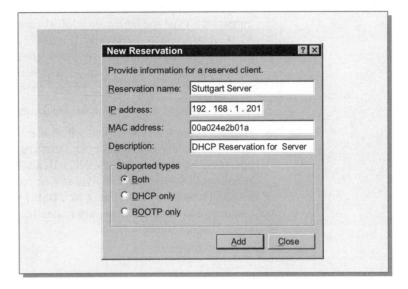

You configure a client reservation to reserve a specific IP address for use by a DHCP client computer so that the client computer always has the same address. For example, the ability to configure a client reservation is useful if you have an application that authenticates a user by IP address.

Note If your network structure allows a client to receive an IP address from multiple DHCP servers, you must configure a client reservation at each of the servers. This prevents the client from obtaining different IP addressing information, depending on which DHCP server responds to the lease request.

To configure a client reservation:

1. Open DHCP from the **Administrative Tools** menu.

2. In the console tree, expand the server that you are configuring, expand the scope where you want to add a reservation, and then click **Reservations**.

3. Right-click **Reservations**, and then click **New Reservation**.

4. In the **New Reservation** dialog box, in the **Reservation name** box, type a name to identify the client.

   The name associates the hardware address of the network adapter to a client.

5. In the **IP address** box, type the IP address that you want to reserve for a specific client.

6. In the **MAC address** box, type the hardware address (MAC address) of the host's network adapter. Do not use dashes in the hardware address.

Important   Type the hardware address carefully. If you type a value in the **MAC Address** box incorrectly, it will not match the value that the DHCP client sends, and the DHCP server will assign to the client any available IP address instead of the IP address that is reserved for that client.

---

7. In the **Comment** box, type an optional comment for the client.

8. Under **Supported types**, click which method the client uses, and then click **Add**. Some older client computers that are running a non-Microsoft operating system may use the older BOOTP instead of DHCP. Also, Windows 2000 Remote Installation Services (RIS) clients use the BOOTP protocol when they initialize. Click **Both**, unless you want the client computers to be able to use only a specific protocol to receive an IP address.

Lab B: Configuring a DHCP Scope

Objectives

After completing this lab, you will be able to:

- Create a DHCP scope.
- Configure DHCP scope options.
- Configure a DHCP reservation.

Prerequisites

Before working on this lab, you must have:

- Knowledge about DHCP scope options.
- Knowledge about DHCP reservations.
- Experience configuring network properties.

Lab Setup

To complete this lab, you need the following:

- A computer running Windows 2000 Advanced Server that is configured as a domain controller in a child domain of the nwtraders.msft domain, has a static IP address, and uses the instructor computer for DNS name resolution.

- A partner with a similarly configured computer.

Important   One computer will be the DHCP server and the other will be the DHCP client. The computer of the student with the lower student number will act as the DHCP server; the computer of the student with the higher student number will act as the DHCP client. Determine the role that your computer will perform before starting the lab.

Scenario

You have installed and authorized a DHCP server on your network. Next, you want to configure a scope to test the service and to make sure that it is operating properly before putting the server into production.

Estimated time to complete this lab: 30 minutes

Exercise 1
Creating, Configuring, and Assigning a Scope

Scenario

You must configure a DHCP scope that has addresses that are valid for the network segment to which the DHCP server is attached. You must configure this scope to provide network configuration information to DHCP client computers.

Goal

The partner on the DHCP server will create a scope; exclude some of the addresses in the scope; and then configure the scope to provide a gateway, the IP address of a DNS server, and the IP address of a WINS server.

The partner on the DHCP client will record the hardware address of his or her network adapter, and then configure his or her TCP/IP properties to receive an IP address from a DHCP server.

Tasks	Detailed Steps
Perform the following procedure only on the computer designated as the DHCP server.	
1. Create a scope for the IP address range 192.168.*x*.1 to 192.168.*x*.254 (where *x* is the third octet of the partner network's IP address). Use the scope name *server* (where *server* is the name of your computer). Exclude the first 50 and last two IP addresses of the scope, and configure the following optional information: Gateway: 192.168.*x*.254 DNS server: 192.168.*x*.254 WINS server: 192.168.*x*.254 (where *x* is the third octet of the partner network's IP address)	**a.** Log on as administrator@*domain*.nwtraders.msft (where *domain* is the name of your domain) with a password of **password**. **b.** Open DHCP from the **Administrative Tools** menu. **c.** In the console tree, click *server* (where *server* is the name of your computer), right-click *server*, and then click **New Scope**. **d.** In the New Scope wizard, click **Next**. **e.** On the **Scope Name** page, in the **Name** box, type *server* (where *server* is the name of your computer), and then click **Next**. **f.** On the **IP Address Range** page, in the **Start IP address** box, type **192.168.*x*.1** (where *x* is the third octet of the IP address of the PartnerNet connection). **g.** In the **End IP address** box, type **192.168.*x*.254** (where *x* is the third octet of the IP address of the PartnerNet connection). *The wizard automatically fills in the correct length of the subnet mask and the IP address of the subnet mask.* **h.** Click **Next**. **i.** On the **Add Exclusions** page, in the **Start IP address** box, type **192.168.*x*.1** and in the **End IP address** box, type **192.168.*x*.50** (where *x* is the third octet of the IP address of the PartnerNet connection), and then click **Add**. **j.** Repeat the preceding step to exclude the address range **192.168.*x*.253** to **192.168.*x*.254** (where *x* is the third octet of the IP address of the PartnerNet connection), click **Add**, and then click **Next**. **k.** On the Lease **Duration** page, read the description of the lease duration, and then click **Next**.

Tasks	Detailed Steps
1. *(continued)*	l. On the **Configure DHCP Options** page, verify that **Yes, I want to configure these options now** is selected, and then click **Next**.
	m. On the **Router (Default Gateway)** page, in the **IP address** box, type **192.168.x.254** (where *x* is the third octet of the IP address of the PartnerNet connection), click **Add**, and then click **Next**.
	n. On the **Domain Name and DNS Servers** page, in the **IP address** box, type **192.168.x.254** (where *x* is the third octet of the IP address of the PartnerNet connection), click **Add**, and then click **Next**.
	o. On the **WINS Servers** page, in the **IP address** box, type **192.168.x.254** (where *x* is the third octet of the IP address of the PartnerNet connection), click **Add**, and then click **Next**.
	p. On the **Activate Scope** page, verify that **Yes, I want to activate this scope now** is selected, and then click **Next**.
	q. On the **Completing the Create Scope Wizard** page, click **Finish**.
	DHCP displays the scope that you created.

 Note: If the DHCP server authorization information has been replicated to your computer, the server icon in the console tree appears with a green arrow when you click it. You do not need to wait for the authorization information to display correctly to complete this lab.

 Perform the following procedure only on the computer designated as the DHCP server.

2. Confirm that the wizard created the scope options correctly, and then add 192.168.x.255 (where *x* is the third octet of the partner network's IP address) as a secondary DNS server.	a. In the console tree, expand the scope that you created, and then click **Scope Options**.
	b. In the details pane, right-click **006 DNS Servers**, and then click **Properties**.
	c. In the **Scope Options** dialog box, in the **IP address** box, type **192.168.x.255** (where *x* is the third octet of the IP address of the PartnerNet connection), and then click **Add**.
	d. Click **OK** to close the **Scope Options** dialog box.

 Perform the following procedure only on the computer that is designated as the DHCP client.

(continued)

Tasks	Detailed Steps
3. Configure your computer to obtain an IP address automatically.	a. Log on as administrator@*domain*.nwtraders.msft (where *domain* is the name of your domain) with a password of **password**. b. At a command prompt, type **ipconfig /all** and then press ENTER. *Ipconfig displays the IP address settings for all network adapters in your computer. Notice that one local area connection is named Classroom, and that the other local area connection is named PartnerNet.* c. Record the IP address of the PartnerNet connection. d. Record the DNS server address of the PartnerNet connection. e. Minimize the command prompt window. f. Right-click **My Network Places**, and then click **Properties**. g. Open the **Properties** dialog box for the PartnerNet connection. h. In the **PartnerNet Properties** dialog box, click **Internet Protocol (TCP/IP)**, but do not clear the check mark next to the option. i. Click **Properties**. j. In the **Internet Protocol (TCP/IP)** dialog box, click **Obtain an IP address automatically**. k. Click **Obtain DNS server address automatically**, and then click **OK**. l. Click **OK** to close the **Properties** dialog box for the PartnerNet connection. m. Restore the command prompt window. n. At the command prompt, type **ipconfig /release** and then press ENTER. o. Type **ipconfig /renew** and then press ENTER. p. Verify that Windows 2000 assigned an address from your partner's DHCP scope to the network adapter that you configured to automatically obtain an IP address. Also confirm that Windows 2000 assigned all of the scope options that your partner configured in the preceding exercise.

Exercise 2
Creating and Testing a Client Reservation

Scenario

One of the servers on your network runs an application that authenticates connections by using the IP address of the computer from which the connection originates. A client computer that connects to this server receives its TCP/IP configuration information from a DHCP server. You must configure a client reservation so that this client computer receives the same IP address each time that it requests an address from the DHCP server.

Goal

In this exercise, you will create a client reservation for a client computer that requires a specific IP address and then test the address assignment.

Tasks	Detailed Steps
✋ Perform the following procedure only on the computer that is designated as the DHCP client.	
1. Record the MAC address of your computer.	a. At a command prompt, type **ipconfig /all** and then press ENTER. b. Record the physical address for the Ethernet adapter **PartnerNet**.
✋ Perform the following procedure only on the computer designated as the DHCP server.	
2. Configure DHCP to assign the IP address 192.168.*x*.200 to your partner's computer (where *x* is the third octet of the IP address of the PartnerNet connection).	a. In DHCP, in the console tree, under the scope that you created in the preceding exercise, click **Reservations**. b. Right-click **Reservations**, and then click **New Reservation**. c. In the **New Reservation** dialog box, in the **Reservation name** box, type *partner_server* (where *partner_server* is the name of your partner's computer). d. In the **IP address** box, type **192.168.*x*.200** (where *x* is the third octet of the IP address of the PartnerNet connection). e. In the **MAC address** box, type the address of your partner's network adapter (which your partner recorded in the previous task), without the dashes. For example, for the physical address 00-aa-00-4b-ad-14, type **00aa004bad14** f. Click **Add**, and then click **Close**. g. Close DHCP.
✋ Perform the following procedure on only the computer that is designated as the DHCP client.	

(continued)

Tasks	Detailed Steps
3. Obtain a new IP address and confirm that the DHCP server assigned the IP address 192.168.*x*.200 to your computer.	a. At a command prompt, type **ipconfig /release** and then press ENTER. b. Type **ipconfig /renew** and then press ENTER. c. Confirm that Windows 2000 assigned the IP address 192.168.*x*.200 to your computer. d. Close the command prompt window.
4. Configure your computer to use the static IP address that you recorded in the first exercise.	a. Right-click **My Network Places**, and then click **Properties**. b. In Network and Dial-up Connections, right-click **PartnerNet**, and then click **Properties**. c. In the **PartnerNet Properties** dialog box, click **Internet Protocol (TCP/IP)**, and then click **Properties**. d. In the **Internet Protocol (TCP/IP)** dialog box, click **Use the following IP address**. e. In the **IP address** box, type the IP address that you recorded in Exercise 1. f. In the **Subnet mask** box, type **255.255.255.0**. g. Verify that **Use the following DNS server addresses** is selected, and in the **Preferred DNS server** box, type the DNS server address that you recorded in Exercise 1, and then click **OK**. h. Click **OK** to close the **PartnerNet Properties** dialog box. i. Close all open windows.

Exercise 3
Removing DHCP

Scenario

After you have tested a DHCP configuration for your organization, you must restore your original configuration.

Goal

In this exercise, you will restore the original computer configuration.

Tasks	Detailed Steps
🛑 Perform the following procedure on both computers. If you intend to complete the "If Time Permits" exercise, perform this procedure after you complete the "If Time Permits" exercise.	
1. Remove the DHCP service.	a. In Control Panel, double-click **Add/Remove Programs**. b. In Add/Remove Programs, click **Add/Remove Windows Components**.
ℹ️ **Note:** In the next detailed step, click the text **Networking Services** rather than the check box to avoid selecting all options under **Networking Services**.	
1. *(continued)*	c. In the Windows Components wizard, on the **Windows Components** page, click **Networking Services**, and then click **Details**. d. In the **Networking Services** dialog box, clear the **Dynamic Host Configuration Protocol (DHCP)** check box, and then click **OK**. e. On the **Windows Components** page, click **Next**. f. When the configuration process is complete, click **Finish**. g. Close all open windows, and then log off.

If Time Permits
Configuring a Second DHCP Server

Reverse roles with your partner and repeat all of the steps in exercise 1, "Creating, Configuring, and Assigning a Scope," and exercise 2, "Creating and Testing a Client Reservation," so that the computer that you configured as a DHCP client the first time that you completed the exercise is now configured as a DHCP server. Complete exercise 3, "Removing DHCP," after you have completed exercises 1 and 2.

◆ Customizing DHCP Functionality

- **Using Option Classes**
- **Combining Scopes by Using Superscopes**
- **Issuing Multicast Addresses by Using Multicast Scopes**

By creating option classes, you can customize a DHCP server to issue configuration information to a specific client computer or to a group of client computers. You can also customize DHCP to function in a routed network without having to configure a DHCP server on each physical segment. The Windows 2000 implementation of DHCP also supports superscopes, which combine two or more scopes, and multicast scopes, which issue multicast addresses to DHCP clients.

By customizing DHCP functionality, you can reduce administrative overhead, automate configuration for select groups of clients, and minimize the number of DHCP servers that are required in a routed network environment.

Using Option Classes

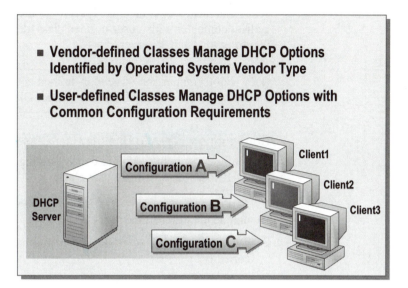

You use option classes to provide unique configurations to specific types of client computers. The Windows 2000 implementation of DHCP supports two types of option classes: vendor-defined classes and user-defined classes.

Vendor-defined classes

Vendor-defined classes identify a DHCP client's operating system vendor type and configuration. You can configure vendor-defined classes to manage DHCP options that you want to assign to clients based on the operating system. For example, you can configure a vendor-defined class to provide a custom configuration for computers that are running a specific operating system, such as Windows 98 or Windows 2000 Professional.

DHCP servers and clients use the identifier in the TCP/IP networking software to take advantage of vendor-defined classes. The DHCP server automatically recognizes the identifiers sent by computers running Windows 2000 and Windows 98. You can also define additional vendor identifiers on the DHCP server. Before you configure additional vendor options, you must determine which identifier, if any, a specific vendor uses by contacting the vendor of the client operating system or network software.

User-defined classes

User-defined classes identify a DHCP client by its type. A client *type* refers to characteristics such as a dial-up connection or portable computer. You configure user-defined classes to manage DHCP options that you want to assign to clients that require a common configuration. For example, you can configure a user-defined class to provide a configuration for computers that require Internet access.

User-Defined Identifiers

You assign user-defined options to a client based on an identifier. The client sends this identifier to the DHCP server to identify itself. You need to configure a client computer with a user-defined class identifier before it will send this identifier to a DHCP server.

Note   For a comparison of vendor-defined classes and user-defined classes, see the topic "Understanding User and Vendor Classes" in Windows 2000 Help.

Configuring Clients to Use the User Class

To configure a client computer that is running Windows 2000 to identify itself to a DHCP server by using a user class:

1. At a command prompt, type **ipconfig /setclassid** *class* (where *class* is the unique identifier of the user class).

2. Type **ipconfig /showclassid** to confirm that the user class was configured correctly.

Note   You can type **ipconfig /?** at a command prompt to learn more about how to configure user-defined identifier options.

Creating a New Vendor or User Class

To create a new vendor or user class:

1. Open DHCP from the **Administrative Tools** menu.

2. In the console tree, right-click the DHCP server on which you want to create a new class, and then, to create a new vendor class, click **Define Vendor Classes**. To create a new user class, click **Define User Classes**.

3. In the **DHCP Vendor Classes** or **DHCP User Classes** dialog box, click **Add**.

4. In the **New Class** dialog box, type a display name, an optional description and an identifier that uniquely identifies the class.

   After you have created a new vendor or user class, you can assign DHCP options to the class. These options are sent to clients that identify themselves by using the class ID.

Combining Scopes by Using Superscopes

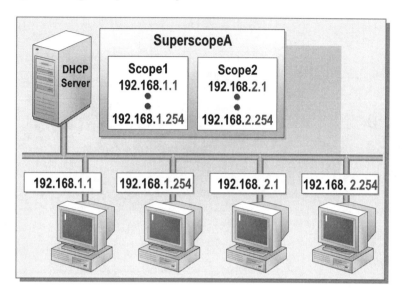

A *superscope* is a group of two or more scopes that are combined so that you can manage them as a single unit. When you configure a superscope on a DHCP server, that server can issue addresses from any participating scope to clients on the same physical subnet.

Superscopes are helpful in a variety of situations, such as when:

- You need to add more hosts than were originally planned on a subnet.

- You replace existing address ranges with new address ranges.

- The IP addresses that your organization owns are not in a contiguous range.

In each case, configuring a superscope eliminates the need to delete and re-create the existing scopes.

Note A DHCP server treats all included addresses as belonging to the same scope when it assigns addresses. You cannot ensure that certain clients receive an address from one of the included address ranges and not from another.

To create a superscope:

1. Open DHCP from the **Administrative Tools** menu.

2. In the console tree, click the name of the DHCP server for which you want to create a superscope, right-click the name of the DHCP server, and then click **New Superscope**.

3. In the New Superscope wizard, type the superscope name, and then specify two or more existing scopes to include in the superscope.

Issuing Multicast Addresses by Using Multicast Scopes

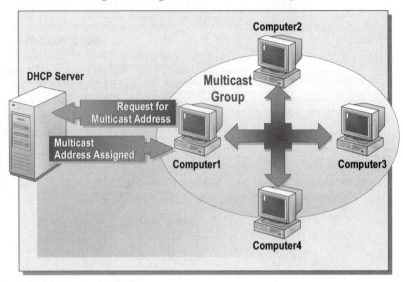

You use a multicast scope to issue a multicast address to selected computers on a network. When you use DHCP to configure client computers with a multicast address, those clients can participate in collaborative application sessions. Typically, audio and conferencing applications, such as Microsoft Windows Media™, use multicasting technology for deploying information from a single point to multiple computers at one time.

You can configure several computers with the same multicast address in addition to each computer's individual IP address. All computers configured with the same multicast address receive IP packets that are sent to that address. For multicasting to work correctly, all routers between the server that is sending packets to the multicast address and the receiving client computers must be configured to recognize the multicast address.

Configuring a multicast scope to issue a multicast address eliminates the need for users to specify the address manually. To take advantage of dynamic multicast IP addressing, you must configure a multicast scope on a DCP server, and multicast applications on client computers must be able to use the Multicast Address Dynamic Client Allocation Protocol (MADCAP).

Note For more information about multicast addresses, see RFCs 1112, 2236, and 2730 under **Additional Reading** on the Student Materials compact disc.

To create a multicast scope:

1. Open DHCP from the **Administrative Tools** menu.

2. In the console tree, right-click the name of the DHCP server on which you want to create a multicast scope, and then click **New Multicast Scope**.

3. In the New Multicast Scope wizard, on the **Multicast Scope Name** page, type the name and an optional description of the multicast scope, and then click **Next**.

4. On the **IP Address Range** page, type the start IP address and the end IP address, and then click **Next**.

    The range of multicast addresses that you select must be in the range of valid multicast addresses, 224.0.0.0 to 239.255.255.255.

5. Select a Time to Live (TTL), which is the number of routers through which multicast traffic can pass, and then click **Next**.

6. On the **Add Exclusions page**, specify any excluded IP addresses, and then click **Next**.

7. On the **Lease Duration** page, specify the lease duration.

8. On the **Activate Multicast Scope page**, click **Yes**, and then click **Next**.

9. On the **Completing the New Multicast Scope Wizard** page, click **Finish**.

Configuring DHCP in a Routed Network

- **Routed Network Configuration Options**
- **Using a DHCP Relay Agent**

Routers separate subnets in large network environments. One of the functions of a router is to contain broadcast traffic to a given subnet. As a result, routers are typically configured to not forward broadcast messages to other subnets.

However, DHCP is a broadcast-based service. As a result, DHCP communication is limited to a single subnet unless you configure it to work in a routed network environment.

Routed Network Configuration Options

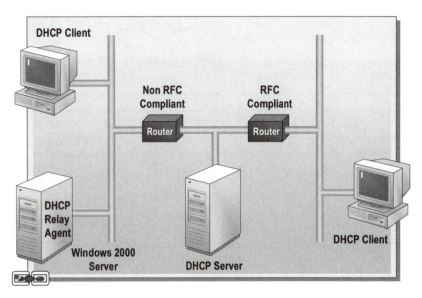

You configure DHCP functionality in a routed network in one of three ways:

- *Include at least one DHCP server on each subnet.* This method supplies DHCP functionality to each subnet. However, it requires significant administrative overhead because of the additional equipment and the need to configure scopes on each DHCP server. In addition, you should configure at least two DHCP servers per subnet for fault tolerance. Placing two DHCP servers on each subnet is often too expensive.

- *Configure an RFC 1542–compliant router to forward DHCP messages between subnets.* An RFC 1542–compliant router that is configured for BOOTP forwarding selectively forwards DHCP broadcasts to another subnet, but it does not forward other broadcast messages. Although this option is preferable to using DHCP servers on each subnet, it can complicate router configuration, and DHCP communication across multiple subnets is slow.

- *Configure a DHCP relay agent on each subnet to forward DHCP messages between subnets.* Configuring a DHCP relay agent on each subnet has several advantages over the other options. Configuring a DHCP relay agent is generally easier than configuring other options, and using a DHCP relay agent limits broadcasts to the subnet in which they originate. By adding DHCP relay agent to multiple subnets, a single DHCP server can provide IP addresses to multiple subnets more efficiently than when using RFC 1542-compliant routers. Configuring a DHCP relay agent can also provide fault tolerance.

Using a DHCP Relay Agent

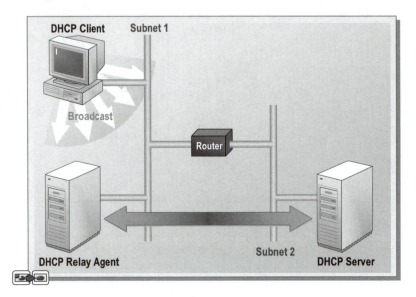

On a local subnet, a DHCP relay agent intercepts DHCP client address request broadcast messages and forwards them to a DHCP server on another subnet. The DHCP server responds to the relay agent by using a directed packet. The relay agent then broadcasts the response on the local subnet for use by the requesting client.

Installing a DHCP Relay Agent

To install a DHCP relay agent:

1. Open Routing and Remote Access from the **Administrative Tools** menu.

2. In the console tree, expand the server icon, and then click **IP Routing**.

3. In the details pane, right-click **General**, and then click **New Routing Protocol**.

4. In the **New Routing Protocol** dialog box, click **DHCP Relay Agent**, and then click **OK**.

5. Open the **Properties** dialog box for the DHCP relay agent, in the **Server Address** box, type the IP address of a DHCP server, and then click **Add**.

Configuring a DHCP Relay Agent

Before a DHCP relay agent forwards DHCP requests from clients on any of its network interfaces, you must configure the relay agent to respond to these requests. When enabling relay agent functionality, you can also specify time-out values for a hop count threshold and a boot threshold.

The *hop count threshold* determines the number of subnets on which the packet can exist as a broadcast before being discarded. Setting this number too high can result in excess network traffic when relay agents are incorrectly configured.

The *boot threshold* determines how long the DHCP relay agent will wait for a local DHCP server to respond to client requests before forwarding the request. If you have a DHCP server on the local subnet, this number should be high enough so that the local DHCP server responds to client broadcasts before the DHCP relay agent forwards client requests. Then the DHCP relay agent only contacts a remote DHCP server if the local DHCP server is not available. This mechanism provides for fault tolerance because a correctly configured DHCP relay agent on a network segment with a DHCP server only contacts a DHCP server on a remote network when the local DHCP server does not respond. If you notice that the DHCP relay agent forwards client requests even though there is a DHCP server on the local network, increase the boot threshold.

Important   When you configure a DHCP relay agent to provide fault tolerance, the DHCP on the remote network must configure a scope that is valid for the subnet on which the DHCP clients are located. For more information about configuring DHCP for fault tolerance, see "Planning for DHCP" and "DHCP Scenarios" in the Windows 2000 Server Resource Kit.

To configure a DHCP relay agent:

1. Open Routing and Remote Access from the **Administrative Tools** menu.

2. In the console tree, expand the server icon, expand **IP Routing**, and then expand **General**.

3. Right-click **DHCP Relay Agent**, and then click **New Interface**.

4. Click the interface that you want to add, and then click **OK**.

5. In the **DHCP Relay Properties** dialog box, on the **General** tab, verify that the **Relay DHCP packets** check box is selected.

6. If needed, in **Hop-count threshold** and **Boot threshold (seconds)**, click the arrows to modify the thresholds, and then click **OK**.

Note   Routing and Remote Access must be enabled to configure a DHCP relay agent. For more information on enabling Routing and Remote Access, see module 7, "Configuring Remote Access," in course 2153, *Implementing a Microsoft Windows 2000 Network Infrastructure*.

◆ Supporting DHCP

- **Monitoring the DHCP Server Service**
- **Troubleshooting DHCP Database Problems**
- **Removing a DHCP Server from Service**

The DHCP service can be configured to log events on the server. You can then monitor these event logs to look for errors or potential problems. Understanding how to use these event logs will help you support DHCP on your network.

Monitoring the DHCP Service

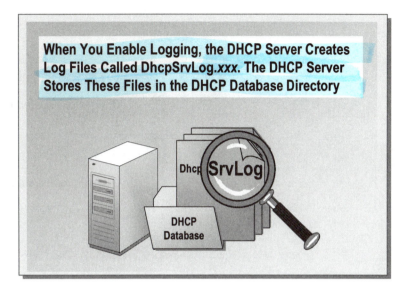

The DHCP service records service startup and shutdown events in addition to critical errors in the Windows system log. You can monitor the details of DHCP operations by enabling detailed event logging.

When you enable logging, DHCP server creates detailed log files of its activity in files called DhcpSrvLog.*xxx* (where *xxx* are the first three letters of the day of the week), which it places in the DHCP database directory. You can review these files to view errors that DHCP server may have encountered.

Important   Because of the system overhead of detailed logging, enable this setting only to troubleshoot DHCP.

To enable logging in DHCP:

1. Right-click the server that you are configuring, and then click **Properties**.
2. In the **DHCP Properties** dialog box, on the **General** tab, click **Enable DHCP audit logging**.

Note   For more information about DHCP audit logging, see "Audit Logging" in Windows 2000 Help.

Troubleshooting DHCP Database Problems

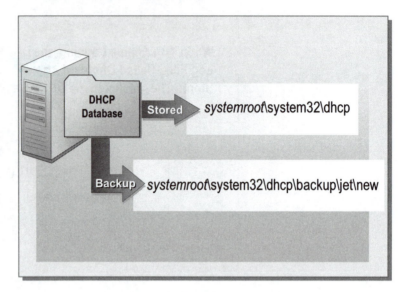

Windows stores the DHCP database in the directory *systemroot*\system32\dhcp. By default, the database is automatically backed up to the backup\jet\new directory, which is located in the database directory. When the DHCP service starts, and periodically thereafter, DHCP performs a consistency check of its database and attempts to fix any errors that it encounters.

If the event log contains Jet database messages that indicate a corruption of the DHCP database, you can repair the database by using the Jetpack program that is included with Windows 2000 Server. On busy DHCP servers with large databases, you should also perform this procedure once per month to compact the database thoroughly.

To run the Jetpack program:

1. Stop the DHCP service.

2. At a command prompt, change to the directory where the DHCP database is located (by default *systemroot*\system32\dhcp).

3. Type **jetpack dhcp.mdb** *temp* (where *temp* is a file name for a temporary database location that is used during repair), and then press ENTER.

4. Start the DHCP service.

Important Before running the Jetpack program, rule out other sources for the errors, such as disk problems, and back up the DHCP database files to a separate location.

If the Jetpack program does not repair the database, you can restore the database from the backup directory. If restoring the DHCP database from these backup files is unsuccessful, you must restore the files from a recent backup tape.

Note For more information about how to force the DHCP server to load the database from the backup directory, see "Restoring Server Data" in Windows 2000 Help.

Removing a DHCP Server from Service

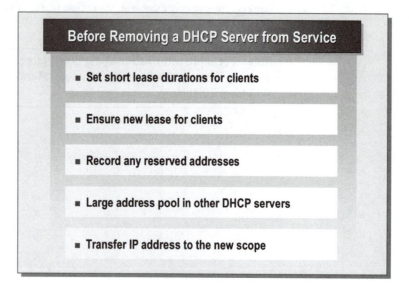

When you remove a DHCP scope from a server or remove a DHCP server from service, you need to take the following steps to ensure that clients continue to be able to connect to network resources:

- *Short lease duration for clients.* To prepare for removing a DHCP scope, set the lease duration for the scope to a short period. This ensures that clients receive only a short lease, which expires soon after the scope is removed.

- *New lease for clients.* Ensure that all clients have received a lease with the new period by waiting until the previous lease period has expired.

- *Record any reserved addresses.* Record any reserved addresses so that you can re-create them on another DHCP server that will assign addresses for the subnet.

- *Sufficiently large address pool on the new DHCP server.* Ensure that another DHCP server that assigns addresses for the subnet has a large enough address pool to assign IP addresses to all clients on the subnet.

- *Transfer IP address to the new scope.* Before allocating any IP addresses of the current scope to another scope, wait until the lease period has expired. This ensures that no DHCP server assigns addresses that are still used by clients that received the address from the scope that you are removing.

Review

- **Overview of DHCP**

- **Requirements for DHCP Servers and Clients**

- **Installing the DHCP Service**

- **Authorizing the DHCP Service**

- **Creating and Configuring a Scope**

- **Customizing DHCP Functionality**

- **Supporting DHCP**

1. What are the steps in the DHCP lease process?

2. What must you configure on a computer running Windows 2000 Server before you can install the DHCP service?

3. How does a DHCP server in a Windows 2000 network determine its authorization status and what are the possible results of that determination?

4. After you create a scope, how can you modify the subnet mask in the scope?

5. What types of option classes does Windows 2000 support and how are they different?

6. Your network consists of multiple network segments that are connected by routers. How should you configure the network so that all client computers can receive IP addresses by using DHCP?

MULTICAST .224 → .239

→ 224.0.0.1

SERVER
↓
SCOPE
↓
VENDOR
↓
USER.

NBNS → NET BIOS NAME SERVICE
NBT → NET BIOS TCP

OBTAIN IP ADDRESS FIRST TIME
_____

D ISCOVER (CLIENT)
O FFER   (SERVER OFFERS IP ADDRESS)
                 INC SERVER ID #
R EQUEST (CLIENT, REQUEST IP ADDRS
              FROM BASED ON
                     OFFER)
A OK
                     INCLUDES SERVER ID #

              → ACKNOWLEDGMENT FROM
                 SERVER VALID IP
                 ADDRESS TO BE ASSIGN

OBTAIN IP ADDRESS 2nd ...
_____

DHCP RELAY AGENT
    ROUTER NEEDS RFC 1542 COMPATABILITY.

                    DHCP
                    SERVER
              _____
   _____(2)_____
  | | |
 PC   DHCP
         RELAY
         AGENT (SIDE OF PC)

Microsoft®
Training &
Certification

Module 3: Implementing Name Resolution by Using DNS

Contents

Overview

- Overview of the DNS Query Process

- Installing the DNS Server Service

- Configuring Name Resolution for Client Computers

- Creating Zones

- Configuring Zones

- Configuring DNS for Internal Use

- Integrating DNS and DHCP

- Maintaining and Troubleshooting DNS Servers

The Domain Name System (DNS) is an integral part of client/server communications in Internet Protocol (IP) networks. DNS is a distributed database that is used in IP networks to translate, or resolve, computer names into IP addresses. Microsoft® Windows® 2000 uses DNS as its primary method for name resolution.

Windows 2000–based clients use the DNS Server service for name resolution and to locate services, including domain controllers that provide user authentication.

At the end of this module, you will be able to:

- Describe the DNS query process.

- Install the DNS Server service.

- Configure name resolution for client computers.

- Create zones.

- Configure zones.

- Configure DNS for internal use by configuring a root zone.

- Configure Dynamic Host Configuration Protocol (DHCP) for DNS integration.

- Maintain and troubleshoot DNS servers.

Multimedia: Basics of the Domain Name System (DNS)

Before you begin the process of installing and configuring the DNS Server service in Windows 2000, it is important to review some basic concepts of DNS.

Note The purpose of this presentation is to review basic DNS concepts prior to learning about the features in the Windows 2000 DNS Server service. To view the Basics of the Domain Name System (DNS) multimedia presentation, open the Web page on the Student Materials compact disc, click **Multimedia Presentations**, and then click **Basics of the Domain Name System (DNS)**.

Review the following key points after you view the multimedia presentation:

- DNS is a distributed database system that can serve as the foundation for name resolution in an IP network.
- The hierarchical structure of the domain namespace is such that the root domain is at the top of the domain structure and is represented by a period. Below the root domain, top-level domains can be represented by an organizational type, such as com or edu, or a geographic location, such as au for Australia. Second-level domains are registered to individuals or organizations and can have many subdomains.
- The fully qualified domain name (FQDN) describes the exact relation of a host to its domain. DNS uses the FQDN to resolve a host name to an IP address.
- The name-to-IP address data for computers that are located in a zone is stored in a zone file on a DNS server.
- A forward lookup query is a request to resolve a name to an IP address.
- When a client sends a forward lookup query to request an IP address from a domain for which the local DNS server does not have authority, the local DNS server sends a query to a DNS server that hosts the root zone.

Overview of the DNS Query Process

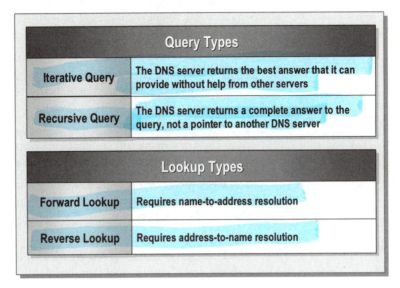

DNS uses a client/server model in which the DNS server contains information about a portion of the DNS namespace and provides this information to clients. A DNS client queries a DNS server for information about the DNS namespace. This server can, in turn, query other DNS servers to provide an answer to the query from the client.

When a DNS server receives a DNS request, it attempts to locate the requested information within its own database. If the request fails, further communication with other DNS servers is necessary.

Query Types

There are two types of queries that can be performed in DNS:

- *Iterative*. A query made from a client to a DNS server in which the server returns the best answer that it can provide based on its cache or zone data. If the queried server does not have an exact match for the request, it provides a pointer to an authoritative server in a lower level of the domain namespace.

  The client then queries the authoritative server to which it was referred. The client continues this process until it locates a server that is authoritative for the requested name, or until an error occurs or time-out condition is met.

- *Recursive*. A query made from a client to a DNS server in which the server assumes the full workload and responsibility for providing a complete answer to the query. The server will then perform separate iterative queries to other servers (on behalf of the client) to assist in answering the recursive query.

Query Process

Client computers typically send recursive queries to DNS servers. The DNS servers then use iterative queries to provide an answer to the client. For example, when a client computer issues a request to a DNS server to resolve the address www.microsoft.com, the following process takes place:

1. The client computer generates a request for the IP address of www.microsoft.com by sending a recursive query to the DNS server that it is configured to use.

2. The DNS server that received the recursive query is unable to locate an entry for www.microsoft.com in its database, so it sends an iterative query to a DNS server that is authoritative for the root domain.

3. The DNS server that is authoritative for the root domain is unable to locate an entry for www.microsoft.com in its database, so it sends a reply to the querying DNS server with the IP addresses of DNS servers that are authoritative for the com domain.

4. The DNS server that received the recursive query sends an iterative query to a server that is authoritative for the com domain.

5. The DNS server that is authoritative for the com domain is unable to locate an entry for www.microsoft.com in its database, so it sends a reply to the querying DNS server with the IP addresses of DNS servers that are authoritative for the microsoft.com domain.

6. The DNS server that received the recursive query sends an iterative query to a server that is authoritative for the microsoft.com domain.

7. The DNS server that is authoritative for the microsoft.com domain locates an entry for www.microsoft.com in its database and sends a reply to the querying DNS server with the IP address of www.microsoft.com.

8. The DNS server that received the recursive query sends a reply to the client computer with the IP address of www.microsoft.com.

Lookup Types

The zone lookup type determines the tasks that a DNS server will perform. When you create a zone, you specify whether the zone will be used for resolving forward or reverse lookup queries by specifying the zone type. Iterative and recursive queries can be associated with either of the following lookup types:

- *Forward lookup*. A request to map a name to an IP address. This is the most common type of lookup, and is used to locate a server's IP address so that a connection can be made to it. This type of request requires name-to-address resolution.

- *Reverse lookup*. A request to map an IP address to a name. This is most commonly used when you know an IP address, but you want to know the domain name that is associated with the IP address. For example, if you monitor IP connections that are made to a server, you can use a reverse lookup to locate the domain name associated with the IP address of the connecting computer. This type of request requires address-to-name resolution.

Installing the DNS Server Service

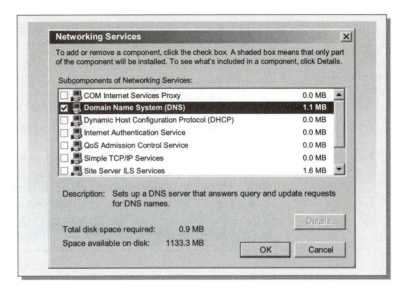

You create a DNS server by installing the DNS Server service on a computer running Windows 2000 Server.

Computers running Windows 2000 are configured to receive Transmission Control Protocol/Internet Protocol (TCP/IP) configuration information from a DHCP server by default. You must configure TCP/IP with a static IP address before you install the DNS Server service.

Configuring TCP/IP

To configure TCP/IP, you must assign a static IP address in the **Internet Protocol (TCP/IP) Properties** dialog box on the computer on which you are installing the DNS Server service.

Microsoft also recommends that you configure the domain name on the computer on which you are installing the DNS Server service.

To configure the domain name:

1. Open the **Properties** dialog box for the network connection that you are configuring.

2. Click **Internet Protocol (TCP/IP)**, and then click **Properties**.

3. In the **Internet Protocol (TCP/IP) Properties** dialog box, click **Advanced**.

4. On the **DNS** tab of the **Advanced TCP/IP Settings** dialog box, verify that the DNS address in the **DNS server addresses, in order of use** box is correct.

5. Type the domain name in the **DNS suffix for this connection** box, and then click **OK**.

DNS Server Service Installation Process

To install the DNS Server service:

1. In Control Panel, click **Add/Remove Programs**, and then click **Add/Remove Windows Components**.

2. On the **Windows Components** page of the Windows Components wizard, click **Networking Services**, and then click **Details**.

3. Select the **Domain Name System (DNS)** check box, and then click **OK**.

4. Click **Next**, and then click **Finish** to complete the Windows Components wizard.

Note The Active Directory™ directory service relies on DNS for name resolution and for the location of Active Directory components in a network. You must configure the DNS infrastructure prior to installing Active Directory or let Active Directory automatically configure the DNS server.

Configuring Name Resolution for Client Computers

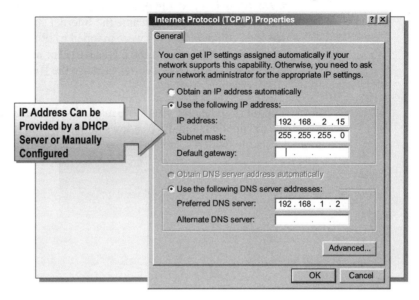

A DNS client uses a DNS server to resolve queries and locate resources on IP networks. In Windows 2000, configuring a computer as a DNS client involves only one configuration parameter: the IP address of the DNS server.

Note   The networking component that performs DNS lookups is sometimes referred to as a *resolver*.

Configuring Client Computers

To configure a client to use a DNS server for name resolution, open the **Properties** dialog box for the connection, and then open the **Internet Protocol (TCP/IP) Properties** dialog box:

- If you want DNS server addresses to be provided by a DHCP server, click **Obtain DNS server address automatically**.

- If you want to manually configure an IP address for a DNS server, click **Use the following DNS server addresses**. Type the IP address of the primary server in the **Preferred DNS server** box. If you are configuring a second DNS server, type the IP address of the additional DNS server in the **Alternate DNS server** box.

Note   Windows 2000 uses the second (or alternate) DNS server only when it cannot contact the primary DNS server.

Configuring the Hosts file

A *Hosts file* is a text file that contains static mappings of host names to IP addresses. Before DNS became the Internet standard for name resolution services, computer names were mapped to IP addresses by using Hosts files. Windows 2000 can use a local Hosts file for name resolution, which provides a faster response to DNS queries because the Hosts file is queried before any DNS servers.

You must update the Hosts file manually, because the mappings in the Hosts file are not dynamic. In Windows 2000, you can use any text editor to edit the Hosts file, which is located in the *systemroot*\system32\drivers\etc folder.

◆ Creating Zones

- **Identifying Zone Types**
- **Examining the Zone File**
- **Creating Lookup Zones**

A *zone* is a contiguous portion of the domain namespace for which a DNS server has authority to resolve DNS queries. You can divide the DNS namespace into zones, which store name information about one or more DNS domains or portions of a DNS domain. For each DNS domain name included in a zone, the zone becomes the authoritative source for information about that domain.

Before you create zones, you must understand the following concepts:

- *Zone types*. DNS servers can host different types of zones. To limit the number of DNS servers on your network, you can configure a single DNS server to support, or host, multiple zones. You can also configure multiple servers to host one or more zones to provide fault tolerance and distribute the name resolution and administrative workloads.

- *Zone file*. The resource records that are stored in a zone file define a zone. The zone file stores information that is used to resolve host names to IP addresses and IP addresses to host names. If you use Active Directory-integrated zones, you can also store zone information in Active Directory, not only in zone files on a DNS server.

Important   To create zones and administer a DNS server that is not running on a domain controller, you must be a member of the Administrators group on that computer. To configure a DNS server that is running on a domain controller, you must be a member of the DNSAdmins, Domain Admins, or Enterprise Admins groups.

Identifying Zone Types

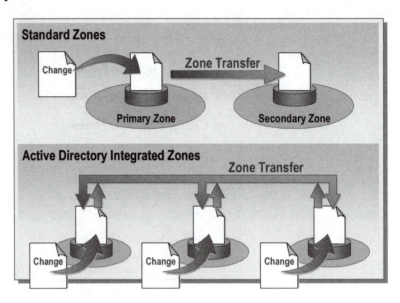

The following table describes the three types of zones that you can configure, and the zone files associated with them.

Zone type	Description
Standard primary	Contains a read/write version of the zone file that is stored in a standard text file. Any changes to the zone are recorded in that file. You must create a standard primary zone each time you create a new zone.
Standard secondary	Contains a read-only version of the zone file that is stored in a standard text file. Any changes to the zone are recorded in the primary zone file and replicated to the secondary zone file. Create a standard secondary zone to create a copy of an existing zone and its zone file. This allows the name resolution workload to be distributed among multiple DNS servers.
Active Directory integrated	Stores the zone information in Active Directory, rather than a text file. Updates to the zone occur automatically during Active Directory replication. Create an Active Directory integrated zone to simplify planning and configuration of a DNS namespace. You do not need to configure DNS servers to specify how and when updates occur because Active Directory maintains zone information.

Examining the Zone File

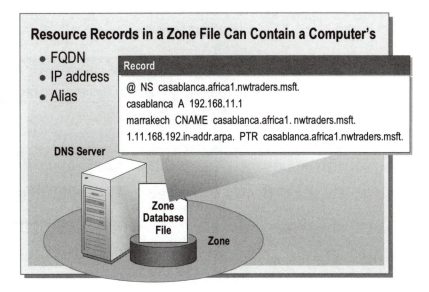

Resource Records in a Zone File Can Contain a Computer's

- FQDN
- IP address
- Alias

Record

@ NS casablanca.africa1.nwtraders.msft.

casablanca A 192.168.11.1

marrakech CNAME casablanca.africa1. nwtraders.msft.

1.11.168.192.in-addr.arpa. PTR casablanca.africa1.nwtraders.msft.

DNS Server

Zone Database File

Zone

Zone files contain the necessary information that a DNS server references to perform two different tasks: resolving host names to IP addresses or resolving IP addresses to host names. This information is stored as resource records that populate the zone file.

A zone file contains the name resolution data for a zone, including resource records that contain information for answering DNS queries. *Resource records* are database entries that contain various attributes, such as the host name or the FQDN of a computer, an IP address, or an alias.

Creating Lookup Zones

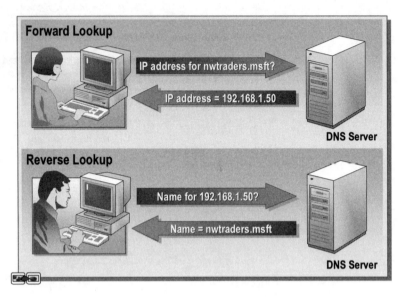

In most DNS lookups, clients typically perform a forward lookup, which is a request to map a computer name to an IP address. DNS also provides a reverse lookup process, which enables clients to request a computer name based on the computer's IP address.

Creating a Forward Lookup Zone

To create a forward lookup zone, click **Forward lookup** on the **Select the Zone Lookup Type** page of the New Zone wizard. The wizard guides you through the process of naming the zone and the zone file. The wizard automatically creates the zone, the zone file, and the necessary resource records for the DNS server on which you create the zone.

Creating a Reverse Lookup Zone

To create a reverse lookup zone, click **Reverse lookup** on the **Select the Zone Lookup Type** page of the New Zone wizard. The wizard guides you through the process of specifying the network identification or zone name, and verifying the name of the zone file based on the network identification information. The wizard automatically creates the zone, the zone file, and the necessary resource records for the DNS server on which you create the zone.

The in-addr.arpa domain is a special top-level DNS domain that is reserved for reverse mapping of IP addresses to DNS host names. To create the reverse namespace, you form subdomains within the in-addr.arpa domain by using the reverse ordering of the numbers in the dotted-decimal notation of IP addresses.

To comply with RFC standards, the reverse lookup zone name requires the in-addr.arpa domain suffix. When you create a reverse lookup zone, the in-addr.arpa suffix is automatically appended to the end of the network identification. For example, if the network uses the class B network identifier of 172.16.0.0, the reverse lookup zone name becomes 16.172.in-addr.arpa.

Note For more information about the in-addr.arpa domain suffix, see RFC 2317 under **Additional Reading** on the Web page on the Student Materials compact disc.

◆ Configuring Zones

- **Configuring Standard Zones**
- **Zone Transfer Process**
- **Configuring Zone Transfers**
- **Creating a Subdomain**
- **Configuring Active Directory Integrated Zones**
- **Migrating Zones to the Windows 2000 DNS Server service**

A zone is defined by the information that is stored in the zone file on the DNS server. DNS servers reference this information to perform name resolution.

You must configure a zone to enable the authoritative DNS server to provide name resolution for DNS clients and other DNS servers. When you configure a zone, you determine the type of zone file that is stored on a DNS server, in addition to how the zone file is updated.

Configuring Standard Zones

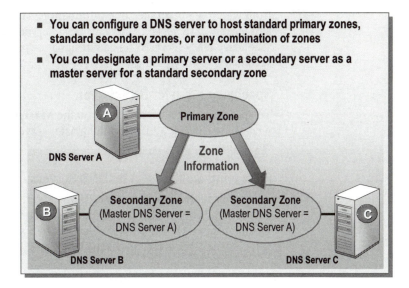

For each zone, the server that maintains the standard primary zone files is called the *primary server*, and the servers that host the standard secondary zone files are called *secondary servers*. A DNS server can host the standard primary zone file (as the primary server) for one zone and the standard secondary zone file (as the secondary server) for another zone.

You can configure a single DNS server or multiple DNS servers to host:

- One or more standard primary zones.
- One or more standard secondary zones.
- Any combination of standard primary and standard secondary zones.

Note You must create a standard primary zone before you can create a standard secondary zone.

Specifying a Master DNS Server for a Secondary Zone

When you add a standard secondary zone, you must designate a DNS server from which to obtain the zone information. The designated server is referred to as a *master DNS server*. A master DNS server transfers zone information to the secondary DNS server. You can designate a primary server or another secondary server as a master DNS server for a standard secondary zone.

Specifying a Master DNS Server

To specify a master DNS server, on the **Master Servers** page of the New Zone wizard, type the IP address of the master server in the **IP address** box, and then click **Add**.

Specifying Multiple Master DNS Servers

To specify more than one master DNS server, use the same procedure to add additional master DNS server IP addresses to the list. You can sort the list into the order in which you want the master DNS servers to be contacted. To sort the list, click an IP address, and then click **Up** or **Down**.

Lab A: Installing and Configuring the DNS Server Service

Objectives

After completing this lab, you will be able to:

- Install the DNS Server service.
- Delegate authority for a domain.
- Create forward and reverse lookup zones.
- Enable dynamic updates.

Prerequisite

Before working on this lab, you must be familiar with DNS concepts and operations.

Lab Setup

To complete this lab, you need the following:

- A computer running Microsoft Windows 2000 Advanced Server that is configured as a domain controller.

- A static IP address and subnet mask.

- A lab partner. One partner will create the primary zone; the other will create a secondary zone and designate his or her partner's computer as the master DNS server.

- An FQDN. Refer to the Student Computer IP Addresses and FQDNs section of the lab for this information.

- The IP address of the instructor computer. This is 192.168.z.200, where z is the assigned classroom number.

Important   The lab does not reflect the real-world environment. It is recommended that you always use complex passwords for any administrator accounts, and never create accounts without a password.

Important   Outside of the classroom environment, it is strongly advised that you use the most recent software updates that are necessary. Because this is a classroom environment, we may use software that does not include the latest updates.

Student Computer IP Addresses and FQDNs

The following table provides the IP address and FQDN of each student computer in the fictitious domain nwtraders.msft.

Find the student number that the instructor has assigned to you, and make a note of the IP address (where x is the assigned classroom number) and FQDN for your student number.

Student number	IP address	FQDN
1	192.168.x.1	vancouver.namerica1.nwtraders.msft
2	192.168.x.2	denver.namerica1.nwtraders.msft
3	192.168.x.3	perth.spacific1.nwtraders.msft
4	192.168.x.4	brisbane.spacific1.nwtraders.msft
5	192.168.x.5	lisbon.europe1.nwtraders.msft
6	192.168.x.6	bonn.europe1.nwtraders.msft
7	192.168.x.7	lima.samerica1.nwtraders.msft
8	192.168.x.8	santiago.samerica1.nwtraders.msft
9	192.168.x.9	bangalore.asia1.nwtraders.msft
10	192.168.x.10	singapore.asia1.nwtraders.msft
11	192.168.x.11	casablanca.africa1.nwtraders.msft
12	192.168.x.12	tunis.africa1.nwtraders.msft
13	192.168.x.13	acapulco.namerica2.nwtraders.msft
14	192.168.x.14	miami.namerica2.nwtraders.msft
15	192.168.x.15	auckland.spacific2.nwtraders.msft
16	192.168.x.16	suva.spacific2.nwtraders.msft
17	192.168.x.17	stockholm.europe2.nwtraders.msft
18	192.168.x.18	moscow.europe2.nwtraders.msft
19	192.168.x.19	caracas.samerica2.nwtraders.msft
20	192.168.x.20	montevideo.samerica2.nwtraders.msft
21	192.168.x.21	manila.asia2.nwtraders.msft
22	192.168.x.22	tokyo.asia2.nwtraders.msft
23	192.168.x.23	khartoum.africa2.nwtraders.msft
24	192.168.x.24	nairobi.africa2.nwtraders.msft

[handwritten margin note: NAMERICA . NWTRADERS . MSFT]

Scenario

Your company, Northwind Traders, is migrating to Windows 2000, and part of that migration involves configuring DNS domains for use across the organization. Your company domain name is nwtraders.msft, and the different geographic regions in your company have been assigned subdomains.

Estimated time to complete this lab: 45 minutes

Exercise 1
Installing the DNS Server Service

Scenario

Your organization currently has DNS servers installed to manage the zones for your domain, nwtraders.msft. You are responsible for installing and configuring the DNS servers for your subdomain, and these servers will host your regional subdomain.

Goal

In this exercise, you will configure the domain name of your computer and install the DNS Server service.

Tasks	Detailed Steps
1. Install the DNS Server service.	a. Log on as administrator@*domain*.nwtraders.msft (where *domain* is the name of your domain) with a password of **password**.
	b. In Control Panel, double-click **Add/Remove Programs**, and then click **Add/Remove Windows Components**.
⚠ **Important:** In the following detailed step, click the text **Networking Services** rather than the check box to avoid selecting all options under **Networking Services**.	
1. *(continued)*	c. In the Windows Components wizard, on the **Windows Components** page, under **Components**, click **Networking Services**, and then click **Details**.
	d. In the **Networking Services** dialog box, select the **Domain Name System (DNS)** check box, and then click **OK**.
	e. In the Windows Components wizard, click **Next**.
	f. If the **Files Needed** dialog box appears, type **\\London\Setup\Winsrc** and then click **OK**.
	g. When the configuration process is complete, click **Finish**, and then close all open windows.

Exercise 2
Delegating Authority for a Domain

Scenario

You are going to create a new subdomain for your region, and this subdomain will be hosted on your server. So that the DNS hierarchy will be able to locate your domain, you must now delegate authority from the parent domain, nwtraders.msft, to your domain.

Goal

In this exercise, you will delegate authority from the instructor DNS server to the student DNS server that will host the primary zone for the new subdomain.

Tasks	Detailed Steps
✋ Perform the following procedure on the computer of the partner with the lower student number.	
1. Add the instructor's DNS server to your DNS console.	a. Click **Start**, point to **Programs**, point to **Administrative Tools**, right-click **DNS**, and then click **Run as**. *ADMINISTRATOR*
	b. In the **Run As Other User** dialog box, type **admin@nwtraders.msft** in the **User name** box, type **password** in the **Password** box, delete the contents of the **Domain** box, and then click **OK**.
	c. In the console tree, right-click **DNS**, and then click **Connect To Computer**.
	d. In the **Select Target Computer** dialog box, click **The following computer**, type **London** in the text box, and then click **OK**.
2. Delegate authority for *domain*.nwtraders.msft to your DNS server.	a. In the console tree, expand **London**, expand **Forward Lookup Zones**, and then expand **nwtraders.msft**.
	b. In the console tree, right-click **nwtraders.msft**, and then click **New Delegation**.
	c. On the **Welcome to the New Delegation Wizard** page, click **Next**.
	d. On the **Delegated Domain Name** page, in the **Delegated domain** box, type *domain* (where *domain* is the name of your domain), and then click **Next**.
	e. On the **Name Servers** page, click **Add**.
	f. In the **New Resource Record** dialog box, in the **Server name** box, type the FQDN of your computer, click **Resolve**, and then click **OK**.
	g. On the **Name Servers** page, click **Add**.
	h. In the **New Resource Record** dialog box, in the **Server name** box, type the FQDN of your partner's computer, click **Resolve**, and then click **OK**.
	i. On the **Name Servers** page, click **Next**.
	j. On the **Completing the New Delegation Wizard** page, click **Finish**.

Exercise 3
Creating Forward and Reverse Lookup Zones

Scenario

Now that you have delegated authority for your subdomain to your server, you must create the lookup zones to host the DNS records for your subdomain.

Goal

In this exercise, you will create forward and reverse lookup zones.

Tasks	Detailed Steps
✋ Perform the following procedure on the computer of the partner with the lower student number.	
1. Add a standard primary forward lookup zone for *domain*.nwtraders.msft	a. In the console tree, click *server* (where *server* is your computer name), right-click *server*, and then click **Configure the server**.
	b. On the **Welcome to the Configure DNS Server Wizard** page, click **Next**.
	c. On the **Forward Lookup Zone** page, ensure that **Yes, create a forward lookup zone** is selected, and then click **Next**.
	d. On the **Zone Type** page, verify that **Standard primary** is selected, and then click **Next**.
	e. On the **Zone Name** page, in the **Name** box, type *domain*.**nwtraders.msft** (where *domain* is the name of your domain), and then click **Next**.
	f. On the **Zone File** page, verify that **Create a new file with this file name** is selected, and then click **Next**.
2. Add a standard secondary reverse lookup zone for your subnet.	a. On the **Reverse Lookup Zone** page, verify that **Yes, create a reverse lookup zone** is selected, and then click **Next**.
	b. On the **Zone Type** page, click **Standard secondary**, and then click **Next**.
	c. On the **Reverse Lookup Zone** page, in the **Network ID** box, type the first three octets of the IP address of your Classroom connection, and then click **Next**. (For example, if your Classroom adapter has an IP address of 192.168.1.1, type **192.168.1**)
	d. On the **Master DNS Servers** page, in the **IP address** box, type the IP address of the instructor computer, click **Add**, and then click **Next**.
	e. On the **Completing the Configure DNS Server Wizard** page, click **Finish**.
✋ Perform the following procedure on the computer of the partner with the higher student number.	

(*continued*)

Tasks	Detailed Steps
3. Add a standard secondary forward lookup zone for *domain.*nwtraders.msft and a standard secondary reverse lookup zone for your subnet.	a. Open DNS from the **Administrative Tools** menu. b. Right-click *server* (where *server* is your computer name), and then click **Configure the server**. c. On the **Welcome to the Configure DNS Server Wizard** page, click **Next**. d. On the **Forward Lookup Zone** page, verify that **Yes, create a forward lookup zone** is selected, and then click **Next**. e. On the **Zone Type** page, click **Standard secondary**, and then click **Next**. f. On the **Zone Name** page, type *domain.***nwtraders.msft** (where *domain* is the name of your domain), and then click **Next**. g. On the **Master DNS Servers** page, in the **IP address** box, type the IP address of your partner's Classroom connection, click **Add**, and then click **Next**. h. On the **Reverse Lookup Zone** page, verify that **Yes, create a reverse lookup zone** is selected, and then click **Next**. i. On the **Zone Type** page, click **Standard secondary**, and then click **Next**. j. On the **Reverse Lookup Zone** page, in the **Network ID** box, type the first three octets of the IP address of your Classroom connection, and then click **Next**. (For example, for an IP address of 192.168.1.1, type **192.168.1**) k. On the **Master DNS Servers** page, in the **IP address** box, type the IP address of the instructor's computer, click **Add**, and then click **Next**. l. On the **Completing the Configure DNS Server Wizard** page, click **Finish**. m. Close DNS.

Exercise 4
Enabling Dynamic Update

Scenario

You want DHCP and client computers to update DNS records automatically to decrease the administrator's workload.

Goal

In this exercise, you will enable dynamic update on the DNS server.

Tasks	Detailed Steps
✋ Perform the following procedure on the computer of the partner with the lower student number.	
1. Enable dynamic update on the forward lookup zone for *domain*.nwtraders.msft.	a. In the console tree, expand *server* (where *server* is your computer name), expand **Forward Lookup Zones**, and then click *domain*.**nwtraders.msft** (where *domain* is the name of your domain).
	b. Right-click *domain*.**nwtraders.msft** (where *domain* is the name of your domain), and then click **Properties**.
	c. In the *domain*.**nwtraders.msft Properties** box, in the **Allow dynamic updates** box, click **Yes**, and then click **OK**.
	d. Close DNS.
✋ Perform the following procedure on the computer with the higher student number.	
2. Configure the secondary zone *domain*.nwtraders.msft to allow zone transfers.	a. Open DNS from the **Administrative Tools** menu.
	b. In the console tree, expand *server*, expand **Forward Lookup Zones**, and then click *domain*.**nwtraders.msft**
	c. Right-click *domain*.**nwtraders.msft**, and then click **Properties**.
	d. On the **Zone Transfers** tab, click **Allow zone transfers**, and then click **OK**.
	e. Close DNS.
✋ Perform the following procedure on both student computers.	

(continued)

Tasks	Detailed Steps
3. Configure the TCP/IP properties for both adapters so that your computer is a client of the DNS Server service on your computer.	a. Right-click **My Network Places**, and then click **Properties**.
	b. Open the **Properties** dialog box for the Classroom connection.
	c. Click **Internet Protocol (TCP/IP)**, and then click **Properties**.
	d. In the **Internet Protocol (TCP/IP) Properties** dialog box, verify that **Use the following DNS server addresses** is selected, type the IP address of your Classroom connection in the **Preferred DNS server** box, and then click **OK**.
	e. Click **OK** to close the **Classroom Properties** dialog box.
	f. Repeat steps b through e to change the DNS server address for the PartnerNet connection.
	g. Close all open windows, and then log off.

Zone Transfer Process

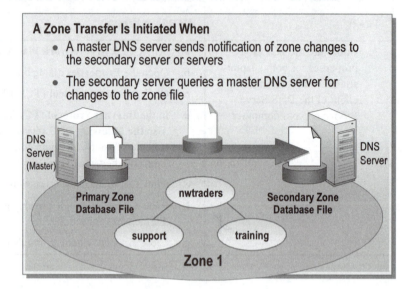

A Zone Transfer Is Initiated When
- A master DNS server sends notification of zone changes to the secondary server or servers
- The secondary server queries a master DNS server for changes to the zone file

DNS Server (Master)   Primary Zone Database File   nwtraders   Secondary Zone Database File   DNS Server

support   training

Zone 1

To provide availability and fault tolerance when resolving name queries, zone data should be available from more than one DNS server on a network. For example, if a single DNS server is used and that server is not responding, name queries will fail. When more than one server is configured to host a zone, zone transfers are required to replicate and synchronize zone data among all of the servers that are configured to host the zone.

Zone Transfer

Zone transfer is the process of replicating a zone file to another DNS server. Zone transfers occur when names and IP address mappings change within your domain. When this happens, the changes to the zone are copied from a master server to its secondary servers.

Incremental Zone Transfer

In Windows 2000, zone information is updated by *incremental zone transfer (IXFR)*, which only replicates changes to the zone file, instead of replicating the entire zone file. DNS servers that do not support IXFR request the entire contents of a zone file when they initiate a zone transfer.

Note For more information about IXFR, see RFC 1995 under **Additional Reading** on the Web page on the Student Materials compact disc.

The zone transfer process begins when one of the following occurs:

- A master server sends a notification of a change in the zone to one or more secondary servers. When the secondary server receives the notification, it queries the master server for the changes.

- Each secondary server periodically queries a master server for changes to the zone file, even if the secondary servers have not been notified of a change. This occurs when the DNS Server service on the secondary server starts, or when the refresh interval on the secondary server expires.

Configuring Zone Transfers

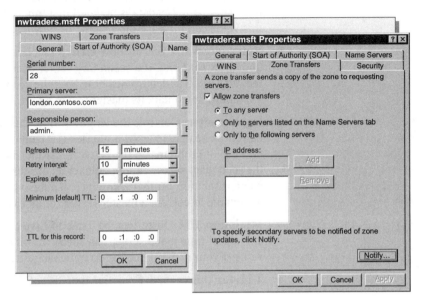

You can control how often and when a zone transfer occurs by modifying the SOA (Start of Authority) resource record. The SOA record specifies the domains for which the zone is authoritative, and the parameters for how zone transfers occur. It also contains administrative information about the zone.

Modifying the SOA Resource Record

To modify the SOA resource record, change any of the following settings on the **Start of Authority (SOA)** tab in the **Properties** dialog box for the zone:

- **Serial number**. Tracks updates to the zone file. Each time the zone database is modified, the serial number is incremented. When a secondary server queries its primary server for updates, it uses the serial number to determine whether changes have been made to a zone. If the number has changed, a zone transfer occurs to update the records on the secondary server.

- **Primary Server**. Specifies the FQDN of the primary server.

- **Responsible Person**. Specifies the Simple Mail Transfer Protocol (SMTP) e-mail address of the person who is responsible for the server. This value should contain the e-mail address of someone who is available and who will check e-mail regularly. If zone transfers are not working properly, users can use the nslookup utility to locate the e-mail address of the responsible person and e-mail a description of the problem.

Note Replace the @ symbol, which appears in the nslookup response, with a period when typing the e-mail address of the responsible person.

- **Refresh interval**. Controls how often a secondary server queries its master server for new data. If DNS data is constantly changing, decrease this value to ensure that DNS data is updated in a timely manner. However, decreasing this value can increase the volume of network traffic.

- **Retry interval**. Controls how often a secondary server will attempt to update its zone file. If a secondary server cannot contact its master server, the retry interval determines how long the secondary server waits before attempting to contact its master server again.

- **Expires after**. Controls the length of time that a secondary server uses its current zone data to answer queries if it cannot contact its master server because of problems on the network. At the end of the expiration interval, if the secondary server cannot contact its master server, it stops performing name resolution for that zone. Increase this value if your secondary servers are unable to contact a master server for an extended period of time.

- **Minimum TTL**. Specifies the Time to Live (TTL) interval, or the minimum amount of time that a server can cache information for a zone. Increase this value if your network names do not change frequently.

- **TTL for this record**. Specifies the TTL of the SOA resource record.

Configuring Zone Transfer Security

You can specify the servers that are authorized to receive zone transfers for the zone by configuring one of the following options on the **Zone Transfers** tab of the **Properties** dialog box for the zone:

- **To any server**. Enables zone information to replicate to any server.

- **Only to servers listed on the Name Servers tab**. Enables zone information to replicate only to the servers that are listed on the **Name Servers** tab of the **Properties** dialog box for the zone. The **Name Servers** tab contains a list of servers that are in the same domain as the zone.

- **Only to the following servers**. Specifies whether you want to allow zone transfers only to the servers that you list under **IP address** on the **Zone Transfers** tab of the **Properties** dialog box for the zone.

Configuring Notification

You can also configure a master DNS server to include a list of one or more secondary servers that should be notified when a zone file is updated. If a secondary server receives notification from its master DNS server that changes have been made to the zone file, it initiates a zone transfer to update its records. It is recommended that on the **Name Servers** tab, you configure master DNS servers to allow zone transfers to only designated DNS servers.

DNS Notify allows you to configure a master server to notify one or more secondary servers whenever changes to the zone occur. The secondary server then sends a request to its master DNS server for the updated information. Whenever a change is made to the primary zone, DNS updates the serial number of the zone file. When this happens, a master DNS server notifies any secondary servers that are included in its notify list, and the secondary servers that receive the notification then retrieve the updated information.

Note For more information about DNS Notify, see RFC 1996 under **Additional Reading** on the Web page on the Student Materials compact disc.

To configure the notify list, open the **Properties** dialog box for the zone, click the **Zone Transfers** tab, and then click the **Notify** button. Then, specify the secondary server or servers that the master server will automatically notify of updates to the zone.

Creating a Subdomain

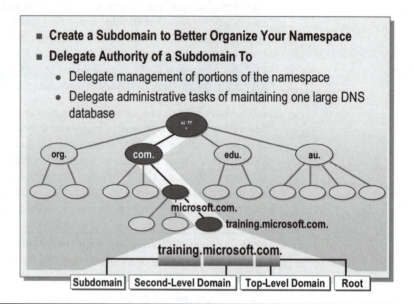

- ■ **Create a Subdomain to Better Organize Your Namespace**
- ■ **Delegate Authority of a Subdomain To**
  - • Delegate management of portions of the namespace
  - • Delegate administrative tasks of maintaining one large DNS database

A subdomain, also called a child domain, is a DNS domain that is located directly beneath another domain in the DNS hierarchical structure. The domain located immediately above the subdomain in the DNS hierarchical structure is called the parent domain. For example, training.microsoft.com is a subdomain of the microsoft.com domain.

Creating a Subdomain in an Existing Zone

You can create subdomains to better organize a zone and provide structure to your namespace. Dividing your namespace to include subdomains can be compared to creating folders and subfolders on a hard disk. Subdomains are generally based on departmental or geographic divisions within an organization.

To create a subdomain, open DNS, and then expand the **Forward Lookup Zones** or **Reverse Lookup Zones** folder. Click the name of the zone in which you want to create a subdomain, right-click the zone name, and then click **New Domain**. Type the name of the subdomain in the **New Domain** dialog box, and then click **OK**.

Creating a Subdomain in a New Zone

You can delegate authority of a subdomain to a DNS server that you want to manage that portion of your DNS namespace. Delegation of authority allows you to:

- Delegate the management of a DNS domain to a number of departments (subdomains) within an organization.

- Delegate the administrative tasks of maintaining one large DNS database. You can assign different administrators to manage the DNS servers in the subdomain.

To delegate authority of a subdomain, open the DNS console, and then expand **Forward Lookup Zones** or **Reverse Lookup Zones**. Click the name of the domain for which you want to delegate authority. Right-click the domain name, point to **New**, and then click **Delegation**.

The Add New Delegation wizard guides you through the process of specifying the name of the domain to which you are delegating authority. The wizard also guides you through the process of adding the name and IP address of the server or servers that will host the delegated domain.

Configuring Active Directory Integrated Zones

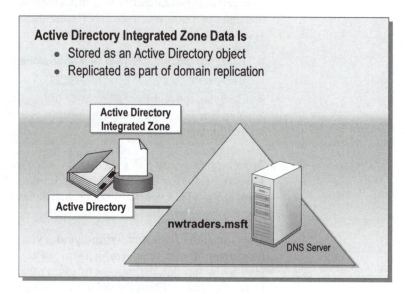

Active Directory Integrated Zone Data Is
- Stored as an Active Directory object
- Replicated as part of domain replication

**Active Directory
Integrated Zone**

Active Directory

nwtraders.msft

DNS Server

In Active Directory integrated zones, zone data is stored as an Active Directory object and is replicated as part of domain replication. Active Directory integrated zones provide the following advantages:

- *No single point of failure.* With Active Directory integrated zones, changes made by using the dynamic update protocol can be made to any server that hosts the Active Directory integrated zone, rather than to a single server.

- *Fault tolerance.* All Active Directory integrated zones are primary zones. Therefore, each domain controller that hosts an Active Directory integrated zone maintains the zone information. Only domain controllers that reside in the Active Directory domain in which the zone data is stored can host the zone.

- *Single replication topology.* Zone transfers occur automatically as part of Active Directory replication, eliminating the need to configure replication for DNS and Active Directory separately.

- *Secure dynamic updates.* With Active Directory integrated zones, you can set permissions on zones and records within those zones. Also, updates that use the dynamic update protocol can only come from authorized computers.

Note You can only create Active Directory integrated zones on servers that are configured as domain controllers and that have the DNS Server service installed on them.

Creating Active Directory Integrated Zones

To create an Active Directory integrated zone, use the same procedure that you would use to create a standard zone, but click **Active Directory integrated** on the **Zone Type** page of the New Zone wizard.

Converting Existing Zones

Before you convert an existing zone to an Active Directory integrated zone, it is important to be aware of the following information:

- The server that is running the DNS Server service must be configured as a domain controller.

- Active Directory integrated zones are stored in Active Directory. When you store a zone in Active Directory, the zone file is copied into Active Directory and deleted on the primary server for the zone.

You can convert a standard primary zone to an Active Directory integrated zone. To do this, open the **Properties** dialog box for the zone that you want to convert. Click the **General** tab, and then click **Change**. In the **Change Zone Type** dialog box, click **Active Directory integrated**, and then click **OK**.

Note   The **Active Directory integrated** option is not available in the **Change Zone Type** dialog box until you implement Active Directory.

Migrating Zones to the Windows 2000 DNS Server Service

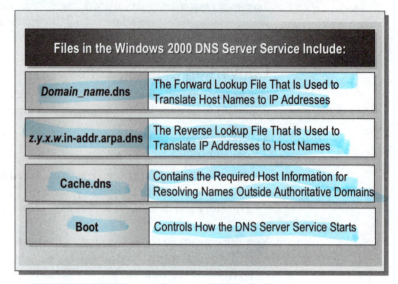

Files in the Windows 2000 DNS Server Service Include:	
Domain_name.dns	The Forward Lookup File That Is Used to Translate Host Names to IP Addresses
z.y.x.w.in-addr.arpa.dns	The Reverse Lookup File That Is Used to Translate IP Addresses to Host Names
Cache.dns	Contains the Required Host Information for Resolving Names Outside Authoritative Domains
Boot	Controls How the DNS Server Service Starts

The DNS Server service installation process creates the *systemroot*\System32\Dns folder. This folder contains the DNS database files described in the following table.

File type	Description
Domain_name.dns	The forward lookup file that is used to translate host names to IP addresses.
z.y.x.w.in-addr.arpa.dns	The reverse lookup file that is used to translate IP addresses to host names.
Cache.dns	The cache file that contains the required host information for resolving names outside authoritative domains. The default file contains records for all of the servers that host the root zone on the Internet.
Boot	The boot file that controls how the DNS Server service starts. In Windows 2000, the Boot file is optional because the boot settings are stored in the registry.

Migrating From a BIND-Based DNS Server

When migrating from a DNS server running Berkeley Internet Name Domain (BIND) to a Windows 2000–based DNS server, you need to rename any BIND-created zone or boot files and copy them to the folder that is used by the Windows 2000 DNS Server service.

If you continue to use a BIND boot file to provide the initial configuration settings that are used when the DNS Server service starts, you must change the boot method that the DNS Server service uses.

Renaming Zone Files

BIND zone files on UNIX-based DNS servers use a different naming convention from the naming convention that the Windows 2000 DNS Server service uses. Therefore, you must copy and rename zone files on UNIX-based DNS servers that use BIND to the computer running Windows 2000 Server.

The following table compares the file names on a UNIX-based DNS server that uses BIND with the file names that the Windows 2000 Server service uses.

File type	UNIX file name	Windows 2000 file name
Boot file	named.boot	Boot
Forward lookup zone file	db.*domain_name*	*Domain_name*.dns
Reverse lookup zone file	db.*w.x.y*	*y.x.w*.in-addr.arpa.dns

Note The Boot file is a part of the BIND-specific implementation of DNS. If you are migrating from a DNS server running BIND, copying the Boot file allows easy migration of your existing configuration.

For more information about BIND, see the Internet Software Consortium (ISC) Web site at http://www.isc.org

Configuring DNS for Internal Use

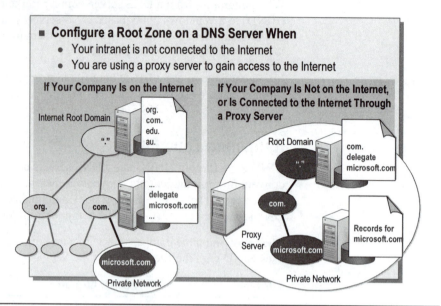

DNS is the hierarchical structure that defines the Internet's namespace. The Internet's root domain contains information about various attributes of the top-level DNS servers (for example, the servers in the com domain). The top-level DNS servers contain information about the second-level DNS servers (for example, the servers in the microsoft.com domain).

To resolve a host name on the Internet, a DNS server begins its search in its own database. If unsuccessful, it then starts at the root, and continues searching through the top-level and second-level servers, until it can resolve the host name.

There are two instances in which you would configure a root zone on a DNS server on your intranet to enable name resolution to start at your internal root domain rather than at the Internet's root domain. It is necessary for you to configure a root zone if:

- Your intranet is not connected to the Internet.

- Your organization is connected to the Internet through a proxy server.

To configure a root zone on a DNS server, use the New Zone wizard to create a root zone that is represented by a period (.).

Important   To allow your DNS server to perform name lookups on the Internet, ensure that you have not configured a root zone on the server, and that the **Root Hints** tab in the **Properties** dialog box of the server contains a list of servers that are authoritative for the root zone of the Internet.

◆ Integrating DNS and DHCP

- Overview of Dynamic Updates
- Configuring Dynamic Updates
- Securing Dynamic Updates

By default, Windows 2000–based clients can update DNS with their name-to-IP address mapping information whenever a DHCP server assigns an IP address to them. However, computers running previous versions of Windows, such as Microsoft Windows NT® and Windows 98, do not have this capability. To resolve this problem, you can configure a DHCP server to update the DNS server database with the name-to-IP address mapping information of client computers. The DHCP server uses the dynamic update protocol to update the DNS server.

Overview of Dynamic Updates

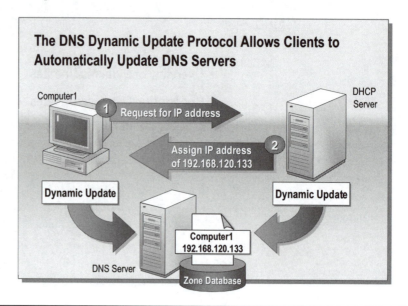

You can configure DHCP servers to automatically assign IP addresses to client computers. When a client receives a new IP address from a DHCP server, the name-to-IP address mapping information that is stored on a DNS server must be updated. In Windows 2000, DHCP servers and clients can register with and dynamically update name-to-IP address mapping information on DNS servers that are configured to support dynamic updates.

Important   Static DNS servers are incapable of interacting dynamically with DHCP when client configurations change. Therefore, Microsoft recommends that you upgrade all DNS servers to Windows 2000 to enable them to support dynamic updates.

Dynamic Update Protocol

The dynamic update protocol enables client computers to automatically update their resource records on a DNS server without administrator intervention. Windows 2000-based computers that are configured with a static IP address are, by default, also configured to perform dynamic updates on the DNS server. In this case the client will update both the forward and reverse lookup entries.

Note   For more information about the DNS dynamic update protocol, see RFC 2136 or the white paper *Windows 2000 DNS* under **Additional Reading** on the Web page on the Student Materials compact disc.

Dynamic Update Process

When a DHCP server assigns an IP address to a Windows 2000–based DHCP client, the following process occurs:

1. The client initiates a DHCP request message to the DHCP server, requesting an IP address. This message includes the FQDN.

2. The DHCP server returns a DHCP acknowledgment message to the client, granting an IP address lease.

3. The client sends a DNS update request to the DNS server for its own forward lookup record, the A resource record.

Note As an alternative to this step, you can configure the DHCP client and the DHCP server to enable the DHCP server to send updates on behalf of the client.

---

4. The DHCP server sends updates for the DHCP client's reverse lookup record, the PTR (pointer) resource record. The DHCP server uses the FQDN that it obtained in the first step to perform this operation.

Dynamic Updates for Clients Running Previous Versions of Windows

Client computers running previous versions of Windows do not support dynamic updates and are unable to interact dynamically with the DNS server. You must configure the DHCP server to always update A and PTR records for these clients, in which case the following process occurs:

1. The client initiates a DHCP request message to the server, requesting an IP address. Unlike DHCP request messages from Windows 2000–based DHCP clients, the request does not include an FQDN.

2. The server returns a DHCP acknowledgment message to the client, granting an IP address lease.

3. The DHCP server sends updates to the DNS server for the client's A and PTR resource records.

Configuring Dynamic Updates

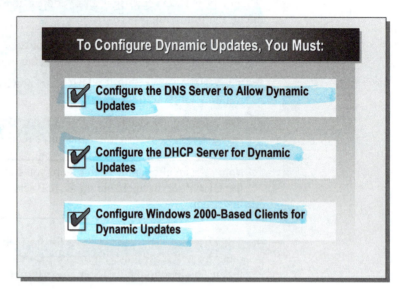

To enable dynamic updates, you must configure the DNS server to allow dynamic updates, and configure the DHCP server and the client computers to update the DNS database.

Configuring the DNS Server to Allow Dynamic Updates

To configure a DNS server to allow dynamic updates, open the **Properties** dialog box for the zone on the DNS server that you want to configure. On the **General** tab, click **Yes** in the **Allow dynamic updates** list box. The following table describes the available options for dynamic updates.

Option	Description
No	Disables dynamic updates for the zone.
Yes	Enables dynamic updates for the zone.
Only secure updates	Enables secure dynamic updates from authorized client computers to an Active Directory integrated zone.

Configuring the DHCP Server for Dynamic Updates

To configure the DHCP server to update the DNS database:

1. In DHCP, open the **Properties** dialog box for the server that you are configuring, and then click the **DNS** tab.

2. Select the **Automatically update DHCP client information in DNS** check box, and then click one of the following options to specify how you want the DHCP server to interact with the DNS server:

   - **Update DNS only if DHCP client requests**. Specifies that the DHCP server update the DNS database based on the client settings. By default, Windows 2000–based clients register their A resource records and request that the DHCP server update its PTR resource record. This option is the default setting for the DHCP server.

- **Always update DNS**. Specifies that the DHCP server update the client's A and PTR resource records in the DNS database, regardless of the client settings.

Note   If you do not want the DHCP server to register and update client information in the DNS database, clear the **Automatically update DHCP client information in DNS** check box.

---

3. To specify how the DHCP server functions when a client's lease expires, perform one of the following steps:

    - Verify that the **Discard forward (name-to-address) lookups when the lease expires** check box is selected if you want the DHCP server to send updates to the DNS database to discard the client's A resource record when the lease expires. This is the default setting for the DHCP server.

    - Clear the **Discard forward (name-to-address) lookups when the lease expires** check box to prevent the DHCP server from sending updates to the DNS database to discard the client's A resource record when the lease expires.

4. To enable the DHCP server to update the DNS database with the A and PTR resource records of clients that are running previous versions of Windows, select the **Enable updates for DNS clients that do not support dynamic update** check box.

5. When you have finished configuring the DHCP server, click **OK**.

Configuring Windows 2000–Based Clients for Dynamic Updates

To configure Windows 2000–based clients to update their A resource records in the DNS database:

1. In Networking and Dial-up Connections, right-click the connection that you want to configure, and then click **Properties**.

2. In the **Properties** dialog box for the connection, click **Internet Protocol (TCP/IP)**, and then click **Properties**.

3. In the **Internet Protocol (TCP/IP) Properties** dialog box, click **Advanced**.

4. In the **Advanced TCP/IP Settings** dialog box, on the **DNS** tab, select the appropriate check boxes:

    - **Register this connection's address in DNS**. Enables the client to register resource records in DNS by using the full computer name and the IP address of the network connection.

    - **Use this connection's DNS suffix in DNS registration**. Enables the client to register resource records in DNS by using the first label of the computer name in addition to the DNS suffix for the connection. Use this option only if the DNS suffix differs from the domain name.

5. Click **OK** three times.

Securing Dynamic Updates

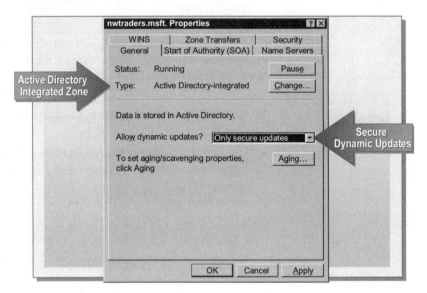

You can configure the DNS server to perform secure dynamic updates for Active Directory integrated zones. With secure dynamic updates, the authoritative DNS server only accepts new registrations from computers that have a computer account in Active Directory, and only accepts updates from the computer that originally registered the record.

Benefits of Secure Dynamic Updates

Secure dynamic updates provide the following benefits:

- Protection of zones and resource records against modification by unauthorized computers.

- The ability to specify the computers and groups that are authorized to modify zones and resource records.

Configuring Secure Dynamic Updates

To configure secure dynamic updates on the DNS server:

1. In DNS, open the **Properties** dialog box for the Active Directory integrated zone on the DNS server that you want to configure.

2. On the **General** tab, click **Only secure updates** in the **Allow dynamic updates** list, and then click **OK**. This option appears in the list only if the zone type is Active Directory integrated.

Note For more information about secure dynamic updates, see RFC 2137 under **Additional Reading** on the Web page on the Student Materials compact disc.

◆ Maintaining and Troubleshooting DNS Servers

- **Reducing Network Traffic by Using Caching-Only Servers**

- **Maintaining DNS Zones**

- **Monitoring DNS Servers**

- **Verifying Resource Records by Using Nslookup**

- **Troubleshooting Name Resolution Problems**

DNS servers are critical to a network; therefore, you must maintain and troubleshoot them to ensure that they are functioning properly and to optimize network performance. For example, you can improve DNS performance by configuring a caching-only server to reduce the amount of DNS-related network traffic, and maintaining resource records to ensure that the name resolution data on a DNS server is current.

Windows 2000 provides several utilities for monitoring and troubleshooting DNS servers. These utilities include:

- The DNS in Microsoft Management Console (MMC), which you can use to test DNS servers and monitor their ability to process and resolve queries.

- Command-line utilities, such as Nslookup, which you can use to verify resource records and troubleshoot DNS problems.

- Logging features, such as the DNS server log, which you can view by using Event Viewer.

Reducing Network Traffic by Using Caching-Only Servers

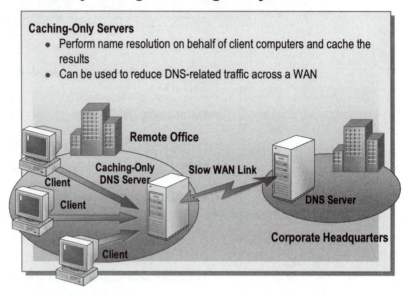

Caching-only servers perform name resolution on behalf of clients and then cache, or store, the results. They are not configured to be authoritative for a zone, so they do not store standard primary or standard secondary zones. The cache is populated with the most frequently requested names. These names and their associated IP addresses are available from the cache for answering subsequent client queries.

When a remote office has a limited amount of available bandwidth for connecting to a corporate office, a caching-only server should be configured at the remote office to send recursive queries to a DNS server at the corporate office. A recursive query is one in which the DNS server assumes the full workload and responsibility for providing a complete answer to the query. The DNS server at the corporate office is better equipped to handle recursive queries because it has a greater amount of available bandwidth for connecting to the Internet or an intranet.

Caching-only servers help to reduce traffic across a wide area network (WAN) in the following ways:

- A caching-only server attempts to locate information in its cache to resolve client requests. If the required information is not in its cache, the caching-only server performs a query across the WAN to locate the necessary information and update its cache. The greater the amount of information that is stored in its cache, the less likely it is that the caching-only server will need to perform a query, thus reducing traffic across the WAN.

- A caching-only server neither maintains zone files, as does a primary DNS server, nor does it store a copy of a zone file, as does a secondary DNS server. Therefore, caching-only servers do not generate zone transfer traffic.

Configuring a Caching-Only Server

To configure a caching-only server, install the DNS Server service on a computer running Windows 2000 Server, and do not configure any forward or reverse lookup zones.

Configuring Forwarders

You should configure a caching-only server to perform recursive rather than iterative queries by configuring it to use forwarders. A *forwarder* is a DNS server that other DNS servers designate to forward queries for resolving external domain names. This reduces the amount of traffic across the WAN for performing name resolution.

To forward queries to another server:

1. Open DNS from the **Administrative Tools** menu.
2. Right-click the server on which you want to configure forwarding, and then click **Properties**.
3. On the **Forwarders** tab, select the **Enable Forwarders** check box.
4. Type the IP address of the server to which you want to forward, click **Add**, and then click **OK**.

Note   You can also configure forwarders on a server that hosts zones. In this case, the DNS server responds to all queries that it can resolve from its zone files and forwards all other queries.

Maintaining DNS Zones

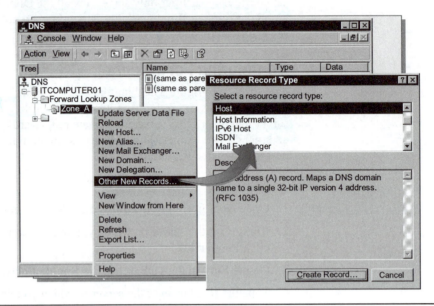

Resource records contain data that is used to configure a DNS server or to provide the information that DNS servers use when resolving queries from hosts and other servers. There are various resource record types that are defined for a zone. Each type of resource record contains different types of data.

DNS servers can contain the following types of resource records:

Record Type	Purpose
A (address)	Contains name-to-IP address mapping information. You must manually add A records to a DNS database if you have clients that do not register their names in the DNS database by using the DNS dynamic update protocol, such as clients running Windows NT version 4.0. An A record is also referred to as a host record.
NS (name server)	Defines the servers that are authoritative for a certain zone or contain the zone file for that domain.
CNAME (canonical name)	Allows you to provide additional names to a server that already has a name in an A record. For example, if the server called webserver1.nwtraders.msft hosts the Web site for nwtraders.msft, this server should have the common name www.nwtraders.msft. To do this, create a CNAME record that maps the name www to webserver1. An A record is also referred to as alias record.
MX (mail exchanger)	Specifies the server to which e-mail applications can deliver mail. For example, if you have a mail server running on a computer named mail1.nwtraders.msft and you want all mail for *user_name*@nwtraders.msft to be delivered to this mail server, you need to add an MX record to the zone for nwtraders.msft that points to the mail server for that domain.

(*continued*)

Record Type	Purpose
SOA (start of authority)	Indicates the starting point or original point of authority for information stored in a zone. The SOA resource record is the first resource record created when you add a new zone. It also contains several parameters used by other computers that use DNS to determine how long they will use information for the zone and how often updates are required.
PTR (pointer)	Used in a reverse lookup zone created within the in-addr.arpa domain to designate a reverse mapping of a host IP address to a host DNS domain name.
SRV (service)	Registered by services so that clients can locate a service by using DNS. For example, a Windows 2000 domain controller has many network services that perform functions such as verifying user logon and checking group membership. Domain controllers register these services by creating the appropriate SRV record in the DNS database. A client computer can then find a domain controller by looking up the necessary information in the DNS database.
	You are not normally required to add SRV resource records, because the service creates them automatically and adds them to the DNS database by using the dynamic update protocol.

Creating Resource Records

To create a new resource record, open DNS. Right-click the name of the zone to which you want to add the new resource record, and then click the type of record that you want to create, or click **Other New Records** for a complete list of resource records.

Removing a DNS Server From the Network

You must update your DNS configuration when removing a DNS server from your network. To remove a DNS server from the network, make the following changes in any zone for which the DNS server is authoritative:

- Remove the A resource record for the server.

- Delete the server name from the NS resource records.

- If the server is the primary server for a standard zone, revise the owner field of the SOA resource record for the zone to point to the new primary DNS server for the zone.

Note   This step is not necessary for Active Directory integrated zones.

- Verify that all records (NS or A resource records) that are used for delegation to the zone are revised and no longer point to the removed server.

Monitoring DNS Servers

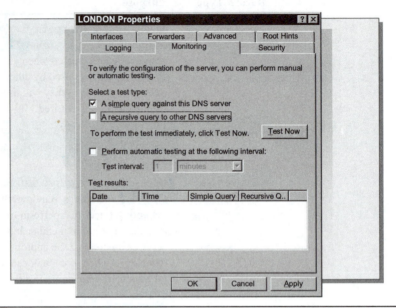

After you install DNS, test the configuration before activating it on your network to prevent problems with name resolution. The Windows 2000 DNS Server service provides the capability to test and monitor DNS by using the DNS administrative tool.

Testing the DNS Server Service

You can configure the DNS Server service to perform queries immediately or on a scheduled basis to ensure that the service is operating correctly. In DNS, open the **Properties** dialog box for the server that you want to monitor, and then click the **Monitoring** tab. You can test a DNS server by performing two types of queries:

- *Simple query*. This type of query performs a local test by using the DNS client to query a DNS server.

- *Recursive query*. This type of query tests a DNS server by forwarding a recursive query to another DNS server.

Under **Tests Performed**, select the **Simple query** check box, the **Recursive query** check box, or both, and then click **Test Now**. The test results appear under **Test results**.

To perform tests on a scheduled basis, select the **Perform automatic testing at the following interval** check box, and then select an interval.

Tip   You may receive incorrect results if you verify the operation of a DNS server immediately after adding or removing zones. If this occurs, either right-click the DNS server in the console tree, and then click **Refresh**, or close and then reopen DNS.

Monitoring the DNS Server Service By Using Event Viewer

You can use Event Viewer to view the DNS server event log. This information is particularly useful when you need detailed information about server performance.

Enabling DNS Server Debug Logging Options

For advanced troubleshooting purposes, you can configure a DNS server to record detailed information about all operations. To enable logging, on the **Logging** tab of the **Properties** dialog box of the DNS server, select the appropriate check boxes for the events that you want to record. By default, the DNS server records logging information in the file *\systemroot*\system32\dns\dns.log.

Important   Enable logging for troubleshooting purposes only. Logging can be resource intensive, which can affect overall server performance and consume disk space.

Verifying Resource Records by Using Nslookup

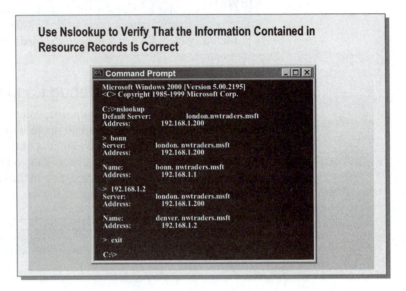

Use Nslookup to Verify That the Information Contained in Resource Records Is Correct

```
Command Prompt                                    _ □ ✕

Microsoft Windows 2000 [Version 5.00.2195]
<C> Copyright 1985-1999 Microsoft Corp.

C:\>nslookup
Default Server:        london.nwtraders.msft
Address:          192.168.1.200

> bonn
Server:        london. nwtraders.msft
Address:          192.168.1.200

Name:          bonn. nwtraders.msft
Address:          192.168.1.1

> 192.168.1.2
Server:        london. nwtraders.msft
Address:          192.168.1.200

Name:          denver. nwtraders.msft
Address:          192.168.1.2

> exit

C:\>
```

After you add resource records, you can use Nslookup to verify that the resource records are correct. Nslookup has two modes:

- *Interactive.* Use interactive mode when you require more than one piece of data. To run interactive mode, at the command prompt, type **nslookup**

  To exit interactive mode, type **exit**

- *Non-Interactive.* Use non-interactive mode when you require a single piece of data, or to include an Nslookup command in a command or batch file. Type the Nslookup syntax at the command prompt, and the data is returned.

The following table describes the Nslookup syntax:
nslookup [*–option* ...] [*computer_to_find* | – [*server*]]

Syntax	Description
-option...	Specify one or more Nslookup commands. For a list of available commands, type a question mark (?).
computer_to_find	If you specify the IP address of a computer, Nslookup returns the host name. If you specify the host name of a computer, Nslookup returns the IP address. If the computer that you want to find is a host name and does not have a trailing period, the default DNS domain name is appended to the name. To find a computer outside the current DNS domain, append a period to the name.
-server	Specify the server to use as the DNS server. If you omit the server, the currently configured default DNS server is used.

Note For Nslookup to work properly, a PTR resource record must exist for the server on which you perform a lookup. At startup, Nslookup performs a reverse lookup on the IP address of the server that is running the DNS Server service and reports an error if it cannot resolve the address to a name.

Troubleshooting Name Resolution Problems

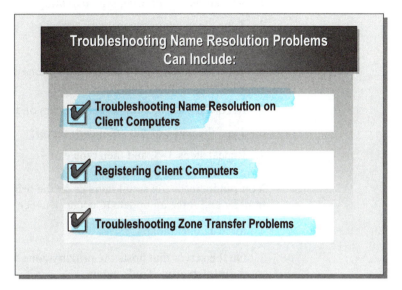

Name resolution problems can occur if a client computer is resolving names incorrectly, or if the client computer name is not registered with the DNS servers on your network. Other name resolution problems can occur when the zone transfer process is not working properly.

Troubleshooting Name Resolution on Client Computers

DNS clients cache query responses from DNS servers and use this information to answer future queries locally. When a query cannot be resolved locally, the client queries DNS servers to resolve a name. If you determine that the client computer is resolving names incorrectly, you can use the Ipconfig utility to flush and reset the cache on the client computer. At a command prompt, type **ipconfig /flushdns** to flush the cache.

Registering Client Computers

Client computers use the dynamic update protocol to register their names with DNS servers. If a client's name records are missing from the servers, use the Ipconfig utility to refresh all DHCP leases and register any related DNS names. at a command prompt, type **ipconfig /registerdns** to force the client to renew its registration.

Troubleshooting Zone Transfer Problems

A secondary server queries its primary server for updates to a zone file, and uses the serial number in the SOA resource record to determine whether changes have been made to the zone. If the serial number has changed, a zone transfer occurs to update the records on the secondary server.

When a secondary server is not receiving updates from its master server, you can use the Nslookup utility to compare the serial numbers in each server's SOA resource record.

To compare serial numbers by using the Nslookup utility:

1. At a command prompt, type **nslookup**

2. Type the name of the primary server.

3. Type **set type=SOA**

4. Type *domain name* (where *domain name* is the name of the domain in which the primary server resides).

5. Record the serial number that appears on the SOA record.

6. Type the name of the secondary server.

7. Repeat steps 3–5, and then type **exit**

You can increase the serial number on the primary server to initiate a zone transfer and force an update to occur between a primary and a secondary server.

To force a zone transfer:

1. On the server that hosts the primary zone file, open DNS from the **Administrative Tools** menu.

2. Open the **Properties** dialog box for the zone, and then click the **Start of Authority** tab.

3. Click **Increment** to increase the serial number, and then click **OK**.

Tip   For more information about advanced DNS troubleshooting, see Windows 2000 Help and the Windows 2000 Server Resource Kit.

Lab B: Maintaining and Troubleshooting a DNS Server

Objectives

After completing this lab, you will be able to:

- Monitor the DNS Server service.
- Troubleshoot the DNS Server service by using Nslookup.
- Enable event DNS logging.

Prerequisite

Before working on this lab, you must be familiar with DNS concepts and operations.

Lab Setup

To complete this lab, you need the following:

- A computer running Microsoft Windows 2000 Advanced Server that is configured as a domain controller.

- A static IP address and subnet mask.

- A lab partner. One partner will create the primary zone; the other will create a secondary zone and designate his or her partner's computer as the master DNS server.

- An FQDN. Refer to the Student Computer IP Addresses and FQDNs section of the lab for this information.

Scenario

Your company has configured DNS servers for your domain, and you are responsible for making sure that these servers are functioning correctly. Also, you are responsible for maintaining the DNS servers in your domain, so you must be able to determine when a server is not functioning correctly, and correct the problem quickly.

Estimated time to complete this lab: 45 minutes

Exercise 1
Monitoring the DNS Server Service

Scenario

You have just installed a DNS server, and you want to test it to ensure that it is functioning correctly.

Goal

In this exercise, you will test the DNS Server service to determine that it is functioning correctly.

Tasks	Detailed Steps
🖐 Perform the following procedure on both computers.	
1. In DNS, perform simple query and recursive query tests.	**a.** Log on as administrator@*domain*.nwtraders.msft (where *domain* is the name of your domain) with a password of **password**.
	b. Open DNS from the **Administrative Tools** menu.
	c. In the console tree, right-click *server* (where *server* is the name of your computer), and then click **Properties**.
	d. In the *server* **Properties** dialog box, on the **Monitoring** tab, under **Select a test type**, select the check boxes for both query types, and then click **Test Now**.
	e. Verify that **PASS** appears in both columns, click **OK** to close the *server* **Properties** dialog box, and then minimize DNS.
2. Disable all network adapters and clear the DNS cache. Perform the simple and recursive query tests again.	**a.** Right-click **My Network Places**, and then click **Properties**.
	b. In Network and Dial-up Connections, right-click **Classroom**, and then click **Disable**.
⚠ **Important:** If your partner has already disabled the PartnerNet network connection on his or her computer, your PartnerNet network interface appears as disconnected.	
2. *(continued)*	**c.** Right-click **PartnerNet**, and then click **Disable**.
	d. Restore DNS.
	e. In the console tree, right-click *server* (where *server* is the name of your computer), and then click **Clear cache**.
	f. Right-click *server*, and then click **Properties**.
	g. On the **Monitoring** tab, under **Select a test type**, verify that the check boxes for each query type are selected, and then click **Test Now**.
ℹ **Note:** You may have to wait up to one minute for the results of the query tests to appear. This is because of the time-out values for DNS queries.	

(continued)

Tasks	Detailed Steps
❷	The **Simple Query** column lists **PASS**, and the **Recursive Query** column lists **FAIL**. If the recursive query fails but the simple query passes, as in this test, what is the most likely cause of the failure? A. The DNS server is unable to contact any of the servers listed in **Root Hints**. B. The DNS server SOA record has an incorrect entry on the **Name Servers** tab. C. The IP address of this computer is incorrect. D. There are no forward lookup zones configured. _____ _____
3. Enable the network adapters and try the recursive and simple queries again.	a. Click **OK** to close the *server* **Properties** dialog box. b. Minimize DNS. c. Right-click **Classroom**, and then click **Enable**. d. Right-click **PartnerNet**, and then click **Enable**.
⚠	**Important:** If your partner has not enabled the PartnerNet network connection yet, you may receive a message stating that the connection failed. You can ignore this message.
3. *(continued)*	e. Close Network and Dial-up Connections. f. Restore DNS. g. Right-click *server* (where *server* is the name of your computer), and then click **Clear cache**. h. In the console tree, right-click *server*, and then click **Properties**. i. On the **Monitoring** tab, under **Select a test type**, verify that the check boxes for each query type are selected, and then click **Test Now**. 💻 *PASS should appear the **Simple Query** and **Recursive Query** columns of the **Test results** box, indicating that the test was successful.* j. Click **OK** to close the *server* **Properties** dialog box, and then close DNS.

Exercise 2
Examining Resource Records by Using Nslookup

Scenario

You have received reports of DNS servers not resolving names correctly in all locations. You suspect that this may be a result of zone transfers not working correctly, or that it may be due to invalid resource records.

Goal

In this exercise, you will use Nslookup to verify resource records on your server and your partner's server. You will also use Nslookup to determine whether a zone transfer has taken place.

Tasks	Detailed Steps
1. Using Nslookup, examine the A (host), NS (name server) and SOA (start of authority) records for your domain.	a. At a command prompt, type **nslookup** and then press ENTER.
ℹ **Note:** If you receive a message "Can't find server name for address 192.168.1.200: Timed out," ignore this message for this lab (note that the address may be 192.168.*z*.200, where *z* is the number for your classroom). This message appears because Nslookup attempts to use reverse lookup to determine the validity of the address. If there is no reverse lookup zone for this subnet, which in this case would be 1.168.192.in-addr.arpa, the reverse lookup query will fail, and this message will appear. This message does not imply that Nslookup will not work.	
1. *(continued)*	b. To set the default server to your server, type **server** *server*.*domain*.**nwtraders.msft** (where *server* is the name of your computer and *domain* is the name of your domain), and then press ENTER.
	c. Type **ls –t a** *domain*.**nwtraders.msft** and then press ENTER.
	🖥 *Nslookup displays a list of the A records for the domain domain.nwtraders.msft. Using the ls –t command within nslookup is a quick way of viewing resource records in a domain. Next you are going to look at the NS and SOA records for the domain domain.nwtraders.msft.*
	d. Type **set type=NS** and then press ENTER.
	e. Type *domain*.**nwtraders.msft** and then press ENTER.
	f. Type **set type=SOA** and then press ENTER.
	g. Type *domain*.**nwtraders.msft** and then press ENTER.

(*continued*)

Tasks	Detailed Steps
The details for the SOA record for your domain are displayed. Which part of the SOA record can you use to determine whether the data in the primary and secondary zone files is up-to-date? A. Refresh B. Default TTL C. Serial D. Expire	

 Perform the following procedure on the computer with the lower student number.

2. Increment the serial number for the SOA record for your domain.	**a.** Minimize the command prompt. **b.** Open DNS from the **Administrative Tools** menu. **c.** Expand *server* (where *server* is the name of your computer), expand **Forward Lookup Zones**, and then click *domain*.**nwtraders.msft** (where *domain* is the name of your domain). **d.** In the console tree, right-click *domain*.**nwtraders.msft**, and then click **Properties**. **e.** On the **Start of Authority (SOA)** tab, click **Increment** twice, and then click **OK**. **f.** Close DNS.

 Perform the following procedure on both computers.

3. Using Nslookup, verify that the two name servers in your domain have the same serial number.	**a.** Restore the command prompt. **b.** Type *domain*.**nwtraders.msft** (where *server* is the name of your computer and *domain* is the name of your domain), and then press ENTER. **c.** Type *partner_server*.*domain*.**nwtraders.msft** (where *partner_server* is the name of your partner's computer and *domain* is the name of your domain), and then press ENTER.

(*continued*)

Tasks	Detailed Steps
❓	The serial number for both servers' SOA records should be the same. If the serial numbers are not the same after you wait a short time, what can you do to determine why zone transfer has not occurred? Select all that apply. A. Examine the System Log in Event Viewer B. Examine the DNS Server log in Event Viewer C. Examine all A (host) records in DNS D. Ping both servers E. Examine Zone Transfers and SOA tabs for your domain in DNS _____ _____ _____
3. *(continued)*	**d.** Close the command prompt window.

Exercise 3
Examining the DNS Server Event Logs

Scenario

You are monitoring your DNS server to determine when changes that cause zone transfers occur, and when changes are written to the hard disk for ongoing performance management. You also want to monitor the DNS server to determine whether any errors are occurring.

Goal

In this exercise, you will examine the contents of the DNS Server event logs and DNS trace logs to determine the possible causes of an error.

Tasks	Detailed Steps
1. Open Computer Management and examine the DNS Server event log.	**a.** Open Computer Management from the **Administrative Tools** menu. **b.** In the console tree, expand **Event Viewer**, and then click **DNS Server**. **c.** In the details pane, double-click the first event log entry.
❓ What was the last version of the zone that was written to the zone file? _____ _____	
1. *(continued)*	**d.** Click **OK** to close the **Event Properties** dialog box. **e.** Close Computer Management.
2. Configure the DNS Server service to log updates to the zone database file.	**a.** Open DNS from the **Administrative Tools** menu. **b.** In the console tree, right-click *server* (where *server* is the name of your computer), and then click **Properties**. **c.** On the **Logging** tab, **select** the **Update** check box, and then click **OK**.
⚠ **Important:** Perform the following procedure only on the computer with the lower student number.	

(*continued*)

Tasks	Detailed Steps
3. Increment the serial number for your domain's primary zone database file, and then update the Server Data files. Stop the DNS Server service.	a. In the console tree, expand *server*, and then expand **Forward Lookup Zones**. b. Right-click *domain*.**nwtraders.msft** (where *domain* is the name of your domain), and then click **Properties**. c. On the **Start of Authority (SOA)** tab, click **Increment**, and then click **OK**. d. Right-click *server*, and then click **Update Server Data Files**. e. Right-click *server*, point to **All Tasks**, and then click **Stop**.
4. Examine the contents of the log file c:\winnt\ system32\dns\dns.log.	a. Click **Start**, and then click **Run**. b. In the **Open** box, type **c:\winnt\system32\dns\dns.log** and then click **OK**.

❓   What information can you find in the log?

_____

_____

4. *(continued)*	c. Close the dns-Notepad window. d. Right-click *server*, (where *server* is the name of your computer), point to **All Tasks**, and then click **Start**.

✋   Perform the following procedure on both computers.

5. Close all open windows.	a. Close all open windows.

Exercise 4
Removing the DNS Server Service

Scenario

You are now going to remove the DNS Server service, because you are going to decommission this server and configure another server as the DNS server for your domain.

Goal

In this exercise, you will remove the DNS Server service and configure its TCP/IP properties.

Tasks	Detailed Steps
✋ Perform the following procedure on both computers.	
1. Configure the server to use the instructor computer as the DNS server.	a. Right-click **My Network Places**, and then click **Properties**.
	b. Open the **Properties** dialog box for the **Classroom** connection.
	c. Click **Internet Protocol (TCP/IP)**, and then click **Properties**.
	d. In the **Preferred DNS server** box, type **192.168.z.200** (where z is the number of your classroom), and then click **OK**.
	e. Click **OK** to close the **Classroom Properties** dialog box.
	f. Open the **Properties** dialog box for the **PartnerNet** connection.
	g. Click **Internet Protocol (TCP/IP)**, and then click **Properties**.
	h. In the **Preferred DNS server** box, type **192.168.z.200** and then click **OK**.
	i. Click **OK** to close the **PartnerNet Properties** dialog box, and then close Network and Dial-up Connections.
✋ Perform the following procedure only on the computer with the lower student number.	
2. Remove the delegation of authority for your domain at the nwtraders.msft domain.	a. Click **Start**, point to **Programs**, point to **Administrative Tools**, right-click **DNS**, and then click **Run as**.
	b. In the **Run As Other User** dialog box, type **eadmin@nwtraders.msft** in the **User name** box, type **password** in the **Password** box, delete the contents of the **Domain** box, and then click **OK**.
	c. In the console tree, expand **London**, expand **Forward Lookup Zones**, and then expand **nwtraders.msft**.
	d. In the console tree, right-click *domain*.**nwtraders.msft**, (where *domain* is the name of your domain), and then click **Delete**.
	e. Click **OK** to close the **DNS** message box.
	f. Close DNS.
✋ Perform the following procedures on both computers.	

(continued)

Tasks	Detailed Steps
3. Remove the DNS Server service.	a. In Control Panel, double-click **Add/Remove Programs**, and then click **Add/Remove Windows Components**.
	b. In the Windows Components wizard, on the **Windows Components** page, under **Components**, click **Networking Services**, and then click **Details**.
	c. Clear the **Domain Name System (DNS)** check box, and then click **OK**.
	d. Click **Next**.
	e. When the configuration process is complete, click **Finish**.
	f. Close all open windows.
4. Refresh the DNS entries for your computer by running ipconfig /registerdns, and then log off.	a. At a command prompt, type **ipconfig /registerdns** and then press ENTER.
	b. Type **net stop netlogon** and then press ENTER.
	c. Type **net start netlogon** and then press ENTER.
	d. Close the command prompt window, and then log off.

Review

- Overview of the DNS Query Process

- Installing the DNS Server Service

- Configuring Name Resolution for Client Computers

- Creating Zones

- Configuring Zones

- Configuring DNS for Internal Use

- Integrating DNS and DHCP

- Maintaining and Troubleshooting DNS Servers

1. Describe the difference between an iterative query and a recursive query.

2. What must you do before installing the DNS Server service?

3. How do you configure name resolution on a client computer?

4. What is a zone?

5. What is the difference between a standard primary zone and a standard secondary zone?

6. When is it necessary to create a root zone?

7. How can a caching-only server be used to help reduce traffic across a WAN?

NSLOOKUP

RECURSIVE → SERVER DOES WORK. SERVERS QUERY SERVER

ITERATIVE → PC DOES WORK OF QUERY EACH DNS SERVICE.

AUTHORITIVE → SERVER GIVING INFO

NON AUTHORITIVE → SERVER RELIES ON ANOTHER DNS SERVER FOR ANSWER.

FQDN   FULLY QUALIFIED DOMAIN NAME

NAME SERVER → ALL AUTHORITY SERVERS FOR ZONE.

                SECONDARY (NEW DOMAIN)
                          TUP
                ↙   ↙
TRAINING. MICROSOFT. COM .
        ↑   ↑
      SUB   ROOT

2 DNS SERVERS FOR AUTHORITY.

NEW DELAGATION →

DNS

   WHEN CONNECTING TO ~~SELF~~ INTERNET REMOVE ROOT DIRECTORY
      - CLOSE DNS
      - OPEN DNS
      - ENABLE FORWARDER (FROM SERVER PROPERTIES) TO DNS SERVER ON INTRANET.
                          DNS
            FOR ISP DNS SERVICE
            167. 206. 112.3 // .4   CABLEVISION DNS

DC PROMO. EXE → CREATE DOMAIN CONTROLLER.

Microsoft®
Training &
Certification

Module 4: Implementing Name Resolution by Using WINS

Contents

HOSTS → DNS → FQN → IP

LMHOSTS. → WINS   NET BIOS → IP.

Overview

- **Connecting to NetBIOS-Based Networks**
- **WINS Overview**
- **Configuring WINS Servers and Clients**
- **Configuring Support for Non-WINS Clients**
- **Enabling WINS Database Replication**
- **Maintaining the WINS Server Database**

In Microsoft® Windows® 2000, the primary means for client computers to locate and communicate with other computers on an Internet Protocol (IP) network is by using the Domain Name System (DNS). However, clients using previous versions of Windows, such as computers running Microsoft Windows 98 or Microsoft Windows NT® version 4.0, also use network basic input/output system (NetBIOS) names for network communication. As a result, these clients require a method of resolving NetBIOS names to IP addresses.

You can install Windows Internet Name Service (WINS) to register NetBIOS computer names and resolve them to IP addresses. Implementing WINS in a Windows 2000 network ensures that clients using previous versions of Windows can locate and communicate with network resources as needed.

At the end of this module, you will be able to:

- Explain how to connect to NetBIOS-based networks.
- Explain the WINS name resolution process.
- Configure computers as WINS servers and clients.
- Configure support for non-WINS clients.
- Enable WINS database replication.
- Maintain the WINS database.

◆ Connecting to NetBIOS-Based Networks

- **NetBIOS Names**

- **NetBIOS Name Registration, Discovery, and Release**

- **NetBIOS Name Resolution**

- **NetBIOS over TCP/IP Name Resolution Nodes**

- **The Lmhosts File**

NetBIOS provides programs with a uniform set of commands for requesting the lower-level network services that are required to manage names, conduct sessions between nodes on a network, and transmit information.

It is important to understand NetBIOS name resolution concepts and methods to understand WINS functionality, because previous versions of Windows and some Windows-based applications rely on NetBIOS names to identify network resources.

NetBIOS Names

- **NetBIOS Names Are Registered Dynamically and Can Be:**
  - Used only once within a network
  - Registered as unique names or group names
- **Use a NetBIOS Scope to Group Computers in a Network**
- **Use Browsing to Locate Shared Resources on the Network**

NetBIOS names are a more limiting alternative for naming computers to DNS names. Windows 2000 can use DNS names for most functions, but a NetBIOS name resolution method must exist on any network with computers that are running earlier versions of Windows and applications that depend on NetBIOS names.

NetBIOS names are 16 bytes in length, and the NetBIOS namespace has only one level. This means that NetBIOS names can be used only once within a network. In contrast, the DNS namespace has multiple levels because DNS uses a fully qualified domain name (*FQDN*), which combines the host name with the name of its domain.

NetBIOS Name Registration

NetBIOS names are registered dynamically when computers and services start and when users log on. A NetBIOS name can be registered as a unique name, which maps to a single address, or as a group name, which maps to multiple addresses.

Important Because multiple services that are running on the same computer can register a computer's NetBIOS name, several NetBIOS name registrations can be generated for the same computer name. The registered name is the 15-character computer name plus a sixteenth character. The sixteenth character uniquely identifies each service that uses the computer name to build its NetBIOS name.

Example of NetBIOS Name Registration

An example of a service that uses a NetBIOS name is the Server service in Windows 2000, which provides file and printer sharing. When you start your computer, the service registers a unique NetBIOS name that is based on the computer name. The registered name is the 15-character computer name plus a sixteenth character of 0x20. The sixteenth character uniquely identifies the Server service.

When you attempt to connect to a shared folder by using a NetBIOS name, a name query is initiated to search for the NetBIOS name of the Server service. Communication is established when the NetBIOS name is located, and then you can connect to the server on which the shared folder is stored.

NetBIOS Scope

A NetBIOS name can also contain extra characters that make up a scope. A NetBIOS *scope* is an optional extension to a computer name. You can use a NetBIOS scope to group computers in a network. Only computers with the same NetBIOS scope name can locate each other by using the NetBIOS name. Computers that are outside the scope cannot access computers that are within the scope.

Note   NetBIOS scopes are used to segment a large NetBIOS-based network; however, the use of NetBIOS scopes is not recommended.

For more information about configuring NetBIOS scopes, see RFC 1001 under **Additional Reading** on the Web page on the Student Materials compact disc.

Browsing

Windows 2000 creates lists of registered NetBIOS names to enable users to locate computers that contain shared resources on the network. The process of building these lists is called *browsing*.

To access these shared resources:

1. Open My Network Places, and then double-click **Entire Network**.

2. Click **entire contents**.

3. Double-click **Microsoft Windows Network**.

4. Double-click the appropriate domain or workgroup, and then double-click the name of computer on which the resource is stored.

Note   Open Network Neighborhood to access browsing information on computers running earlier versions of Windows.

For more information about browsing, see the appendix *Computer Browser Service*, under **Additional Reading** on the Web page on the Student Materials compact disc, and the appendix *Windows 2000 Browser Service*, in the Windows 2000 Server Resource Kit.

NetBIOS Name Registration, Discovery, and Release

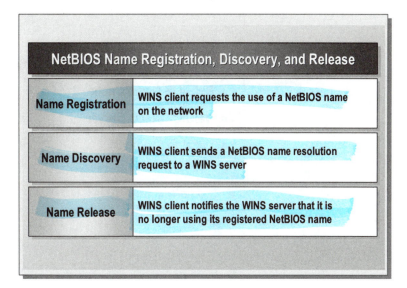

Computers running Windows 2000 support several methods for name registration, name discovery, and name release. These methods are used for interacting with other NetBIOS-based hosts.

Name Registration

Large or routed networks use the NetBIOS over Transmission Control Protocol/Internet Protocol (TCP/IP) component of NetBIOS. When a NetBIOS over TCP/IP (NetBT) host initializes, it registers its NetBIOS name by using a NetBIOS name registration request. This registration uses a broadcast or a directed message to a NetBIOS name server.

If another host has registered the same NetBIOS name, either that host or a NetBIOS name server responds to the request with a negative name registration response. Because the initiating host cannot use a name that is already in use, it receives an initialization error and is unable to communicate by using NetBIOS.

Name Discovery

Local broadcasts or a NetBIOS name server perform name discovery. When a computer running Windows 2000 communicates with another TCP/IP host, it broadcasts a NetBIOS name query request containing the destination NetBIOS name on the local network, or sends the request to a NetBIOS name server for resolution. If the NetBIOS name is in use, either the host that owns the NetBIOS name or a NetBIOS name server responds by sending a positive name query response.

Name Release

Name release occurs automatically whenever a NetBIOS application or service is shut down properly. For example, when a service on a host stops, the host will not send a negative name registration response when another user tries to use the NetBIOS name. The NetBIOS name is released and is available for another host to use.

NetBIOS Name Resolution

Standard Methods of NetBIOS Name Resolution Include:

- **NetBIOS Name Cache**
- **NetBIOS Name Server**
- **Local Broadcast**

NetBIOS name resolution is the process of mapping a computer's NetBIOS name to an IP address. A computer's NetBIOS name must be resolved to an IP address before the IP address can be resolved to a hardware address. The Microsoft implementation of TCP/IP uses several methods to resolve NetBIOS names.

NetBIOS Name Cache

The NetBIOS name cache contains the NetBIOS names that the local computer recently resolved and the name resolution results. Name resolution is performed more quickly because the cached results are accessed for name resolution. However, name resolution data is limited to recently resolved names.

You can use the Nbtstat utility to view the contents of the NetBIOS name cache by typing **nbtstat –c** at a command prompt.

NetBIOS Name Server

A NetBIOS name server maintains a database of NetBIOS names and IP addresses and responds to client name resolution requests. In Windows 2000, a WINS server is a NetBIOS name server that handles name registration requests from WINS clients, registers their names and IP addresses, and responds to NetBIOS name queries.

Note For more information about NetBIOS name servers, see RFC 1001 and RFC 1002 under **Additional Reading** on the Web page on the Student Materials compact disc.

Local Broadcast

A NetBIOS client can issue a broadcast on the local network for the IP address of the destination NetBIOS name. The host that owns the NetBIOS replies with its IP address, and the host that initiated the broadcast can then connect to the host that owns the NetBIOS name.

Note Avoid configuring NetBIOS name resolution for local broadcasts because they can create excessive network traffic. Also, most routers are configured not to forward NetBIOS broadcasts, which limits NetBIOS name resolution to a single network.

NetBIOS over TCP/IP Name Resolution Nodes

NetBIOS over TCP/IP Name Resolution Nodes	
B-node	Uses broadcasts for name registration and resolution
P-node	Uses a NetBIOS name server such as WINS to resolve NetBIOS names
M-node	Combines B-node and P-node, and functions as a B-node by default
H-node	Combines P-node and B-node, and functions as a P-node by default

The different methods that a computer can use to resolve a NetBIOS name into an IP address are referred to as nodes. The nodes that Windows 2000 supports include:

- *B-node (broadcast)*. Uses broadcasts for name registration and resolution.

  Note In a large network, broadcasts can increase the network load. In addition, routers typically do not forward broadcasts, so only computers on the local network can respond.

- *P-node (peer-to-peer)*. Uses a NetBIOS name server such as WINS to resolve NetBIOS names. P-node does not use broadcasts because it queries the name server directly, enabling computers to span routers. P-node requires that all computers be configured with the IP address of the NetBIOS name server. If the NetBIOS name server is not functioning, computers will not be able to resolve the name.

- *M-node (mixed)*. Combines B-node and P-node, and functions as a B-node by default. If M-node is unable to resolve a name by broadcast, it uses the NetBIOS name server of P-node.

- *H-node (hybrid)*. Combines P-node and B-node, and functions as a P-node by default. If H-node is unable to resolve a name by using the NetBIOS name server, it uses a broadcast to resolve the name.

Note For more information about NetBIOS over TCP/IP nodes, see RFC 1001 and RFC 1002 under **Additional Reading** on the Web page on the Student Materials compact disc.

Configuring Node Types

The system defaults to B-node if there are no WINS servers configured. If there is at least one WINS server configured, the system defaults to H-node. You can configure the NetBIOS name resolution method that Windows 2000 employs by using Dynamic Host Configuration Protocol (DHCP) to assign a node type, or by editing the following registry value:

**HKEY_LOCAL_MACHINE\SYSTEM\CurrentControlSet\Services\
Netbt\Parameters\NodeType**

The following table lists the registry values that correspond to each node type:

Node type	Value
B-node	1
P-node	2
M-node	4
H-node	8

The Lmhosts File

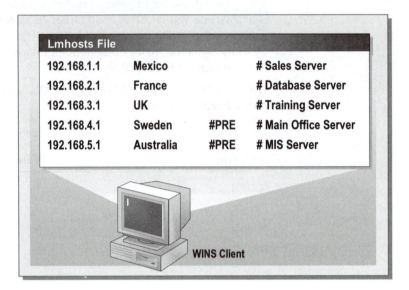

An Lmhosts file is a local text file that contains NetBIOS name-to-IP address mapping information. The Lmhosts file helps computers to resolve the NetBIOS names of other computers that cannot respond to NetBIOS name query broadcasts, such as a computer that is located on a remote network. The Lmhosts file is similar in functionality to the Hosts file in DNS, except that the Hosts file is used for mapping IP addresses for host names in the DNS namespace, rather than NetBIOS names.

Note Avoid using an Lmhosts file for regular name resolution because you must manually maintain a separate Lmhosts file on each computer.

Creating an Lmhosts File

When you create an Lmhosts file, Windows 2000 automatically queries the file to resolve NetBIOS names when other name resolution methods fail.

By default, Lmhosts files do not exist on computers running Windows 2000. Therefore, you must create the file and save it in the *systemroot*\System32\Drivers\Etc folder. This folder also includes a sample Lmhosts file (Lmhosts.sam), which you can use as a template to create an Lmhosts file.

You can use any text editor to create an Lmhosts file. Save the file with the file name **Lmhosts**, and without a file extension.

Note Some text editors may automatically assign a file extension. Therefore, you must verify the file name in the *systemroot*\System32\Drivers\Etc folder. If necessary, remove the file extension.

Preconfigured Entries in an Lmhosts File

Computers running Windows 2000 can load preconfigured entries from the Lmhosts file into the NetBIOS name cache when TCP/IP is initialized. For example, entries in the Lmhosts file that are designated with **#PRE** are added to the NetBIOS name cache when TCP/IP initializes. This can increase the speed of name resolution, because names in the cache are resolved first.

An Lmhosts file can contain predefined keywords that begin with a number sign (#). The following table lists the keywords that you can add to an Lmhosts file:

Predefined keyword	Description
#PRE	Defines the entries that are initially preloaded as permanent entries in the name cache. Entries with a **#PRE** tag are loaded automatically when TCP/IP initializes, or manually by typing **nbtstat –R** at a command prompt.
#DOM:[domain_name**]**	Indicates that the computer is a domain controller. Facilitates domain activity, such as logon validation over a router, account synchronization, and browsing.
#INCLUDE	Loads and searches NetBIOS entries in a separate file from the default Lmhosts file. Typically, the **#INCLUDE** file is a centrally located shared Lmhosts file. Refer to the **#INCLUDE** file by using a universal naming convention (UNC) path. Any computer referred to in the UNC path must also have a name-to-IP address mapping in the Lmhosts file. This enables Windows 2000 to resolve a computer's NetBIOS name when it reads the **#INCLUDE** file.
#BEGIN_ALTERNATE **#END_ALTERNATE**	Defines a redundant list of alternate locations for Lmhosts files. When you include multiple **#INCLUDE** lines between **#BEGIN_ALTERNATE** and **#END_ALTERNATE**, Windows 2000 includes the first file that it can locate in the list.
#MH	Adds multiple entries for a multihomed computer. A multihomed computer is a computer that contains IP addresses that belong to different networks.

Note The NetBIOS name cache and file are always read sequentially. Add the most frequently accessed computers to the top of the list. Add the **#PRE**-tagged entries near the bottom, because they are loaded when TCP/IP initializes and are not accessed again.

Disabling an Lmhosts File

To disable the use of an Lmhosts file:

1. In the **Internet Protocol (TCP/IP) Properties** dialog box, click **Advanced**.

2. In the **Advanced TCP/IP Settings** dialog box, on the **WINS** tab, clear the **Enable LMHOSTS lookup** check box.

◆ WINS Overview

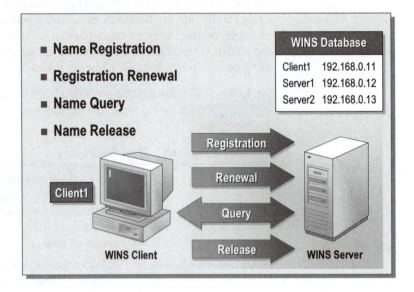

- Name Registration
- Registration Renewal
- Name Query
- Name Release

WINS Database

Client1	192.168.0.11
Server1	192.168.0.12
Server2	192.168.0.13

Client1

Registration
Renewal
Query
Release

WINS Client   **WINS Server**

WINS is a method of NetBIOS name resolution that reduces broadcast traffic and enables clients to resolve NetBIOS names of computers that are on different network segments. For WINS to function properly on a network, each client must register its name in the WINS database. The client can then perform a name query to locate and establish communication with other computers that are registered in the database.

For example, each time a WINS client starts, it registers its NetBIOS name and IP address with a configured WINS server. When a WINS client initiates a command to communicate with another host, the client sends a name query request directly to the WINS server instead of broadcasting it on the local network. The WINS server searches its database for a registration from the host. If the WINS server finds a registration, and it is active, WINS returns the destination host's IP address to the WINS client.

WINS name registrations are temporary, so clients must periodically renew their registrations. In addition, the client computer issues a name release request to delete its registration from the WINS database when it no longer requires a name registration, such as when the client computer shuts down.

Name Registration

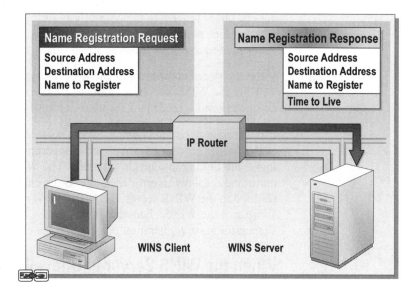

The WINS configuration of a computer includes the IP address of a primary WINS server and, optionally, a secondary WINS server. When a client computer starts, it registers its NetBIOS name and IP address by sending a name registration request directly to the primary WINS server.

If the WINS server is available and another WINS client has not registered the name already, the WINS server returns a successful registration message to the client. This message contains the amount of time that the NetBIOS name is registered to the client, specified as the Time to Live (TTL). In addition, the WINS server stores the NetBIOS name-to-IP address mapping of the client in its database. Whenever a WINS client's addressing information changes, the client automatically requests that the WINS server update its database.

Note Typically, computers request more than one entry in the WINS database. For example, a computer running Windows 2000 registers with a WINS server the Workstation, Server, and Messenger services; the workgroup or domain to which the computer belongs; and the name of the user currently logged on. Registration of services instead of computer names only allows WINS clients to query a WINS server for computers with specific capabilities. Registration of the Messenger service and the user name allow other users to send network messages to the registered computer or user.

When a Name Is Already Registered

If the name is already registered in the WINS database, the WINS server sends a name query request to the currently registered owner of the name to determine whether the computer that owns the record is still active. The WINS server sends the request three times at 500-millisecond intervals.

If the registered computer has multiple network adapters that are bound to TCP/IP, the WINS server attempts to contact each IP address that it has for the computer until it receives a response, or until it has tried all of the IP addresses.

If the current registered owner responds successfully to the WINS server, the WINS server sends a negative name registration response to the WINS client that is attempting to register the name. The WINS client then does not use the name and displays an error message. If the current registered owner does not respond to the WINS server, the WINS server registers the name with the IP address of the WINS client that is attempting to register the name, and sends a successful name registration response to the client.

When the WINS Server Is Unavailable

A WINS client makes three attempts to find its primary WINS server. If the client fails after the third attempt, it sends the name registration request to the secondary WINS server (if one is configured for the client).

If neither server is available, the WINS client sends the name registration to any other WINS server that is configured on the client. If no WINS server is available, the client initiates a broadcast to register its name.

Registration Renewal

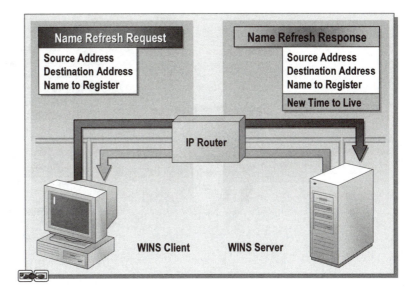

Client name registrations with a WINS server are temporary, and from time to time a WINS client must renew its name or the lease will expire. If a client does not renew its lease before it expires, the WINS server marks the database records that represent the client for deletion and no longer replies to queries for that client.

Name Refresh Request

When a client computer first registers with a WINS server, the WINS server returns a message with a TTL value that indicates when the client registration expires or needs to be renewed. If renewal does not occur by that time, the name registration expires on the WINS server and the name entry is eventually removed from the WINS database.

The default renewal interval for entries in the WINS database is six days. Renewal occurs every three days for most WINS clients because WINS clients attempt to renew their registrations when 50 percent of the TTL value has elapsed. A WINS client sends a name refresh request to the WINS server to renew its name in the WINS database.

Name Refresh Response

When a WINS server receives the name refresh request, it sends to the client a name refresh response with a new TTL.

Name Query

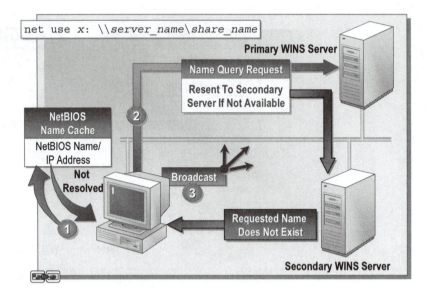

A WINS client can use the NetBIOS name of another WINS client to obtain the IP address of that client from the WINS server. The client can then use the IP address of the other client to establish a connection with that client.

By default, a WINS client attempts to resolve the NetBIOS name of another computer to an IP address in the following way:

1. The client checks its NetBIOS name cache for the NetBIOS name-to-IP address mapping of the destination computer.

2. If the client cannot resolve the name from its cache, it sends a name query request directly to its primary WINS server. If the primary WINS server is unavailable, the client resends the request two more times.

3. If the client does not receive a response from the primary WINS server, the client resends the request to any additional WINS servers that are configured on the client. If a WINS server resolves the name, it responds to the client with the IP address for the requested NetBIOS name.

4. The client initiates a network broadcast if it does not receive a response from any WINS servers, or if a WINS server indicates that it cannot resolve the name by sending a Requested Name Does Not Exist message.

5. If there is no reply to the broadcast, the client searches the Lmhosts file for the name that is trying to resolve. The client only checks the Lmhosts file if it is configured to do so.

Name Release

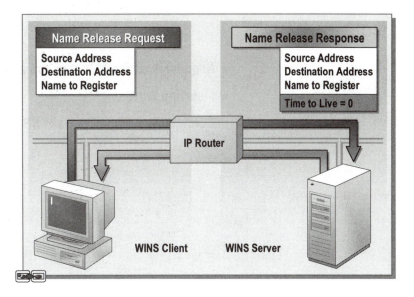

When a WINS client no longer requires a name, the client sends a message instructing the WINS server to release the name.

Name Release Request

When you shut down a WINS client properly by using the operating system shutdown sequence or by stopping a registered network service, the client sends a name release request directly to the WINS server for each registered name. The request includes the IP address and the NetBIOS name of the client so that the server can remove the mappings for the client from the WINS database.

Note   When a WINS client is not shut down properly, it does not release its name registration and the WINS database contains outdated information. When another WINS client receives an outdated IP address for the WINS client that is still registered, the requesting client may make an attempt to connect to that outdated address and will eventually time out.

Name Release Response

When the WINS server receives the name release request, it checks its database for the specified name. If the WINS server finds an entry for the specified name, the WINS server sends a positive name release response, and then the server designates the specified name as released in its database. The name release response contains the released NetBIOS name and a TTL value of zero.

If the WINS server does not find an entry for the specified name or if the name maps to a different IP address from that of the computer requesting the release, the WINS server sends a negative name release response to the WINS client.

◆ Configuring WINS Servers and Clients

- **Requirements for WINS Servers and Clients**

- **Installing WINS**

- **Configuring Computers As WINS Clients**

WINS has certain installation requirements for both servers and clients. If you are installing WINS on a server, you must configure that server with a static IP address so that WINS clients can contact it. In addition, you will need to configure the WINS clients so that they recognize the IP address of the server.

Requirements for WINS Servers and Clients

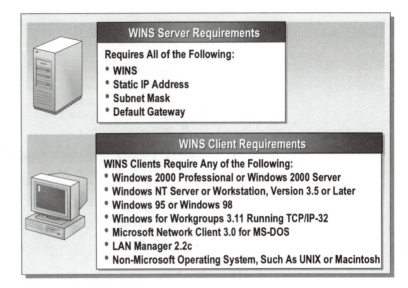

Before you implement WINS, you must ensure that the servers and client computers meet certain requirements.

WINS Server Requirements

To configure a computer running Windows 2000 Server as a WINS server, you must:

- Install WINS.

- Configure a static IP address, subnet mask, and default gateway.

WINS Client Requirements

WINS clients must be configured with the static IP address of a WINS server, and must be computers running any of the following supported operating systems:

- Windows 2000 Professional or Windows 2000 Server

- Windows NT Server or Windows NT Workstation, version 3.5 or later

- Microsoft Windows 95 or Windows 98

- Microsoft Windows for Workgroups version 3.11 running Microsoft TCP/IP-32

- Microsoft MS-DOS® with the Microsoft Network Client version 3.0 for MS-DOS that is configured with the real-mode TCP/IP driver

- Microsoft LAN Manager version 2.2c (LAN Manager 2.2c for OS/2 is not supported)

- Some non-Microsoft operating systems, such as versions of UNIX or Macintosh

Installing WINS

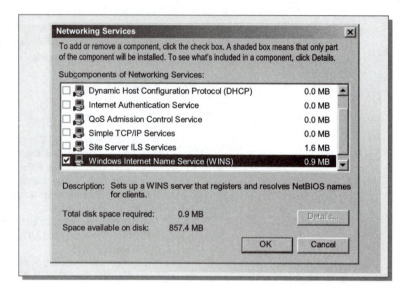

To create a WINS server, install WINS on a computer running Windows 2000 Server.

To install WINS:

1. In Control Panel, double-click **Add/Remove Programs**.

2. Click **Add/Remove Windows Components**.

3. In the Windows Components wizard, on the **Windows Components** page, under **Components**, click **Networking Services**, and then click **Details**.

4. In the **Networking Services** dialog box, under **Subcomponents of Networking Services**, select the **Windows Internet Name Service (WINS)** check box, click **OK**, and then click **Next**.

Important You must configure the advanced TCP/IP settings on a WINS server so that it is a WINS client of itself. This ensures that the WINS server registers itself in its own database.

Configuring Computers As WINS Clients

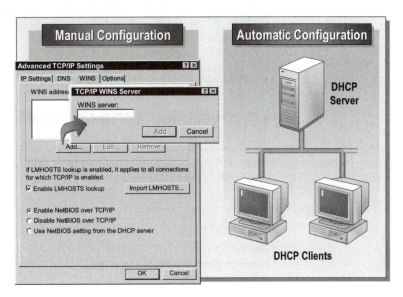

After you install WINS to create a WINS server, you can configure WINS clients in one of two ways: manually by configuring the TCP/IP properties on each client, or automatically by configuring DHCP scope options.

Manually Configuring WINS Clients

To configure a WINS client manually:

1. In the **Internet Protocol (TCP/IP) Properties** dialog box, click **Advanced**.

2. In the **Advanced TCP/IP Settings** dialog box, on the **WINS** tab, click **Add**.

3. Type the IP address of the WINS server, and then click **Add**.

4. Repeat steps 2 and 3 to add additional WINS servers.

Note   Typically, you do not need to configure a WINS client for more than two WINS servers. If you require a high level of fault tolerance because of unreliable connections to WINS servers, you can specify up to 12 WINS servers on a WINS client. The first and second WINS servers are the primary and secondary servers, and any remaining servers are backup WINS servers.

Automatically Configuring WINS Clients

If a computer is a DHCP client, you can configure DHCP scope options to provide WINS configuration information to DHCP clients automatically. To configure a DHCP server for WINS support, use the following DHCP scope options when configuring a DHCP scope:

- **044 WINS/NBNS Servers**. Configure the address of primary and secondary servers.

- **046 WINS/NBT Node Type**. Configure to 0x8 (H-node).

Note   For more information about node types, see RFC 1001 and RFC 1002 under **Additional Reading** on the Web page on the Student Materials compact disc.

When the DHCP client leases an address or renews a lease and you configured the WINS/NBNS Servers and WINS/NBT Node Type scope options, the client receives the settings that you configured. When the client applies these settings, it becomes a WINS client.

Important   If you manually configure WINS client computers with IP addresses of a primary and secondary WINS server, those values take precedence over the same parameters that a DHCP server provides.

◆ Configuring Support for Non-WINS Clients

- Overview of WINS and DNS Interoperability
- Integrating DNS and WINS
- Enabling WINS Lookup on DNS Zones
- Configuring DNS to Forward Queries to WINS Servers
- Configuring Static Mappings
- Configuring a WINS Proxy

Microsoft Windows 2000 uses DNS as its primary method of name resolution, whereas computers running previous versions of Windows use WINS. When most of the client computers on your network are configured to use DNS as the primary method for name resolution, you must configure DNS to use a WINS server to resolve client queries.

A DNS server can forward queries that it is unable to resolve to a WINS server, which enables DNS clients to use DNS for name resolution and still have access to records in a WINS database.

In a WINS environment, you can also provide support for clients that do not use WINS by using static mappings and configuring a WINS proxy. By understanding how to configure a static mapping and a WINS proxy, you can ensure efficient communication between the WINS clients and non-WINS clients on your network.

Overview of WINS and DNS Interoperability

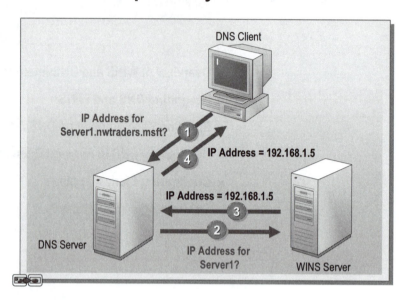

WINS is required in a mixed environment where computers running Windows 2000 interoperate with computers running Windows NT, Windows 98, and Windows for Workgroups. In such a mixed environment, a computer running Windows 2000 might need to resolve the name of a computer running a previous version of Windows and registered with WINS.

Integrating WINS with DNS name resolution enables client computers to use DNS exclusively for name resolution. Clients gain access to data in a WINS database through the DNS server. However, if the DNS server cannot locate the mapping information for the requested name, it may need to query a WINS server for the information. The client communicates only with the DNS server, even if the DNS server forwards the client request to a WINS server.

In Windows 2000, you can configure interoperability between WINS and DNS to enable non-WINS clients to resolve NetBIOS names by querying a DNS server. For example, if a Windows 2000–based client needs to access a shared folder on a server running Windows NT, the client computer can query the DNS server. The DNS server then queries a WINS server, and the name is resolved and returned to the client. This is more efficient than configuring all client computers as WINS clients.

Integrating DNS and WINS

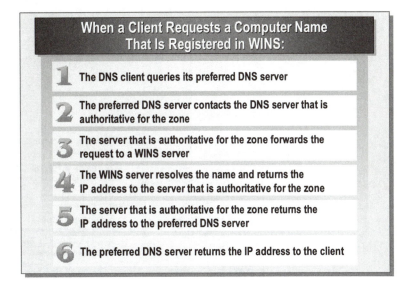

When a Client Requests a Computer Name That Is Registered in WINS:

1. The DNS client queries its preferred DNS server

2. The preferred DNS server contacts the DNS server that is authoritative for the zone

3. The server that is authoritative for the zone forwards the request to a WINS server

4. The WINS server resolves the name and returns the IP address to the server that is authoritative for the zone

5. The server that is authoritative for the zone returns the IP address to the preferred DNS server

6. The preferred DNS server returns the IP address to the client

---

When you configure a DNS server to forward queries to a WINS server, DNS clients can query the DNS server to request computer names that are registered in WINS. For example, the following process takes place when a client requests the IP address for a computer named server1.nwtraders.msft:

1. The DNS client queries its preferred DNS server for the IP address of the computer named server1.nwtraders.msft.

2. The preferred DNS server contacts the DNS server that is authoritative for the zone nwtraders.msft.

3. The server that is authoritative for the zone forwards the request to a WINS server.

4. The WINS server resolves the name and returns the IP address to the DNS server that is authoritative for the zone.

Note   If the WINS server is unable to resolve the name, it sends a message to the DNS server.

---

5. The DNS server that is authoritative for the zone returns the IP address to the preferred DNS server.

6. The preferred DNS server returns the IP address information to the client.

Only the DNS server that is authoritative for the zone needs to be configured for WINS lookup. The client and any intermediate DNS servers are unaware that the IP address maps to a name that is registered in WINS.

Enabling WINS Lookup on DNS Zones

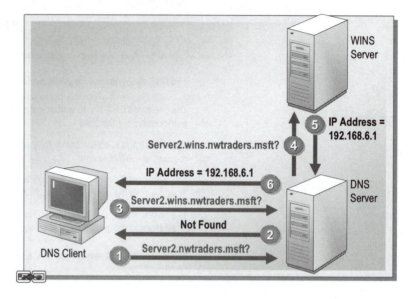

When you configure a DNS zone to use WINS lookup, Windows 2000 creates nonstandard DNS resource records. Make only DNS servers running Windows 2000 or Windows NT 4.0 authoritative for such a zone, because DNS servers running other versions of Windows cannot use these records or perform WINS lookups.

Note   If you use a mixture of Windows-based and other DNS servers to host a zone, it is recommended that you enable the **Do not replicate this record** check box option for any primary zones in which you use the WINS lookup record. This prevents the WINS lookup record from being included in zone transfers to other DNS servers that do not support or recognize the WINS lookup record.

Enabling WINS Lookup with Third-Party DNS Servers

Although you can enable any zone for WINS lookup, creating a separate DNS zone for WINS lookup facilitates interoperability with third-party DNS servers. To use a separate zone for WINS lookups:

- Create a DNS zone without host records and enable it for WINS lookup. For example, assign the name wins.nwtraders.msft to the DNS zone.

- For each client computer, on the **DNS** tab of the **Advanced TCP/IP Properties** dialog box, add the name of the zone that you created to the **Append these DNS suffixes (in order)** box.

This configuration allows for WINS lookup and allows third-party DNS servers to be authoritative for the domain nwtraders.msft.

WINS Lookup Process

When a client computer in the domain nwtraders.msft queries for a server called server2, the following process occurs:

1. The DNS client queries the DNS server for the IP address of server2.nwtraders.msft.

2. The DNS server that is authoritative for the zone returns a negative response to the client.

3. The client immediately issues another name query to the DNS server for the IP address of server2.wins.nwtraders.msft.

4. The DNS server that is authoritative for the zone wins.nwtraders.msft performs a WINS lookup by querying the WINS server.

5. The WINS server returns the correct IP address to the DNS server.

6. The DNS server returns the correct IP address to the client.

Configuring DNS to Forward Queries to WINS Servers

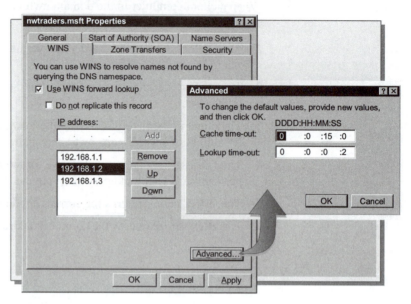

You can configure DNS to forward queries to WINS servers. To configure a DNS zone to use WINS lookup:

1. Open DNS from the **Administrative Tools** menu.

2. In DNS, expand the server that is authoritative for the zone, expand **Forward Lookup Zones**, and then click the name of the zone that you are configuring.

3. Right-click the zone that you are configuring, and then click **Properties**.

4. In the **Properties** dialog box for the zone, on the **WINS** tab, select the **Use WINS forward lookup** check box.

5. If there are third-party DNS servers that are authoritative for the zone, select the **Do not replicate this record** check box.

6. In the **IP address** box, type the IP address of the WINS server that will provide lookups, and then click **Add**.

Note   For fault tolerance, repeat this step if you add any additional WINS servers. To set the preferred order of use, click the IP address that you want to move up or down in the list of IP addresses, and then click the **Up** or **Down** button.

7. Click **Advanced** if you want to change the following values:

   - **Cache time-out**. The length of time for which the DNS server caches WINS lookup results. Increasing this time reduces the number of WINS lookups but may result in outdated responses.

   - **Lookup time-out**. The length of time for which the DNS server waits for a response from a WINS server. Increase this value if the WINS server is taking longer than two seconds to respond.

8. Click **OK**.

Configuring Static Mappings

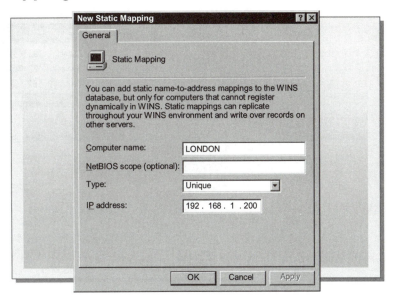

A *static mapping* is a manual entry in the WINS database that maps a NetBIOS name to an IP address. You can configure static mappings on a WINS server to add name resolution information for NetBIOS-based computers that are not WINS clients to the WINS server database. When you configure static mappings, WINS clients can resolve the NetBIOS names of these computers by querying the WINS server.

To configure a static mapping for a computer that is not a WINS client:

1. Open WINS from the **Administrative Tools** menu.

2. In the console tree, expand the entry for the WINS server on which you want to create a static mapping.

3. Right-click **Active Registrations**, and then click **New Static Mapping**.

4. In the **New Static Mapping** dialog box, in the **Computer name** box, type the name of the non-WINS client.

5. In the **NetBIOS scope** box, you have the option to specify a scope.

6. Under **Type**, specify the type of entry that you are creating. For a computer, click **Unique**.

7. In the **IP Address** box, type the IP address of the non-WINS client, and then click **OK**.

Note   Windows 2000 adds static mappings to the WINS database as soon as you click **OK**. If you provide incorrect information for a static mapping, you must delete the entry for the mapping from the list of active registrations for the specific WINS server and then create a new static mapping.

Configuring a WINS Proxy

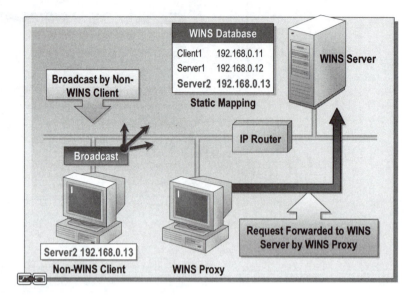

A WINS proxy is a computer configured to forward broadcast name resolution requests to a WINS sever for name resolution. A NetBIOS-based computer that is not a WINS client registers its name on the network by broadcasting its name registration, and resolves NetBIOS names to IP addresses by broadcasting name resolution requests. A WINS proxy extends the name resolution capabilities of a WINS server to non-WINS clients by listening for broadcasts that indicate name registrations and name resolution requests, and then forwarding them to a WINS server.

Note   Configure at least one but not more than two WINS proxies on a subnet with non-WINS clients. Configuring more than two WINS proxies can result in excessive network traffic and WINS server workloads.

NetBIOS Name Registration

When a non-WINS client broadcasts a name registration request, the WINS proxy forwards the request to the WINS server. A WINS proxy agent does not participate in the name registration process, nor does it check for duplicate names in the WINS server database for the b-node client.

NetBIOS Name Resolution

When a WINS proxy detects a name resolution broadcast, it checks its NetBIOS name cache and attempts to resolve the name. If the name is not in its cache, the WINS proxy sends a name resolution request to a WINS server. The WINS server sends the IP address for the requested NetBIOS name to the WINS proxy. The WINS proxy then returns this information to the non-WINS client.

To configure a computer as a WINS proxy, edit the registry and set the value for the **EnableProxy** entry to **1**, and then restart the computer. The **EnableProxy** entry is located in the registry under the following subkey:

HKEY_LOCAL_MACHINE\SYSTEM\CurrentControlSet\Services \NetBT\Parameters

◆ Enabling WINS Database Replication

- Overview of WINS Replication
- Examining Replication Partners
- Configuring WINS Replication

Although a single WINS server can support more than 5,000 clients under typical workloads, always install a second WINS server on a network to provide fault tolerance for NetBIOS name resolution. This way, if one of the WINS servers fails, the remaining server continues to provide NetBIOS name resolution on the network.

Each WINS server on a network maintains its own WINS database. As a result, if there are multiple WINS servers on your network, configure each of them to replicate the records in their databases to the other WINS servers. Understanding the function and configuration of WINS replication helps to ensure the maintenance and distribution of a consistent set of WINS database information throughout a network.

Overview of WINS Replication

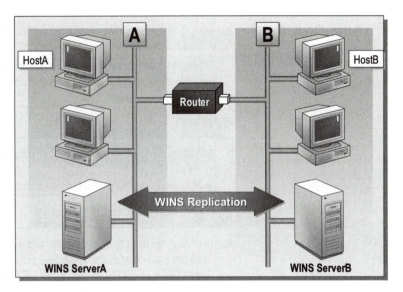

Replication of WINS databases ensures that a name that is registered with one WINS server is replicated to all other WINS servers on the network. As a result, a WINS client can resolve any NetBIOS name in the network, regardless of the WINS server on which the name was registered. For example:

- HostA on SubnetA registers with the WINS ServerA on SubnetA.

- HostB on SubnetB registers with the WINS ServerB on SubnetB.

- WINS replication occurs, and each WINS server updates its database with the new entry from the other server's database.

As a result of replication, both WINS servers have information about both hosts, and HostA and HostB can resolve each other's names by contacting their local WINS servers.

Note Rather than replicate the entire database, WINS servers only replicate changes to their database.

Examining Replication Partners

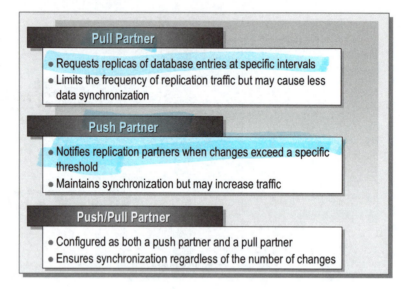

For replication to occur, you must configure each WINS server with at least one replication partner. When you configure a replication partner for a WINS server, you can specify the partner as a pull partner, a push partner, or a push/pull partner in the replication process.

Pull Partner

A *pull partner* requests replicas of new database entries from its replication partners at specific, configurable intervals. For example, you can configure a pull partner to request database changes every eight hours.

Configure a replication partner as a pull partner if slow communication links connect the servers. This configuration limits the frequency of replication traffic across the link, although a slower replication frequency causes the WINS databases to become increasingly less synchronized. When a WINS server has incomplete data, some name resolution attempts may fail. Configure pull replication across slow links to restrict replication to specific times.

Push Partner

A *push partner* notifies its replication partners when the number of changes to its WINS database surpasses a specific, configurable threshold. For example, you can configure a push partner to notify replication partners when 50 changes have occurred to the WINS database. When replication partners respond to the notification with a replication request, the push partner sends replicas of its new database entries.

Configure a replication partner as a push partner if fast communication links connect the servers. This ensures that the WINS databases maintain a high level of synchronization, although the replication traffic generally increases as a result.

Important By default, WINS replication between two WINS servers only occurs when both servers are configured for replication and when one of them is configured as a pull partner and the other is configured as a push partner.

Push/Pull Partner

A *push/pull partner* is configured as both a push partner and a pull partner. WINS replication partners are, by default, configured as push/pull partners.

Configure a replication partner as a push/pull partner if you want to specify both a replication threshold and a replication interval for the partner. This ensures that the WINS databases remain synchronized regardless of the number of changes that occur. In effect, replication occurs when either the threshold of changes has been reached, or when a maximum period between replication notifications has been exceeded. When configuring a WINS server as a push/pull partner of another WINS server, you typically configure each of the WINS servers as a push/pull partner of the other server.

Tip Configure the primary and secondary WINS servers of any client as push/pull partners of each other to ensure that the databases on these servers are close to identical at any given time.

Configuring WINS Replication

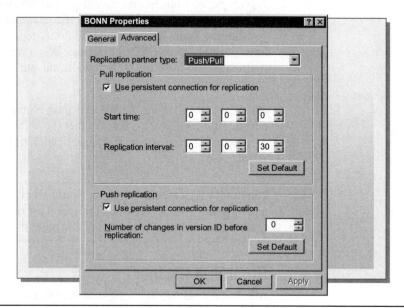

To enable replication, you must add replication partners to a WINS server, and then configure the pull and push parameters on each partner as needed. You can also configure WINS servers for automatic discovery of replication partners.

Adding a Replication Partner

To add a replication partner for a WINS server:

1. Open WINS from the **Administrative Tools** menu.

2. In the console tree, expand the entry for the WINS server for which you want to add a replication partner.

3. Right-click **Replication Partners**, and then click **New Replication Partner**.

4. In the **New Replication Partner** dialog box, in the **WINS server** box, type the computer name or IP address of the WINS server that you want to configure as a replication partner, and then click **OK**.

Configuring Push and Pull Parameters

To customize WINS replication on your network, specify push parameters and pull parameters for each configured replication partner. You configure pull and push parameters on the **Advanced** tab in the **Properties** dialog box for a WINS replication partner.

The following table explains the options for WINS replication.

Option	Explanation
Replication partner type	The WINS server that you are configuring contacts a pull partner for updates at specified intervals, sends an update to a push partner after a number of updates has occurred, and performs both types of replication with a push/pull partner.
Use persistent connection for replication	Maintains connections between WINS servers. Persistent connections increase the speed at which each replication occurs because no new connection needs to be established. Disable persistent connections for replication across slow wide area network (WAN) links.
Start time and replication interval	Set the times at which replication occurs. For example, if you set the start time to midnight and the replication interval to 12 hours, the WINS server contacts this pull partner at midnight and noon every day. Set the pull replication values to minimize the impact of replication on other network traffic and to avoid having a WINS server replicate with multiple WINS server at the same time.
Number of changes in version ID before replication	A low number of updates that are required for replication ensures frequent replication but leads to more network traffic. Setting this value to 0 disables any push replication but leaves the replication partner configured to exchange data with its corresponding pull partner.

Note   Use the **Replication Partners Properties** dialog box to configure a replication partner that you have already added, and to configure the default replication settings for replication partners that you will add in the future.

Automatic Replication Partner Discovery

If your network supports multicasting, you can configure your WINS servers to find other WINS servers on the network automatically. When enabled, WINS servers use the multicast address 224.0.1.24 to discover other WINS servers. If routers do not support multicasting, WINS servers only find other WINS servers on the same subnet. WINS servers that locate each other by using multicasting act as push/pull partners with replication set to occur every two hours.

To enable automatic replication partner discovery, in the **Replication Partners Properties** dialog box, on the **Advanced** tab, click **Enable automatic partner configuration**, and then configure the length of time between discovery multicasts. To open the dialog box, in WINS, expand the WINS server, right-click **Replication Partners**, and then click **Properties**.

Initiating Replication

To initiate replication with a partner, in WINS, expand your WINS server, expand **Replication Partners**, right-click the replication partner, and then click **Start Pull Replication** or **Start Push Replication**. You can choose whether you want to push database changes only to this replication partner, or whether you want to propagate the changes by initiating a push replication from your pull partner to all of its configured push partners. Forcing propagation ensures that updates are quickly replicated throughout the network, but this can result in excessive network traffic.

To enable replication even when only one computer is configured as a replication partner, in the **Replication Partners Properties** dialog box, on the **General** tab, clear the **Replicate only with partners** check box.

◆ Maintaining the WINS Server Database

- **Reconciling WINS Database Records**

- **Compacting the WINS Database**

- **Removing Records from the WINS Database**

- **Verifying WINS Database Consistency**

- **Configuring Advanced WINS Server Options**

- **Backing Up and Restoring the WINS Database**

The WINS database stores and replicates the NetBIOS name-to-IP address mappings for your network. The WINS database changes over time as clients log on and log off the network. Therefore, it is important to maintain the WINS server database to ensure that the data is valid.

To maintain the WINS server database, it is important to know how to reconcile WINS database records to ensure database integrity among WINS servers in a large network. You must also be able to compact the WINS database to recover unused space, remove records to delete obsolete information, and back up and restore the WINS database to prevent loss of data or recover lost data.

Reconciling WINS Database Records

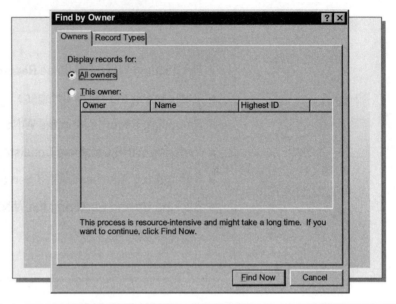

WINS in Microsoft Management Console (MMC) enables you to view the contents of the WINS database and search for specific entries.

Opening the WINS Database

To open the WINS database:

1. In WINS, expand the name of the server, and then click **Active Registrations**.

2. Right-click **Active Registrations**, and then click **Find by Owner**.

3. In the **Find by Owner** dialog box, on the **Owners** tab, click **All owners**, and then click **Find Now**.

Note To view only those entries that originate from a specific WINS server, click **This owner**, and then select the WINS Server. To view only certain record types, on the **Record Types** tab, select the check boxes for the types of records that you want to view, and clear the check boxes for all other record types.

Updating the List of Owners

If the **Find by Owner** dialog box does not display all owners of database records, you can update the list. To update the list of owners, in the console tree, right-click the server, and then click **Refresh**.

WINS Record Information

WINS displays all records in the database and organizes WINS record information into the following columns:

- *Record Name*. The registered NetBIOS name, which can be a unique name or can represent a group, internet group, or multihomed computer.

- *Type*. The service that registered the entry, including the hexadecimal type identifier.

Note   For a list of identifiers, see "NetBIOS Names Reference" in Windows 2000 Server Help.

- *IP Address*. The IP address that corresponds to the registered name.

- *State*. The state of the database entry, which can be active, released, or tombstoned. A tombstoned entry is no longer active and will be removed from the database.

- *Static*. Indicates whether the mapping is static.

- *Owner*. The WINS server from which the entry originates. Because of replication, this is not necessarily the same server on which you view the database.

- *Version*. A unique hexadecimal number assigned by the WINS server during name registration. It is used by the server's pull partner during replication to find new records.

- *Expiration*. Shows when the entry will expire. When a replica is stored in the database, its expiration data is set to the current time on the receiving WINS server, plus the renewal interval that is set on the client.

Deleting WINS Records

Occasionally you may have to delete incorrect records from the WINS database. There are two methods that you can use to delete a WINS record.

To delete a WINS record:

1. Open WINS, and verify that the details pane displays the contents of the WINS database.

2. Right-click the record that you want to delete, and then click **Delete**.

3. In the **Delete Record** dialog box, click one of the following options:

   - **Delete the record only from this server**. Removes the record from the database of the WINS server that you are configuring. Select this option when the database of the WINS server that you are configuring contains incorrect information, but other WINS servers contain the correct information.

   - **Replicate deletion of the record to other servers (tombstone)**. Removes the record from the database of the WINS server that you are configuring, and deletes the record on other WINS servers. Select this option when the databases of all of the WINS servers contain incorrect information. This type of deletion is called *tombstoning*.

     When you mark a record as tombstoned, it remains in the database, but it is no longer active. The WINS server no longer responds to queries for the name, and the status of the record is replicated to other WINS servers. To prevent deleted records from reappearing in WINS after subsequent replication with other servers, you must delete the record on the WINS server that is listed as the record's owner.

4. Click **OK**.

Compacting the WINS Database

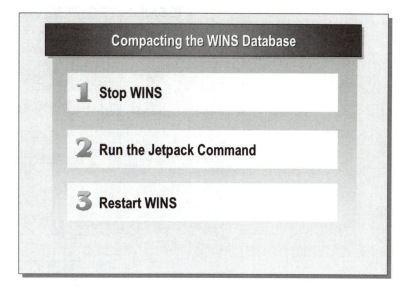

By default, Windows 2000 compacts the WINS database automatically. You can compact the database manually by using the **jetpack** command that Windows 2000 Server includes.

To compact the WINS database:

1. Stop WINS.

2. From the *systemroot*\system32\wins directory, run the Jetpack.exe command-line utility by using the following command syntax:

   jetpack wins.mdb *temporary_name*.**mdb** (where *temporary_name* is any file name that you assign)

   This compacts the contents of **wins.mdb** in *temporary_name*.**mdb**, copies the temporary file to **wins.mdb**, and deletes the temporary name.

3. Restart WINS.

Removing Records from the WINS Database

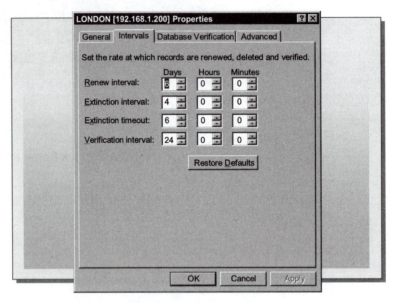

When WINS database records are marked as released, the records remain in the database to inform replication partners of the record's status. Therefore, you must periodically clear each WINS database of released entries, in addition to entries that were registered at another WINS server but were never removed.

Clearing WINS Database Entries

To manually clear entries in the WINS database, open WINS, right-click the server name, and then click **Initiate Scavenging**. You can also configure WINS to automatically remove entries in the database at configured intervals.

Configuring Intervals

To configure the interval that is used for WINS operations:

1. Open WINS, right-click the server name, and then click **Properties**.

2. In the **Properties** dialog box, on the **Intervals** tab, specify the intervals for each of the following options:

   - **Renewal interval**. The frequency at which a WINS client renews its name registration with the WINS server. The default value is six days.

   - **Extinction interval**. The interval between the time when an entry is marked as *released* (no longer registered) and the time when it is marked as *extinct*. The default value is four days.

   - **Extinction timeout**. The interval between the time when an entry is marked *extinct* and the time when the entry is scavenged (removed) from the WINS database. The default is the same as the renewal interval, and cannot be less than 24 hours.

   - **Verification interval**. The time after which the WINS server will verify that those names that it does not own—those replicated from other WINS servers—are still active. The minimum value is 24 days.

Verifying WINS Database Consistency

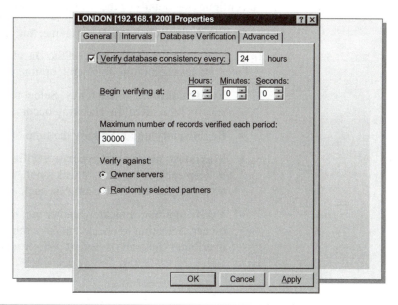

Verifying WINS database consistency enables you to determine whether the WINS database contains incorrect entries. When a WINS server verifies its database, it compares all of its entries with entries on other WINS servers that belong to the same replication topology. It compares all records that it pulls from remote databases with records in the local database, as follows:

- If the record in the local database is identical to the record pulled from the owner database, its time stamp is updated to that of the owner database.

- If the record that is pulled from the owner database has a higher version identifier (ID) than the record in the local database, the pulled record is added to the local database, and the original local record is marked for deletion.

Initiating WINS Database Consistency Verification

To verify WINS database consistency, open WINS, and then click the server name. Click **Action**, and then click **Verify Database Consistency**.

Note   Consistency verification of a large database is resource intensive and can increase network traffic. Schedule the verification process for off-hours and restrict how many records are checked at any given time.

Configuring WINS Database Consistency Verification

To configure the details of the database verification:

1. In WINS, right-click the server name, and then click **Properties**.

2. In the **Properties** dialog box, on the **Database Verification** tab, specify the intervals for each of the following options:

    *   **Verify database consistency**. Select to enable consistency checking and specify how often the checking occurs.

    *   **Begin verifying at**. Specify the time of day at which verification begins.

    *   **Maximum number of records verified each period**. Use this number to keep each consistency check small. Increasing this number can be taxing on the server's resources, such as memory and processor load.

    *   **Verify against**. Indicate whether records are verified against their owner. Selecting to check against a randomly selected WINS server distributes the load on remote WINS servers more evenly.

Configuring Advanced WINS Server Options

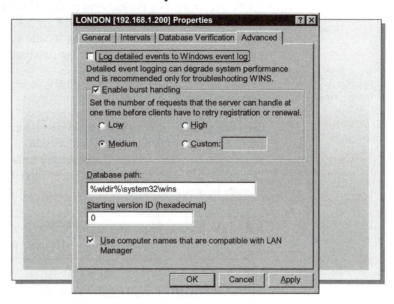

The **Advanced** tab of the **Properties** dialog box for a WINS server contains the following options through which you can specify how the WINS server operates.

Log Detailed Events to Windows Event Log

This option logs detailed events about WINS server operations to the Windows system log. Consider the impact on WINS server operation and increase the size of the system log before you enable this option.

Enable Burst Handling

WINS servers can support handling of high-volume (burst) server loads. The **Enable burst handling** option configures a WINS server to respond to client requests even when there is a temporary increase in the number of client requests. When burst handling is enabled, and WINS cannot update its database quickly enough to keep up with client requests, the WINS server issues short leases to clients and does not record these leases in the database. If the WINS server is less busy when the clients renew these leases, the server issues a new lease and updates its database.

Enabling burst handling eliminates errors on WINS clients that occur when a WINS server is too busy to reply. The default burst handling setting is **Medium**. On slow WINS servers, you can decrease the setting to **Low**. On a fast server, increase the setting to **High**.

Database Path

This option specifies the location of the WINS database and log files. The default location is *systemroot*\system32\wins. When changing this path, ensure that the database files are in the new location and initiate replication with all partners to rebuild the contents of the database. Changing this value requires restarting WINS.

Starting Version ID

This option specifies the highest version ID number for the database. This number is used to determine which version of a record is most recent during replication between servers that store the same record. Usually, you do not need to change this value unless you want to force the update and replication of records between servers.

Note   For more information about how to use the starting version ID, see the topic "Increase the Starting Version Count" in Windows 2000 Server Help.

Use Computer Names That Are Compatible With LAN Manager

This option restricts the NetBIOS names that clients can register to 15 characters. Leave this setting enabled if only computers running Microsoft-based operating systems will register names with the WINS server. Non-Microsoft operating systems may register names that are 16 characters long. If you have clients that register long names, disable this setting.

Backing Up and Restoring the WINS Database

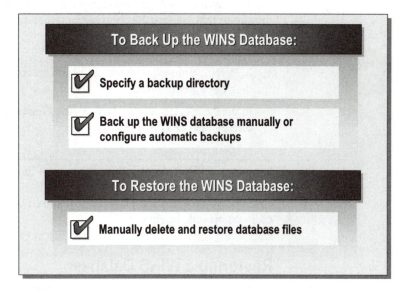

It is important to back up the WINS database in the event of system failure or database corruption, because you can use the backup to restore the database. To back up the WINS database, you need to specify a directory for the backup and initiate a manual backup. You can also specify settings for automatic backups.

Specifying a Backup Directory

To specify a backup directory:

1. In WINS, right-click the name of the server that you are configuring, and then click **Properties**.

2. In the **Properties** dialog box, on the **General** tab, in the **Default backup path** box, type the name of the directory that the WINS server uses for database backups.

   When WINS backs up the server database, it creates a Wins_bak\New folder under the backup folder that you specified. Actual backups of the WINS database (Wins.mdb) are stored in this folder. By default, the backup path is the root folder on your system partition. The backup folder must be on the local computer. After you specify a backup directory, WINS performs a complete backup to that directory every three hours.

Backing Up a WINS Database

To back up the WINS database manually, open WINS, right-click the name of the server that you are configuring, and then click **Back Up Database**.

To configure automatic backups of the WINS database:

1. In WINS, right-click the name of the server that you are configuring, and then click **Properties**.

2. In the **Properties** dialog box, on the **General** tab, click **Back up database during server shutdown**.

Important   WINS stores information about its configuration and replication partners in the registry. As part of your WINS disaster-recovery strategy, make sure that you always have a recent backup of your registry; for example, as part of a system state backup.

Restoring a WINS Database

In the event that the WINS database becomes corrupt and cannot be repaired, restore the WINS database from a recent backup.

To restore a WINS database from a recent backup:

1. Stop WINS.

   Wait for WINS to completely stop before proceeding. A busy server might require several minutes before it can stop WINS and you can proceed with restoring the database.

2. Delete all files in the folder path on the WINS server computer where you are restoring the database. This path is determined by the current setting of **Database path**, which is located on the **Advanced** tab in the **Properties** dialog box for the server.

3. In WINS, right-click the name of the server that you are configuring, and then click **Restore Database**.

   The **Restore Database** option is only available when viewing a computer on which WINS is stopped. In some cases, you might need to refresh the WINS console to activate the restore option. If necessary, right-click the server, and then click **Refresh** to refresh the server node so that WINS detects that WINS is stopped on the server.

4. In the **Browse for Folder** dialog box, click the folder that you used previously to back up the local WINS database, and then click **OK**.

   When you restore the database, WINS requires that the backup path used for restoration match the path that was originally specified in *server* **Properties** as the **Backup path**.

Lab A: Installing and Configuring WINS

Objectives

After completing this lab, you will be able to:

- Install WINS.
- Manually configure a client computer to use WINS.
- Add static entries to the WINS database.
- Configure replication between WINS servers.
- Remove records from the WINS database.

Prerequisite

Before working on this lab, you must be familiar with WINS concepts.

Lab Setup

To complete this lab, you need the following:

- A computer running Windows 2000 Advanced Server
- A partner with a similarly configured computer

Important The lab does not reflect the real-world environment. It is recommended that you always use complex passwords for any administrator accounts, and never create accounts without a password.

Important Outside of the classroom environment, it is strongly advised that you use the most recent software updates that are necessary. Because this is a classroom environment, we may use software that does not include the latest updates.

Scenario

Your organization has multiple subnets with client computers running Windows 98 and Windows 2000 Professional. Several applications that users are running use NetBIOS names for connections to servers. You must configure your network so that all computers can resolve NetBIOS names. You must also ensure that these computers can do this without using an Lmhosts file or contacting WINS servers that are in a remote location.

Estimated time to complete this lab: 45 minutes

Exercise 1
Installing WINS

Scenario

To allow client computers to resolve NetBIOS names, you need to configure a server as a WINS server.

Goal

In this exercise, you will install the WINS Server service and configure your computer to use WINS for NetBIOS name resolution.

Tasks	Detailed Steps
1. Add WINS.	**a.** Log on as administrator@*domain*.nwtraders.msft (where *domain* is the name of your domain) with a password of **password**.
	b. In Control Panel, double-click **Add/Remove Programs**.
	c. In Add/Remove Programs, click **Add/Remove Windows Components**.
ⓘ **Note:** In the next detailed step, click the text **Networking Services** rather than the check box to avoid selecting all options under **Networking Services**.	
1. *(continued)*	**d.** In the Windows Components wizard, on the **Windows Components** page, click **Networking Services**, and then click **Details**.
	e. In the **Networking Services** dialog box, select the **Windows Internet Name Service (WINS)** check box, and then click **OK**.
	f. Click **Next**.
	g. In the **Files Needed** dialog box, type **London\Setup\Winsrc** and then click **OK**.
	h. When the configuration process is complete, click **Finish**, and then close all open windows.

(continued)

Tasks	Detailed Steps
2. Configure the TCP/IP properties of your computer so that it is a WINS client of itself.	a. Right-click **My Network Places**, and then click **Properties**. b. In Network and Dial-up Connections, right-click **Classroom**, and then click **Properties**. c. In the **Classroom Properties** dialog box, click **Internet Protocol (TCP/IP)**, and then click **Properties**. d. In the **Internet Protocol (TCP/IP) Properties** dialog box, click **Advanced**, and then on the **WINS** tab, click **Add**. e. In the **TCP/IP WINS Server** dialog box, type the IP address of your PartnerNet connection, and then click **Add**. f. Click **OK** to close the **Advanced TCP/IP Settings** dialog box. g. Click **OK** to close the **Internet Protocol (TCP/IP) Properties** dialog box. h. Click **OK** to close the **Classroom Properties** dialog box. i. Complete steps b through h to configure the properties of the PartnerNet connection. j. Close Network and Dial-up Connections.
❓ Why would you configure a WINS server to be a WINS client of itself? _____ _____ _____ _____	
3. Verify that your computer is registered in the WINS database.	a. Start WINS from the **Administrative Tools** menu. b. In the console tree, expand *server* (where *server* is the name of your computer), and then click **Active Registrations**. c. Right-click **Active Registrations**, and then click **Find by Owner**. d. In the **Find by Owner** dialog box, on the **Owners** tab, click **All owners**, and then click **Find Now**.
❓ Why are multiple names listed for your IP address? _____ _____ _____ _____	

Exercise 2
Administering WINS

Scenario

Your organization has NetBIOS clients in addition to some older NetBIOS-based servers that do not register themselves with WINS servers. You have configured multiple WINS servers on your network, and users with computers running Windows 2000 must be able to connect to all servers by using a NetBIOS name, regardless of the part of the network to which their computers are connected. You also need to ensure that the WINS database does not contain outdated records.

Goal

In this exercise, you will create static WINS records, configure a WINS server for replication, and delete WINS records.

Tasks	Detailed Steps
1. Add a static WINS record for SERVER*x* (where *x* is your student number) with an IP address of 192.168.200.*x* (where *x* is your student number).	**a.** In WINS, in the console tree, right-click **Active Registrations**, and then click **New Static Mapping**.
	b. In the **New Static Mapping** dialog box, type **SERVER*x*** (where *x* is your student number) in the **Computer name** box, verify that **Unique** is selected in the **Type** box, type **192.168.200.***x* (where *x* is your student number) in the **IP address** box, and then click **OK**.
	c. Minimize WINS.
	d. At a command prompt, type **ping server***x* (where *x* is your student number), and then press ENTER.
	*Because the computer SERVERx is not a computer on your network, there is no reply. However, the **ping** command displays the correct IP address of the server, which confirms that name resolution was successful.*
	e. Close the command prompt window.
2. Configure Push/Pull replication with your partner's WINS server, and then initiate replication.	**a.** Restore WINS, and then in the console tree, click **Replication Partners**.
	b. Right-click **Replication Partners**, and then click **New Replication Partner**.
	c. In the **New Replication Partner** dialog box, type the IP address of your partner's PartnerNet network connection, and then click **OK**.
	d. In the details pane, right-click your partner's computer name, and then click **Properties**.

Tasks	Detailed Steps
2. *(continued)*	**e.** In the **Properties** dialog box for your partner's computer, on the **Advanced** tab, verify that the replication partner type is Push/Pull, and then verify that persistent connections are used both for pull and push replication. **f.** If your student number is lower than your partner's, set the start time for pull replication to 18:00:00 (6:00 P.M.) and the replication interval to 12 hours. If your student number is higher than your partner's, set the start time for pull replication to 21:00:00 (9:00 P.M.) and the replication interval to 12 hours. **g.** In the **Number of changes in version ID before replication** box, type **200**

❓   Explain the impact of the replication setting that you configured.

_____

_____

_____

_____

Tasks	Detailed Steps
2. *(continued)*	**h.** Click **OK** to close the **Properties** dialog box for the replication partner. **i.** In the console tree, right-click **Replication Partners**, and then click **Replicate Now**. **j.** In the **WINS** message box, click **Yes**. **k.** In the **WINS** message box, click **OK**.

✋   Wait for your partner to complete the preceding step before continuing with the next step.

Tasks	Detailed Steps
2. *(continued)*	**l.** In the console tree, click *server* (where *server* is the name of your computer). **m.** On the **Action** menu, click **Refresh** to update the console with the names of all replication partners. **n.** In the console tree, click **Active Registrations**. **o.** Right-click **Active Registrations**, and then click **Find by Owner**. **p.** In the **Find by Owner** dialog box, on the **Owners** tab, click **All owners**, and then click **Find Now**. 🖥️ *If the static entries that your partner created do not appear, wait for one minute, and then repeat the preceding step.*

(continued)

Tasks	Detailed Steps
3. Delete the WINS records that you created. Perform the deletion both with and without tombstoning.	a. In the details pane, right-click the WorkStation WINS record for SERVER*x* (where *x* is your student number), and then click **Delete**.
	b. In the **Delete Record** dialog box, click Replicate deletion of this record to other servers (tombstone), and then click **OK**.
	c. In the **WINS** message box, click **Yes**.
	d. Right-click the Messenger WINS record for SERVER*x* (where *x* is your student number), and then click **Delete**.
	e. In the **Delete Record** dialog box, click Replicate deletion of this record to other servers (tombstone), and then click **OK**.
	f. In the **WINS** message box, click **Yes**.
	g. Right-click the File Server WINS record for SERVER*x* (where *x* is your student number), and then click **Delete**.
	h. In the **Delete Record** dialog box, verify that **Delete the record only from this server** is selected, and then click **OK**.
	i. In the console tree, right-click **Replication Partners**, and then click **Replicate Now**.
	j. In the **WINS** message box, click **Yes**.
	k. In the **WINS** message box, click **OK**.
	l. In the console tree, click **Active Registrations**.
	m. Right-click **Active Registrations**, and then click **Find by Owner**.
	n. In the **Find by Owner** dialog box, verify that **All owners** is selected, and then click **Find Now**.
	If the deletions that your partner made do not appear, wait for one minute and then repeat the preceding two steps.
	o. Compare the WINS records on your server with the WINS records on your partner's server.
❓ Why is there a discrepancy between the WINS records on your partner's server and the records on your server?	
	_____
	_____
	_____
	_____
3. *(continued)*	p. Close WINS.

Exercise 3
Removing WINS

Scenario

After you have tested a WINS configuration for your organization, you must restore your original configuration.

Goal

In this exercise, you will restore the original computer configuration.

Tasks	Detailed Steps
🖐 Do not start the following procedure until your partner has completed the preceding procedure.	
1. Remove WINS from your computer.	a. In Control Panel, double-click **Add/Remove Programs**.
	b. In Add/Remove Programs, click **Add/Remove Windows Components**.
ℹ **Note:** In the next detailed step, click the text **Networking Services** rather than the check box to avoid selecting all options under **Networking Services**.	
1. *(continued)*	c. In the Windows Components wizard, on the **Windows Components** page, click **Networking Services**, and then click **Details**.
	d. In the **Networking Services** dialog box, clear the **Windows Internet Name Service (WINS)** check box, and then click **OK**.
	e. On the **Windows Components** page, click **Next**.
	f. When the configuration process is complete, click **Finish**, and then close all windows.
2. Configure the TCP/IP properties of your computer so that it is no longer a WINS client.	a. Right-click **My Network Places**, and then click **Properties**.
	b. In **Network and Dial-up Connections**, right-click **Classroom**, and then click **Properties**.
	c. In the **Classroom Properties** dialog box, click **Internet Protocol (TCP/IP)**, and then click **Properties**.
	d. In the **Internet Protocol (TCP/IP) Properties** dialog box, click **Advanced**.
	e. In the **Advanced TCP/IP Settings** dialog box, on the **WINS** tab, click the IP address of your computer, click **Remove**, and then click **OK**.
	f. In the **Microsoft TCP/IP** dialog box, click **Yes**.
	g. Click **OK** to close the **Internet Protocol (TCP/IP) Properties** dialog box.
	h. Click **OK** to close the **Classroom Properties** dialog box.
	i. Complete steps b through h to configure the properties of the PartnerNet connection.
	j. Close all open windows, and then log off.

Review

- **Connecting to NetBIOS-Based Networks**
- **WINS Overview**
- **Configuring WINS Servers and Clients**
- **Configuring Support for Non-WINS Clients**
- **Enabling WINS Database Replication**
- **Maintaining the WINS Server Database**

1. What processes does a WINS client use to interact with a WINS server?

2. What are the steps that you must perform to configure a computer running Windows 2000 as a WINS server?

3. What must you do to ensure that computers that use NetBIOS and are not WINS clients can resolve NetBIOS names of servers that are registered with a WINS server?

4. You are concerned that replication traffic between WINS servers across a slow network link might cause other network traffic to slow down. What can you do to manage WINS replication traffic?

5. You are troubleshooting network problems and you notice that computers in one branch office are resolving NetBIOS names to incorrect IP addresses when they connect to several servers on your network. Client computers in other locations are resolving the NetBIOS names correctly. What is the most likely cause of the problem, and how can you resolve it?

RENEW → RENEWS WINS RECORDS

EXTINCTION → CLEARS USELESS RECORDS

EXTINCION → REMOVES RECORDS.

VERIFICATION → VERIFIES IF IT WAS REMOVED. ACCROSS ALL CONFIGURE WINS SERVERS.

PULL → CLOCK.
PUSH → # CHANGES

Microsoft®
Training &
Certification

Module 5: Configuring Network Security by Using Public Key Infrastructure

Contents

Simulations and interactive exercises were built with Macromedia Authorware

Overview

- **Introduction to Public Key Infrastructure (PKI)**
- **Deploying Certificate Services**
- **Using Certificates**
- **Managing Certificates**
- **Configuring Active Directory for Certificates**
- **Troubleshooting Certificate Services**

Your organization's network may consist of intranets, Internet sites, and extranets—all of which are potentially susceptible to access by unauthorized individuals who may maliciously view or alter your digital information assets. A well-planned Public Key Infrastructure (PKI) can help you to secure data and distribute and manage identification credentials across your organization. The Microsoft® Windows® 2000 operating system includes a native PKI that is designed to take full advantage of the Windows 2000 security architecture.

At the end of this module, you will be able to:

- Define PKI concepts.
- Deploy Certificate Services.
- Use certificates.
- Manage certificates.
- Configure the Active Directory™ directory service for certificates.
- Troubleshoot Certificate Services.

Note This module provides an overview of PKI concepts. For more information about cryptography basics, see the Microsoft Windows 2000 Public Key Infrastructure white paper at http://www.microsoft.com/windows2000/techinfo/planning/security/pki.asp.

◆ Introduction to Public Key Infrastructure (PKI)

- **Public Key Encryption**
- **Public Key Authentication**
- **Certificate Authority**
- **Certificate Hierarchies**
- **Windows 2000 PKI**

Public key cryptography is an important technology for e-commerce, intranets, extranets, and Web-enabled applications. The two fundamental operations associated with public key cryptography include encryption and authentication. Windows 2000 uses public key cryptography in areas such as smart card logon, Encrypting File System (EFS), and Internet Protocol Security (IPSec).

Note   The PKI in Windows 2000 supports the standards developed by the Internet Engineering Task Force (IETF) and RSA Data Security, Inc. These include Public Key Infrastructure, X.509 draft standards, and Public Key Cryptography Standards, respectively.

For more information about Internet drafts and for RFCs about PKI, see www.ietf.org/.

Public Key Encryption

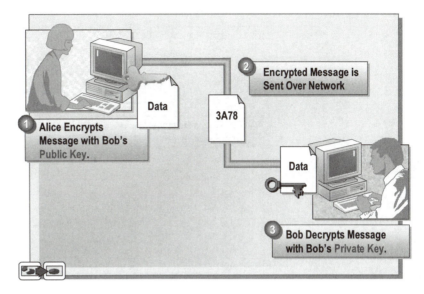

Public key cryptography provides privacy through data encryption, whether the data is in the form of e-mail messages, credit-card numbers sent over the Internet, or network traffic. Because public keys can be posted freely, complete strangers can establish private communications over public networks merely by retrieving each other's public keys and encrypting the data.

Using Public Keys and Private Keys

Public key encryption uses two keys that are mathematically related. A *key* is a random string—such as a number, ASCII value, word, or phrase—that is used in conjunction with an algorithm. For public key encryption, every user has a pair of mathematically related keys, including:

- A *private key*, which is kept confidential.

- A *public key*, which is freely given out to all potential correspondents.

The goal of encryption is to obscure data in such a way that it can only be read by the intended party. In a typical scenario, a sender uses the recipient's public key to encrypt a message. Only the recipient has the related private key to decrypt the message. By making your public key available, other people can send you encrypted data that can only be decrypted by using your private key. The use of keys in PKI-enabled programs that provide data encryption is typically transparent to the user.

Encrypting and Decrypting Text

The fundamental property of public key encryption is that the encryption and decryption keys are different Encryption with a public key is a one-way function. When you encrypt a document with a public key, *plaintext* turns into *cipher text*. A decryption key, which is related but not identical to the encryption key, is needed to turn the cipher text back into plaintext. If someone intercepts an encrypted message in transmission, the message is in cipher text and is unreadable.

Public Key Authentication

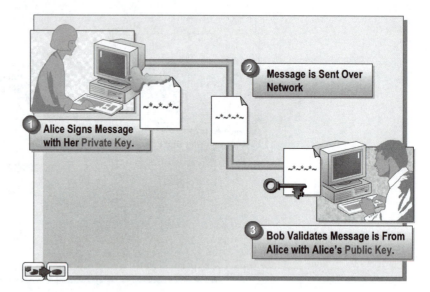

Public key authentication uses public key cryptography to authenticate and verify the originator of electronic data in e-mail, e-commerce, and other electronic transactions. Like public key encryption, public key authentication uses a key pair. However, instead of using the sender's private key to decrypt a message, the sender's public key is used to authenticate and validate the sender of the message. A string of characters that uniquely identifies the contents of the message is encrypted with the private key to create a *digital signature*. A digital signature swaps the role of the private and public keys.

Digital Signatures

A digital signature is a means for the originator of a message, file, or other digitally encoded information to bind his or her identity to the information. The signature itself is a sequence of bits appended to a digital document. A digital signature ensures that:

- Only someone possessing the private key could have created the digital signature.

- Anyone with access to the corresponding public key can verify the digital signature.

For example, when you visit a Web site and you are prompted to download a file, a dialog box informs you that the file has been digitally signed by an entity that you can trust. A digital signature assures you that a file or program that you are about to download has come from a reputable source.

Hash Algorithms

A digital signature uses an algorithm called a *hash algorithm*. Hash algorithms are designed to guarantee that if a single byte changes, processing the document generates a completely different hash. When a hash is encrypted by using a public key, any modification of the signed data invalidates the digital signature.

Certification Authority

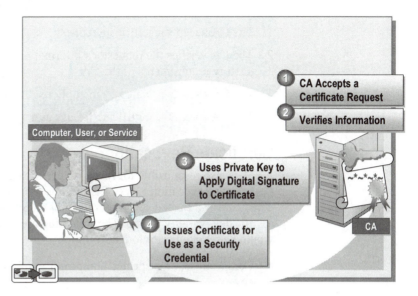

A certification authority (CA) is responsible for providing and assigning the keys for encryption, decryption, and authentication. A CA distributes keys by issuing *certificates*, which contain the public key and a set of attributes. A CA can issue certificates to a computer, a user account, or a service.

Certificates

Certificates are signed documents that match public keys to other information, such as a name or an e-mail address. Certificates are signed by CAs that issue certificates. A CA's signature guarantees that the public key does indeed belong to the party that presents it.

External and Internal CAs

A CA can be an external issuing company, such as a large commercial CA that issues certificates to millions of users. Or a CA can be internal, such as department within a company that has installed its own server for issuing and verifying certificates. Each CA decides what attributes it includes in a certificate and what mechanism it uses to verify those attributes before issuing the certificate.

Important An organization can set its own policy for its internal CA. Be aware that other organizations may have very different policies from your own organization. The use of certificates requires that you trust the policies of the organization that issues the certificates.

Additionally every CA has a certificate to confirm its own identity, issued by another trusted CA or by itself. By trusting a CA, you implicitly trust the policies and procedures that the CA has in place for confirming the identity of the entities that are issued certificates.

The Process for Issuing Certificates

The process for issuing a certificate has four basic steps:

1. The CA accepts a certificate request.
2. The CA verifies the requester's information according to the proof-of-identity requirements of the CA.
3. The CA uses its private key to apply its digital signature to the certificate.
4. The CA issues the certificate for use as a security credential within a PKI.

Certificate Revocation

A CA is also responsible for revoking certificates and for publishing a Certificate Revocation List (CRL). Revocation of a certificate invalidates the certificate as a trusted security credential before the expiration of the certificate's validity period. The following are some reasons why a certificate would be revoked prior to its expiration:

- Compromise, or suspected compromise, of the certificate subject's private key
- Discovery that a certificate was obtained fraudulently
- Change in the status of the certificate subject as a trusted entity

---

Note   If a CA's certificate is revoked, then all certificates that the CA issued are also revoked.

Certificate Hierarchies

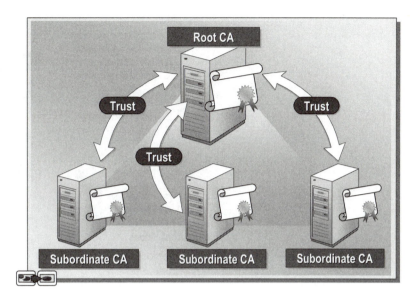

A certificate hierarchy is a model of trust in which certification paths are created through the establishment of parent/child relationships between CAs. A root CA, the subordinate CAs that have been certified by the root, and subordinate CAs that have been certified by other subordinate CAs, form a certificate hierarchy. You can only trust root CAs, not subordinate CAs. You trust the policies and procedures defined by the root CA, because all subordinate CAs must also follow these rules.

Root CA

A *root CA*, sometimes called a root authority, is meant to be the most trusted type of CA in an organization's PKI. Typically, both the physical security and the certificate issuance policy of a root CA are more rigorous than those for subordinate CAs. If the root CA is compromised or issues a certificate to an unauthorized entity, all certificate-based security in your organization is suddenly vulnerable. Although root CAs can be used to issue certificates to end users for such tasks as sending secure e-mail, in most organizations they are only used to issue certificates to other CAs, called subordinate CAs.

Subordinate CA

A *subordinate CA* is a CA that has been certified by another CA in your organization. Typically, a subordinate CA issues certificates for specific uses, such as secure e-mail, Web-based authentication, or smart card authentication. Subordinate CAs can also issue certificates to other, more subordinate CAs.

Windows 2000 PKI

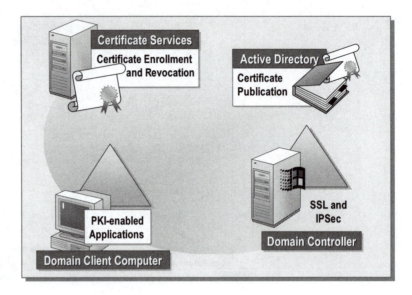

To use the benefits of public-key cryptography, an organization needs a supporting infrastructure. The PKI supplied by Windows 2000 consists of a set of services that are provided by a group of interconnected components. These components work together to provide public key–based security services to users and applications.

Windows 2000 PKI Primary Components

The primary components of the Windows 2000 PKI are:

- *Certificate Services*. The core operating system service that allows businesses to act as their own CAs and to issue and manage digital certificates.

- *Active Directory*. The publication service for PKI. Certification publication makes certificates and CRLs publicly available within an organization.

Note   Certificates can also be published on Web pages or distributed on smart cards, disks, or compact discs. Certificate Revocation Lists are published at URLs.

- *PKI-enabled applications*. The applications that use PKI for encryption and authentication. These include Microsoft Internet Explorer, Microsoft Money, Microsoft Internet Information Services (IIS), Microsoft Outlook®, Microsoft Outlook Express, and third-party applications.

Security Protocols

In addition, Windows 2000 PKI components use industry security protocols, including:

- *Secure Sockets Layer (SSL).* A protocol developed by Netscape Communications Corporation for ensuring security and privacy in Internet communications. SSL supports authentication of client, server, or both, in addition to encryption during a communications session.

- *Internet Protocol Security (IPSec).* A set of protocols being developed by the IETF to support secure exchange of packets at the IP layer.

- *Transport Layer Security (TLS).* A protocol that provides privacy and security between two applications communicating over a network.

Use of Certificates

Security services and programs in Windows 2000 use certificates to provide authentication, data integrity, and secure communications across nonsecure networks such as the Internet. Certificates provide the following:

- *Server authentication.* Uses certificates to authenticate servers to clients. E-commerce is an example.

- *Client authentication.* Uses certificates to authenticate clients to servers. Remote access functionality and smart card authentication are examples.

- *Code signing.* Uses certificates associated with key pairs to sign active content.

- *Secure e-mail.* Uses certificates associated with key pairs to sign e-mail messages.

- *EFS.* Uses two certificates associated with key pairs. One certificate is for encryption and decryption and one certificate is used for EFS recovery.

- *IPSec.* Uses certificates associated with key pairs to encrypt IP-based network traffic.

◆ Deploying Certificate Services

- **Choosing a Certificate Authority (CA) Model**
- **Installing Certificate Services**
- **Creating a Subordinate CA**
- **Backing up and Restoring Certificate Services**

By installing Certificate Services, you can create a CA for issuing certificates that are needed to run a PKI. In Windows 2000 Server, the certification authority is one of two types: *enterprise* or *stand-alone*. Within each type, there can be a root CA and one or more subordinate CAs.

Typically, you must install an enterprise CA if you plan to issue certificates to users or computers inside a single Windows 2000 network. An enterprise CA requires that all users and computers requesting certificates have an account in Active Directory.

You must install a stand-alone CA if you plan to issue certificates to users or computers outside a single Windows 2000 network. A stand-alone CA does not require Active Directory.

Whichever type of CA you choose, backing up the CA database, certificates, and keys is essential to protecting your organization against the loss of critical data.

Note For more information about using Certificate Services as part of a PKI infrastructure, see the white paper *Windows 2000 Certificate Services* under **Additional Reading** on the Web page on the Student Materials compact disc.

Choosing a CA Model

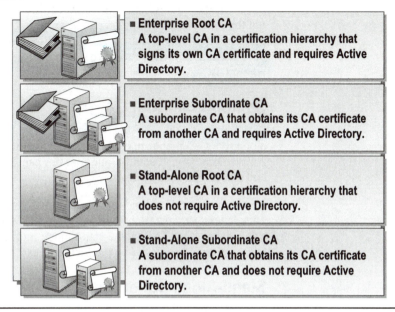

- **Enterprise Root CA**
  A top-level CA in a certification hierarchy that signs its own CA certificate and requires Active Directory.

- **Enterprise Subordinate CA**
  A subordinate CA that obtains its CA certificate from another CA and requires Active Directory.

- **Stand-Alone Root CA**
  A top-level CA in a certification hierarchy that does not require Active Directory.

- **Stand-Alone Subordinate CA**
  A subordinate CA that obtains its CA certificate from another CA and does not require Active Directory.

The first choice that you make when implementing Certificate Services is deciding which CA model to use. When you install Certificate Services, you can select from one of four different CA models, each of which causes the CA to have different characteristics and performance. You choose the model that you want to use, based on how you need the CA to perform, given its role in your PKI.

Enterprise Root CA

An enterprise root CA is the top-level CA in a certificate hierarchy. An enterprise root CA uses Active Directory to determine the identity of the requester and to determine whether the requester has the security permissions to request a particular certificate type. You should set up an enterprise root CA if you will issue certificates only to users and computers within your organization. Typically, the enterprise root CA issues certificates only to subordinate CAs.

To install an enterprise root CA, you must have the following:

- *Active Directory*. The enterprise policy used by Certificate Services places information into Active Directory.

- *DNS Server service*. Active Directory requires the DNS service.

- *Administrative privileges on the DNS, Active Directory, and CA servers*. This is especially important because Setup modifies information in places that may require domain administrative privileges. Also, to install an enterprise CA, you must be a member of the Enterprise Admins group.

Important   To publish certificates in Active Directory, the server on which the CA is installed must be a member of the Cert Publishers group.

Enterprise Subordinate CA

An enterprise subordinate CA issues certificates within an organization, but is not the most trusted CA. You can use an enterprise subordinate CA to issue certificates for specific uses, such as secure e-mail, Web-based authentication, or smart card authentication. An enterprise subordinate CA must have a parent CA.

Stand-Alone Root CA

A stand-alone root CA is the top-level CA in a certificate hierarchy. A stand-alone root CA may or may not be a member of a domain and does not require Active Directory. A stand-alone root CA can be disconnected from the network and placed in a secure area.

You should install a stand-alone root CA if you will issue certificates to entities outside your organization. Typically, a root CA only issues certificates to subordinate CAs. To install a stand-alone root CA, you must have administrative privileges on the local server.

Stand-Alone Subordinate CA

A stand-alone subordinate CA operates as a solitary certificate server within a CA trust hierarchy. You should set up a stand-alone subordinate CA if you will issue certificates to entities outside an organization.

To install a stand-alone subordinate, you must have the following:

- A parent CA, such as an external commercial CA, that will process the subordinate CA's certificate requests.
- Administrative privileges on the local server.

Installing Certificate Services

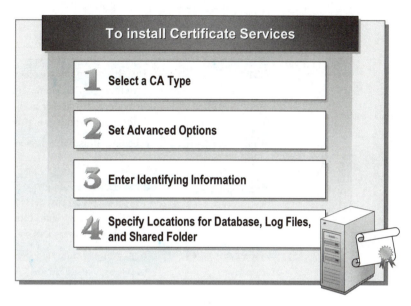

Although Certificate Services is a Windows 2000 service and is included with Windows 2000 server products, it is not installed by default. You can install Certificate Services during or after Windows 2000 setup. To install Certificate Services during Windows 2000 installation, select Certificate Services from the optional components list that displays during setup. You can install Certificate Services after Windows 2000 setup, by using Add/Remove Programs in Control Panel. During Certificate Services setup, you must configure several options and settings.

Important A computer cannot be renamed, or joined to or removed from a domain after Certificate Services is installed. To perform any of these actions, you first need to remove Certificate Services from the computer.

Selecting a CA Type

First, you must select one of the following CA types: enterprise root CA, enterprise subordinate CA, stand-alone root CA, or stand-alone subordinate CA.

Setting Advanced Options

To change default cryptographic settings, click **Advanced options**, and then select from the following settings.

Setting	Description
CSP	Use this setting to specify a third-party cryptographic service provider (CSP). The default is Microsoft Base Cryptographic Provider v 1.0. Refer to the CSP vendor's documentation for information about using the CSP with Certificate Services.
Hash algorithm	The default is SHA-1 (Secure Hash Algorithm 1).
Key length	The default key length is 512 bit when using Microsoft Base Cryptographic Providers. For a root CA, you should use a key length of at least 2048 bits. This setting is not available if you are using existing keys.
Use existing keys	Select this option when you are relocating or restoring a previously installed CA. Also, select **Use the associated certificate** to ensure that the CA has a certificate that is identical to the previous CA.

Entering Identifying Information

Enter the required information to identify your CA, according to the following guidelines:

Field	Description
CA name	The name to identify the CA object that will be created in Active Directory. Active Directory object names are limited to 64 characters by the Lightweight Directory Access Protocol (LDAP) standard. Refer to Windows 2000 Help for information about names with special characters.
Country/Region	The two-character country/region code, as required by the X.500 Naming Scheme standard. For example, the country/region code for the United States is US, and the code for Germany is DE.
Valid for	The field can be set only for a root CA. The validity duration you choose for the CA determines when the CA expires. Typically, a time period of two years is recommended.

Specifying Locations for the Database and Log Files

Certificate Services uses local storage for its database, configuration data, backup data, and log files. You can specify locations for the database and log files during CA setup. By default, the certificates that a CA issues are stored in *systemroot*\System32\CertLog. You can improve performance by storing the files on different physical hard drives.

You can also store configuration data in a shared folder. By default, the shared folder is *systemroot*\CAConfig.

You can also specify a shared folder where the CA stores information about the CA and its root CA certificate. Create the shared folder if you want to allow users to retrieve information about the CA and the root CA certificate from a shared folder instead of using a Web browser to retrieve this information. If you specify a shared folder, Certificate Services shares the folder and assigns to it the name CertConfig.

Installation Components

Certificate Services adds the following components after installation:

- *Certification Authority.* A console for managing CAs on servers on which Certificate Services is installed. You access Certification Authority through the **Administrative Tools** menu. You use Certification Authority to issue certificates, revoke certificates, change policy settings, view a list of certificates issued, and to perform other administrative tasks.

- *Certificates.* A snap-in that you add to Microsoft Management Console (MMC) to manage existing certificates for user accounts, computers, and services.

- *Certificate Services Web enrollment support.* Web pages provided for users and administrators to request certificates. These Web pages are located at http://*server*/certsrv, where *server* is the name of the server running Windows 2000 that hosts the CA.

Creating a Subordinate CA

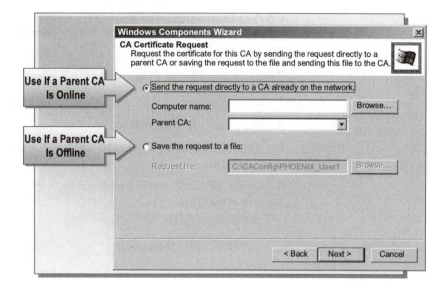

A subordinate CA must be associated with a CA that processes the subordinate CA's certificate requests. Depending on the type of CA, this can be another CA in your organization or an external third-party CA. Typically, a subordinate CA issues certificates for specific uses, such as secure e-mail, Web-based authentication, or smart card authentication. Subordinate CAs can also issue certificates to other, more subordinate CAs. When you install a subordinate CA, you must obtain a certificate from a parent CA.

Obtaining a Certificate for a Subordinate CA

To obtain a certificate if a parent CA is available online:

1. On the **CA Certificate Request** page, click **Send the request directly to a CA already on the network**.

2. In the **Computer Name** box, type or browse to the name of the computer on which the parent CA is installed.

3. In the **Parent CA** list, click the name of the parent CA.

To obtain a certificate if a parent CA is not available online:

On the **CA Certificate Request** page, click **Save the request to a file**. In the **Request file** box, type the path and file name of the file that will store the request. You then must obtain the certificate from the parent CA. As a minimum, the file from the parent CA should contain the subordinate CA's certificate and the full certification path.

Installing a Certificate from a File

When you create a certificate request file during installation of a subordinate CA, you must submit the file to your parent CA. Your parent CA will provide you with a certificate for this file. After you receive your certificate, you must install the certificate.

To install a certificate from a file:

1. Open Certification Authority from the **Administrative Tools** menu.

2. In the console tree, click the name of the CA.

3. On the **Action** menu, point to **All Tasks**, and then click **Install CA Certificate**.

4. Locate the certificate file received from the parent CA, click this file, and then click **Open**.

Backing Up and Restoring Certificate Services

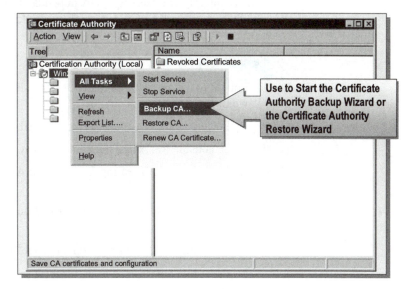

The purpose of performing backup and restore operations is to protect the CA and its operational data from accidental loss due to hardware or storage media failure. The recommended method for backing up a CA is to use Windows 2000 Backup to back up the entire server. When backing up a server, the CA is backed up as part of the system state. It is also possible to back up and restore a CA by using Certification Authority, but this method is intended for use only when you do not want to back up the entire server on which the CA is installed.

Important Upon restoring a CA, the IIS metabase must also be restored if it has been damaged or lost. If a damaged or missing IIS metabase is not restored, IIS will fail to start, and that will result in the failure of Certificate Services to start.

Backing up a CA

How frequently you back up a CA depends on the number of certificates issued. The more certificates a CA issues, the more frequently you should back up the CA.

To back up a CA:

1. Log on to the system as a member of the Backup Operators or Administrators groups.

2. Open Certification Authority from the **Administrative Tools** menu.

3. In the console tree, click the name of the CA.

4. Right-click the name of the CA, point to **All Tasks**, and then click **Backup CA**.

5. Follow the instructions in the Certification Authority Backup wizard. They include:

   - Selecting the data to back up and specifying a backup location.

   - Providing a password to gain access to the private key and CA certificate.

Restoring a CA

To restore a CA from a backup copy:

1. Log on to the system as a member of the Backup Operators or Administrators groups.

2. Open Certification Authority.

3. In the console tree, click the name of the CA.

4. Right-click the name of the CA, point to **All Tasks**, and then click **Restore CA**.

5. Follow the instructions in the Certification Authority Restore wizard. They include:

   - Selecting the data to restore and specifying the restore location.

   - Providing a password to gain access to the private key and CA certificate.

◆ Using Certificates

- **Using the Certificate Request Wizard**
- **Using the Certificate Services Web Pages**
- **Viewing Certificates**

There are two primary ways to explicitly request certificates in Windows 2000: by using the Certificate Request wizard or by using the Certificate Services Web pages. The Certificate Request wizard is only available if you are requesting a certificate from an enterprise CA. You can use the Certificate Services Web pages to request certificates from a stand-alone CA or from an enterprise CA.

Using the Certificate Request Wizard

- **Using Certificate Templates**
- **Requesting a Certificate**

The Certificate Request wizard is available only for requesting a certificate from an enterprise CA. When requesting a certificate, a user can select from different certificate types. The user can select from certificates types for which they have Read or Enroll permissions. After a user submits a certificate request, the request is either immediately denied or granted. If it is granted, the user is prompted to install the certificate.

Using Certificate Templates

As part of its policy settings, an enterprise CA can issue specific certificate types. The certificate types are based on *certificate templates*. Certificate templates are predefined configurations that provide common settings for the certificate request. The following are examples of some commonly used certificate templates.

Certificate Template	Description
Administrator	Allows use of a certificate for code signing, certificate trust list signing, EFS, secure e-mail, and client authentication
Domain Controller	Allows use of a certificate for client authentication and server authentication
Computer	Allows use of a certificate for client authentication and server authentication
Basic EFS	Allows use of a certificate for EFS only
EFS Recovery Agent	Allows use of a certificate for file recovery
User	Allows use of a certificate for EFS, secure e-mail, and client authentication
Web Server	Allows use of a certificate for server authentication.

Requesting a Certificate

To request a certificate by using the Certificate Request wizard:

1. Open an MMC console that contains the Certificates snap-in.

2. In the **Certificates snap-in** dialog box, select **My user account**, **Service account**, or **Computer account** , and then click **Finish**.

3. Close the **Add Stand-alone snap-in** dialog box, and then click **OK**.

4. In the console tree, expand **Certificates Current User**, **Certificates (Local Computer)**, or the node for the selected service.

5. In the console tree, click a logical store name (for example, **Personal)**, right-click, point to **All Tasks**, click **Request New Certificate** to start the Certificate Request wizard, and then click **Next**.

6. On the **Certificate Template** page, select a certificate template.

7. If necessary, click **Advanced options** to specify the following information:

   - The cryptographic service provider (CSP).

   - Whether to enable strong private key protection.

     Enabling strong private key protection ensures that you are prompted for a password every time the private key is used. This is useful if you want to make sure that the private key is not used without your knowledge.

   - The name of the CA that issues the certificate, if more than one CA is available.

8. Type a display name for the certificate.

9. When the Certificate Request wizard is finished, click **Install Certificate**.

Note   You can automate the process of requesting, receiving, and installing a certificate by using automatic certificate settings in public key policies. This enables automatic certificate enrollment for computers associated with a Group Policy, which eliminates the need for an administrator to explicitly enroll each computer-related certificate.

Using the Certificate Services Web Pages

- **Submitting a Certificate Request**
- **Submitting an Advanced Certificate Request**
- **Checking a Pending Request**

Each CA that is installed on a Windows 2000–based server has Web pages that users can access to submit basic and advanced certificate requests. The Web pages are the only way that users can request certificates from a stand-alone CA. Web pages are optional for users who want to request certificates from enterprise CAs.

Submitting a Certificate Request

To submit a certificate request through the Web:

1. In Internet Explorer, connect to http://*server*/certsrv (where *server* is the name of the Windows 2000–based Web server where the CA that you want to access is located).

2. On the **Welcome** page, under **Select a task**, click **Request a certificate**, and then click **Next**.

3. On the **Choose Request Type** page, under **User certificate request**, select the type of certificate that you want to request, and then click **Next**.

4. Type your identifying information for the certificate request if necessary, and then click **Submit**.

   By default, on a stand-alone CA, a certificate is not available to install until the CA has issued the certificate.

   Note An enterprise CA requires the requester to be authenticated and generates a certificate based on the information in Active Directory.

Submitting an Advanced Certificate Request

Many types of certificate requests, such as those for IPSec, client authentication, and server authentication, require the submission of an advanced certificate request. To request an advanced certificate through Web-based enrollment:

1. In Internet Explorer, connect to http://*server*/certsrv (where *server* is the name of the Windows 2000–based Web server where the CA that you want to access is located).

2. On the **Welcome** page, under **Select a task**, click **Request a certificate**, and then click **Next**.

3. On the **Choose Request Type** page, click **Advanced** request, and then click **Next**.

4. On the **Advanced Certificate Requests** page, click **Submit a certificate request to this CA using a form**, and then click **Next**.

5. Type your identifying information for the certificate request if necessary, and then click **Submit**.

Important   When requesting a certificate for a computer, you must select the **Store in local machine store** check box.

By default, on a stand-alone CA, a certificate is not available to install until the CA has issued the certificate.

Checking a Pending Request

To check a pending certificate:

6. In Internet Explorer, connect to http://*server*/certsrv, where *server* is the name of the Windows 2000–based Web server where the CA that you want to access is located.

Important   To check a certificate by using Internet Explorer, you must use the same installation of Internet Explorer that you used to request the certificate.

---

7. On the **Welcome** page, under **Select a task**, click **Check on a pending certificate**, and then click **Next**.

8. Select the certificate request that you want to check, and then click **Next**.

9. Check the pending certificate requests. The status of the pending certificate requests is one of the following:

   - **Still pending.** The administrator of the CA has not yet issued the certificate. Click **Remove** to remove the certificate request.

   - **Issued.** Click **Install this certificate** to install the certificate.

   - **Denied.** Contact the administrator of the CA for further information.

Viewing Certificates

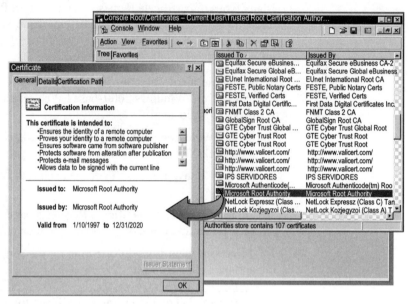

Windows 2000 stores computer certificates locally on the computer that requested the certificate, and stores user certificates in the user's profile. The storage location is called the *certificate store*. Certificates can be displayed by purpose or by logical stores. Displaying certificates by logical stores is the Certificates default.

By opening an MMC console that contains the Certificates snap-in, you can display the certificate store for a user, a computer, or a service, as shown in the following table.

Folder name	Contents
Personal	Certificates associated with private keys to which you have access.
Trusted Root Certification Authorities	Implicitly trusted Certificate Authorities.
Enterprise Trust	Certificate trust lists. A certificate trust list provides a mechanism for trusting self-signed root certificates from other organizations and limiting the purposes for which these certificates are trusted.
Intermediate Certification Authorities	Certificates that a CA issues to a subordinate CA. The subordinate CA could also receive a certificate from either trusted root CAs or other intermediate CAs.
Active Directory User Object	Certificates associated with your user object and published in Active Directory.
REQUEST	Pending or rejected certificate requests.
SPC	Certificates from import files.

You can view information about the fields, extensions, and properties that define an issued certificate by double-clicking any certificate displayed in the certificate store.

◆ Managing Certificates

- Issuing Certificates
- Revoking Certificates
- Publishing a Certificate Revocation List
- Importing and Exporting Certificates

In addition to storing certificates, the Certificates snap-in provides administrative tools to issue, revoke, and publish a CRL, and import and export certificates. Administrators can use the Certificates snap-in to manage certificates for themselves and other users, a computer, or a service.

Issuing Certificates

- **Rejecting a Certificate Request**
- **Issuing a Certificate Request**

When a user submits a certificate request to a stand-alone CA, the request is considered pending until the administrator of the CA approves or rejects it. The user must access the Certificate Services Web pages to check the status of pending certificates.

Note The following procedure applies *only* to a stand-alone CA that is configured to mark every incoming certificate request as pending.

Reviewing Pending Certificate Requests

To review pending certificate requests:

1. Open Certification Authority.

2. In the console tree, click **Pending Requests**.

3. In the details pane, examine the certificate request by noting the values for requester's name, e-mail address, and any other fields that you consider critical information for issuing the certificate, and then perform one of the following:

To	Do this
Reject the certificate request	Right-click the certificate request, point to **All Tasks**, click **Deny**, and then click **Yes**.
Issue the certificate	Right-click the certificate request, point to **All Tasks**, and then click **Issue**.

Revoking Certificates

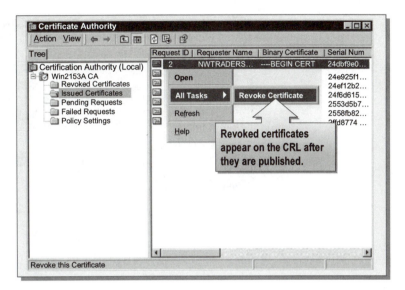

To maintain the integrity of an organization's PKI, the administrator of a CA may need to revoke certificates before they expire. For example, certificates may need to be revoked if the recipient of a certificate leaves an organization, if the private key of a certificate is compromised, or if a security event affects the validity of a certificate.

An administrator revokes certificates in Certification Authority. After a certificate is revoked, it is moved to the Revoked Certificates folder. The revoked certificate will appear on the CRL the next time the CRL is published.

To revoke an issued certificate:

1. Open Certification Authority.

2. In the console tree, click **Issued Certificates**.

3. In the details pane, click the certificate that you want to revoke, right-click the certificate, point to **All Tasks**, and then click **Revoke Certificate**.

4. In the **Reason code** list, select one of the following, and then click **Yes**.

- **Unspecified**

- **Key Compromise**

- **CA Compromise**

- **Affiliation Changed**

- **Superseded**

- **Certificate Hold**

A certificate marked Certificate Hold can be unrevoked, left on Certificate Hold until the certificate expires, or have the reason code changed later.

Publishing a Certificate Revocation List

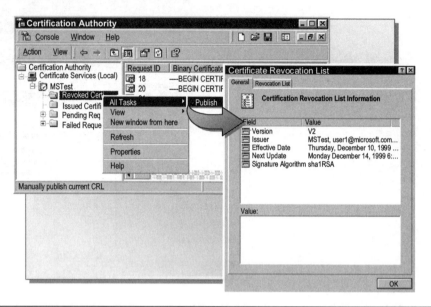

A CA automatically publishes an updated CRL at an interval of time specified by the administrator of the CA. You can also publish a CRL on demand by using the CRL Publishing wizard. If you manually publish a CRL in the middle of a scheduled publish period, the CRL will still be automatically republished at the end of the current publish period.

Important Clients that have a cached copy of the previously published CRL continue to use it until its validity period has expired, even though a new CRL has been published.

To manually publish the CRL:

1. Open Certification Authority.

2. In the console tree, right-click **Revoked Certificates**, point to **All Tasks**, and then click **Publish**.

3. Click **Yes** to overwrite the previously published CRL.

   The CRL is published in *systemroot*\system32\CertSrv\CertEnroll\. If Active Directory is available, the CRL is also published in Active Directory.

To view the newly published CRL, right-click **Revoked Certificates**, and then click **Properties**.

Importing and Exporting Certificates

- **Examining Certificate File Formats**
- **Importing a Certificate**
- **Exporting a Certificate**

The Certificates snap-in provides administrative tools for importing and exporting certificates, including certification paths and private keys. You can import a certificate from another user, computer, or CA. Or, you can export a certificate for use on another computer. You can export certificates to or import certificates from several standard certificate file formats.

Examining Certificate File Formats

You can import and export certificates in the following formats:

- *Personal Information Exchange (PKCS #12)*. Enables the transfer of certificates and their corresponding private keys from one computer to another or from a computer to removable media. If a certificate was issued from a Windows 2000–based CA, the private key for that certificate is only exportable if one of the following is true:

  - The certificate is for EFS or EFS recovery.

  - The certificate was requested through the Advanced Certificate Request Web page with the **Mark keys as exportable** check box selected.

- *Cryptographic Message Syntax Standard (PKCS #7)*. Enables the transfer of a certificate and all of the certificates in its certification path from one computer to another, or from a computer to removable media.

- *DER Encoded Binary X.509*. Supports interoperability for CAs that are not on Windows 2000–based servers. DER certificate files use the .cer extension.

- *Base64 Encoded X.509*. Supports interoperability for CAs that are not on Windows 2000–based servers. Base64 certificate files use the .cer extension.

Importing a Certificate

When you import a certificate, you copy the certificate from a file that uses a standard certificate storage format to a certificate store for your user account or your computer account.

To import a certificate:

1. Open an MMC console that contains the Certificates snap-in.
2. In the console tree, expand **Personal**, and then click **Certificates** below it.
3. Right-click **Certificates**, point to **All Tasks**, and then click **Import**.
4. Provide the following information in the Certificate Import wizard:

   - Specify the name of the file to import.

   - If the file is a PKCS #12 file, type the password used to encrypt the private key. If you want the private key to be exportable, select the appropriate check box, and then select to enable strong private key protection, if necessary.

   - Select the appropriate check box either to automatically place the certificate in a predefined certificate store or to specify another storage location.

Exporting a Certificate

When you export a certificate, you are copying the certificate from its certificate store to a file that uses a standard certificate storage format.

To export a certificate:

1. Open an MMC console that contains the Certificates snap-in.
2. In the console tree, expand **Personal**, and then click **Certificates** below it.
3. Right-click **Certificates**, point to **All Tasks**, and then click **Import**.
4. Provide the following information in the Certificate Export wizard:

   - Select **No, do not export the private key**.

   Note This option appears only if the private key is marked as exportable and you have access to the private key.

   - Select the file format that you want to use to store the exported certificate.

   - If you are exporting the certificate to a PKCS #7 file, you also have the option to include all certificates in the certification path.

   - Specify the name of the file to export.

After the Certificate Export wizard is finished, the certificate will remain in the certificate store. If you want to remove the certificate from the certificate store, you must delete it manually.

Configuring Active Directory for Certificates

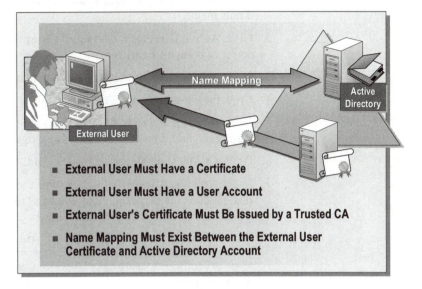

- **External User Must Have a Certificate**
- **External User Must Have a User Account**
- **External User's Certificate Must Be Issued by a Trusted CA**
- **Name Mapping Must Exist Between the External User Certificate and Active Directory Account**

Your organization may need to support authentication of external users—individuals who do not have an account in Active Directory. Authenticating external users requires the following:

- The external user must have a certificate.
- The external user must have a user account.
- The external user's certificate must be issued by a CA that is trusted by, or listed in the certificate trust list for, the site, domain, or organizational unit in which you have created the user account.
- You must create a *name mapping* between the external user certificate and the Active Directory account that you have created for authenticated access.

Any external user whose client program presents a mapped certificate can then access the permitted locations published on the appropriate Web site for your organization. The authentication process is transparent to the external user.

Setting Up a CA Trust

If your organization has its own Windows 2000 enterprise root CA and uses Active Directory, Windows 2000 automatically distributes the root certificates. Distribution of any other root certificates requires Group Policy.

Note For more information about setting up a CA trust, see the white paper *Windows 2000 Certificate Services*, under **Additional Reading** on the Web page on the Student Materials compact disc.

Mapping Accounts to Certificates

1. Open Active Directory Users and Computers from the **Administrative Tools** menu.

2. Click **Active Directory Users and Computers**. On the **View** menu, click to select **Advanced Features**.

3. In the console tree, double-click the domain name.

4. Click the container where the user account is located.

5. In the details pane, right-click the user account to which you want to map a certificate, and then click **Name Mappings**.

6. On the **X.509 Certificates** tab, click **Add**.

7. In the **Add Certificate** dialog box, type the name and path of the .cer file that contains the certificate that you want to map to this user account, click **Open**, and then do one of the following:

To	Do this
Map the certificate to one account (one-to-one mapping)	Confirm that both the **Use Issuer for alternate security identity** and the **Use Subject of alternate security identity** check boxes are selected.
Map any certificate that has the same subject to the user account, regardless of the issuer of the certificate (many-to-one mapping)	Clear the **Use Issuer for alternate security identity** check box and confirm that the **Use Subject of alternate security identity** check box is selected.
Map any certificate that has the same issuer to the user account, regardless of the subject of the certificate (many-to-one mapping)	Clear the **Use Subject of alternate security identity** check box and confirm that the **Use Issuer for alternate security identity** check box is selected.

Troubleshooting Certificate Services

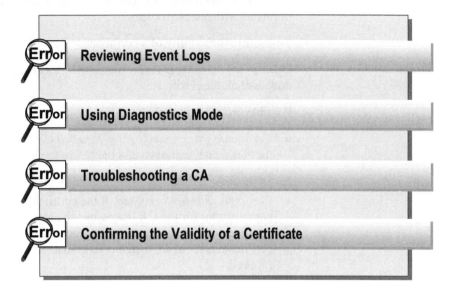

Determining the validity of the certificates issued is an important troubleshooting task for administering Certificate Services. Troubleshooting may also involve verifying the public/private key combination.

Reviewing Event Logs

The first step in troubleshooting Certificate Services is to review the Windows 2000 event logs for any indication of what the problem is.

Using Diagnostics Mode

You can obtain detailed diagnostics information about Certificate Services by running Certificate Services in diagnostics mode.

Note For more information about diagnostics mode, see "Troubleshooting under Certificate Services" in Windows 2000 Help.

Troubleshooting a CA

If you cannot access the Certificate Services Web pages, or you cannot create certificates by using the Web pages, check the authentication methods for your Web server.

Note For more information about troubleshooting a CA, see "Troubleshooting under Certificate Services" in Windows 2000 Help.

Confirming the Validity of a Certificate

The **Certificate** dialog box lists the details of the certificates, including any problems with the certificates.

To confirm the validity of a certificate:

Open an MMC console that contains the Certificates snap-in, and then double-click the certificate.

Possible problems include:

- *Certificate was created by a nontrusted CA.* If a nontrusted CA has issued the certificate, you must add the CA to the list of trusted CAs.

- *Certificate has expired.* If the CA has expired, you must renew it.

- *Certificate has been revoked.* If the certificate has been revoked, contact an administrator for the CA that issued the certificate to determine why the certificate was revoked, and then request a new certificate. If a CA certificate is revoked, then any CAs that stem from that CA are also revoked.

Lab A: Installing and Configuring Certificate Services

Objectives

After completing this lab, you will be able to:

- Install a stand-alone CA.
- Request a certificate from a CA.
- Issue a certificate.

Prerequisite

Before working on this lab, you must have knowledge about the roles that CAs have in Windows 2000.

Lab Setup

To complete this lab, you need the following:

- A computer running Windows 2000 Advanced Server that is configured as a domain controller

- A partner with a similarly configured computer

Important   One computer will hold a stand-alone root CA, and the other computer will hold a stand-alone subordinate CA. The computer of the student with the higher student number will act as the stand-alone root CA; the computer of the student with the lower student number will act as the stand-alone subordinate CA. Determine the role that your computer will have before you start the lab.

Important   The lab does not reflect the real-world environment. It is recommended that you always use complex passwords for any administrator accounts, and never create accounts without a password.

Important   Outside of the classroom environment, it is strongly advised that you use the most recent software updates that are necessary. Because this is a classroom environment, we may use software that does not include the latest updates.

Scenario

Your organization requires business partners to access a database of product specifications at Northwind Traders over the Internet. You must ensure that the information remains confidential. To ensure security of the network traffic between the computers that will communicate across the Internet, you will use certificates to encrypt IP traffic between these computers. Northwind Traders' specifications for a PKI structure call for a stand-alone root CA and stand-alone subordinate CAs. You must install the required CAs. You must also ensure that all computers that communicate with each other across the Internet have a valid certificate so that all IP traffic between these computers can be encrypted.

Estimated time to complete this lab: 45 minutes

Exercise 1
Creating a Stand-Alone Root CA

Scenario

Northwind Traders requires a stand-alone root CA. This CA will be at the top of the certification chain for other CAs that will issue certificates for Northwind Traders.

Goal

In this exercise, you will create a stand-alone root CA.

Tasks	Detailed Steps
✋	Complete the following procedure only on the computer that will hold the root CA.
1. Create a stand-alone root CA that has the name of your computer.	**a.** Log on as administrator@*domain*.nwtraders.msft (where *domain* is the name of your domain) with a password of **password**. **b.** In Control Panel, double-click **Add/Remove Programs**. **c.** In Add/Remove Programs, click **Add/Remove Windows Components**. **d.** In the Windows Components wizard, on the **Windows Components** page, select the **Certificate Services** check box. **e.** In the **Microsoft Certificate Services** message box, click **Yes**, and then click **Next**. **f.** On the **Certification Authority Type** page, verify that **Stand-alone root CA** is selected, and then click **Next**. **g.** On the **CA Identifying Information** page, enter the following information: **CA name**: *server* **CA** (where *server* is the name of your computer) **Organization**: the name of your company or organization **Organizational unit**: the name of your organizational unit or department **City**: the name of your city **State or province**: the name of your state or province **Country/region**: the two-letter code of your country or region **E-mail**: your e-mail address **CA description**: **Certification Authority for Windows 2000 class** **Valid for**: 2 Years **h.** Click **Next**. **i.** On the **Data Storage Location** page, click **Next**. **j.** In the **Microsoft Certificate Services** dialog box, click **OK** to stop Internet Information Services. **k.** In the **Files Needed** dialog box, type **\\London\Setup\Winsrc** and then click **OK**. **l.** When the configuration process is complete, click **Finish**. **m.** Close all open windows.

Exercise 2
Creating a Stand-Alone Subordinate CA

Scenario

Northwind Traders requires a stand-alone subordinate CA. This CA will issue certificates for Northwind Traders that business partners can use to connect securely to your network.

Goal

In this exercise, you will create a stand-alone subordinate CA.

Tasks	Detailed Steps
✋	Complete the following procedures only on the computer that will hold the subordinate CA. Ensure that your partner has completed the preceding exercise before you continue.
1. Add your partner's CA as a trusted root CA.	a. Log on as administrator@*domain*.nwtraders.msft (where *domain* is the name of your domain) with a password of **password**.
	b. Click **Start**, and then click **Run**.
	c. In the **Open** box, type **http://***partner_server***/certsrv** (where *partner_server* is the name of your partner's computer), and then click **OK**.
	d. If the Internet Connection wizard appears, complete the wizard by specifying that you want to connect through a local area network (LAN). Accept the defaults for a LAN connection, and do not set up an Internet mail account.
	e. In Internet Explorer, on the **Welcome** page, click **Retrieve the CA certificate or certificate revocation list**, and then click **Next**.
	f. On the **Retrieve The CA Certificate or Certificate Revocation List** page, click **Install this CA certification path**.
	g. In the **Root Certificate Store** dialog box, click **Yes**.
	h. When the **CA Certificate Installed** page appears, close Internet Explorer.
2. Create a stand-alone subordinate CA that has the name of your computer. Make the subordinate CA a subordinate of your partner's root CA.	a. In Control Panel, double-click **Add/Remove Programs**.
	b. In Add/Remove Programs, click **Add/Remove Windows Components**.
	c. In the Windows Components wizard, on the **Windows Components** page, select the **Certificate Services** check box.
	d. In the **Microsoft Certificate Services** message box, click **Yes**, and then click **Next**.
	e. On the **Certification Authority Type** page, select the **Stand-alone subordinate CA** check box, and then click **Next**.

(continued)

Tasks	Detailed Steps
2. *(continued)*	**f.** On the **CA Identifying Information** page, type the following information: **CA name**: *server* **CA** (where *server* is the name of your computer) **Organization**: the name of your company or organization **Organizational unit**: the name of your organizational unit or department **City**: the name of your city **State or province**: the name of your state or province **Country/region**: the two-letter code of your country or region **E-mail**: your e-mail address **CA description**: **Certification Authority for Windows 2000 class** **Valid for**: determined by parent CA
	g. Click **Next**.
	h. On the **Data Storage Location** page, click **Next**.
	i. On the **CA Certificate Request** page, in the **Computer name** box, type *partner_server* (where *partner_server* is the name of your partner's computer), and then press **TAB**.
	j. Click **Next**.
	k. In the **Microsoft Certificate Services** dialog box, click **OK** to stop Internet Information Services.
	l. In the **Files Needed** dialog box, type **\\London\Setup\Winsrc** and then click **OK**.
	m. Read the text in the **Microsoft Certificate Services** message box, and then click **OK**.
	n. Read the text in the **Microsoft Certificate Services** message box, and then click **OK**.
	o. When the configuration process is complete, click **Finish**.
✋	Complete the following procedure only on the computer that holds the root CA. Ensure that your partner has completed the preceding procedure before you continue.
3. Issue a certificate for a subordinate CA on the root CA.	**a.** Open Certification Authority from the **Administrative Tools** menu.
	b. In the console tree, expand *server* **CA** (where *server* is the name of your computer), and then click **Pending Requests**.
	c. In the details pane, right-click your partner's certificate request, point to **All Tasks**, and then click **Issue**.
	d. In the console tree, click **Issued Certificates**, and then verify that the certificate for your partner's CA has been issued.
	e. Minimize Certification Authority.
✋	Complete the following procedure only on the computer that holds the root CA. Ensure that your partner has completed the preceding procedure before you continue.

(continued)

Tasks	Detailed Steps
4. Install a certificate for the subordinate CA.	a. Open Certification Authority from the **Administrative Tools** menu.
	b. In the console tree, right-click *server* **CA** (where *server* is the name of your computer), point to **All Tasks**, and then click **Install CA Certificate**.
	c. In the **Select file to complete CA installation** dialog box, click **Cancel**.
	d. In the **CA Certificate Request** dialog box, in the **Computer Name** box, verify that the name of your partner's computer appears.
	e. In the **Parent CA** box, click *partner_server* **CA** (where *partner_server* is the name of your partner's computer), and then click **OK**.
	The CA installation completes and the CA starts.
	f. Minimize Certification Authority.

Exercise 3
Requesting a Computer Certificate

Scenario

After all of the CAs in your organization have been configured, you must assign a computer certificate that allows encrypting of all IP traffic to each computer.

Goal

In this exercise, you will request a computer certificate for your computer.

Tasks	Detailed Steps
🖐 Complete the following procedure on both student computers.	
1. Use Internet Explorer to request an IPSec certificate for your computer from the CA on your computer.	a. Click **Start**, and then click **Run**.
	b. In the **Open** box, type **http://**server**/certsrv** (where *server* is the name of your computer), and then click **OK**.
	c. If the Internet Connection wizard appears, complete the wizard by specifying that you want to connect through a LAN. Accept the defaults for a LAN connection, and do not set up an Internet mail account.
	d. In Internet Explorer, on the **Welcome** page, verify that **Request a certificate** is selected, and then click **Next**.
	e. On the **Choose Request Type** page, click **Advanced request**, and then click **Next**.
	f. On the **Advanced Certificate Requests** page, verify that **Submit a certificate request to this CA using a form** is selected, and then click **Next**.
	g. On the **Advanced Certificate Request** page, enter the following information: **Name**: your name **E-mail**: your e-mail address **Company**: the name of your company or organization **Department**: the name of your department **City**: the name of your city **State or province**: the name of your state or province **Country/Region**: the two-letter code of your country or region.
	h. Under **Intended Purpose**, click **IPSec Certificate**.
	i. Under **Key Options**, select the **Use local machine store** check box, and then click **Submit**.
	j. When the **Certificate Pending** page appears, minimize Internet Explorer.

(continued)

Tasks	Detailed Steps
2. Use Certification Authority to issue the certificate that you requested.	a. Restore Certification Authority. b. In the console tree, expand *server* **CA** (where *server* is the name of your computer) if necessary, and then click **Pending Requests**. c. On the **Action** menu, click **Refresh**. d. In the details pane, right-click your certificate request, point to **All Tasks**, and then click **Issue**. e. In the console tree, click **Issued Certificates**, and then verify that the certificate for your computer has been issued. f. Close Certification Authority.
3. Use Internet Explorer to install the certificate that you issued.	a. Restore Internet Explorer. b. In the **Address** box, type **http://***server*/**certsrv** (where *server* is the name of your computer), and then press ENTER. c. On the **Welcome** page, click **Check on a pending certificate**, and then click **Next**. d. On the **Check On A Pending Certificate Request** page, verify that the certificate request that you submitted is listed, and then click **Next**. e. On the **Certificate Issued** page, click **Install this certificate**. f. When the **Certificate Installed** page appears, close Internet Explorer.

(*continued*)

Tasks	Detailed Steps
4. Create an MMC console that contains the Certificates snap-in for your computer, and then confirm that the IPSec certificate has been issued to your computer.	a. Click **Start**, and then click **Run**.
	b. In the **Open** box, type **mmc** and then click **OK**.
	c. Maximize the Console Root window.
	d. In the Console1 – [Console Root] window, on the **Console** menu, click **Add/Remove Snap-in**.
	e. In the **Add/Remove Snap-in** dialog box, click **Add**.
	f. In the **Add Stand-alone Snap-in** dialog box, click **Certificates**, and then click **Add**.
	g. In the **Certificates snap-in** dialog box, click **Computer account**, and then click **Next**.
	h. In the **Select Computer** dialog box, verify that **Local computer** is selected, and then click **Finish**.
	i. Click **Close** to close the **Add Stand-alone Snap-in** dialog box.
	j. Click **OK** to close the **Add/Remove Snap-in** dialog box.
	k. On the **Console** menu, click **Save As**.
	l. Save the console file as **Computer Certificates** in the default location.
	m. In the console tree, expand **Certificates**, expand **Personal**, and then under **Personal**, click **Certificates**.
	n. On the **Action** menu, click **Refresh**.
	o. In the details pane, right-click the certificate that you issued to name (where name is your name), and then click **Open**.
	p. In the **Certificate** dialog box, verify that the certificate is intended to allow secure communication on the Internet and that the certificate is valid, and then click **OK**.
	q. Close Computer Certificates without saving changes.

Exercise 4
Removing Certificate Services

Scenario

The computers that host the CA at Northwind Traders will be removed from the network and replaced with other computers. After explaining to management that you should remove the current certification path from all computers in your company as soon as new CAs have been established, you proceed to remove all existing CAs.

Goal

In this exercise, you will remove Certificate Services from your computer.

Task	Detailed Steps
1. Remove Certificate Services.	a. In Control Panel, double-click **Add/Remove Programs**.
	b. In Add/Remove Programs, click **Add/Remove Windows Components**.
	c. In the Windows Components wizard, on the **Windows Components** page, clear the **Certificate Services** check box, and then click **Next**.
	d. When the configuration process is complete, click **Finish**.
	e. Close all open windows, and then log off.

Review

- **Introduction to Public Key Infrastructure (PKI)**
- **Deploying Certificate Services**
- **Using Certificates**
- **Managing Certificates**
- **Configuring Active Directory for Certificates**
- **Troubleshooting Certificate Services**

1. Which of the following functions can a PKI perform?

   a. Authentication of the originator of a message or a computer.

   b. Confirmation of the physical location of a computer.

   c. Confidentiality of a message.

   d. Confirmation of the security privileges that a user has.

2. What needs to be present before you can install an enterprise subordinate CA?

3. What are the methods for requesting a certificate, and which types of CAs support each of them?

4. You revoke a certificate, but it does not appear in the CRL. What is the problem?

5. You have requested a certificate from a stand-alone CA. What must you do before you can use the certificate?

Microsoft®
Training &
Certification

Module 6: Configuring Network Security by Using IPSec

Contents

Overview

- **Introduction to IPSec**
- **Implementing IPSec**
- **Configuring TCP/IP for Server Security**
- **Troubleshooting Network Protocol Security**

Because the loss of proprietary information can compromise an organization's success, an organization needs to have reliable network security for sensitive information, such as product data, financial reports, and marketing plans. Internet Protocol Security (IPSec) is a framework of open standards for ensuring secure, private communications over Internet Protocol (IP) networks by using cryptographic security services.

You can implement IPSec in a Microsoft® Windows® 2000 network to authenticate computers and encrypt data for transmission between hosts in a network, intranet, or extranet, including workstation-to-server and server-to-server communications.

At the end of this module, you will be able to:

- Describe the use of IPSec in a network.
- Implement IPSec.
- Configure IPSec for server security.
- Troubleshoot network protocol security.

◆ Introduction to IPSec

- **Identifying Security Issues with Networks**
- **Examining the Role of IPSec in a Network**

Without security, both public and private networks are susceptible to unauthorized monitoring and access. Internal attacks might be a result of minimal or nonexistent intranet security, whereas risks from outside the private network stem from connections to the Internet and extranets. IPSec protects private data in a public environment by providing a strong, cryptography-based defense against network attacks.

Note   IPSec is an Internet Engineering Task Force (IETF) proposal and is not yet an IETF standard. For more information about IPSec, see RFC 2411 and RFC 2401 under **Additional Reading** on the Student Materials compact disc.

For a more extensive list of applicable RFCs, see the "Internet Protocol Security" section of the Windows 2000 Server Resource Kit.

Identifying Security Issues with Networks

Common Types of Network Attacks

- Network monitoring
- Data modification
- Passwords
- Address spoofing
- Application-layer
- Man-in-the-middle
- Denial-of-service

Whether over the Internet, an intranet, or to and from branch-office or remote employees, sensitive information is constantly crossing the networks. The challenge for network administrators is to ensure that this data is:

- Safe from modification while in transit.
- Safe from interception, viewing, or copying.
- Safe from being accessed by unauthenticated parties.

You can implement IPSec to secure communications within an intranet and to create secure virtual private network (VPN) solutions across the Internet. IPSec can protect communication between workgroups, local area network (LAN) computers, domain clients and servers, branch offices that are physically remote, extranets, remote clients, and remote administration of computers.

Common Types of Network Attacks

Without security measures and controls in place, your data might be vulnerable to an attack. Some attacks are passive, meaning that an unknown outsider is monitoring your information; others are active, meaning that an assailant is altering information with the intent to corrupt or destroy the data or the network itself. Below is a partial list of the most common network attacks:

- *Network monitoring*. A network monitor is an application or device that can observe and read network packets. If the packets are not encrypted, a network-monitoring tool provides a full view of the data inside the packet. Such applications are useful for diagnostic purposes, but they can be misused to obtain unauthorized access to data. Microsoft Network Monitor is an example of a network-monitoring tool.

- *Data modification*. An attacker can modify a message in transit and send counterfeit data, which can prevent the receiver from receiving the correct information or can allow the attacker to obtain secure information.

- *Passwords*. An attacker can use a stolen password or key, or attempt to decipher the password if it is a simple password.

- *Address spoofing*. An attacker can use special programs to construct IP packets that appear to originate from valid addresses inside the trusted network.

- *Application-layer*. This attack targets application servers by exploiting weaknesses in server operating systems and applications.

- *Man-in-the-middle*. In this attack, someone between the two communicating computers actively monitors, captures, and controls the data transparently (for example, the attacker can reroute a data exchange).

- *Denial-of-service*. The goal of this attack is to prevent normal use of computers or network resources. For example, denial-of-service attacks may occur when e-mail accounts are flooded with more unsolicited messages then the system can handle, which can subsequently shut down the server.

Examining the Role of IPSec in a Network

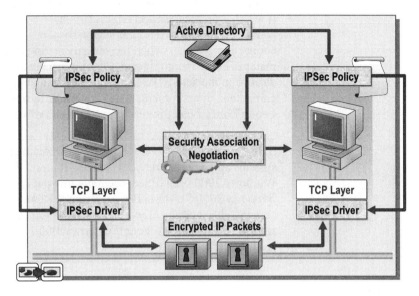

The primary goal of IPSec is to provide protection for IP packets. IPSec is based on an end-to-end security model, meaning that the sender and the receiver are the only hosts that must know about the IPSec protection. Each computer handles security at its own end under the assumption that the medium over which the communication takes place is not secure. Computers that only route data from source to destination are not required to support IPSec.

Enhanced Network Security

IPSec enhances network data security by:

- Mutually authenticating computers prior to data exchange.

- Establishing a security association between the two computers.

- Encrypting exchanged data.

IPSec uses standard IP packet formats when authenticating or encrypting data. Therefore, intermediary network devices, such as routers, do not have to handle IPSec packets differently from standard IP packets.

IPSec Policies

IPSec is implemented by using an IPSec *policy*. Policies are security settings, or *rules*, that define the level of security that you want, in addition to the addresses, protocols, Domain Name System (DNS) names, subnets, or connection types to which the security settings will apply. The IPSec *driver* matches every incoming and outgoing packet against the security settings defined in the active IPSec policy. You can apply IPSec policies to local computers, domain members, domains, or to multiple computers by using a Group Policy object in the Active Directory™ directory service.

Note Several vendors are working on implementing IPSec in other operating systems and network devices, such as routers. For more information about how Windows 2000 uses IPSec, see the white paper *IP Security for Microsoft Windows 2000 Server* under **Additional Reading** on the Student Materials compact disc and the *Step-by-Step Guide to Internet Protocol Security (IPSec)* at http://www.microsoft.com/windows2000/library/technologies/ security/default.asp.

◆ Implementing IPSec

- ■ Enabling IPSec

- ■ Configuring IPSec for Security Between Computers

- ■ Configuring IPSec for Security Between Networks

- ■ Customizing IPSec Policies

- ■ Choosing an Encryption Scheme

- ■ Testing an IPSec Policy Assignment

- ■ Optimizing IPSec Performance

Although stronger security methods based on cryptography have become necessary to fully protect communication, implementing these methods can greatly increase administrative overhead. Windows 2000 provides policy-based administration to implement IPSec services. Policies enable an administrator to configure security settings automatically. A network security administrator can configure IPSec policies to meet the security requirements of a user, group, domain, site, or enterprise. Windows 2000 provides an administrative interface, called IPSec Policy Management, to define IPSec policies for computers at the Active Directory level for any domain members or on the local computer for nondomain members.

Enabling IPSec

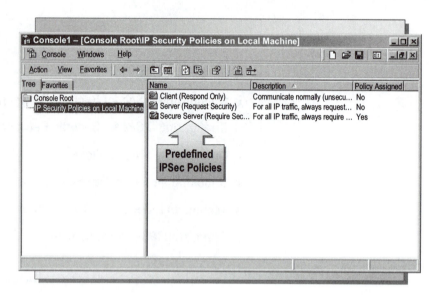

You control IPSec by using a policy configuration that you manage in IP Security Policy Management. You use IP Security Policy Management to manage IPSec policies centrally for Active Directory clients, locally for the computer on which you are running the console, or remotely for a computer or domain.

Note   To configure IPSec policies for computers, you must have the appropriate administrator rights to Group Policy or be a member of the local system's Administrators group.

Managing IPSec Policies

You manage IPSec policies by adding the IP Security Policy Management snap-in to a Microsoft Management Console (MMC) console. After adding the IP Security Policy Management snap-in to a console, select the computer for which you want to manage IPSec policies:

To	Do this
Manage only the computer on which the console is running	Click **Local Computer**.
Manage IPSec policies for any domain members	Click **Manage domain policy for this computer's domain**.
Manage IPSec policies for a domain of which the computer that is running this console is not a member	Click **Manage domain policy for another domain**.
Manage a remote computer	Click **Another computer**.

You can then save the customized console so that it is available to you again at any time.

Using Predefined IPSec Policies

Windows 2000 provides a set of predefined IPSec policies. By default, all predefined policies are designed for computers that are members of a Windows 2000 domain. You can assign predefined policies without further action, or you can modify them , or use them as a template for defining custom policies.

Client (Respond Only)

This policy is for computers that do not require secure communications; for example, intranet clients that only use IPSec when requested by another computer. This policy enables the computer to respond appropriately to requests for secured communications. The policy contains a default response rule, which enables negotiation with computers requesting IPSec.

Server (Request Security)

This policy is for computers that require secure communications most of the time; for example, servers that transmit sensitive data. This policy enables the computer to accept unsecured traffic, but always attempts to secure additional communications by requesting security from the original sender. This policy allows the entire communication to be unsecured if the other computer is not enabled for IPSec.

Secure Server (Require Security)

This policy is for computers that always require secure communications. For example, the secure server policy is useful for servers that transmit highly sensitive data, or for a security gateway that protects the intranet from the outside. This policy rejects unsecured incoming communications, and outgoing traffic is always secured. Unsecured communication will not be allowed, even if a peer is not IPSec enabled.

Activating an IPSec Policy

To activate an IPSec policy on a computer:

1. In IP Security Policy Management, click **IP Security Policies on Local Machine**.

2. In the details pane, right-click the policy that you want to assign, and then click **Assign**.

Note   You can also assign an IPSec policy to a computer by using Group Policy. For more information about Group Policy, see module 7, "Implementing Group Policy," in course 2154, *Implementing and Administering Microsoft Windows 2000 Directory Services.*

Configuring IPSec for Security Between Computers

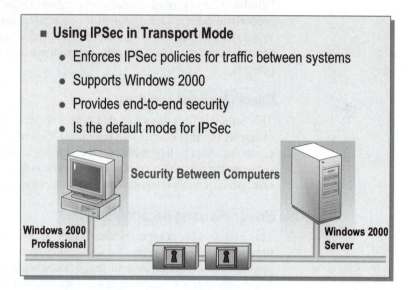

- ■ **Using IPSec in Transport Mode**
  - ● Enforces IPSec policies for traffic between systems
  - ● Supports Windows 2000
  - ● Provides end-to-end security
  - ● Is the default mode for IPSec

Security Between Computers

Windows 2000
Professional

Windows 2000
Server

For secured communications between computers running Windows 2000, configure IPSec for transport mode.

Using IPSec in Transport Mode

The transport mode authenticates and encrypts data flowing between any two computers running Windows 2000. The transport mode provides security for the network and can potentially support a secure connection with more than one other computer. Transport mode is the default IPSec mode.

To specify transport mode:

1. Open IP Security Policy Management.

2. In the details pane, right-click the policy that you want to modify, and then click **Properties**.

3. Click the rule that you want to modify, and then click **Edit**.

4. On the **Tunnel Setting** tab, click **This rule does not specify a tunnel**.

Note   You can also specify transport mode when you create a new rule by using the Security Rule wizard.

Configuring IPSec for Security Between Networks

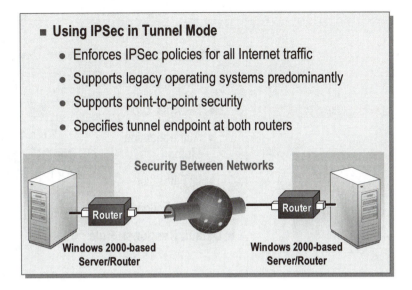

To create secured communications between remote networks, configure IPSec for tunnel mode. The advantage of tunnel mode is that data is secure between the two tunnel ends, regardless of the ultimate destination. When you configure IPSec for tunnel mode, all communications between networks are secure, without requiring you to configure IPSec on each computer. Tunnel mode does not provide security within each network.

Using IPSec in Tunnel Mode

The tunnel mode for IPSec authenticates and encrypts data flowing within an IP tunnel that is created between two routers. Windows 2000 requires Routing and Remote Access to implement tunnel mode for IPSec.

You enable tunnel mode in IPSec Management. When configuring tunnel mode settings, IPSec requires an IP address for each end of the tunnel.

To specify an IPSec tunnel:

1. Open IP Security Policy Management.

2. In the details pane, right-click the policy that you want to modify, and then click **Properties**.

3. Click the rule that you want to modify, and then click **Edit**.

4. On the **Tunnel Setting** tab, click **The tunnel endpoint is specified by this IP Address**, and then specify the IP address of the tunnel endpoint.

Windows 2000 supports multiple tunnel mode connections, but only one tunnel at a time. Each tunnel connection requires a separate rule.

Note You can also specify an IPSec tunnel when you create a new rule by using the Security Rule wizard.

Customizing IPSec Policies

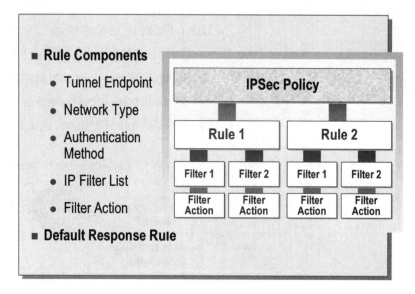

You can create customized IPSec policies to select which computers require encryption and the security methods that are used for encryption. IPSec policies use rules to govern how and when a policy is invoked. A rule provides the ability to initiate and control secure actions based on the source, destination, and type of IP traffic.

Each IPSec policy may contain one or more rules. Any number of the rules may be active simultaneously. Default rules are provided that encompass a variety of client and server-based communications. You can create new rules or modify the default rules to meet your network requirements.

Rule Components

A rule consists of the following components:

- **Tunnel Endpoint**. Defines the tunneling computer closest to the IP traffic destination, as specified by the associated IP filter list. There must be two rules to define an IPSec tunnel, one for each direction.

- **Network Type**. Applies to connections configured in Network and Dial-up Connections. Select one of the following options:

  - **All network connections**

  - **Local area network (LAN)**

  - **Remote access**

- **Authentication Method**. Defines the method for verifying the identity of a user. Windows 2000 supports three authentication methods:

  - **Windows 2000 default (Kerberos V5 protocol)**. Uses the Kerberos V5 security protocol for authentication. You can use this method for any clients that are running the Kerberos V5 protocol (whether or not they are Windows-based clients) that are clients in the same forest or from a trusted Kerberos realm.

  - **Use a certificate from this Certificate Authority (CA)**. Requires that a trusted CA has been configured. Windows 2000 supports X.509 Version 3 certificates, including CA certificates generated by commercial CAs.

  - **Use this string to protect the key exchange (preshared key)**. Specifies a secret, shared key that two users agree upon and manually configure prior to use.

- **IP Filter List**. Defines which traffic will be secured with this rule. You can use the default filters or create policy-specific filters for certain types of IP traffic or specific subnets. Default filters include:

  - **All ICMP traffic**

  - **All IP traffic**

- **Filter Action**. Lists the security actions that will occur when traffic matches an IP filter. The action specifies whether to permit the traffic, block the traffic, or negotiate the security for the given connection. You can specify one or more negotiated filter actions. The filter actions appear as a list, with the first method listed taking precedence. If a filter action cannot be negotiated, the next filter action will be attempted.

To edit the rule properties, click the rule in the **Properties** dialog box for an IPSec policy, and then click **Edit**. To edit the default IP filter list and actions, right-click **IP Security Policies**, and then click **Manage IP filter lists and filter actions**.

Default Response Rule

A computer uses the default response rule to respond to requests for secure communication. If a rule is not defined for secure communication requests, the default response rule is applied and security is negotiated. This rule is designated for all defined policies, but may not be active.

When creating a new policy, the wizard presents the choice of using the default response rule. If the default response rule is activated, the wizard allows the administrator to set the authentication method for the rule.

You can restore the original, predefined configurations, if you modify or delete them beyond regression. Any current modifications that you have made to any of the default policies and rules will be lost.

To restore default policies:

1. Open IP Security Policy Management.

2. In the console tree, click **IP Security Policies Local Machine**, right-click, point to **All Tasks**, click **Restore Default Policies**, and then click **Yes**.

Choosing an IPSec Encryption Scheme

To Choose an Authentication and Encryption Scheme:

- **Authentication Encryption**
  - SHA
  - MD5
- **Packet Encryption**
  - 56-bit DES
  - 40-bit DES
  - 3DES

The method chosen for authentication and packet encryption may vary according to the sensitivity of the information and any government standards. IPSec offers a variety of authentication and data encryption algorithms.

To view encryption security methods, open the properties of the selected policy, click the **General** tab, click **Advanced**, and then click **Methods**.

Authentication Encryption

The following table summarizes the authentication encryption choices: Secure Hash Algorithm (SHA) and Message Digest 5 (MD5).

Method	Description
SHA	Federal Information Processing Standards (FIPS) accepted for U.S. government contracts. This high-security method uses a 160-bit key.
MD5	Most widely used method for commercial applications. This high-security method uses a single 128-bit key and has a lower performance overhead.

Packet Encryption

The following table summarizes the data encryption choices.

Method	Description
56-bit DES	Method used for most exported applications and low-security business traffic, such as e-mail. This low-security method uses a single 56-bit key.
40-bit DES	Method supported for application exports to France. This low-security method uses a single 40-bit key. The 40-bit Data Encryption Standard (DES) is not RFC compliant.
3DES	Most secure method. Uses three 56-bit keys. 3DES processes each block three times, using a unique key each time. This high-security method increases processor utilization by a factor of about 2.5 compared with other DES encryption.

Testing an IPSec Policy Assignment

- **Using the Ping Command to Verify That a Valid Network Connection**

- **Using IPSec Monitor to Verify That a Policy Has Been Assigned**

Before secured data can be exchanged, a *security association* (SA) between the two computers must be established. In an SA, both computers negotiate how to exchange and protect information. The initiating computer sends an offer list of potential security levels to the responding peers. The responder either sends a reply accepting the offer, or discards the offer and sends back a message indicating that no offer was chosen. If the active policies allow unsecured communications with non-IPSec-capable computers, a *soft* SA is established. If active policies are compatible, a secured, or *hard*, SA is established.

To make sure that an SA can be established and IPSec-secured communication can be successful, use the **ping** command to verify a valid network connection and use IPSec Monitor to verify a valid policy assignment.

Using the Ping Command to Verify That a Valid Network Connection

When testing an IPSec policy assignment, use the ping command to verify a valid network connection. Using ping to verify a valid network connection allows you to separate network problems from IPSec issues.

To verify a valid network connection:

Open a command prompt, type **ping** *IP address* where *IP address* is the IP address of the computer with which you are trying to communicate, and then press ENTER.

If there is a valid network connection, you should receive four replies to the ping. This verifies that you can communicate with the destination IP address. IPSec does not block the ping command if you are using the default policies unmodified.

If there are problems with establishing a secure channel, you will see the response "Negotiating IP Security." You can expect this response while the secure channel is established, but subsequent output from the ping command should include replies from the remote host.

Important   If you create custom policies and do not exempt the Internet Control Message Protocol (ICMP) used by the ping command, using the ping command may present erroneous results.

Using IPSec Monitor to Verify That a Policy Has Been Assigned

IPSec Monitor displays the active security associations on local or remote computers. For example, you can use IPSec Monitor to determine whether there is a pattern of authentication or security association failures, possibly indicating incompatible security policy settings.

To start IPSec Monitor:

- Click **Start**, click **Run**, and then type **ipsecmon** *ComputerName* where *ComputerName* is the computer that you want to monitor.

When IPSec Monitor opens, you see a message in the lower-right corner indicating whether IPSec is enabled on the computer. For IPSec to be enabled, you must assign a policy. However, no policies are listed in the IPSec Monitor Security Association list unless an SA with another computer is currently active.

Optimizing IPSec Performance

> **To Ensure High Availability of IPSec Service, Consider:**
>
> - **Level of Security Required**
> - **Security Requirements of the Computer**
> - **Number of IPSec Policy Filter Entries**

Prior to implementing IPSec in an enterprise network, you should consider the following performance issues.

Level of Security Required

The sensitivity of most data on many enterprise networks may not require the level of security that IPSec provides. When you enable IPSec, processor utilization, IP packet traffic, and IP packet size all increase. You should consider whether a particular host sufficiently benefits from enhanced security before implementing IPSec on that platform.

Note Some vendors offer network adapters that perform the IPSec encryption tasks on the network adapter. Performing the IPSec encryption by using dedicated hardware can significantly increase performance.

Security Requirements of the Computer

Certain data may be sensitive, yet you will only access it with a subset of the computers on the network. Identify the server and client computers requiring access to the sensitive data and enable IPSec on only those computers.

Number of IPSec Policy Filter Entries

IPSec can block unauthorized access through the use of IP filters and negotiation policies. Use wildcard filters to reduce the number of IP filter entries. Negotiation policies should be restrictive enough to ensure that authorized computers have access but unauthorized computers do not. You can design your IPSec configuration with IP filters, negotiation policies, or both.

Configuring TCP/IP for Server Security

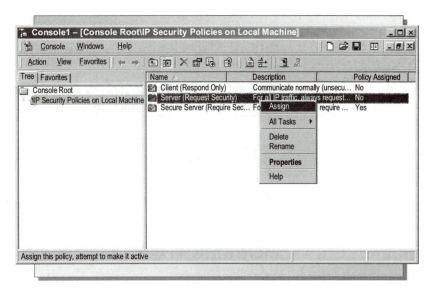

IPSec at the IP transport level provides protection for server applications and services, without modifying those server applications and services that use IP for transport of data. You can enable IPSec to provide secure end-to-end communication of IP-based traffic on a private network or on the Internet. You enable IP Security for Transmission Control Protocol/Internet Protocol (TCP/IP) by assigning the Secure Server policy. By default, the Secure Server policy is disabled.

To enable IP security for TCP/IP:

1. Open IP Security Policy Management.

2. In the console tree, click **IP Security Policies on Local Machine**.

3. In the details pane, right-click **Secure Server (Require Security)**, and then click **Assign**.

Troubleshooting Network Protocol Security

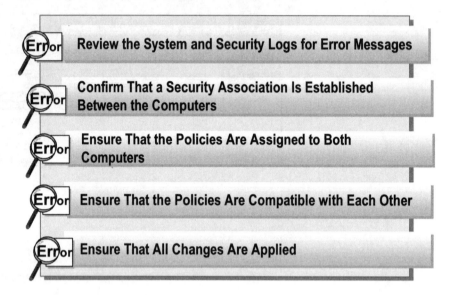

The most common symptom of problems with network protocol security is that two or more computers that are configured to use IPSec cannot communicate with each other. When troubleshooting network protocol security, begin by isolating the problem.

Isolating the Problem

When troubleshooting IPSec problems, it is important to isolate the problem. A Communication problem may be due to general network problem or a problem with security settings. Stop the IPSec policy agent on both computers, and then verify communications between computers. If there is a communications problem even with the policy agent stopped, then general network issues are the cause.

To stop the policy agent:

1. Open Services from the **Administrative Tools** menu.

2. In the console tree, right-click **IPSec Policy Agent**, and then click **Stop**.

After you confirm that a problem is related to network security, be sure to restart the IPSec policy agent to continue troubleshooting.

Verifying the IPSec Policy

After you have confirmed that you can communicate with the remote computer, use the following methods to find the problem:

- Review the system logs and security logs for error messages.

- Use IPSec Monitor to confirm that a security association is established between the computers to ensure that the IPSec policy is in effect.

- Use IP Security Policy Management to ensure that the policies have been assigned to both computers.

- Use IP Security Policy Management to review the policies on both computers and ensure that the policies are compatible with each other.

- Restart the IPSec Security Monitor to ensure that all changes that you have made are applied.

Note For more information about troubleshooting IPSec, see "Troubleshooting IP Security" in Windows 2000 Help.

Lab A: Configuring TCP/IP for Secure Connections by Using IPSec

Objectives

After completing this lab, you will be able to:

- Configure an IPSec policy.
- Assign an IPSec policy.

Prerequisites

Before working on this lab, you must have:

- Knowledge of how IPSec works.
- Knowledge of the role of IPSec policies in securing network traffic.

Lab Setup

To complete this lab, you need the following:

- A computer running Windows 2000 Advanced Server and configured as a domain controller.
- A partner with a similarly configured computer.
- Certificates that are assigned to your computer and your partner's computer. Both certificates must be from CAs in a certification authority path that both student computers trust.
- The IP address of the instructor's computer.

Important   The lab does not reflect the real-world environment. It is recommended that you always use complex passwords for any administrator accounts, and never create accounts without a password.

Important   Outside of the classroom environment, it is strongly advised that you use the most recent software updates that are necessary. Because this is a classroom environment, we may use software that does not include the latest updates.

Scenario

Your organization is working on a project that includes business partners. Work on the project requires extreme confidentiality. Your business partners will access data on some of your servers by using the Internet. You must ensure that all network traffic between the computers in your organization and your business partners' computers is encrypted. Your organization has an existing Public Key Infrastructure (PKI) that includes CAs. You have also issued certificates to all of the computers in your organization that your business partners will access and to the computers that your business partners will use to access your servers.

Estimated time to complete this lab: 45 minutes

Exercise 1
Creating and Assigning an IPSec Policy

Scenario

As part of a joint development project with a business partner, you must ensure that all network traffic between servers on your network and your partners' computers is encrypted. To ensure this, you must use IPSec and computer certificates that you have issued to all computers.

Goal

In this exercise, you will work with a partner to configure and test an IPSec policy for two computers by using certificates.

Tasks	Detailed Steps
1. Use the Ping utility to test communications with your partner.	a. Log on as administrator@*domain*.nwtraders.msft (where *domain* is the name of your domain) with a password of **password**. b. At a command prompt, type **ping 192.168**.*z.y* (where *z* is your assigned classroom number and *y* is your partner's student number), and then press ENTER. *You should receive four replies from your partner's computer.* c. Minimize the command prompt window.
2. Add the IP Security Policy Management snap-in to an MMC console. Configure IP Security: **Tunnel Endpoint**: no tunnel **Network Type**: all connections **Authentication Method**: certificate from the same certification authority that your partner selects **IP Filter List**: All IP Traffic **Filter Action**: Require Security	a. Click **Start**, and then click **Run**. b. In the **Open** box, type **mmc** and then click **OK**. c. Maximize the Console Root window. d. In the Console1 – [Console Root] window, on the **Console** menu, click **Add/Remove Snap-in**. e. In the **Add/Remove Snap-in** dialog box, click **Add**. f. In the **Add Standalone Snap-in** dialog box, click **IP Security Policy Management**, and then click **Add**. g. In the **Select Computer** dialog box, verify that Local computer is selected, and then click **Finish**. h. In the **Add Standalone Snap-in** dialog box, click **Services**, and then click **Add**. i. In the **Services** dialog box, verify that **Local computer** is selected, and then click **Finish**. j. Click **Close** to close the **Add Standalone Snap-in** dialog box, and then click **OK** to close the **Add/Remove Snap-in** dialog box. k. In the console tree, click **IP Security Policies on Local Machine**. l. In the details pane, right-click **Secure Server (Require Security)**, and then click **Properties**. m. In the **Secure Server (Require Security) Properties** dialog box, click **Add**.

Tasks	Detailed Steps
2. *(continued)*	**n.** Complete the Security Rule wizard by using the following information Accept the defaults where no information is provided (accept the defaults where no information is provided): **Tunnel Endpoint** page: Verify that **This rule does not specify a tunnel** is selected. **Network Type** page: Verify that **All network connections** is selected. **Authentication Method** page: Click **Use a certificate from this Certificate Authority (CA)**, click **Browse**, and then click *server* **CA** (where *server* is the name of a computer that holds a trusted root CA, which normally is your computer or your partner's computer). Ask your instructor if you are unsure about which CA to select. **IP Filter List** page: Click **All IP Traffic**. **Filter Action** page: Click **Require Security**.
	o. Click **Finish** to close the wizard. 💻 *Four rules appear in the **IP Security Rule** box.*
	p. In the **Secure Server (Require Security) Properties** dialog box, clear the check boxes for all of the rules except the one that displays **Certificate** in the **Authentication** column.
	q. Click **Close** to close the **Secure Server (Require Security) Properties** dialog box.

ℹ	**Note:** You have just created a new security rule for the Secure Server policy. The rule uses the default settings, with the exception of using a certificate.

Tasks	Detailed Steps
2. *(continued)*	**r.** In the details pane, right-click **Secure Server (Require Security)**, and then click **Assign**.

✋	Wait until your partner has completed the previous procedures before starting the following procedure.

Tasks	Detailed Steps
3. Test IPSec by using the **ping** command and IP Security Monitor.	**a.** In the console tree, click **Services (Local)**, and in the details pane, right-click **IPSEC Policy Agent**, and then click **Restart**.
	b. Minimize the Console1 window.
	c. Restore the command prompt window, type **ping 192.168**.*x*.*y* (where *x* is your assigned classroom number and *y* is your partner's student number), and then press ENTER. 💻 *One or both partners will see "Negotiating IP Security" messages. If you receive "Negotiating IP Security" messages, repeat the **ping** command until you receive replies from your partner's computer.*
	d. At the command prompt, **ping** the IP address of the instructor computer several times. 💻 *There is no reply from the instructor computer because that computer is not configured for IPSec.*
	e. At the command prompt, type **ipsecmon** and then press ENTER. 💻 *IP Security Monitor starts, showing the IPSec activity.*
	f. In IP Security Monitor, click **Options**.

Tasks	Detailed Steps
3. *(continued)*	**g.** In the **IP Security Monitor Options** dialog box, in the **Refresh Seconds** box, type **1** and then click **OK**.
	h. Arrange the windows on your screen so that you can see the **IPSec Statistics** box in IP Security Monitor and the command prompt window.
	i. **Ping** your partner's computer a few more times, while viewing the results in the **IPSEC Statistics** box in IP Security Monitor.
	*Notice that the **IPSEC Statistics** box displays an active association and indicates that the number of confidential and authenticated bytes sent and received is increasing while you are using the **ping** command.*
	j. Close IP Security Monitor, close the command prompt window, and then restore the Console1 window.
4. Remove the Security Association.	**a.** In the console tree, click **IP Security Policies on Local Machine**, and in the details pane, right-click **Secure Server (Require Security)**, and then click **Un-assign**.
	*The **Policy Assigned** status will change from **Yes** to **No**, indicating that there are no active IP Security policies.*
	b. In the console tree, click **Services (Local)**, and in the details pane, right-click **IPSEC Policy Agent**, and then click **Restart**.
	c. Close the Console1 window without saving the changes, and then log off.

Review

■ **Introduction to IPSec**

■ **Implementing IPSec**

■ **Configuring TCP/IP for Server Security**

■ **Troubleshooting Network Protocol Security**

1. How can IPSec prevent network security breaches that are caused by network monitoring and address spoofing?

2. How do the predefined policies Server (Require Security) and Server (Request Security) differ from each other?

3. When do you use transport mode, and when do you use tunnel mode?

4. What are the authentication methods that you can use for IPSec?

5. When troubleshooting IPSec, how do you determine whether a problem is caused by security settings or by general network problems?

Microsoft®
Training &
Certification

Module 7: Configuring Remote Access

Contents

Overview

- **Examining Remote Access in Windows 2000**

- **Configuring Inbound Connections**

- **Configuring Outbound Connections**

- **Configuring Multilink Connections**

- **Configuring Authentication Protocols**

- **Configuring Encryption Protocols**

- **Configuring Routing and Remote Access for DHCP Integration**

Remote access allows users to connect to your network from a remote location. The primary tasks for enabling remote access are configuring Routing and Remote Access, creating appropriate remote access connections on remote access clients, and configuring users' access rights to the remote access server.

After you install and configure Routing and Remote Access, there are several ways to enhance remote access to your Microsoft® Windows® 2000 network. You can configure authentication and encryption protocols to increase the security of your remote access connections, and use Dynamic Host Configuration Protocol (DHCP) to provide Internet Protocol (IP) addresses to dial-up clients.

At the end of this module, you will be able to:

- Describe the remote access process and protocols.

- Configure inbound connections on a remote access server.

- Configure outbound connections on a remote access client.

- Configure Multilink connections.

- Configure authentication protocols for remote access sessions.

- Configure encryption protocols for remote access sessions.

- Configure Routing and Remote Access for DHCP integration.

◆ Examining Remote Access in Windows 2000

- Establishing a Remote Access Connection
- Data Transport Protocols
- Virtual Private Network Protocols

Windows 2000 allows remote clients to connect to remote access servers through a variety of hardware, including analog modems, Integrated Services Digital Network (ISDN) adapters, and digital subscriber line (DSL) modems. The remote access server runs Routing and Remote Access, which supports various data transport protocols and virtual private network (VPN) protocols to enable remote connections. Familiarity with the benefits and limitations of these protocols will help you to take advantage of their capabilities and decide which protocols are appropriate for your network.

Establishing a Remote Access Connection

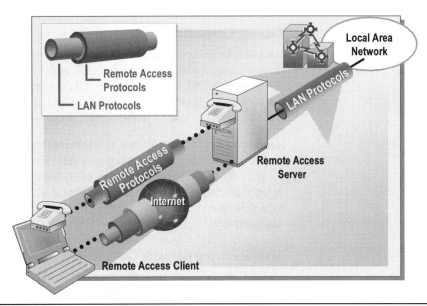

Windows 2000 Server remote access, part of the Routing and Remote Access service, enables remote or mobile workers to connect to corporate networks.

The Remote Access Process

Users run remote access software and initiate a connection to the remote access server. This connection uses a remote access protocol, such as the Point-to-Point Protocol (PPP).

The remote access server, which is a computer running Windows 2000 Server and the Routing and Remote Access service, authenticates users and remote access sessions until terminated by the user or network administrator. The remote access server acts as a gateway by sending data between the client and the local area network (LAN).

Using this connection, the client sends data to and receives data from the remote access server. The data is encoded by a protocol such as Transmission Control Protocol/Internet Protocol (TCP/IP) and is then encapsulated in a remote access protocol.

All services typically available to a LAN-connected user (including file and print sharing, Web server access, and messaging) are enabled for a remote user by means of the remote access connection.

Types of Remote Access Connectivity

Windows 2000 provides two different types of remote access connectivity.

Dial-up Connections

To connect to the network with dial-up remote access, a remote access client uses a communications network, such as the Public Switched Telephone Network (PSTN), to create a physical connection to a port on a remote access server on the private network. This is typically done by using a modem or ISDN adapter to dial in to the remote access server.

Dial-up remote access allows an organization to keep users connected to their network when they are working remotely. However, if your organization has a large number of users traveling to many locations, the expense of long-distance telephone charges will become significant. An alternative to increasing the size of a dial-up remote access network is to consider a VPN solution for remote connectivity.

Virtual Private Network Connections

A VPN provides secure remote access through the Internet, rather than through direct dial-up connections. A VPN client uses an IP internetwork to create an encrypted, virtual, point-to-point connection with a VPN gateway on the private network. Typically, the user connects to the Internet through an Internet service provider (ISP), and then creates a VPN connection to the VPN gateway. By using the Internet in this way, companies can reduce their long-distance telephone expenses and rely on existing infrastructure instead of managing their own infrastructures.

Companies that want to reduce the cost of remote access and increase their network flexibility can take advantage of VPN remote access. Traveling employees can dial the local ISP and then make a VPN connection back to the corporate network. This eliminates the long-distance charges or toll calls associated with a dial-up connection.

Data Transport Protocols

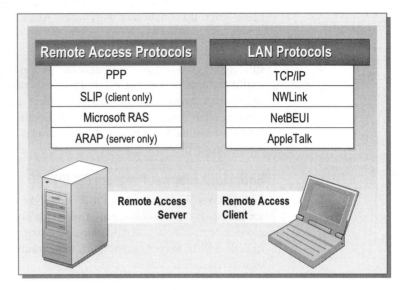

Routing and Remote Access in Windows 2000 uses both remote access protocols and LAN protocols to enable clients to connect to remote access servers. Remote access protocols control transmission of data over wide area network (WAN) links, whereas LAN protocols control transmission of data within the local area network.

Windows 2000 uses a remote access protocol to establish a connection between the remote access devices (usually modems). Windows 2000 then uses LAN protocols to establish communication between the two computers. When a remote access client communicates with a server, Routing and Remote Access encapsulates the data in a LAN protocol packet for transport in the LAN. This packet is then encapsulated in a remote access protocol packet for transport to the server.

When you install and configure Routing and Remote Access, any protocols already installed on the computer are automatically enabled for remote access on inbound and outbound connections. For each LAN protocol, you must also specify whether you want to provide access to the entire network or only the remote access server. By default, access to the entire network is configured. If you provide access to the entire network by using TCP/IP, you must also configure how the server provides IP addresses.

Remote Access Protocols

Windows 2000 supports several remote access protocols to provide clients using a dial-up connection with access to a variety of remote access servers.

PPP

PPP enables remote access clients and servers to operate together in a multivendor network. For example, clients running Windows 2000 can connect to remote networks through any server that uses PPP. Similarly, computers running other remote access software can also use PPP to dial in to a computer running Routing and Remote Access. This is the most commonly used remote access protocol.

Serial Line Internet Protocol (SLIP)

SLIP allows Windows 2000 Professional–based computers to connect to a SLIP server. SLIP is most commonly used with Telnet, and is not suitable for most modern remote access applications. Routing and Remote Access does not include a SLIP server component, so a computer running Windows 2000 cannot be used as a SLIP server.

Microsoft RAS

For client computers running Microsoft Windows NT® version 3.1, Microsoft Windows for Workgroups, Microsoft MS-DOS®, or Microsoft LAN Manager to connect to a remote access server running Windows 2000, the client must use the network basic input/output system (NetBIOS) Enhanced User Interface (NetBEUI) protocol. The remote access server uses the Microsoft RAS protocol to act as a gateway for the remote access client, providing access to servers that use the NetBEUI, TCP/IP, or NWLink IPX/SPX/NetBIOS Compatible Transport Protocol (NWLink) protocol. Client computers running Windows 2000 use the Microsoft RAS protocol to connect to remote access servers running Windows NT 3.1, Windows for Workgroups, MS-DOS, or LAN Manager.

AppleTalk Remote Access Protocol (ARAP)

Apple Macintosh clients can connect to a remote access server running Windows 2000 by using the ARAP protocol. Routing and Remote Access includes an ARAP server component but not a client component, so that client computers running Windows 2000 cannot connect to remote access servers that only support ARAP.

LAN Protocols

Routing and Remote Access supports the following LAN protocols:

- TCP/IP
- NWLink
- NetBEUI
- AppleTalk

Support for these protocols enables you to integrate Routing and Remote Access into existing Microsoft-based, UNIX, or Novell NetWare networks by using remote access protocols. For example, a remote access client can connect to a remote access server by using NetBEUI, and can use that server as a gateway to communicate with a UNIX server running TCP/IP or a NetWare server running Internetwork Packet Exchange/Sequenced Packet Exchange (IPX/SPX).

Virtual Private Network Protocols

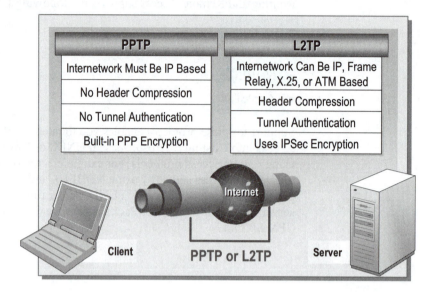

A VPN connection over the Internet is encrypted and secure. The remote access server enforces authentication and encryption protocols. Sensitive data is hidden from Internet users, but made securely accessible to appropriate users through a VPN.

VPN Operation

VPN protocols encapsulate data packets inside PPP data packets. The remote access server performs all security checks and validations, and enables data encryption, making it safer to send data over nonsecure networks such as the Internet. Typically, users will connect to the VPN by first connecting to an ISP and then connecting to the VPN ports through that Internet connection.

Note A VPN does not require a dial-up connection. It only requires IP connectivity between the client and the server. If the client is directly attached to a LAN that uses IP, and it can reach a server through the LAN, you can establish a tunnel across the LAN.

VPNs use either the Point-to-Point Tunneling Protocol (PPTP) or the Layer Two Tunneling Protocol (L2TP) to establish connections. Windows 2000 automatically enables these protocols when you create VPN ports during the installation of Routing and Remote Access.

PPTP and L2TP

Both PPTP and L2TP use PPP to provide an initial envelope for the data and to append additional headers for transport through an internetwork. Some of the key differences between PPTP and L2TP include:

- *Connectivity*. L2TP performs over a wide range of WAN connection media such as IP or frame relay, requiring only that the tunnel media provide packet-oriented, point-to-point connectivity. PPTP requires an IP-based internetwork.

- *Header Compression*. L2TP supports header compression, but PPTP does not. When header compression is enabled, L2TP operates with headers of four bytes, but PPTP operates with six-byte headers.

- *Authentication*. L2TP supports tunnel authentication, but PPTP does not. IPSec provides computer-level authentication, in addition to data encryption, for VPN connections that use the L2TP protocol. IPSec negotiates between your computer and its remote access server before an L2TP connection is established, which secures both passwords and data.

- *Encryption*. PPTP uses PPP encryption. L2TP provides a secure tunnel by cooperating with other encryption technologies, such as Internet Protocol Security (IPSec).

◆ Configuring Inbound Connections

- Configuring Inbound Dial-up Connections

- Configuring Virtual Private Network Ports

- Configuring Modem and Cable Ports

- Configuring User Dial-in Settings

You use the Routing and Remote Access Server Setup wizard to configure common types of remote access servers, such as VPN servers.

When you configure an inbound connection on a remote access server, you enable a port through which a client can connect to your server. You can enable ports for VPN connections, modem connections, and direct cable connections.

If the computer is running Windows 2000 Professional, or is a server that is not a member of a domain, you configure inbound connections by using the Network Connection wizard.

When the computer is a server and a member of a domain, you must use Routing and Remote Access to configure inbound connections. Experience using Routing and Remote Access can help you set up VPNs and modem pools on a remote access server.

Configuring Inbound Dial-up Connections

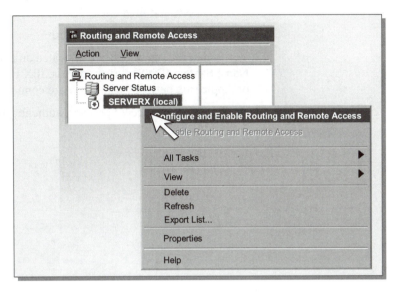

To configure inbound connections on a computer that is a member of a domain, you must use Routing and Remote Access.

To configure remote access on the server:

1. If necessary, verify the compatibility of your hardware by using the Hardware Compatibility List (HCL), and then install the hardware.

2. Install and configure all of the protocols that dial-up users will use, such as TCP/IP, NWLink, NetBEUI, and AppleTalk.

3. Open Routing and Remote Access from the **Administrative Tools** menu.

4. In the console tree, right-click the server name, and then click **Configure and Enable Routing and Remote Access**.

5. In the Routing and Remote Access Server Setup wizard, click **Next**.

6. On the **Common Configuration** page, select **Remote access server**, and then click Next.

7. On the **Remote Client Protocols** page, verify that you have all of the transport protocols that you want to use with remote access, and then click **Next**.

8. On the **Network Selection** page, select the network connection to which the remote access clients will be assigned, and then click **Next**.

9. On the **IP Address Assignment** page, select **Automatically** or **From a specified range of addresses** for assigning IP addresses to the dial-in clients.

10. On the **Managing Multiple Remote Access Servers** page, select whether you want to configure RADIUS (Remote Authentication Dial-In User Service) now, and then click **Next**.

11. Click **Finish** to complete the wizard.

12. Verify that dial-up clients are allocated an appropriate IP address, Domain Name System (DNS) server address, IPX network address, NetBIOS name, or AppleTalk network when they are connected.

13. Configure remote access policies, authentication, and encryption settings.

Configuring Virtual Private Network Ports

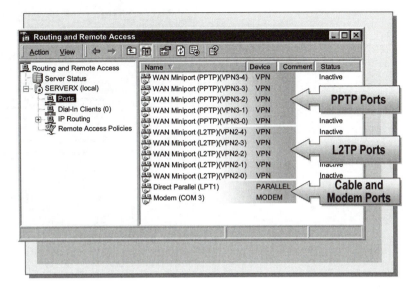

When you start Routing and Remote Access for the first time, Windows 2000 automatically creates five PPTP and five L2TP ports. The number of virtual ports that are available to any remote access server is not limited to availability of hardware. You can increase or decrease the number of available VPN ports to a number that is appropriate for the bandwidth that is available to the remote access server.

Note   If you select the **Virtual private network (VPN)** option in the Routing and Remote Access Setup wizard, Windows 2000 automatically creates 128 PPTP and 128 L2TP ports.

To configure VPN ports on the server:

1. In the console tree of Routing and Remote Access, open the **Properties** dialog box for **Ports**.

2. In the **Ports Properties** dialog box, select a device—for VPN ports, these will appear as **WAN Miniport (PPTP)** and **WAN Miniport (L2TP)**—and then click **Configure**.

3. In the **Configure Ports** dialog box, select the **Remote access (inbound)** check box to enable inbound VPN connections.

4. You can increase or decrease the number of virtual ports available on the server.

5. In the **Configure Device** and **Ports Properties** dialog boxes, click **OK**.

Configuring Modem and Cable Ports

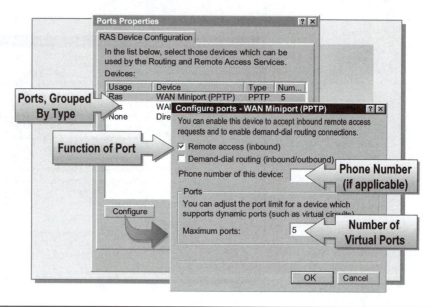

When you start Routing and Remote Access for the first time, Windows 2000 automatically detects any modems that are installed and creates modem ports for them. Windows 2000 also creates ports for each parallel or serial cable connection that it detects. You can also configure these ports manually under **Ports** in the console tree of Routing and Remote Access.

To configure modem or cable ports on the server:

1. In the console tree of Routing and Remote Access, open the **Properties** dialog box for **Ports**.

2. In the **Ports Properties** dialog box, click a device, and then click **Configure**.

   Modem, parallel, and serial ports are listed individually, but are grouped together and can be configured either individually or together. To configure several ports simultaneously, press CTRL while you click multiple ports, and then click **Configure**.

3. In the **Configure Ports** dialog box, select the **Remote access (inbound)** check box to enable inbound connections.

4. If you are configuring a modem port, type a telephone number.

5. In the **Configure Ports** and **Ports Properties** dialog boxes, click **OK**.

Configuring User Dial-in Settings

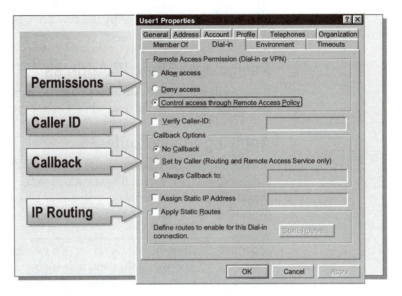

On a stand-alone server, you configure the dial-in settings on the **Dial-in** tab in the **Properties** dialog box for a user account in Local Users and Groups. For an Active Directory™ directory service–based server, you configure the dial-in settings on the **Dial-in** tab in the **Properties** dialog box for a user account in Active Directory Users and Computers.

Setting Remote Access Permissions

The **Remote Access Permission** settings offer the options to **Allow access**, **Deny access**, or **Control access through Remote Access Policy**. If access is explicitly allowed, remote access policy conditions, user account properties, or profile properties can still deny the connection attempt. The **Control access through Remote Access Policy** option is only available on user accounts for stand-alone Windows 2000–based remote access servers or members of a Windows 2000 domain in native mode.

Enabling Caller ID Verification

If the **Verify Caller-ID** option is enabled, the server verifies the caller's telephone number. If the caller's telephone number does not match the configured telephone number, the connection attempt is denied.

All parts of the connection must support caller ID. Caller ID support on the remote access server consists of caller ID answering equipment and the driver that passes caller ID information to Routing and Remote Access. If you configure a caller ID setting for a user and you do not have the driver for passing the caller ID information from the caller to Routing and Remote Access, the connection attempt will be denied.

Setting Callback Options

If the callback property is enabled, the server calls back a specific telephone number (set by the caller or by the network administrator) during the connection process.

Assigning a Static IP Address

If the **Assign Static IP Address** option is enabled, Windows 2000 assigns a specific IP address to the user when a connection is made.

Applying Static Routes

If the **Apply Static Routes** option is enabled, the network administrator defines a series of static IP routes that are added to the routing table of the remote access server when a connection is made. This setting is designed for use with demand-dial routing.

Important   If a remote access server is a member of a Windows NT version 4.0 domain or a Windows 2000 domain in mixed mode, only the **Allow access** and **Deny access** options (under **Remote Access Permission**) and the **Callback Options** dial-in settings are available. You can also use User Manager for Domains in Windows NT to grant or deny dial-in access and set callback options.

◆ Configuring Outbound Connections

- ■ **Exploring Hardware Options**

- ■ **Creating a Dial-up Connection**

- ■ **Connecting to a Virtual Private Network**

- ■ **Connecting Directly Through a Cable**

Outbound connections are connections made from a client to a server. Although it is possible for a computer running Windows 2000 Server to be a client, clients are typically computers running Windows 2000 Professional.

There are three basic types of outbound connections:

- ■ Dial-up connections, which include:
    - • Connections to a private network or server. This can include connections to a stand-alone computer in someone's home or a modem pool in a corporate intranet.
    - • Connections to an ISP.
- ■ Connections to a VPN.
- ■ Direct connections to another computer through a cable.

You configure all outbound connections in Windows 2000 by using the Network Connection wizard. Much of the work of configuring protocols and services is automated when you use this process. Understanding the options in the wizard will help you configure connections efficiently.

Tip Connection Manager provides a graphical user interface so that your customers can connect to your service by using connection features and telephone numbers that you define. The Connection Manager Administration Kit (CMAK) wizard simplifies the customization process because you can use it to specify custom elements for your service, such as dial-up locations, telephone numbers, and VPN settings. It then builds a customized installation package for you.

For more information about using Connection Manager and creating customized profiles with the CMAK wizard, see Windows 2000 Server Help.

Exploring Hardware Options

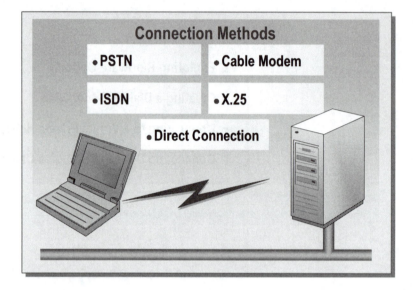

You can connect remote access clients to a remote access server by using any of several types of hardware. Windows 2000 supports connections over the Public Switched Telephone Network (PSTN), ISDN lines, cable modems, an X.25 network, or direct cable connections. When selecting a hardware type to use for remote access, you should consider the advantages and disadvantages of each type of hardware.

Hardware type	Advantages	Disadvantages
PSTN	Universal availability; inexpensive modems; higher speeds available with DSL	Toll charges; low speeds unless using DSL; DSL is not available in all locations and requires expensive modems
ISDN	Faster than most PSTN connections; dedicated lines; wide availability in urban areas	Low speeds compared with DSL or cable modems; expensive adapters
Cable modem	Very fast connections	Lower availability; expensive modems
X.25	Secure, dedicated network	Expensive adapters
Direct connection (parallel cables, serial cables, or infrared sensors)	Simple, secure, dedicated connection; inexpensive cables	Distance between computers limited to length of cable or infrared sensor range

Creating a Dial-up Connection

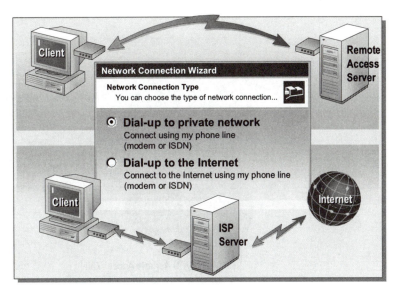

You can use the Network Connection wizard to create and configure an outbound dial-up connection either to a private network or to an ISP.

To create a new outbound connection:

1. Click **Start**, point to **Settings**, and then click **Network and Dial-up Connections**.

2. In Network and Dial-up Connections, double-click **Make New Connection**.

3. In the Network Connection wizard, click **Next**, and then click either **Dial-up to private network** or **Dial-up to the Internet**.

4. Do one of the following:

   - If you clicked **Dial-up to private network**, type the telephone number of the computer to which you are connecting. This may be an ISP for an Internet connection or the modems for your private network.

   - If you clicked **Dial-up to the Internet**, the Internet Connection wizard will start. Complete this wizard to create the connection.

5. If you want this connection to be made available to all users of this computer, click **For all users**, and then click **Next**. If you want to reserve the connection for yourself, click **Only for myself**, and then click **Next**.

6. If you clicked **Only for myself** in the previous step, proceed to the last step. If you clicked **For all users**, and you want to enable other computers to gain access to external resources through this dial-up connection, select the **Enable Internet Connection Sharing for this connection** check box.

7. By default, selecting shared access also enables on-demand dialing. If you want to prevent other computers from automatically dialing this connection, clear the **Enable on-demand dialing** check box, then click **Next**.

8. Type a name for the connection, and then click **Finish**.

Connecting to a Virtual Private Network

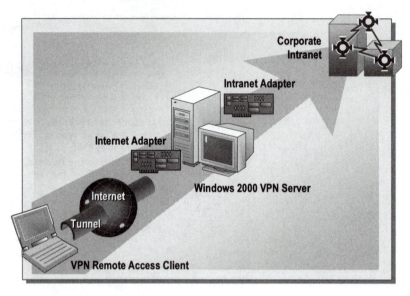

You can also use the Network Connection wizard to create a connection to a VPN. To create a new VPN connection:

1. In Network and Dial-up Connections, double-click **Make New Connection**.

2. In the Network Connection wizard, select **Connect to a private network through the Internet**, click **Next**, and then do one of the following:

   - If you must establish a connection with your ISP or some other network before connecting to the VPN, click **Automatically dial this initial connection**, click a connection on the list, and then click **Next**.

   - If you do not want to establish an initial connection automatically, click **Do not dial the initial connection**, and then click **Next**.

3. Type the host name or IP address of the computer to which you are connecting, and then click **Next**.

4. If you want this connection to be made available to all users of this computer, click **For all users**, and then click **Next**. If you want to reserve the connection for yourself, click **Only for myself**, and then click **Next**.

5. If you selected **Only for myself** in the previous step, proceed to the last step. If you selected **For all users**, and you want to enable other computers to gain access to external resources through this dial-up connection, select the **Enable Internet Connection Sharing for this connection** check box.

6. By default, selecting shared access also enables on-demand dialing. If you want to prevent other computers from automatically dialing this connection, clear the **Enable on-demand dialing** check box, and then click **Next**.

7. Type a name for the connection, and then click **Finish**.

Connecting Directly Through a Cable

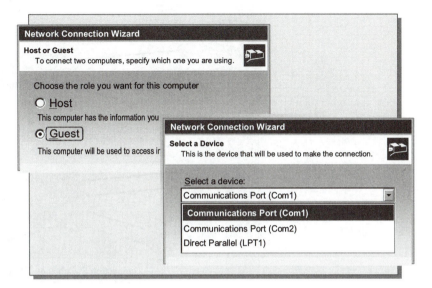

You can use the Network Connection wizard to create a direct (cable or infrared) connection to another computer. However, if you are a member of a domain and want to host a direct connection, use Routing and Remote Access instead of configuring the port as you would for a modem port.

To create a direct connection to another computer:

1. In Network and Dial-up Connections, double-click **Make New Connection**.

2. In the Network Connection wizard, click **Connect directly to another computer**, click **Next**, and then do one of the following:

   • If your computer will be the host for the connection, click **Host**, and then click **Next**.

   • If your computer will be the guest for the connection, click **Guest**, and then click **Next**.

3. Choose the port that is connected to the other computer, and then click **Next**.

4. If you want this connection to be made available to all users of this computer, click **For all users**, and then click **Next**. If you want to reserve the connection for yourself, click **Only for myself**, and then click **Next**.

5. If you clicked **Only for myself** in the previous step, proceed to the next step. If you clicked **For all users**, and you want to enable other computers to gain access to resources through this dial-up connection, select the **Enable shared access for this connection** check box, and then click **Next**.

6. Type a name for the connection, and then click **Finish**.

Configuring Multilink Connections

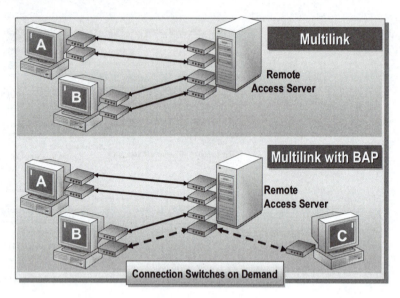

Multilink allows users to combine analog modem paths, ISDN paths, and even mixed analog and digital communications links on client and server computers. Multilinking combines multiple physical links into a logical bundle to increase bandwidth.

Multilink enables your computer to use two or more communications ports as if they were a single port of greater bandwidth. This means that if you use two modems to connect to the Internet, you can connect at double the speed of a single modem. For example, a computer with four modems operating at 33.6 kilobits per second (Kbps), and a telephone line for each modem, can connect to a remote access server with multiple modems and maintain a sustained transfer rate of 134.4 Kbps. Four 128-Kbps ISDN lines would return a throughput rate of 512 Kbps. To dial multiple devices, your connection and your remote access server must both have Multilink enabled.

The Multilink feature in Routing and Remote Access uses the PPP Multilink protocol. Windows 2000 also supports the Bandwidth Allocation Protocol (BAP) for dynamic multilinking.

PPP Multilink

The PPP Multilink protocol combines the bandwidth of two or more communication lines to create a single virtual data connection, providing scalable bandwidth based on the volume of data. Routing and Remote Access can use Multilink over multiple modems, ISDN, or X.25 cards. Both the client and remote access server must have Multilink enabled.

BAP

BAP enhances Multilink by dynamically adding or dropping links on demand. BAP is especially valuable to operations that have carrier charges based on bandwidth utilization. BAP is a PPP control protocol that works with PPP to provide bandwidth on demand.

Note   For more information about Multilink, see RFC 1990, and for more information about BAP, see RFC 2125 under **Additional Reading** on the Web page on the Student Materials compact disc.

Configuring Multilink and BAP on the Remote Access Server

You can enable the PPP Multilink and BAP protocols on a serverwide basis on the **PPP** tab in the **Properties** dialog box for each remote access server. Select the **Multilink connections** and **Dynamic bandwidth control (BAP/BACP)** check boxes to enable PPP Multilink and BAP, respectively. This is the only configuration necessary for the server to accept Multilink connections.

Configuring Multilink on the Remote Access Client

To configure an outbound connection with multiple devices:

1. Right-click the connection on which you want to enable the dialing of multiple devices, and then click **Properties**.

2. On the **General** tab, select the check boxes for all the devices that you want the connection to use.

3. On the **Options** tab, in **Multiple devices**, do one of the following:

   a. If you want Windows 2000 to dial only the first available device, click **Dial only first available device**, and then click **Configure**.

   b. If you want Windows 2000 to use all of your devices, click **Dial all devices**, and then click **Configure**.

   c. If you want Windows 2000 to dynamically dial and hang up devices as needed, click **Dial devices only as needed**, and then click **Configure**.

      i. In the **Automatic Dialing and Hanging Up** dialog box, click the **Activity at least** percentage and **Duration at least** time that you want to set. Another line is dialed when connection activity reaches this level for the amount of time that you specify.

      ii. In the **Automatic hangup** dialog box, click the **Activity no more than** percentage and **Duration at least** time that you want to set. A device is hung up when connection activity decreases to this level for at least the amount of time that you specify, and then click **OK**.

4. Click **OK**.

Lab A: Configuring a VPN Connection

Objectives

After completing this lab, you will be able to:

- Install Routing and Remote Access.

- Configure Routing and Remote Access to allow incoming VPN connections.

- Configure and test an outgoing VPN connection by using the Network Connection wizard.

Prerequisite

Before working on this lab, you must be familiar with remote access concepts and VPN concepts.

Lab Setup

To complete this lab, you need the following:

- A computer running Windows 2000 Advanced Server that is configured as a domain controller

- A static IP address and subnet mask

- A lab partner with a similarly configured computer

You will also need the following information. If you are unsure about any of these values, please ask your instructor.

Number	Record value here
Your student number	$x=$
Your partner's student number	$y=$
Your classroom number (usually 1)	$z=$

Important   The lab does not reflect the real-world environment. It is recommended that you always use complex passwords for any administrator accounts, and never create accounts without a password.

Important   Outside of the classroom environment, it is strongly advised that you use the most recent software updates that are necessary. Because this is a classroom environment, we may use software that does not include the latest updates.

Scenario

Your company, Northwind Traders, has employees that travel to remote locations. You do not have the resources to set up a worldwide network to allow dial-up connections to these locations, so you are going to configure a VPN server on the Internet and allow your staff to connect to your network through the VPN connection.

Estimated time to complete this lab: 45 minutes

Exercise 1
Configuring Inbound VPN Connections

Scenario

The sales staff at Northwind Traders has started traveling to remote locations. Although the traveling sales force will have access to the Internet at all of the remote locations, they still need access to your network for demonstration purposes. You need to enable secure remote access to your network over the Internet for these traveling users.

Goal

In this exercise, you will set up Routing and Remote Access, create VPN ports, and grant access permissions to the Administrator account for testing purposes.

Tasks	Detailed Steps
1. Install Routing and Remote Access. Use the Configuration wizard to configure the remote access server with the following values: For the IP address, use **10.x.0.10** (where *x* is your student number). Address range: **5** addresses.	a. Log on as administrator@*domain*.nwtraders.msft (where *domain* is the name of your domain) with a password of **password**. b. Open Routing and Remote Access from the **Administrative Tools** menu. c. In the console tree, right-click *server* (where *server* is the name of your computer), and then click **Configure and Enable Routing and Remote Access**. d. In the Routing and Remote Access Server Setup wizard, click **Next**. e. On the **Common Configurations** page, click **Remote access server**, and then click **Next**. f. On the **Remote Client Protocols** page, click **Next**. g. On the **Network Selection** page, under **Name**, verify that **Classroom** is selected, and then click **Next**. h. On the **IP Address Assignment** page, click **From a specified range of addresses**, and then click **Next**. i. On the **Address Range Assignment** page, click **New**. j. In the **Start IP address** box, type **10.x.0.10** (where *x* is your student number), and then in the **Number of addresses** box, type **5** k. Click **OK**, and then click **Next**. l. On the **Managing Multiple Remote Access Servers** page, verify that **No, I don't want to set up this server to use RADIUS now** is selected, click **Next**, and then click **Finish**. m. Click **OK** to close the **Routing and Remote Access** message box, and then close Routing and Remote Access.

(continued)

Tasks	Detailed Steps
2. Grant dial-in permissions to the Administrator account.	a. Open Active Directory Users and Computers from the **Administrative Tools** menu.
	b. In the console tree, expand *domain* (where *domain* is the name of your domain), click **Users**, and then in the details pane, double-click **Administrator**.
	c. On the **Dial-in** tab, verify that **Allow access** is selected, and then click **OK**.
	d. Close Active Directory Users and Computers.

Exercise 2
Configuring and Testing Outbound VPN Connections

Scenario

To verify that remote access works for the traveling users, you need to connect to the remote access server that you have installed and configured.

Goal

In this exercise, you will create and test a VPN connection to your partner's remote access server.

Tasks	Detailed Steps
🖐 Both partners must complete the previous procedure before either partner can continue.	
1. Use the Network Connection wizard to configure a VPN connection to your partner's computer. **Area Code**: Location area code. **Network Connection Type**: Connect to a private network through the Internet. **Destination Address**: **192.168.** *z.y* (where *z* is your assigned classroom number and *y* is your partner's student number). **Connection Availability** page: **Only for myself**.	a. Right-click **My Network Places**, and then click **Properties**. b. In Network and Dial-up Connections, double-click **Make New Connection**. c. On the **Location Information** page, type an area code, click **OK**, and then click **OK** to close the **Phone And Modem Options** dialog box. d. In the Network Connection wizard, click **Next**. e. On the **Network Connection Type** page, click **Connect to a private network through the Internet**, and then click **Next**. f. On the **Destination Address** page, type **192.168.***z.y* (where *z* is your assigned classroom number and *y* is your partner's student number), and then click **Next**. g. On the **Connection Availability** page, click **Only for myself**, click **Next**, and then click **Finish**.
2. Initiate a connection to your partner's computer, logging on as Administrator.	a. In the **Connect Virtual Private Connection** dialog box, verify that the user name is **Administrator**, and in the **Password** box, type **password** and then click **Connect**. 🖥 *After connecting to your partner's computer, a message appears indicating that Virtual Private Connection is connected. Notice that there is an icon in the system tray representing the new connection.* b. Click **OK** to close the "Connection Complete" message. c. Close Network and Dial-up Connections.

*(**continued**)*

Tasks	Detailed Steps
3. Use the Ipconfig utility to verify that you have established a VPN connection and received an IP address for that connection.	a. At a command prompt, type **ipconfig** and then press ENTER. *Notice that there are four network adapters: the Classroom network adapter, the PartnerNet network adapter, the remote access server connection, and the Virtual Private Network connection. The IP address for the VPN connection was assigned from the static address pool on your partner's computer.* b. Close the command prompt window.
4. Close the connection.	a. In the system tray, double-click the **Connection** icon. b. In the **Virtual Private Connection Status** dialog box, click **Disconnect**. c. Close all open windows.

◆ Configuring Authentication Protocols

- **Standard Authentication Protocols**
- **Extensible Authentication Protocols**

Remote access servers use authentication to determine the identity of users attempting to connect to the network remotely. After a user is authenticated, the user receives the appropriate access permissions and is allowed to connect to the network.

The correct and secure authentication of user accounts is critical for the security of a network. Without authentication, a potentially large number of unauthorized users can access your network.

Routing and Remote Access uses several protocols to perform authentication, and also allows for the use of Extensible Authentication Protocols, through which you can load third-party protocols.

Standard Authentication Protocols

Protocol	Security	Use when
PAP	Low	The client and server cannot negotiate using more secure validation
SPAP	Medium	Connecting a Shiva LANRover and Windows 2000–based client or a Shiva client and a Windows 2000–based remote access server
CHAP	Medium	You have clients that are not running Microsoft operating systems
MS-CHAP	High	You have clients running Windows NT version 4.0 and later or, Microsoft Windows 95 and later
MS-CHAP v2	High	You have dial-up clients running Windows 2000, or VPN clients running Windows NT 4.0 or Windows 98

Windows 2000 supports many different authentication protocols that have varying levels of security. You enable standard authentication protocols in Routing and Remote Access by selecting the appropriate check boxes on the **Security** tab in the **Properties** dialog box for the remote access server. Only those protocols that you select on this tab can be used to authenticate users to the remote access server.

PAP

The Password Authentication Protocol (PAP) uses clear-text passwords. If the passwords match, the server grants access to the remote access client. This protocol provides little protection against unauthorized access.

SPAP

The Shiva Password Authentication Protocol (SPAP) is a two-way reversible encryption mechanism employed by Shiva, a hardware manufacturer. SPAP encrypts the password data that is sent between the client and server and is, therefore, more secure than PAP.

CHAP

The Challenge Handshake Authentication Protocol (CHAP) (also known as Message Digest 5 [MD5]–CHAP) is a challenge-response authentication protocol. CHAP uses the industry-standard MD5 one-way encryption scheme to encrypt the response, providing a medium level of protection against unauthorized access. The authentication process works as follows:

1. The remote access server sends a challenge—consisting of a session identifier and an arbitrary challenge string—to the remote access client.

2. The remote access client sends a response that contains the user name and a one-way encryption of the challenge string, the session identifier, and the password.

3. The remote access server checks the response, and, if valid, allows the connection.

MS-CHAP

Microsoft Challenge Handshake Authentication Protocol (MS-CHAP) is a one-way, encrypted password authentication protocol. If the server uses MS-CHAP as the authentication protocol, it can use Microsoft Point-to-Point Encryption (MPPE) to encrypt data to the client or server. On a remote access server running Windows 2000, MS-CHAP is enabled by default.

MS-CHAP v2

A new version of MS-CHAP, MS-CHAP v2, is available. This new protocol provides mutual authentication, stronger initial data encryption keys, and different encryption keys for sending and receiving.

For VPN connections, Windows 2000 Server offers MS-CHAP v2 before offering MS-CHAP. Windows 2000 dial-up and VPN connections can use MS-CHAP v2. Computers running Windows NT 4.0 and Microsoft Windows 98 can use MS-CHAP v2 authentication for VPN connections only.

Selecting Authentication Protocols

The following table describes the situations in which you use these protocols.

Protocols	Security	Use when
PAP	Low	The client and server cannot negotiate by using a more secure form of validation.
SPAP	Medium	Connecting to a Shiva LanRover, or when a Shiva client connects to a Windows 2000–based remote access server.
CHAP	Medium	You have clients that are not running Microsoft operating systems.
MS-CHAP	High	You have clients running Windows 2000, Windows NT 4.0, or Microsoft Windows 95 or later.
MS-CHAP v2	High	You have dial-up clients running Windows 2000, or VPN clients running Windows NT 4.0 or Windows 98. MS-CHAP v2 is the most secure form of authentication.

Extensible Authentication Protocols

- **Allows the Client and Server to Negotiate the Authentication Method That They Will Use**

- **Supports Authentication by Using**
    - MD5-CHAP
    - Transport Layer Security
    - Additional third-party authentication methods

- **Ensures Support of Future Authentication Methods Through an API**

The Extensible Authentication Protocol (EAP) allows for customized authentication to remote access servers. The client and the remote access server negotiate the exact authentication method to be used. EAP supports authentication by using:

- *MD5-CHAP*. This protocol encrypts user names and passwords with an MD5 algorithm.

- *Transport Layer Security*. Transport Layer Security (TLS) is used for smart card (and other) intermediary security devices. Smart cards require a card and reader. The smart card electronically stores the user certificate and private key.

- *Additional, third-party authentication methods*. EAP allows vendors to add their own authentication methods, such as token cards. Token cards are physical cards that provide passwords and may use several authentication methods, including the use of codes that change with each use.

Through the use of the EAP application programming interfaces (APIs), independent software vendors can supply new client and server authentication methods for technologies such as token cards, smart cards, biometric hardware (such as retina or fingerprint scanners), and authentication technologies that are not yet developed.

To enable EAP authentication, open **Routing and Remote Access**, right-click your server, and then click **Properties**. The configuration settings are on the **Security** tab. You enable and configure specific EAP types on the **Authentication** tab of the **Edit Dial-in Profile** dialog box for the remote access policy.

Note   For more information about EAP, see RFC 2284 and RFC 2716 under **Additional Reading** on the Web page on the Student Materials compact disc.

Configuring Encryption Protocols

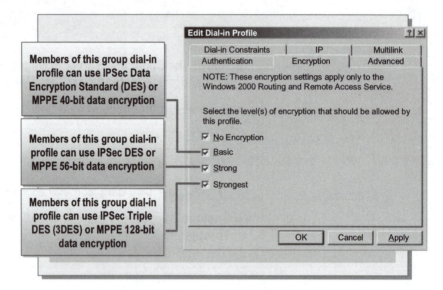

Data encryption provides security by encrypting, or encoding, data that is sent between a remote access client and a remote access server. For installations that require the highest degree of security, the administrator can set the server to force encrypted communications. Clients connecting to that server must encrypt their data or the server will refuse their connection.

You enable encryption protocols on the **Encryption** tab in the **Edit Profile** dialog box for the remote access policy.

Important Data encryption is only available if you use MS-CHAP (v1 or v2) or TLS (an EAP protocol) as the authentication protocol.

There are two methods of encrypting the data that is transmitted over a Windows 2000 remote access connection: MPPE and IPSec.

Encrypting Data by Using MPPE

MPPE encrypts data that moves between a PPTP connection and the VPN server. It has three levels of encryption: strongest (128-bit), strong (56-bit), and basic (40-bit) schemes.

Note For 128-bit encryption, you must download the Windows 2000 high encryption pack from the Windows Update Web site.

Encrypting Data by Using IPSec

IPSec is a framework of open standards for ensuring secure private communications over IP networks by using encryption. IPSec provides aggressive protection against private network and Internet attacks. IPSec is also easy to use. Clients negotiate a security association that acts as a private key to encrypt the data flow.

You use IPSec policies to configure IPSec security services. IPSec security services provide protection for most types of network traffic. Your network security administrator can configure IPSec policies to meet the security requirements of a user, group, application, domain, site, or global enterprise network.

You create and manage IPSec policies by using IP Security Policy Management, which is a snap-in that you can add to Microsoft Management Console (MMC).

Note   For more information about configuring IPSec policies, see module 6, "Configuring Network Security by Using IPSec," in course 2153, *Implementing a Microsoft Windows 2000 Network Infrastructure*.

◆ Configuring Routing and Remote Access for DHCP Integration

- **Assigning IP Addresses to Remote Access Clients by Using DHCP**
- **Configuring Routing and Remote Access to Use DHCP**

When you configure a remote access server to allow clients to connect to a corporate network by using dial-up networking, you select how clients will receive an IP address from one of the following options:

- *Static IP Address*. You configure the IP address on the client computer. When clients use preassigned IP addresses, you need to ensure that the IP address is valid for each network to which the client connects and that no other client uses the same address. Because of this, it is not recommended that you use static IP addresses for dial-up networking.

- *From a Range of IP Addresses*. A remote access server can assign an IP address from a range of addresses that you configure. If you choose this option, you need to ensure that you have a sufficient number of IP addresses allocated exclusively for the remote access server to assign to client computers.

- *From the DHCP Server*. A remote access server can obtain IP addresses from a DHCP server and assign the IP addresses to dial-up clients. This is the most versatile configuration, because you do not have to reserve IP addresses for use by dial-up clients, and you only need to maintain one address pool.

Note For more information about how dial-up clients obtain a subnet mask and addresses of DNS servers and WINS server, see the "DHCP Option Parameters" topic in the Windows 2000 Server Resource Kit.

Tip When using DHCP to obtain IP addresses for dial-up clients, you can reduce the number of required IP addresses by setting a short lease duration, such as one hour. Configuring a short lease duration allows you to support many dial-up clients while keeping the number of allocated IP addresses low. A remote access server only requires as many IP addresses as there are simultaneously connected clients.

Assigning IP Addresses to Remote Access Clients by Using DHCP

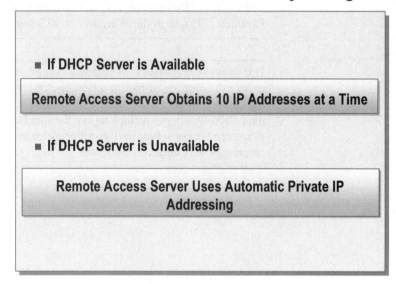

- **If DHCP Server is Available**

Remote Access Server Obtains 10 IP Addresses at a Time

- **If DHCP Server is Unavailable**

Remote Access Server Uses Automatic Private IP Addressing

If the remote access server is configured to use DHCP to obtain IP addresses, the remote access server initially obtains 10 IP addresses from a DHCP server. The remote access server uses the first IP address obtained from DHCP for itself and allocates subsequent addresses to TCP/IP-based remote access clients as they connect. IP addresses that are released when remote access clients disconnect are reused. When all 10 IP addresses are used, the remote access server obtains 10 more. When the Routing and Remote Access service is stopped, all IP addresses obtained through DHCP are released.

If a DHCP server is not available when Routing and Remote Access is started, Automatic Private IP Addressing addresses in the range from 169.254.0.1 through 169.254.255.254 are used. Because this may prevent client computers from accessing computers on your network other than the remote access server, you should ensure that a DHCP server is always available.

The remote access server uses a specific LAN adapter to obtain DHCP-allocated IP addresses for remote access clients. The IP addresses that the remote access server receives are valid for the network segment to which the adapter is attached. You can select which adapter you want to use. By default, Routing and Remote Access randomly picks a LAN adapter to use. For a remote access server with multiple adapters, you should select the adapter that is connected to a network segment where DHCP-allocated addresses can be obtained.

Tip   You can assign DHCP options to dial-up clients that differ from the options that you assign to clients that are directly connected to the network. To do this, use the Default Routing and Remote Access Class user class.

For more information about DHCP, see module 2, "Automating IP Address Assignment by Using DHCP," in course 2153, *Implementing a Microsoft Windows 2000 Network Infrastructure*.

Configuring Routing and Remote Access to Use DHCP

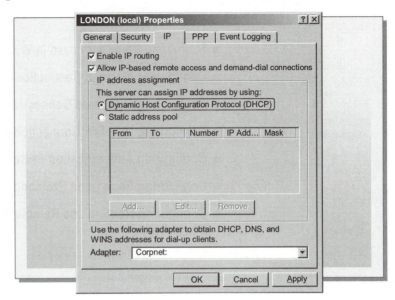

You can configure Routing and Remote Access to obtain IP addresses from a DHCP server.

To configure a remote access server to obtain IP addresses from a DHCP server:

1. Open Routing and Remote Access from the **Administrative Tools** menu.

2. Right-click the server name for which you want to view properties, and then click **Properties**.

3. In the **Properties** dialog box for the remote access server, on the **IP** tab, click **Dynamic Host Configuration Protocol (DHCP)**.

4. In the **Adapter** box, click the network adapter from which you want the remote access server to obtain IP addresses by using DHCP.

5. Click **OK**.

Review

- Examining Remote Access in Windows 2000
- Configuring Inbound Connections
- Configuring Outbound Connections
- Configuring Multilink Connections
- Configuring Authentication Protocols
- Configuring Encryption Protocols
- Configuring Routing and Remote Access for DHCP Integration

1. What are the advantages of using L2TP rather than using PPTP?

2. In the Network Connection wizard, you must configure two settings regarding sharing the connection and its associated resources. Describe the difference between these two settings.

3. Your organization has many employees that are connecting to your network by modems over the telephone system, but are requesting more bandwidth so that they can be more productive. High-speed connections such as ISDN and DSL are not currently available in your area. What can you do to increase bandwidth for people working remotely?

4. People in your organization use a number of different operating systems to connect to your network by remote access. You want a remote access authentication protocol that is very secure but will allow all of your client operating systems to connect. What is the best authentication protocol to select?

5. You are configuring a remote access server for your organization, and you want to make sure that users who are using the remote access server get only specified IP addresses, and that these addresses are always available to the remote access server. How can you do this?

6. Help desk has received a call from a user who is dialing into your network by using remote access. The user connects successfully, but is unable to access any resources on the network. You ask the user to use Ipconfig to verify the IP address for the connection, and the user reports that she has an IP address of 169.254.5.23. What is a likely cause of this problem? Why?

Microsoft®
Training &
Certification

Module 8: Supporting Remote Access to a Network

Contents

Simulations and interactive exercises were built with Macromedia Authorware

Overview

- Examining Remote Access Policies
- Examining Remote Access Policy Evaluation
- Creating a Remote Access Policy
- Troubleshooting Remote Access

In Microsoft® Windows® 2000, you can define and create remote access policies to control the level of remote access that a user or group of users has to the network. Remote access policies are a set of conditions and connection settings that give network administrators more flexibility in granting remote access permissions and usage. The Windows 2000 Routing and Remote Access service and Windows 2000 Internet Authentication Service (IAS) both use remote access policies to determine whether to accept or reject connection attempts. As the administrator, you are also required to troubleshoot and maintain the remote access server for optimum performance.

At the end of this module, you will be able to:

- Explain remote access policy and profile concepts.
- Describe the process of remote access policy evaluation.
- Create a remote access policy and configure a remote access profile.
- Maintain and troubleshoot remote access.

Examining Remote Access Policies

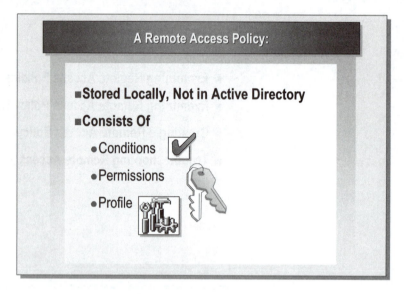

You can use remote access policies to assign settings to a connection, based on the user that is connecting and the properties of the connection. Understanding how policies are applied will help you provide customized access to the various users and groups in your organization. It is likely that the default policy settings are adequate for your remote access needs. However, it is important that you become familiar with remote access policies because using them effectively provides you with flexibility in granting remote access permissions and usage.

Policies are Stored Locally

Windows 2000 stores remote access policies on the remote access server, not in the Active Directory™ directory service, so that policies can vary according to remote access server capabilities.

Note You can centralize remote access policies through the use of IAS. For more information about IAS, see module 9, "Extending Remote Access Capabilities by Using IAS," in course 2153, *Implementing a Microsoft Windows 2000 Network Infrastructure*.

Components of a Policy

A remote access policy consists of three components that cooperate with Active Directory to provide secure access to remote access servers. The three components of a remote access policy are its conditions, permissions, and profile.

Conditions

The conditions of remote access policies are a list of parameters, such as the time of day, user groups, caller IDs, or Internet Protocol (IP) addresses, that are matched to the parameters of the client that is connecting to the server. The first set of policy conditions that match the parameters of the incoming connection request is processed for access permission and configuration.

Permissions

Remote access connections are permitted based on a combination of the dial-in properties of a user account and remote access policies. The permission setting on the remote access policy works with the user's dial-in permissions in Active Directory.

For example, a policy can grant access to all users in Group A from 8:00 A.M. through 5:00 P.M. However, the permissions for User X in Group A can be set to deny access in Active Directory, whereas the permissions for User Y in Group A can be set to allow access at all times. As a result, most users in Group A are controlled by the policy setting and can gain access only from 8:00 A.M. through 5:00 P.M. However, User X is denied access completely, and User Y is granted 24-hour access.

Profile

Each policy includes a profile of settings, such as authentication and encryption protocols, that are applied to the connection. The settings in the profile are applied to the connection immediately, and may cause the connection to be denied. For example, if the profile settings for a connection specify that the user can only connect for 30 minutes at a time, the user will be disconnected from the remote access server after 30 minutes.

◆ Examining Remote Access Policy Evaluation

- Following Policy Evaluation Logic
- Examining Default and Multiple Policies

It is important to understand how remote access policies are evaluated, so that you can determine the settings that will apply to incoming connections and plan your policies appropriately. Remote access policies are evaluated according to a logical flow that depends on whether the Windows 2000 domain is in mixed or native mode. (A mixed mode domain allows domain controllers to run Windows 2000 or Microsoft Windows NT® version 4.0. A native mode domain requires that all domain controllers run Windows 2000.) Familiarity with the logic of remote access policy evaluation, the features of the default policy, and the interaction of multiple policies will help you design effective remote access policies.

Following Policy Evaluation Logic

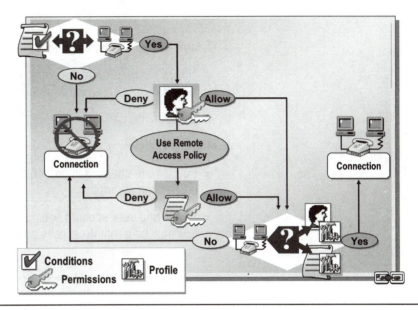

Windows 2000 evaluates a connection attempt based on logic that incorporates policy conditions, user and remote access permissions, and profile settings.

Remote access policies are evaluated as follows:

1. Routing and Remote Access matches the conditions of the remote access policy to the conditions of the attempted connection:

   - If there is no policy defined, all access is denied.

   - If there is no policy that matches, the access is denied.

   - If there is a match, the policy is used to determine access.

2. Routing and Remote Access checks the user account's dial-in permissions:

   - If the permission is set to **Deny access**, the user is denied access.

   - If the permission is set to **Allow access**, the user is granted access and the profile for the policy is applied.

   - If the permission is set to **Control access through Remote Access Policy**, the policy's permission setting determines user access.

3. Routing and Remote Access applies the settings in the policy's profile to the incoming connection.

   - The connection may not be allowed if a critical setting in the profile does not match a setting on the remote access server. For example, the profile for an incoming connection may specify that a group can only connect at night. If a user in that group tries to connect during the day, the connection attempt will be denied.

   - The connection may be disconnected at a later stage due to a setting in the profile, such as a time restriction on connecting.

Examining Default and Multiple Policies

- **Default Remote Access Policy**
  - Native mode (default policy denies all attempts unless User's account is set to **Allow Access**)
  - Mixed mode (default policy overridden)
- **Multiple Policies**
  - Policies are checked in order until a policy matches the connection attempt
  - Profile and user account settings are checked for the first matching remote access policy only

---

The default remote access policy will have no effect on incoming connections when the domain is in mixed mode, and the remote access policy has no profile settings associated with it. The default policy will be applied to all connection attempts that do not match any other policies. You should be aware of the settings of this policy and the implications of using the default policy in native mode and mixed mode domains. You should also understand how multiple policies interact.

Default Remote Access Policy

The default policy, called **Allow access if dial-in permission is enabled**, is created when Routing and Remote Access is installed. This policy controls access through the user's dial-in permission. The following table describes the settings of the default policy.

Setting	Value
Conditions	Current date/time = any day, any time
Permissions	Deny access
Profile	None

Native Mode and Standalone Servers

When your domain is running in native mode, or if your remote access server is a standalone server, setting the dial-in permission on every user account to **Control access through Remote Access Policy** will result in the rejection of all connection attempts if you do not change the default remote access policy. However, if you set one user's dial-in permission to **Allow access**, that user's connection attempts will be accepted. If you change the permission setting on the default policy to **Grant remote access permission**, all connection attempts are accepted.

Mixed Mode

The default policy is always overridden in a mixed mode domain because the user's dial-in permission, **Control access through Remote Access Policy**, is not available in mixed mode. However, the remote access server still applies remote access policies to users in a mixed mode domain. If the user's dial-in permission is set to **Allow access**, the user still must meet the conditions of a policy to gain access.

Important When converting from mixed mode to native mode, the permissions for all users with a dial-in setting of **Deny access** will be changed to **Control access through Remote Access Policy**. Permissions for all users with a dial-in setting of **Allow access** will remain set to **Allow access**. As a result, if the default remote access policy remains unaltered and no other policies exist, the conversion to native mode will have no effect on users' remote access permissions.

Multiple Policies

Many organizations will have different remote access requirements for different groups in the organization. These organizations will require multiple remote access policies. You should create these policies carefully. If a connection attempt does not match any of the remote access policies, the connection attempt is rejected, even when a user's dial-in permission is set to **Allow access**.

When a user attempts to connect, the first policy in the ordered list of remote access policies is checked. If all of the conditions of the policy do not match the connection attempt, the next policy in the ordered list is checked, until a policy matches the connection attempt.

The connection attempt is then evaluated against the profile and user account settings of that profile. If the connection attempt does not match the profile or user account settings of the first remote access policy that matches the connection attempt, the connection attempt is rejected. No other policies are checked.

You can modify the order of remote access policies. For example, you might want the remote access policy that applies to the majority of your users to be checked first, so that fewer connection attempts must be evaluated against more than one policy.

To modify the order of remote access policies:

1. In Routing and Remote Access, in the console tree, click **Remote Access Policies**.

2. In the details pane, right-click the policy that you want to move, and then click either **Move Up** to move the policy up one level, or **Move Down** to move the policy down one level.

Important Because Routing and Remote Access requires that the conditions of at least one policy be matched, if the default policy is removed and there are no other policies, all connection attempts will be rejected. In most situations, you should leave the default policy unaltered to provide access for users who are explicitly granted access through their user permissions.

◆ Creating a Remote Access Policy

- **Configuring Remote Access Policy Conditions**
- **Configuring Remote Access Profile Settings**

You can create detailed rules for remote access that are as simple or as complex as your organization needs. A remote access policy consists of user dial-in settings, remote access policy conditions, and remote access policy settings. Although they do not need to be completed in any particular order, it is important to include all three components in your planning.

Note   For more information about user dial-in settings, see module 7, "Configuring Remote Access," in course 2153, *Implementing a Microsoft Windows 2000 Network Infrastructure.*

Configuring Remote Access Policy Conditions

Examples of Connection Attempt Conditions

- **Is Between 8 A.M. and 5 P.M., Monday–Friday**

  AND

- **Is from Any IP Address That Matches 192.168.*.***

  AND

- **Is from Any User in the Sales Group**

Remote access policy *conditions* are attributes that are compared to the settings of a connection attempt. If there are multiple conditions in a policy, all of the conditions must match the settings of the connection attempt, or the next policy is evaluated.

The following table lists the conditions that you can set for a remote access policy.

Note Some of these conditions apply to Remote Authentication Dial-In User Service (RADIUS). For more information about RADIUS, see module 9, "Extending Remote Access Capabilities by Using IAS," in course 2153, *Implementing a Microsoft Windows 2000 Network Infrastructure.*

Condition name	Description	Wildcard okay (*)	Used by IAS
NAS IP Address	A character string that identifies the IP address of the network access server (NAS).	Yes	Yes
Service Type	The type of RADIUS service that is requested. Examples include framed (such as Point-to-Point Protocol [PPP] connections) and logon (such as Telnet connections). For more information about RADIUS service types, see RFC 2138 under **Additional Reading** on the Web page on the Student Materials compact disc.	No	Yes
Framed Protocol	The type of framing for incoming packets. Examples include PPP, AppleTalk, Serial Line Internet Protocol (SLIP), Frame Relay, and X.25.	No	Yes
Called Station ID	A character string that identifies the telephone number of the NAS.	Yes	No

(continued)

Condition name	Description	Wildcard okay (*)	Used by IAS
Calling Station ID	A character string that identifies the telephone number that the caller uses. The telephone line, hardware, and hardware driver must support reception of caller ID data.	Yes	No
NAS Identifier	A character string that identifies the NAS from which the request originated.	Yes	No
NAS Port Type	The type of media that the caller uses. Examples include analog telephone lines (or Async), Integrated Services Digital Network (ISDN), and virtual private networks (VPNs).	No	No
Day and Time Restrictions	The day of the week and the time of day of the connection attempt.	No	No
Client IP Address	A character string that identifies the IP address of the RADIUS client.	Yes	Yes
Client Vendor	The manufacturer of the NAS that is requesting authentication.	No	Yes
Client Friendly Name	A character string that identifies the name of the RADIUS client that is requesting authentication.	Yes	Yes
Windows Groups	The names of the Windows 2000 groups to which the user who is attempting the connection belongs. For a remote access server in a domain in native mode or an IAS server, use universal groups. There is no condition for a specific user name.	No	No
Tunnel Type	Tunneling protocols for incoming packets, such as Layer Two Tunneling Protocol (L2TP).	No	No

You can create a remote access policy and an associated profile under **Remote Access Policies** in the console tree of Routing and Remote Access.

To add a remote access policy:

1. Open Routing and Remote Access from the **Administrative Tools** menu.

2. Right-click **Remote Access Policies**, and then click **New Remote Access Policy**.

3. In the Add Remote Access Policy wizard, type the name of the profile in the **Policy friendly name** box, and then click **Next**.

4. To configure a new condition, click **Add**.

5. In the **Select Attribute** dialog box, click the attribute to add, and then click **Add**.

6. In the *attribute* dialog box (the name of this dialog box will vary according to the attribute selected), enter the information that the attribute requires, and then click **OK**.

7. Click **Add** to add another condition, or click **Next** to continue with the wizard.

8. To grant access to callers matching these conditions, click **Grant remote access permission**, or to deny access, click **Deny remote access permission**, and then click **Next**.

9. You can then create a profile, or click **Finish** to create a policy without a profile. You can add a profile after the policy is created.

Configuring Remote Access Profile Settings

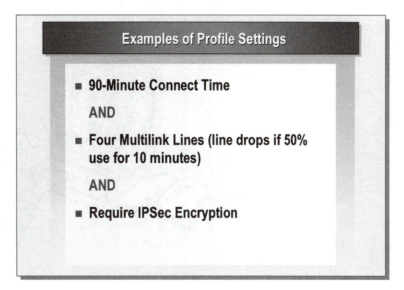

The remote access profile specifies what kind of access the user will be given if the conditions match. Access will be granted only if the connection attempt does not conflict with the settings of the user account or the profile. You can configure a profile in the **Edit Dial-in Profile** dialog box by clicking **Edit Profile** in the **Properties** dialog box for a policy. You can configure the following settings in the dialog box:

- **Dial-in Constraints**. You can use these settings to determine the amount of idle time before disconnection; the maximum session time; and the days, times, telephone numbers, and media types (ISDN, VPN, and so on) that are allowed.

- **IP**. You can configure client IP address assignment and Transmission Control Protocol/Internet Protocol (TCP/IP) packet filtering on this tab. You can define separate filters for inbound or outbound packets.

- **Multilink**. You can configure Multilink and Bandwidth Allocation Protocol (BAP) on this tab. Use these settings to disconnect a line if bandwidth falls below a certain level for a given length of time. Multilink can also be set to require the use of BAP.

- **Authentication**. You can use these settings to define the authentication protocols that are allowed for connections that use this policy. Make sure that any protocols that you select here are also enabled in the **Properties** dialog box for the server.

- **Encryption**. You can use this tab to specify the types of encryption that are prohibited, allowed, or required.

- **Advanced**. You can use this tab to configure additional network parameters that can be sent from RADIUS servers running non-Microsoft operating systems.

Lab A: Creating a Remote Access Policy and Profile

Objectives

After completing this lab, you will be able to:

- Create a remote access policy.
- Create a remote access profile.
- Test a policy and a profile.

Prerequisite

Before working on this lab, you must have a familiarity with remote access policy and profile concepts.

Lab Setup

To complete this lab, you need the following:

- Successful completion of Lab A, "Configuring a VPN Connection," in module 7, "Configuring Remote Access" of course 2153, *Implementing a Microsoft Windows 2000 Network Infrastructure*.

- A computer running Windows 2000 Advanced Server that is configured as a domain controller in native mode.

- A lab partner with a similarly configured computer.

- You will also need the following information. If you are unsure about any of these values, please ask your instructor.

Number	Record value here
Your student number	$x=$
Your partner's student number	$y=$

Important The lab does not reflect the real-world environment. It is recommended that you always use complex passwords for any administrator accounts, and never create accounts without a password.

Important Outside of the classroom environment, it is strongly advised that you use the most recent software updates that are necessary. Because this is a classroom environment, we may use software that does not include the latest updates.

Scenario

Your company needs to have more control over which employees have access to its network remotely, and it also needs more control over how those employees connect to the network. To accomplish this, you are going to configure remote access policies to control access to your network.

In this lab, you will work with a partner to configure remote access policies. You will create a user account, and configure its dial-in properties and group membership. You will then create a remote access policy for this group, and configure access by using that policy. Your partner will then use the user account that you created to dial in to your computer by a VPN connection, to test the use of the policy.

Estimated time to complete this lab: 45 minutes

Exercise 1
Configuring and Testing Remote Access Policies

Scenario

Northwind Traders has implemented remote access servers for the sales force, to allow for secure access to the company network from the Internet. As the administrator for the remote access servers on your network, you need to implement a remote access policy that grants access to the sales groups and denies access to everyone else. Before you set up the actual remote access policy, you will create a test user and a test group.

Goal

In this exercise, you will create a test user in a test group, verify that the default policy denies access to the test user, and then create and test a remote access policy that grants access to members of the test group.

Tasks	Detailed Steps
🖐 Perform the following procedures on both computers.	
1. Create a user called RemoteUser*x* (where *x* is your student number), with a password of password. Configure the user properties to allow dial-in access.	a. Log on as administrator@*domain*.nwtraders.msft (where *domain* is the name of your domain) with a password of **password**.
	b. Open Active Directory Users and Computers from the **Administrative Tools** menu.
	c. In the console tree, under *domain*, right-click **Users**, point to **New**, and then click **User**.
	d. In the **New Object – User** dialog box, in the **First name** box, type **RemoteUser***x* (where *x* is your student number).
	e. In the **User logon name** box, type **RemoteUser***x*
	f. Click *domain*.**nwtraders.msft**, and then click **Next**.
	g. Set the password for the new user account to **password**, click **Next**, and then click **Finish**.
	h. In the details pane, right-click **RemoteUser***x*, and then click **Properties**.
	i. On the **Dial-in** tab, click **Allow access**, and then click **OK**.

(continued)

Tasks	Detailed Steps
2. Create a new global group called RemoteGroup*x*. Add the user that you just created to the group.	**a.** In the console tree, right-click **Users**, point to **New**, and then click **Group**. **b.** In the **New Object – Group** dialog box, in the **Group name** box, type **RemoteGroup*x*** (where *x* is your student number). **c.** Under **Group scope**, verify that **Global** is selected, and under **Group type**, verify that **Security** is selected, and then click **OK**. **d.** Open the **Properties** dialog box for RemoteGroup*x*. **e.** On the **Members** tab, click **Add**. **f.** In the **Select Users, Contacts, Computers, or Groups** dialog box, in the **Look in** box, verify that your domain is displayed. **g.** In the list of objects, click **RemoteUser*x***, click **Add**, and then click **OK**. **h.** Click **OK** to close the **RemoteGroup*x* Properties** dialog box. **i.** Minimize Active Directory Users and Computers.
✋ **Important:** Wait until your partner has completed the previous procedures before starting the following procedure.	
3. Test your dial-in configuration by dialing in to your partner's computer by using the account that your partner created, and then close the connection.	**a.** Right-click **My Network Places**, and then click **Properties**. **b.** In Network and Dial-up Connections, double-click **Virtual Private Connection**. **c.** Connect as RemoteUser*y* (where *y* is your partner's student number) with a password of **password**. **d.** Click **OK** to close the **Connection Complete** message, and then disconnect the VPN connection.
✋ **Important:** You must perform tasks 4 and 5 at the same time as your partner.	
4. Configure the dial-in permissions for RemoteUser*x* to have access controlled through the remote access policy.	**a.** Restore Active Directory Users and Computers, and then open the **Properties** dialog box for RemoteUser*x*. **b.** On the **Dial-in** tab, click **Control access through Remote Access Policy**, and then click **OK**.
ℹ **Note:** The domain controllers must be running in native mode for the **Control access through Remote Access Policy** option to be available on the **Dial-in** tab.	
4. *(continued)*	**c.** Minimize Active Directory Users and Computers.

(continued)

Tasks	Detailed Steps
5. Test your dial-in configuration by dialing in to your partner's computer as RemoteUser*y*.	**a.** In Network and Dial-up Connections, double-click **Virtual Private Connection**, and then connect as RemoteUser*y* (where *y* is your partner's student number) with a password of **password**. *The connection attempt was denied because the default remote access policy denies access to all users. In native mode, if you select **Control access through Remote Access Policy**, you must configure a policy that allows access for your users.* **b.** In the **Error Connecting to Virtual Private Connection** dialog box, click **Cancel**. **c.** Minimize Network and Dial-up Connections.
6. Use Routing and Remote Access to add a new policy called Allow RemoteGroup*x* access, which allows access to users in the RemoteGroup*x* group. Make sure that this policy is evaluated before the default policy.	**a.** Open Routing and Remote Access from the **Administrative Tools** menu. **b.** In the console tree, expand *server* (where *server* is the name of your computer), right-click **Remote Access Policies**, and then click **New Remote Access Policy**. **c.** On the **Policy Name** page, type **Allow RemoteGroup*x* access** (where *x* your student number), and then click **Next**. **d.** On the **Conditions** page, click **Add**, and in the **Select Attribute** dialog box, click **Windows-Groups**, and then click **Add**. **e.** In the **Groups** dialog box, click **Add**. **f.** In the **Select Groups** dialog box, in the **Look in** list, click your domain. **g.** In the **Select Groups** dialog box, under **Name**, click **RemoteGroup*x***, click **Add**, and then click **OK**. **h.** In the **Groups** dialog box, click **OK**. **i.** On the **Conditions** page, click **Next**. **j.** On the **Permissions** page, click **Grant remote access permission**, and then click **Next**. **k.** On the **User Profile** page, click **Finish**. **l.** In Routing and Remote Access, in the console tree, click **Remote Access Policies**, and in the details pane, right-click **Allow RemoteGroup*x* access**, and then click **Move Up**. **m.** Minimize Routing and Remote Access.
Important: Wait until your partner has completed the previous procedure before starting the following procedure.	

(*continued*)

Tasks	Detailed Steps
7. Test your dial-in configuration by dialing in to your partner's computer.	a. Restore Network and Dial-Up Connections, double-click **Virtual Private Network**, and then connect as RemoteUser*y* with a password of **password**. b. Click **OK** to close the **Connection Complete** message, and then disconnect the VPN connection.
8. Configure the order of the remote access policies so that the default policy is evaluated first.	a. Restore Routing and Remote Access. b. In the console tree, click **Remote Access Policies**, and in the details pane, right-click **RemoteGroup***x*, and then click **Move Down**. c. Minimize Routing and Remote Access.
9. Test your dial-in configuration by dialing in to your partner's computer.	a. In Network and Dial-Up Connections, double-click **Virtual Private Network**, and then connect as RemoteUser*x* with a password of **password**. *Notice that this connection attempt fails because the policy denies dial-in permission.* b. In the "Error Connecting to Virtual Private Connection" message, click **Cancel**.

⚠ **Important:** You must perform tasks 10 and 11 at the same time as your partner.

Tasks	Detailed Steps
10. Configure the user dial-in properties of RemoteUser*x* to allow access.	a. Restore Active Directory Users and Computers. b. Open the **Properties** dialog box for RemoteUser*x*. c. On the **Dial-in** tab, click **Allow access**, and then click **OK**. d. Close Active Directory Users and Computers.
11. Test your dial-in configuration by dialing in to your partner's computer.	a. In Network and Dial-Up Connections, double-click **Virtual Private Network**, and then connect as RemoteUser*y* with a password of **password**. b. Click **OK** to close the **Connection Complete** message, and then disconnect the VPN connection.

Exercise 2
Disabling Routing and Remote Access

Scenario

One of your remote access servers is going to be replaced. You need to disable Routing and Remote Access for the server before taking the server offline.

Goal

In this exercise, you will disable Routing and Remote Access on your server and then log off.

Tasks	Detailed Steps
1. Remove the remote access policy that you added in the previous exercise.	a. Restore Routing and Remote Access. b. In the console tree, click **Remote Access Policies**. c. In the details pane, right-click **Allow RemoteGroup*x* access**, and then click **Delete**. d. In the **Delete Policy** box, click **Yes**.
2. Use Routing and Remote Access to disable the service on your computer, close all open windows, and then log off.	a. Right-click *server* (where *server* is the name of your computer), and then click **Disable Routing and Remote Access**. b. In the **Routing And Remote Access** dialog box, click **Yes**. c. Close all open windows, and then log off.

◆ Troubleshooting Remote Access

- **Monitoring Remote Access**

- **Tracing Remote Access Connections**

- **Troubleshooting Communication Hardware**

- **Troubleshooting Communication Lines**

- **Troubleshooting Configuration Settings**

Remote access to your organization requires the successful operation of many components, including computers, communication hardware, communication lines, and in some cases, the Internet. Because the successful operation of remote access relies on such a large number of components to function correctly, operational problems arise occasionally. The ability to diagnose and then fix problems is critical to keeping your local and remote users connected to your network.

Monitoring Remote Access

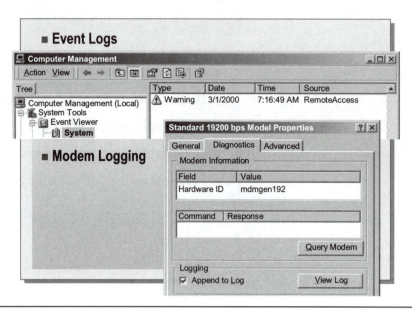

Monitoring the remote access server is the best method you can use to determine the source of problems on a remote access server. There are several tools and logs that can be used to monitor and troubleshoot remote access.

Event Logs

The Windows 2000 event log contains information about system components in Windows 2000 and is one of the first places to check for information about a problem. To access the event log, right-click **My Computer**, and then click **Manage**. Under **Computer Management**, expand **Event Viewer**, and then click **System**. The entries that have RemoteAccess listed in the source column are the event logs related to remote access.

Modem Logging

Windows 2000 Professional automatically records a log of communication made from the computer to a modem during a connection. This log is normally overwritten each time a new connection is made, but can be configured to append the log file. In Windows 2000 Server and Advanced Server, you must manually enable the log file.

To enable modem logging on Windows 2000 Server:

1. In Control Panel, double-click **Phone and Modem Options**.

2. In the **Phone and Modem Options** dialog box, on the **Modems** tab, click the modem that you are configuring, and then click **Properties**.

3. In the **Properties** dialog box for the modem, on the **Diagnostics** tab, click select the **Record a Log** check box, and then click **OK**. (In Windows 2000 Professional, this option appears as **Append to Log**. This means that each connection will not overwrite the existing log file.)

To view the log file, click **View log** on the **Diagnostics** tab.

Tracing Remote Access Connections

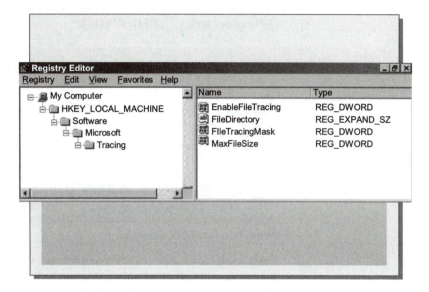

Windows 2000 has an extensive tracing capability that you can use to troubleshoot complex network problems. You can enable the components in Windows 2000 Server to log tracing information to files. You must enable the tracing function by changing settings in the Windows 2000 registry under:

HKEY_LOCAL_MACHINE\SOFTWARE\Microsoft\Tracing

Caution Incorrectly editing the registry may severely damage your system. Before making changes to the registry, you should back up all critical data on the computer.

You enable tracing for each remote access component by setting the registry values described in the following table.

Value	Data type	Description
EnableFileTracing	**REG_DWORD**	You can enable logging tracing information to a file by setting the value of **EnableFileTracing** to 1. The default value is 0.
FileDirectory	**REG_EXPAND_SZ**	You can change the default location of the tracing files by setting **FileDirectory** to the path that you want. The file name of the log file is the name of the component for which tracing is enabled. By default, log files are placed in the *systemroot*\Tracing folder.

(continued)

Value	Data type	Description
FileTracingMask	**REG_DWORD**	**FileTracingMask** determines how much tracing information is logged to the file. The default value is FFFF0000, which is the maximum level of tracing.
MaxFileSize	**REG_DWORD**	You can change the size of the log file by setting different values for **MaxFileSize**. The default value is 65536 bytes (64 kilobytes).

Tracing consumes system resources, so you should use it only when necessary to help identify network problems. After the trace is captured or the problem is identified, you should immediately disable tracing. Do not leave tracing enabled on multiprocessor computers.

The tracing information can be complex and very detailed. Most of the time, this information is useful only to Microsoft Product Support Services engineers or to network administrators who are highly experienced with the Windows 2000–based router.

Troubleshooting Communication Hardware

- **User's Communication Hardware**
  - Refer to manufacturer's guidelines for hardware testing
  - Query modem on **Diagnostics** tab
  - View modem session log
- **Remote Access Server Communication Hardware**
  - Check hardware as you would on user's computer
  - View system event logs

The first step in resolving a problem is to identify its source. After you identify the source of a problem, the solution is usually self-evident. When problems with remote access connections occur, the source may be the hardware on the user's computer or the hardware on the remote access server.

User's Communication Hardware

One of the first remote access components to check is the communication hardware that the user is using to connect remotely. This hardware may be a modem, network card, or some other device. Because most hardware has unique self-test procedures, refer to the hardware manufacturer's guidelines for information about how to check hardware.

If the connection is by a modem, make sure that the modem is configured correctly in Windows 2000, and that the modem's self-test functions correctly.

To check the modem:

1. In Control Panel, double-click **Phone and Modem Options**.

2. On the **Modems** tab, click your modem, and then click **Properties**.

3. Click the **Diagnostics** tab, and then click **Query Modem**.

If the modem is working correctly, a series of diagnostics responses should be returned. If the modem is faulty, try reinstalling the modem, or consult the modem manufacturer for more information.

To get more information about what the modem is doing during a connection attempt, you can view the modem session log information to determine the source of the error.

Remote Access Server Communication Hardware

Another possible source of problems with remote access connections is the communication hardware of the remote access server itself. To determine whether the communication hardware is functioning, check the system event logs for error messages, and use hardware testing methods provided by your hardware manufacturer.

If you suspect a problem with a modem, follow the same troubleshooting steps as for the client computer. Another way of determining a problem with remote access server modems is to call the modem with a normal telephone and hear whether the modem picks up the line and attempts to connect. If the remote access server modem does not try to connect, this is an indication that there is something wrong with the remote access server's modem.

Caution   The noise generated during a connection attempt may be very loud when emitted from a normal telephone receiver. To avoid injury, hold the headset away from your ear.

Troubleshooting Communication Lines

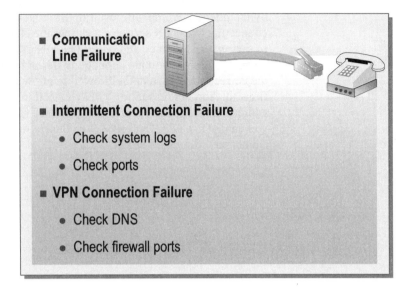

- **Communication Line Failure**

- **Intermittent Connection Failure**
  - Check system logs
  - Check ports
- **VPN Connection Failure**
  - Check DNS
  - Check firewall ports

If the communication hardware is functioning correctly, the next step is to verify that the communication lines are functioning.

Communication Line Failure

If the communication line is not working for some reason, or is not connected correctly, remote access connection attempts will fail. This can be the result of an incorrectly connected cable or disconnected telephone service.

In larger installations, it is common for many telephone lines to be used for remote access connections. Before connecting a telephone line to a modem, always check to make sure that the line is working correctly by using a normal telephone receiver.

Intermittent Connection Failure

Often, in large remote access installations, a single telephone number is used for dial-in and is then split into a number of separate telephone lines by a piece of hardware called a rotary splitter. Modems are then connected to each line. In this situation, it is possible for one modem to be faulty or incorrectly configured. This will give the end-user the appearance that the connection to the remote access server gives intermittent failures, because the connection attempt only fails when the rotary tries to connect the user by using the line connected to the faulty modem.

To identify the intermittent connection problem, use the system event logs; but if the problem is in the remote access hardware itself, check which ports are being used in Routing and Remote Access. The faulty modem port should appear as unused even during busy times.

VPN Connection Failure

When troubleshooting a VPN connection, the communication line is replaced by the Internet, which will result in different errors. If there is a problem connecting to a VPN server, check that the Domain Name System (DNS) name of the server is correct, and check that DNS name resolution is functioning correctly. Also, if you are connecting through a firewall, ensure that you have the correct ports open at the firewall to allow the VPN connection through the firewall. Another reason for VPN connection failure can be the use of network address translation (NAT). If you use NAT to protect internal IP addressing, you cannot use L2TP and IPSec to connect to a remote VPN server. IPSec cannot pass through a NAT.

Troubleshooting Configuration Settings

- **Network Configuration**
  - Check TCP/IP configuration, and DNS and WINS IP addresses
  - PING user
- **Remote Access Server Settings**
  - Check system event log
  - Enable tracing
- **User's Computer Settings**
  - Check configuration
  - Create new setting

After you determine that the source of the problem is not the hardware or communication lines, check the configuration settings.

Network Configuration

Network configuration error occurs when the user successfully connects, and appears to have a valid connection, but is still unable to access resources on the network. Network configuration error is usually due to a problem with the underlying network. It might occur if name resolution is not working correctly, or if some other critical network function, such as routing, is not configured correctly.

When network configuration error occurs, confirm that you can access resources when you are connected directly to the network, and check TCP/IP configuration properties by using the **ipconfig /all** command on the client. Make sure that the DNS and/or Windows Internet Name Service (WINS) server IP addresses are configured and working. Also, attempt to diagnose the problem as if the user's computer were connected directly to the local area network (LAN). Use the **ping** command on the user's computer to determine where the network connectivity problem resides.

Remote Access Server Settings

The settings that you configure on your remote access server can prevent users with incorrect settings from completing a connection. To determine whether a setting on the remote access server is causing a connection to fail, the user must successfully connect to the server and then become disconnected due to one of the configured settings.

To help determine which setting could be at fault, check the system event log on the remote access server and on the computer on which the user dials in. In some cases it may be necessary to enable tracing on the remote access server to determine the cause of the problem.

User Computer Settings

There are a number of settings that can be made to the computer and to the connection properties that will cause a remote access connection to fail. For example, if the computer on which the user dials in only uses the NWLink IPX/SPX/NetBIOS Compatible Transport Protocol (NWLink) and the remote access server only uses TCP/IP, the connection will not be successful.

In the event of a connection failure, if the remote access server and communication lines are tested and found to be working correctly, the cause of the failure is probably in the user's computer settings. Examine the error messages that appear; if they do not show the cause, check the system event log and the modem log, if this is a modem connection.

A common problem with user computer settings occurs when a user has modified the connection properties in such a way that it causes the connection attempt to fail. A quick way to determine whether this is the problem is to re-create the outbound connection by using the Make New Connection wizard. Either create a new connection or instruct the user to create a new connection, and attempt to connect to the remote access server again. If this new connection succeeds, the configuration of the original connection was the problem.

Lab B: Troubleshooting Remote Access (Simulation)

Objectives

After completing this lab, you will be able to:

- Read event logs to determine the cause of an error
- Troubleshoot remote access problems

Prerequisites

Before working on this lab, you must have:

- The ability to configure a remote access connection
- An understanding of how VPN connections work

Lab Setup

This lab is a simulation. To complete this lab, you need the following:

- A computer running Windows 2000, Windows NT 4.0,
  Microsoft Windows 98, or Microsoft Windows 95
- A minimum display resolution of 800 x 600 with 256 colors

▶ **To start the lab**

1. Insert the Student Materials compact disc into your CD-ROM drive.

2. At the root of the compact disc, double-click **Default.htm**.

3. On the Student Materials Web page, click **Lab Simulations**, and then click **Troubleshooting Remote Access**.

4. Read the introductory information, and then click the link to start the lab.

Estimated time to complete this lab: 15 minutes

Review

- **Examining Remote Access Policies**
- **Examining Remote Access Policy Evaluation**
- **Creating a Remote Access Policy**
- **Troubleshooting Remote Access**

1. You have been receiving many help-desk calls lately about users not being able to connect to your remote access servers because all available lines are busy. You monitor the incoming lines, and notice that many people connect and remain connected for many hours, even though they do not transmit or receive any data. How can you reduce the time that users stay connected while idle?

2. You want to allow different time use and Multilink settings for different groups of users connecting to your remote access server. What steps do you need to perform to achieve this?

3. You want to control dial-up access to your remote access server completely through policies, but when you attempt to configure this by using Active Directory Users and Computers, the option to **Control access through remote access policy** is not available. Why?

4. Users are attempting to connect to your remote access server, but are receiving a message that they do not have dial-in permissions. You look up their accounts in Active Directory Users and Computers, and they do have dial-in permissions. What could be causing the problem?

5. A user is calling the help desk to say that he cannot connect to the organization's remote access servers. You look up the event logs on the remote access server for all remote access entries, but find no entries. What components of the remote access connection could be causing this error?

Microsoft®
Training &
Certification

Module 9: Extending Remote Access Capabilities by Using IAS

Contents

Overview

- ■ **Introduction to IAS**
- ■ **Installing and Configuring IAS**

Organizations that outsource dial-up remote access, or perform joint ventures with other organizations, require authentication of user accounts outside the private network. Also, organizations that provide the outsourcing services, such as Internet service providers (ISPs), require remote user connection accounting so that they can charge subscribers.

Remote Authentication Dial-In User Service (RADIUS) is an industry-standard protocol that provides the solution to these authentication and remote user accounting requirements. In Microsoft® Windows® 2000, the combination of Routing and Remote Access and the Internet Authentication Service (IAS) provides support for RADIUS.

At the end of this module, you will be able to:

- ■ Describe the use of IAS in a network.

- ■ Install and configure IAS.

◆ Introduction to IAS

- **IAS and RADIUS in a Windows 2000 Network**
- **Purpose and Use of IAS**

Corporations and ISPs maintaining remote access service for employees and customers face the increasing challenge of managing all remote access from a single point of administration. IAS performs centralized authentication, authorization, auditing, and accounting of connections for dial-up, virtual private network (VPN), and demand-dial connections. IAS enables organizations to centrally manage and control remote access to their networks, and track usage statistics of the network centrally. IAS also enables network administrators to centrally manage remote access permissions and connection properties.

Note For more information about RADIUS, see RFC 2138 and RFC 2139 under **Additional Reading** on the Web page on the Student Materials compact disc.

IAS and RADIUS in a Windows 2000 Network

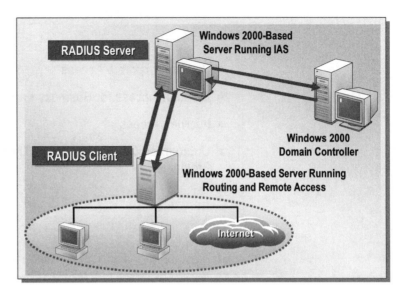

RADIUS is a *client/server protocol* that enables RADIUS clients to submit authentication and accounting requests to a RADIUS server. A RADIUS client can be a network access server (NAS) that accepts Point-to-Point Protocol (PPP) connections and places clients on the network, or it can be a remote access server, such as a Windows 2000–based server running Routing and Remote Access. In a Windows 2000 network infrastructure, the RADIUS server is a Windows 2000–based server running IAS.

The RADIUS Authentication Process

The following steps describe the basic process that remote servers, a RADIUS server, and RADIUS clients use to perform authentication and authorization:

1. A user connects to a Windows 2000–based computer that is running Routing and Remote Access by using a dial-up connection or a VPN connection.

2. The Windows 2000–based computer that is running Routing and Remote Access forwards authentication requests to an IAS server. When doing this, the computer running Routing and Remote Access acts as a RADIUS client.

3. The IAS server accesses the user account information on a domain controller and checks the remote access authentication credentials. When doing this, the IAS server performs the functions of a RADIUS server.

4. If the user's credentials are authenticated and the connection attempt is authorized, the IAS server authorizes the user's access and logs the remote access connections as accounting events.

   During the session, interim accounting packets are sent. When the user disconnects, an accounting-stop packet is sent to the IAS server, indicating the end of the user session. When logging accounting information, the computer running Routing and Remote Access acts as a RADIUS client, and the IAS server acts as a RADIUS server.

Purpose and Use of IAS

- **Dial-up Corporate Access**
- **Extranet Access for Business Partners**
- **Internet Access**
- **Outsourced Corporate Access Through Service Providers**

The main benefit of using RADIUS for authentication and accounting is that it is a standards-based protocol that allows for interoperability with other vendors' solutions.

You can set up IAS to support several business scenarios, including:

- *Dial-up corporate access*. You can set up IAS to support remote employees with authenticated dial-up connections. For example, the IAS server can give access to employees based on the group to which they belong.

- *Extranet access for business partners*. You can set up IAS to make network resources available to other companies with which an organization has partnership agreements. For example, the IAS server can limit a partner's access to corporate network resources.

- *Internet access*. You can set up IAS to support customer-authenticated dial-up connections to an ISP. For example, the IAS server can give access to customers based on the service plan for which they sign up.

- *Outsourced corporate access through service providers*. You can set up IAS to support a company that outsources remote access infrastructure to ISPs but retains control over user authentication, authorization, and accounting. For example, when an employee connects to the remote access server at the ISP, the authentication and usage records are forwarded to the organization's IAS server. The IAS server enables the company to control user authentication, track usage, and control which employees are allowed to gain access to the network.

◆ Installing and Configuring IAS

- **Installing an IAS Server**

- **Configuring an IAS Server**

- **Configuring a Remote Access Server to Use RADIUS Authentication**

- **Configuring a Remote Access Server to Use RADIUS Accounting**

- **Configuring Logs for Accounting Information**

Before you can use IAS, you must install and configure IAS on a computer running Windows 2000 Server. You also must configure servers that have Routing and Remote Access installed to integrate with the IAS servers. You can configure the remote access server to use the IAS server to authenticate remote access users. Although the remote access servers can also authenticate users, each server has its own remote access policy to authorize user access to the network. Integration of these servers with IAS provides centralized authentication and authorization. You can also configure IAS to record the duration of the connection and the volume of data that a user has transferred.

Installing an IAS Server

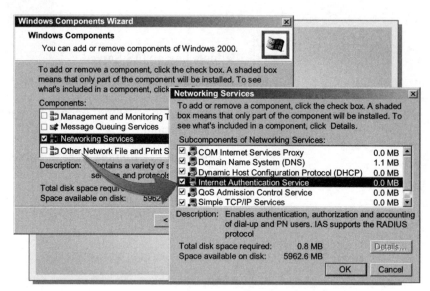

Before a RADIUS client can access an IAS server, you must first install IAS on the server.

To install IAS:

1. In Control Panel, double-click **Add/Remove Programs**.

2. Click **Add/Remove Windows Components**.

3. On the **Windows Components** page, under **Components**, click **Networking Services** (but do not select or clear the check box), and then click **Details**.

4. Select the **Internet Authentication Service** check box, and then click **OK**.

5. Click **Next**, and then click **Finish**.

   When you install the IAS network component, **Internet Authentication Service** is added to the **Administrative Tools** menu.

Configuring an IAS Server

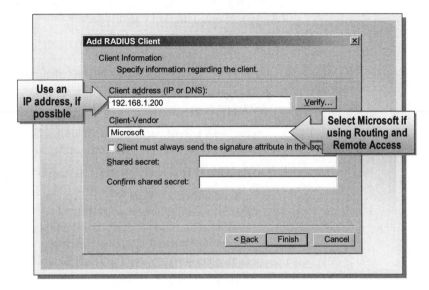

Before you configure the IAS server to authenticate users by using the Active Directory™ directory service, you must authorize the IAS server to ensure that the IAS service has the correct permissions to access account information from Active Directory.

You must also add the RADIUS clients to the IAS server. The RADIUS clients are the remote access servers that will use the IAS server for authentication and authorization. Finally, you can configure the size and location of the logs that store the accounting information collected by an IAS server.

Authorizing an IAS Server

If an IAS server must access Active Directory to authenticate users, you must authorize the IAS server in Internet Authentication Service in Microsoft Management Console (MMC). Only members of the Enterprise Admins group can authorize an IAS server.

To authorize an IAS server in Active Directory:

1. Open Internet Authentication Service from the **Administrative Tools** menu.

2. Right-click **Internet Authentication Service (Local)**, and then click **Register Service in Active Directory**.

3. In the **Register Internet Authentication Service in Active Directory** dialog box, click **OK**.

Note When you authenticate an IAS Server, Windows 2000 adds the server's computer account to the RAS and IAS Servers security group, which has the required Active Directory permissions to access user data in Active Directory.

Configuring RADIUS Clients

After you authorize the IAS server, you must configure the server for the RADIUS clients that will use this server.

To configure the IAS Server for RADIUS clients:

1. Open Internet Authentication Service from the **Administrative Tools** menu.

2. In the console tree, right-click **Clients**, and then click **New Client** to start the Add Client wizard.

3. On the **Add Client** page, in the **Friendly Name** box, type a name for the RADIUS client that you are configuring, and then click **Next**.

4. On the **Client Information** page, specify the following:

   - **Client address (IP or DNS)**. Type the Internet Protocol (IP) address or Domain Name System (DNS) name for the RADIUS client. Typically, it is more efficient to specify an IP address so that IAS does not have to resolve all host names at startup. If you only know a client's DNS name, click **Verify** to resolve the name to an IP address.

   - **Client-Vendor**. Select **Microsoft** if you are adding a Routing and Remote Access server. If you are adding a RADIUS client from a vendor that is not listed, select **RADIUS Standard**.

Note   The Client-Vendor setting is only required if you are using remote access policies that are based on a client-vendor attribute.

   - **Client must always send the signature attribute**. Select this check box if the RADIUS client must send a signature attribute in the Access-Request packet. You must specify a signature attribute if you use Extensible Authentication Protocol (EAP) for authentication.

   - **Shared secret**. Type the secret, and then retype the secret in the **Confirm shared secret** box.

     A *shared secret* is a text string that serves as a password between an IAS server and the remote access servers that forward requests to it. Shared secrets:

     - Must be exactly the same on both servers.

     - Are case sensitive.

     - Can use any standard alphanumeric and special characters. Using combinations of uppercase and lowercase letters, numbers, and special characters will make the shared secret more secure.

     - Can be up to 255 characters long. Long shared secrets are more secure than shorter ones.

5. Click **Finish**.

Configuring a Remote Access Server to Use RADIUS Authentication

To configure a remote access server as a RADIUS client, you must configure the server to forward authentication requests to an IAS server.

To configure RADIUS authentication:

1. Open Routing and Remote Access from the **Administrative Tools** menu.

2. In the console tree, right-click *server* (where *server* is the name of your computer), and then click **Properties**.

3. On the **Security** tab of the **Properties** dialog box for the server, in the **Authentication provider** box, click **RADIUS Authentication**, and then click **Configure**.

4. In the **RADIUS Authentication** dialog box, click **Add**.

5. In the **Add RADIUS Server** dialog box, in the **Server name** box, type the name of the IAS server that you are using for RADIUS authentication.

6. If you have a shared secret configured on the IAS server, click **Change** to set the shared secret on the remote access server.

7. If you are using digital signatures, select the **Always use digital signatures** check box.

   You must specify this option if the RADIUS server is an IAS server and you selected the **Client must always send the signature attribute in the request** option when you added the client to the IAS server.

8. Click **OK** to close all dialog boxes, and then restart Routing and Remote Access.

Configuring a Remote Access Server to Use RADIUS Accounting

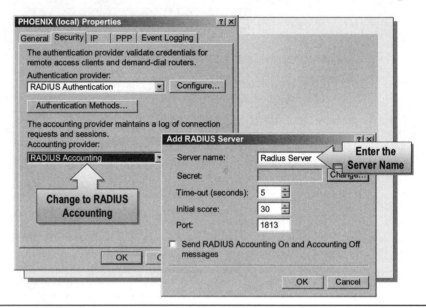

For a remote access server to use RADIUS accounting, you must configure the server to forward accounting requests to an IAS server.

To configure RADIUS accounting:

1. Open Routing and Remote Access from the **Administrative Tools** menu.

2. In the console tree, right-click *server* (where *server* is the name of your computer), and then click **Properties**.

3. On the **Security** tab of the **Properties** dialog box for the server, in the **Accounting provider** box, click **RADIUS Accounting**, and then click **Configure**.

4. In the **RADIUS Accounting** dialog box, click **Add**.

5. In the **Add RADIUS Server** dialog box, in the **Server name** dialog box, type the name of the IAS server that you have configured for RADIUS accounting.

6. If you have a shared secret configured on the IAS server, click **Change** to set the shared secret on the remote access server.

7. Select the **Send RADIUS Accounting On and Accounting Off messages** check box to send messages to the IAS server when you start or stop Routing and Remote Access.

8. Click **OK** to close all dialog boxes, and then restart Routing and Remote Access.

Configuring Logs for Accounting Information

Configure Settings for Accounting Logs:

- **Select Events to Log**
  - Log accounting requests
  - Log authentication requests
  - Log periodic status
- **Select Log File Format**
  - Database-compatible format
  - IAS format
- **New Log Time Period**
- **Log File Directory**

You can configure settings for the accounting information logs, including events to log, file format, time period to log, and location of files. You can configure IAS to create accounting logs, but to analyze the data, you must import the logs into a database program.

Note For more information about importing IAS logs into a database, see "Importing IAS log files into a database" in Windows 2000 Help.

To configure settings for accounting logs:

1. Open Internet Authentication Service from the **Administrative Tools** menu.
2. In the console tree, click **Remote Access Logging**.
3. In the details pane, right-click **Local File**, and then click **Properties**.
4. On the **Settings** tab, select from the following events to log:
   - **Log accounting requests**. Specifies whether the account packets, such as accounting start or stop, are logged in the IAS log file.
   - **Log authentication requests**. Specifies whether the authentication requests, such as access-accept or access-reject, are logged in the IAS log file.
   - **Log periodic status**. Specifies whether interim accounting packets are logged in the IAS log file. This option is not generally recommended because it can fill hard drive space quickly.

5. On the **Local File** tab, specify the following:

- **Log file format**. Click **Database-compatible format** to store information in a comma-delimited format, which you can import into most database programs. Click **IAS Format** to log data in a format that is compatible with IAS servers running Microsoft Windows NT® version 4.0. Click this option only if required for migration or compatibility reasons.

- **New log time period**. Specify when IAS creates a new log file: daily, weekly, monthly, or when the file reaches a certain size.

- **Log file directory**. Select the location for your logs.

6. Click **OK**.

Lab A: Configuring Internet Authentication Service

Objectives

After completing this lab, you will be able to:

- Install IAS.
- Configure Windows 2000 as a RADIUS client.
- Configure RADIUS authentication and accounting.

Prerequisites

Before working on this lab, you must have:

- The ability to install and configure Routing and Remote Access.
- An understanding of how user accounts are authenticated.

Lab Setup

To complete this lab, you need the following:

- A computer running Windows 2000 Advanced Server that is configured as a domain controller in native mode.
- A lab partner with a similarly configured computer.

Important   The lab does not reflect the real-world environment. It is recommended that you always use complex passwords for any administrator accounts, and never create accounts without a password.

Important   Outside of the classroom environment, it is strongly advised that you use the most recent software updates that are necessary. Because this is a classroom environment, we may use software that does not include the latest updates.

Scenario

Your company is increasing the number of remote access servers that it uses, and now you want to centrally control access to these servers through RADIUS. Also, you want centralized logging of remote access accounting information, and centralized authentication.

To achieve this, you are going to configure a server running the IAS, and then configure your remote access servers to use this IAS server for authentication, accounting, and remote access policies.

Estimated time to complete this lab: 30 minutes

Exercise 1
Installing and Configuring Internet Authentication Service

Scenario

You have been asked to centralize the administration and access for your remote access users in your organization. To do this, you have decided to use IAS for authentication of users connecting remotely, and also to use IAS for accounting to track the use of remote access throughout the organization.

Goal

In this exercise, you will install IAS, configure a RADIUS client for this service, and then configure shared secrets for this server.

Tasks	Detailed Steps
1. Install IAS.	a. Log on as administrator@*domain*.nwtraders.msft (where *domain* is the name of your domain) with a password of **password**.
	b. In Control Panel, double-click **Add/Remove Programs**.
	c. In Add/Remove Programs, click **Add/Remove Windows Components**.
ⓘ **Note:** In the next detailed step, click the text **Networking Services** rather than the check box to avoid selecting all options under **Networking Services**.	
1. *(continued)*	d. In the Windows Components wizard, on the **Windows Components** page, click **Networking Services**, and then click **Details**.
	e. In the **Networking Services** dialog box, select the **Internet Authentication Service** check box, and then click **OK**.
	f. On the **Windows Components** page, click **Next**.
	g. If the **Files Needed** dialog box appears, type **London\Setup\Winsrc** and then click **OK**.
	h. When the configuration is complete, click **Finish**, and then close all open windows.

(continued)

Tasks	Detailed Steps
2. Register IAS in Active Directory, and then specify your server as a new RADIUS client. Use **password** as your shared secret.	a. Open Internet Authentication Service from the **Administrative Tools** menu. b. In the console tree, right-click **Internet Authentication Service (Local)**, and then click **Register Service in Active Directory**. c. Click **OK** to close the **Register Internet Authentication Service in Active Directory** dialog box. d. Click **OK** to close the **Service registered** message box. e. In the console tree, under **Internet Authentication Service (Local)**, click **Clients**. f. Right-click **Clients**, and then click **New Client**. g. On the **Name and Protocol** page, in the **Friendly name** box, type *server* (where *server* is the name of your computer), and then click **Next**. h. On the **Client Information** page, in the **Client address (IP or DNS)** box, type the IP address of your computer's Classroom network adapter. i. In the **Client-Vendor** box, click **Microsoft**. j. In the **Shared secret** and **Confirm shared secret** boxes, type **password** and then click **Finish**.
3. Configure IAS to log all accounting requests.	a. In the console tree, click **Remote Access Logging**, and then in the details pane, click **Local File**. b. Right-click **Local File**, and then click **Properties**. c. On the **Settings** tab, select all of the check boxes. d. On the **Local File** tab, under **Log file directory**, type **c:\moc\win2153** and then click **OK**. e. Close Internet Authentication Service.

Exercise 2
Configuring a Windows 2000 RADIUS Client

Scenario

You have installed IAS on a computer running Windows 2000, and you must configure your remote access servers to be RADIUS clients to this server.

Goal

In this exercise, you will configure your computer to be a RADIUS client.

Tasks	Detailed Steps
1. Enable Routing and Remote Access. Use the Configuration wizard to configure the remote access server with the following values: **IP address: 10.*x*.0.10** (where *x* is your student number) **Address Range**: Five addresses	a. Open Routing and Remote Access from the **Administrative Tools** menu. b. In the console tree, right-click *server* (where *server* is the name of your computer), and then click **Configure and Enable Routing and Remote Access**. c. In the Routing and Remote Access Server Setup wizard, click **Next**. d. On the **Common Configurations** page, click **Remote access server**, and then click **Next**. e. On the **Remote Client Protocols** page, click **Next**. f. On the **Network Selection** page, under **Name**, verify that **Classroom** is selected, and then click **Next**. g. On the **IP Address Assignment** page, click **From a specified range of addresses**, and then click **Next**. h. On the **Address Range Assignment** page, click **New**. i. In the **Start IP address** box, type **10.*x*.0.10** (where *x* is your student number), and then in the **Number of addresses** box, type **5** j. Click **OK**, and then click **Next**. k. On the **Managing Multiple Remote Access Servers** page, verify that **No, I don't want to set up this server to use RADIUS now** is selected, click **Next**, and then click **Finish**. l. Click **OK** to close the **Routing and Remote Access** message box.

(continued)

Tasks	Detailed Steps
2. Configure your remote access server to use RADIUS authentication. Specify your server as your own RADIUS server, and use a secret of **password**.	**a.** In Routing and Remote Access, right-click *server*, and then click **Properties**. **b.** In the **Properties** dialog box for your server, on the **Security** tab, in the **Authentication provider** box, click **RADIUS Authentication**, and then click **Configure**. **c.** In the **RADIUS Authentication** dialog box, click **Add**. **d.** In the **Add RADIUS Server** dialog box, in the **Server name** box, type *server*. **e.** To the right of the **Secret** box, click **Change**. **f.** In the **Change Secret** dialog box, in the **New secret** and **Confirm new secret** boxes, type **password** and then click **OK**.
🛈	**Note:** The secret is configured on the RADIUS server for a client, and on the RADIUS client itself. The secret is used in the setup of a secure, authenticated channel between RADIUS client and server.
2. *(continued)*	**g.** Click **OK** to close the **Add RADIUS Server** dialog box, and then click **OK** to close the **RADIUS Authentication** box. **h.** Click **OK** to close the **Routing and Remote Access** dialog box.
⚠	**Important:** Do not restart the Routing and Remote Access service at this time.
3. Configure your remote access server to use RADIUS accounting. Specify your server as your own RADIUS server, and use a secret of **password**.	**a.** In the **Properties** dialog box, on the **Security** tab, in the **Accounting provider** box, click **RADIUS Accounting**, and then click **Configure**. **b.** In the **RADIUS Accounting** dialog box, click **Add**. **c.** In the **Add RADIUS Server** dialog box, in the **Server name** box, type *server*. **d.** To the right of the **Secret** box, click **Change**. **e.** In the **Change Secret** dialog box, in the **New secret** and **Confirm new secret** boxes, type **password** and then click **OK**. **f.** In the **Add RADIUS Server** dialog box, select the **Send RADIUS Accounting On and Accounting Off messages** check box, and then click **OK**. **g.** Click **OK** to close the **RADIUS Accounting** dialog box. **h.** Click **OK** to close the **Routing and Remote Access** message box, and then click **OK** to close the *server* **(local) Properties** dialog box. **i.** Click **OK** to close the **Routing and Remote Access** dialog box. **j.** Click **OK** to close the **Routing and Remote Access** dialog box.
4. Stop and then restart Routing and Remote Access.	**a.** In the console tree, right-click *server*, point to **All Tasks**, and then click **Restart**. **b.** Minimize Routing and Remote Access.

Exercise 3
Monitoring Remote Access by Using RADIUS

Scenario

You need to check usage statistics for your remote access server.

Goal

In this exercise, you will connect to your remote access server and then verify the usage statistics by viewing the RADIUS Accounting log file.

Tasks	Detailed Steps
1. Create a VPN connection called **RADIUS Test** to your server.	a. Right-click **My Network Places**, and then click **Properties**. b. In Network and Dial-up Connections, double-click **Make New Connection**. c. Click **Next**. d. On the **Network Connection Type** page, click **Connect to a private network through the Internet**, and then click **Next**. e. On the **Public Network** page, verify that **Do not dial the initial connection** is selected, and then click **Next**. f. On the **Destination Address** page, type the IP address of your computer's Classroom network adapter, and then click **Next**. g. On the **Connection Availability** page, verify that **For all users** is selected, and then click **Next**. h. On the **Internet Connection Sharing** page, click **Next**. i. On the **Completing the Network Connection Wizard** page, type **RADIUS Test** in the text box, and then click **Finish**.
2. Using the VPN connection that you created in the previous task, connect to your computer, and then disconnect.	a. In the **Connect RADIUS Test** dialog box, verify that **Administrator** appears in the **Username** box. b. In the **Password** box, type **password** and then click **Connect**.
ℹ **Note:** Wait for the VPN connection to be established. This connection will generate a RADIUS accounting log that you will examine in the next step.	
2. (continued)	c. Click **OK** to close the **Connection Complete** message box, and then disconnect the connection. d. Close Network and Dial-up Connections.
3. Open the RADIUS accounting log file at c:\moc\win2153\iaslog.log.	a. Click **Start**, then click **Run**. b. In the **Open** box, type **c:\moc\win2153\iaslog.log** and then click **OK**.

(*continued*)

Tasks	Detailed Steps
❓ What can you use the information in the RADIUS accounting log for? (Select all that apply.) A. Tracking the amount of time that users spend connected to a remote access server. B. Monitoring problems with recursive DNS queries. C. Calculating remote access usage times for a user. D. Performance monitoring of remote access. E. Detecting errors with a remote access server. _____ _____ _____ _____	
3. (*continued*)	c. Close Notepad.

Exercise 4
Removing the Internet Authentication Service

Scenario

You now want to use this server for another purpose, so you need to remove IAS and Routing and Remote Access.

Goal

In this exercise, you will remove IAS and Routing and Remote Access.

Tasks	Detailed Steps
1. Remove IAS.	a. In Control Panel, double-click **Add/Remove Programs**.
	b. In Add/Remove Programs, click **Add/Remove Windows Components**.
ⓘ	**Note:** In the next detailed step, click the text **Networking Services** rather than the check box to avoid selecting all options under **Networking Services**.
1. *(continued)*	c. In the Windows Components wizard, on the **Windows Components** page, click **Networking Services**, and then click **Details**.
	d. In the **Networking Services** dialog box, clear the **Internet Authentication Service** check box, and then click **OK**.
	e. On the **Windows Components** page, click **Next**.
	f. When the configuration process is complete, click **Finish**, and then close all windows.
2. Disable Routing and Remote Access on your computer, close all windows, and then log off.	a. Restore Routing and Remote Access.
	b. Right-click *server* (where *server* is the name of your computer), and then click **Disable Routing and Remote Access**.
	c. In the **Routing And Remote Access** dialog box, click **Yes**.
	d. Close Routing and Remote Access, and then log off.

Review

- **Introduction to IAS**
- **Installing and Configuring IAS**

---

1. You must configure a remote access server to use RADIUS authentication. What steps must you take to do this?

2. Your company has a worldwide remote access infrastructure in place, and you want to be able to track usage statistics for users connecting to all servers worldwide. You also want to be able to control connection properties for users at a central location, instead of at each remote access server. How can you do this?

3. You must create reports on remote access usage in your organization. You have configured all remote access servers as RADIUS clients of an IAS server. What else must you do to create the reports?

Microsoft®
Training &
Certification

Module 10: Configuring a Windows 2000–Based Server as a Router

Contents

Overview

- **Overview of Routers and Routing Tables**
- **Configuring Network Connections**
- **Enabling Routing by Using Routing and Remote Access**
- **Configuring Static Routes**
- **Configuring a Routing Interface**
- **Implementing Demand-Dial Routing**
- **Configuring the Routing Information Protocol**

This module provides the knowledge and skills necessary to configure a computer running Microsoft® Windows® 2000 as a network router. When enabled as a network router, Windows 2000 supports both local routing and remote routing. In addition to physical dial-up, frame relay, Integrated Services Digital Network (ISDN), or X.25 connections, the connection can be a direct connection to the corporate network or a point-to-point, virtual private network (VPN) connection through the Internet.

At the end of this module, you will be able to:

- Explain the function and purpose of routing.
- Configure network connections.
- Enable routing by using Routing and Remote Access.
- Configure static routes.
- Configure a routing interface.
- Implement demand-dial connections.
- Configure the Routing Information Protocol (RIP).

◆ Overview of Routers and Routing Tables

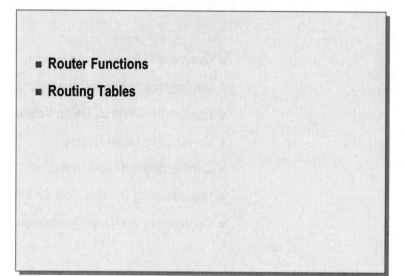

A network consists of a number of different devices such as hubs, bridges, switches, and routers. Routers allow you to scale your network and maintain bandwidth by segmenting network traffic. Routers determine where to forward packets based on routing tables. Routing tables enable routers to make decisions about forwarding traffic to the proper destination for efficient packet delivery. A thorough understanding of routers and routing tables will help you effectively configure routers for your network environment.

Router Functions

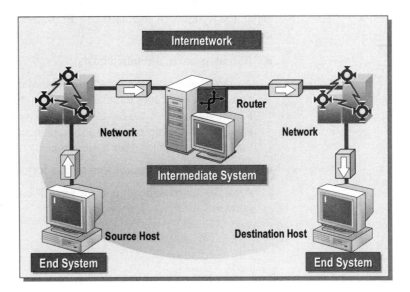

Routing is the process of forwarding packets between connected networks. Routing is part of the Internet Protocol (IP) and is used in combination with other network protocol services to provide forwarding capabilities between hosts that are located on separate network segments within a larger Transmission Control Protocol/Internet Protocol (TCP/IP)–based network. Each incoming or outgoing packet is called an IP *datagram* or a *packet*. An IP datagram contains two IP addresses: the source address of the sending host and the destination address of the receiving host.

Routing Terminology

The following terms are essential to an understanding of routing:

- *End systems.* Network devices without the ability to forward packets between portions of a network. End systems are also known as *hosts*.

- *Intermediate systems.* Network devices with the ability to forward packets between portions of a network. Bridges, switches, and routers are examples of intermediate systems.

- *Network.* A portion of the networking infrastructure that is bound by a network layer intermediate system and that is associated with the same network layer address.

- *Router.* A network layer intermediate system used to connect networks together based on a common network layer protocol.

- *Hardware router.* A router that performs routing as a dedicated function and has specific hardware that is designed and optimized for routing.

- *Software router.* A router that is not dedicated to performing routing but performs routing as one of multiple processes running on the router computer. Windows 2000 Routing and Remote Access is a service that performs routing as one of its multiple processes.

- *Internetwork.* At least two networks that are connected by using routers.

Purpose of Routing

IP routers provide the primary means of joining together two or more physically separated IP network segments. All IP routers share two essential characteristics:

- IP routers are multihomed hosts.

  A *multihomed* host is a network host that uses two or more network connection interfaces to connect to separate network segments. In addition, a multihomed host can have a single network adapter and multiple logical adapters; an example of a multihomed host would be a demand-dial VPN that connects offices over the Internet.

- IP routers provide packet forwarding for other TCP/IP hosts.

  An IP router must be able to forward IP-based communication between networks for other IP network hosts.

Routing Tables

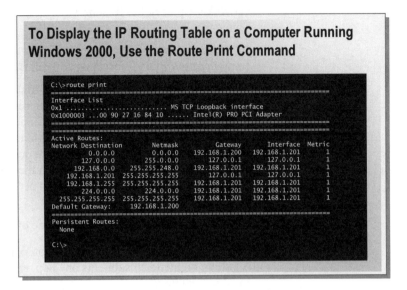

To Display the IP Routing Table on a Computer Running Windows 2000, Use the Route Print Command

```
C:\>route print
===========================================================================
Interface List
0x1 ......................... MS TCP Loopback interface
0x1000003 ...00 90 27 16 84 10 ...... Intel(R) PRO PCI Adapter
===========================================================================
===========================================================================
Active Routes:
Network Destination        Netmask          Gateway       Interface  Metric
          0.0.0.0          0.0.0.0    192.168.1.200   192.168.1.201       1
        127.0.0.0        255.0.0.0        127.0.0.1       127.0.0.1       1
      192.168.0.0    255.255.248.0    192.168.1.201   192.168.1.201       1
    192.168.1.201  255.255.255.255        127.0.0.1       127.0.0.1       1
    192.168.1.255  255.255.255.255    192.168.1.201   192.168.1.201       1
        224.0.0.0        224.0.0.0    192.168.1.201   192.168.1.201       1
  255.255.255.255  255.255.255.255    192.168.1.201   192.168.1.201       1
Default Gateway:       192.168.1.200
===========================================================================
Persistent Routes:
  None

C:\>
```

Routers forward packets between network segments based on rules that allow for efficient packet delivery. Routers use data stored in a routing table to determine the correct destination. The routing table data includes IP information about all of the segments to which the router is connected. The data also includes instructions on how to forward packets destined for other networks that are not directly connected to the router. Typically, a router contains a routing table entry for each network to which it connects. The entry identifies where the router should forward packets that are destined for a given network.

Displaying the IP Routing Table

Every computer that runs TCP/IP makes routing decisions that are controlled by the routing table. The routing table is built automatically, based on the current TCP/IP configuration of a computer.

To display the IP routing table on a computer that is running Windows 2000, type **route print** at a command prompt.

Examining Routing Table Entries

The following describes each of the columns displayed in the IP routing table:

- *Network destination*. Used along with the netmask to match the destination IP address. The network destination can range from 0.0.0.0 for the default route through 255.255.255.255 for a limited broadcast. A computer uses the default route if no other host or network route matches the destination address that is included in an IP datagram.

- *Netmask*. Applied to the destination IP address when matching to the value in the network destination. Netmask is also called a *subnet mask*. A subnet mask distinguishes network identifiers (IDs) and host IDs within an IP address.

- *Gateway.* Indicates the IP address that the local host uses to forward IP datagrams to other IP networks. A gateway is either the IP address of a local network adapter or the IP address of an IP router on the local network segment.

- *Interface.* Indicates the IP address of the network adapter that the local computer uses when it forwards an IP datagram on the network.

- *Metric.* Indicates the cost of a route. If multiple routes to the IP destination exist, the metric is used to decide which route is to be taken. The route with the lowest metric is the preferred route, and other routes are only used if the preferred route becomes unavailable. Metrics can indicate different ways of expressing a route preference. The measurement that is used for the metric depends on the routing protocol: When the routing protocol does not specify how a metric is defined, the administrator who configures the router chooses how the metric is defined.

A metric is commonly defined by using one of the following criteria:

- *Hop count.* Indicates the number of routers in the path to the destination. Anything on the local subnet is one hop, and each router crossed after that is an additional hop.

- *Delay.* Indicates a measure of time that is required for the packet to reach the network ID. Delay is used to indicate the speed of a path or a congested condition of a path; for example, local area network (LAN) links have a low delay, and wide area network (WAN) links have a high delay.

- *Throughput.* Indicates the effective amount of data that can be sent along the path per second.

- *Reliability.* A measure of the path constancy. Some types of links are more prone to link failures than others. For example, with WAN links, leased lines are more reliable than dial-up lines.

Default Routing Table Entries

The following are default routing table entries for a Windows 2000–based computer running TCP/IP. These IP addresses are reserved for use by TCP/IP. A Windows 2000–based router also contains, by default, entries for the network address for all local interfaces.

Network address	Description
0.0.0.0	All IP addresses for which no other routes have been defined, the *default route*
127.0.0.0	The local loopback address
224.0.0.0	IP multicast addresses
255.255.255.255	IP broadcast address

◆ Configuring Network Connections

- ■ **Configuring Network Connection Names**
- ■ **Configuring IP Settings for a Network Adapter**

Configuring a Windows 2000–based server as a router requires a number of steps. After you install networking hardware and configure the relevant drivers, you must configure the IP properties of the network adapter so that the router can communicate with the network. To manage a router with multiple network adapters more easily, you can rename each network adapter connection with a descriptive name.

Configuring Network Connection Names

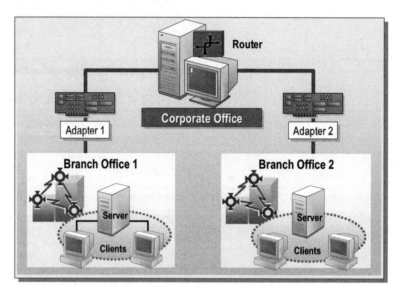

Typically, two or more network adapters are installed in a computer that performs routing. For each adapter, Windows 2000 displays a **local area connection** icon in the Network and Dial-up Connections folder. To eliminate confusion, you can rename each local area connection to reflect the network to which the adapter connects.

To rename a connection, open Network and Dial-up Connections in the Control Panel, right-click the connection that you want to rename, and then click **Rename**.

Configuring IP Settings for a Network Adapter

- **Configuring Settings for a Network Connected to the Internet**
- **Configuring Settings for a Private Network**
- **Verifying the Address Relationship**

In general, when adding a network adapter to a server, you assign a single IP address for each network connection. Each network adapter is uniquely identified by its physical, or media access control (MAC), address. Each network adapter displays in Network and Dial-up Connections as a **local area connection** icon. To match a network adapter to a network interface, you must match the physical address of the adapter to the connection. You can verify the physical address and interface name relationship by using the **ipconfig /all** command.

Configuring Settings for a Network Connected to the Internet

You must manually configure the Windows 2000–based router interfaces with an IP address. You configure the IP address through the properties of the TCP/IP protocol for the connection in Network and Dial-up Connections.

You configure the connection for a Windows 2000–based router with the following:

- *IP address*. Obtained from the address range that you received from the Internet service provider (ISP).

- *Subnet mask*. Obtained from the address range that you received from the ISP.

- *Domain Name System (DNS) server*. Obtained from the IP address that you received from the ISP. This server is required if your router forwards DNS queries to an ISP.

Configuring Settings for a Private Network

For private TCP/IP networks that are not directly or indirectly connected to the Internet, you can use any range of valid IP addresses.

For private TCP/IP networks that are indirectly connected to the Internet by using a network address translator (NAT) or an application layer gateway such as a proxy server, the Internet Assigned Numbers Authority (IANA) recommends that you use the private IP addresses shown in the following table.

Private Network ID	Subnet mask	Range of IP addresses
10.0.0.0	255.0.0.0	10.0.0.1–10.255.255.254
172.16.0.0	255.240.0.0	172.16.0.1–172.31.255.254
192.168.0.0	255.255.0.0	192.168.0.1–192.168.255.254

Important   Even though you can use any addressing scheme when configuring a network that is not connected to the Internet, it is highly recommended that you use private network addresses. Doing so will prevent address conflicts if you ever decide to connect your network to the Internet by indirect means, such as a proxy server.

Verifying the Address Relationship

You can verify the address relationship between the network adapter and the IP settings by using the Ipconfig utility. The Ipconfig utility displays all of the current TCP/IP configuration values, including the physical address and IP address, for the connection. To obtain detailed results, type **ipconfig /all** at a command prompt.

Enabling Routing by Using Routing and Remote Access

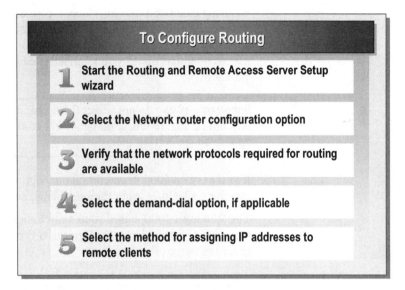

For your Windows 2000–based server to function as a network router, you must enable Routing and Remote Access. Understanding how to configure a network router by using Routing and Remote Access lets you to create versatile connections between branch offices and a corporate network.

Note If the server is a member of an Active Directory™ directory service domain in Windows 2000 and you enable demand-dial routing, you must add the computer account of the server to the RAS and IAS Servers security group before you can use demand-dial routing. When a member of the Domain Admins group enables the Routing and Remote Access service, Windows 2000 adds the server to this group automatically.

Configuring a Windows 2000 Server for Routing

You configure a Windows 2000–based server as a network router by using the Routing and Remote Access Server Setup wizard.

To configure a Windows 2000–based server for routing, open Routing and Remote Access from the Administrative Tools menu, then:

1. In the console tree, right-click *server* (where *server* is the name of your computer), click **Configure and Enable Routing and Remote Access**, and then click **Next** to start the Routing and Remote Access Server Setup wizard.

2. On the **Common Configurations** page, click **Network router**, and then click **Next**.

3. On the **Routed Protocols** page, verify that the network protocols required for routing are available, and then click **Next**.

   The Windows 2000–based router can route IP, Internetwork Packet Exchange (IPX), and AppleTalk traffic.

4. On the **Demand-Dial Connections** page, click **Yes** if you want to use demand-dial connections, and then click **Next**.

   By using a demand-dial interface, a connection becomes active only when data is sent to the remote site. When no data has been sent over the link for a specified amount of time, the link is disconnected. Demand-dial connections use existing dial-up telephone lines instead of leased lines for low-traffic situations.

   Important   If you do not select the demand-dial option in the wizard, you will not be able to create demand-dial connections, although the option will appear on the **Action** menu.

   ---

5. If you have enabled demand-dial connections, click the method for assigning IP addresses to remote clients, and then click **Finish**.

   The Windows 2000–based router can assign IP addresses automatically by using the Dynamic Host Configuration Protocol (DHCP), or from a specified range of addresses.

Configuring a Remote Access Server for Routing

If you have already used Routing and Remote Access to configure remote access functionality, you still need to enable routing for your server.

To enable routing on a remote access server:

1. Open Routing and Remote Access.

2. In the console tree, right-click click *server* (where *server* is the name of your computer), and then click **Properties**.

3. On the **General** tab, select the **Router** check box, click **Local area network (LAN) routing only** or **LAN and demand-dial routing**, and then click **OK**.

◆ Configuring Static Routes

- **Examining a Static Routing Table**
- **Adding a Static Route**

After you configure a Windows 2000–based server as a router, the router includes a number of routing table entries by default. These entries are built from LAN interfaces that are already available on that protocol. For your router to successfully forward packets to networks to which it is not directly connected, you need to create routing table entries for these networks. In a small network, you can add these entries manually by configuring static routes in the routing table of your router.

Examining a Static Routing Table

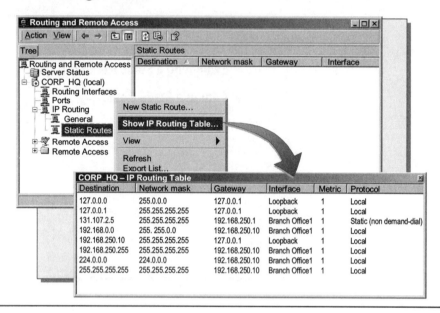

Static routing tables are built and updated manually. If a route changes, the network administrator must manually update the routing tables. Static routes can work well for small internetworks. However, static routes do not scale well because they must be administered manually.

Viewing Static Routing Tables

To view static routing tables:

1. Open Routing and Remote Access.

2. In the console tree, expand *server* (where *server* is the name of your computer), and then expand **IP Routing**.

3. Right-click **Static Routes**, and then click **Show IP routing**.

The IP routing table contains information in the following columns:

- *Destination*. Indicates the destination host, subnet address, network address, or default route. The destination for a default route is 0.0.0.0.

- *Network mask*. Used in conjunction with the destination to determine when a route is used. A mask of 255.255.255.255 means that only an exact match of the destination uses this route. A mask of 0.0.0.0 means that any destination can use this route.

  For example, a destination of 172.16.8.0 has a network mask of 255.255.248.0. This network mask means that the first two octets must match exactly, the first five bits of the third octet must match (248=11111000), and the last octet does not matter. The third octet of 172.16.8.0 (that is, 8) equals **00001**000 in binary. Without changing the first five bits (the masked-off portion shown in **bold**), you can go up to 15, or **00001**111 in binary. So a route with a destination of 172.16.8.0 and a mask of 255.255.248.0 applies to all packets destined for 172.16.**8**.0 through 172.16.**15**.255.

- *Gateway*. Indicates the IP address of the next router where a packet needs to be sent. On a LAN link, the gateway must be directly reachable by the router by using the interface indicated in the **Interface** column. For a demand-dial interface, the gateway address is not configurable.

- *Interface*. Indicates the LAN or demand-dial interface that is to be used to send the packet.

- *Metric*. Indicates the relative cost of using the route to reach the destination. For example, the metric hops indicate the number of routers to cross to reach the destination.

- *Protocol*. Indicates how the route was learned. If the **Protocol** column lists anything other than **Local**, an administrator manually configured the routes or the router is receiving routes from other routers.

Note For more information about IP Addressing, see appendix B, "IP Addressing Basics," under **Appendices** on the Web page on the Student Materials compact disc.

Adding a Static Route

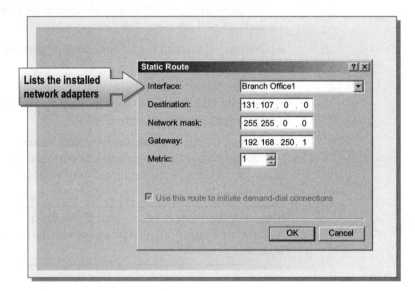

For efficient routing, routers must contain route information for other networks. On an internetwork, it is important to maintain routing tables so that traffic follows the best path and adjusts for out-of-service routers and routes.

Use the **Static Route** dialog box to add static IP routes to the routing table. When your configuration is complete, use the **ping** and **tracert** commands to test connectivity between host computers so that all routing paths are checked.

To add static IP routes to the routing table:

1. Open Routing and Remote Access.

2. In the console tree, expand *server* (where *server* is the name of your computer), expand **IP Routing**, right-click **Static Routes**, and then click **Add Static Route**.

3. Specify the following parameters in the **Static Route** dialog box, and then click **OK** to add the route to the routing table.

Parameter	Description
Interface	The interface that is used to send the packet when using this route.
Destination	The destination network ID, which can be a class-based network ID, a subnetted network ID, a supernetted network ID, or a host ID.
Network mask	The corresponding subnet mask, which must encompass all of the bits in the destination network ID. The network ID cannot be more specific than the subnet mask. For host-specific routes, the network mask is 255.255.255.255.
Gateway	The IP address of the router to which packets for this destination are to be forwarded.
Metric	The "cost" of using this route. The cost can reflect a hop count or a preference for using this route. This value is an integer.

Lab A: Configuring Windows 2000 As a Static Router

Objectives

After completing this lab, you will be able to:

■ Configure Windows 2000 as a router.

■ Add static routes to a Windows 2000–based computer that is configured as a router.

Lab Setup

To complete this lab, you need the following:

■ A computer running Windows 2000 Advanced Server that is configured as a domain controller in native mode

■ A lab partner with a similarly configured computer

■ IP addresses for the two network adapters in your computer

■ IP addresses for the two network adapters in your partner's computer

If you are unsure about any of these values, please ask your instructor.

Adapter	Record IP address here
Your Classroom adapter	
Your PartnerNet adapter	
Your partner's Classroom adapter	
Your partner's PartnerNet adapter	

Important The lab does not reflect the real-world environment. It is recommended that you always use complex passwords for any administrator accounts, and never create accounts without a password.

Important Outside of the classroom environment, it is strongly advised that you use the most recent software updates that are necessary. Because this is a classroom environment, we may use software that does not include the latest updates.

Scenario

Your company is expanding the number of branch offices that are connected to the head-office network, and you are responsible for configuring Windows 2000 as a static router to enable this connectivity.

Estimated time to complete this lab: 30 minutes

Exercise 1
Configuring a Computer Running Windows 2000 As a Static Router

Scenario

Your organization is using a computer running Windows 2000 as a branch-office router for your network, and you need to configure it with a static route to enable routing to take place.

Goal

In this exercise, you will work with your partner to configure a router for your network.

Tasks	Detailed Steps
🛑 **Important:** Perform the following steps only on the computer with the lower student number.	
1. Disable the Classroom network adapter. Set the default gateway for the network adapter PartnerNet to be the IP address of your partner's PartnerNet adapter.	a. Log on as administrator@*domain*.nwtraders.msft (where *domain* is the name of your domain) with a password of **password**. b. Right-click **My Network Places**, and then click **Properties**. c. In Network and Dial-up Connections, right-click **Classroom**, and then click **Disable**. d. Right-click **PartnerNet**, and then click **Properties**. e. In the PartnerNet Properties dialog box, click Internet Protocol (TCP/IP), and then click Properties. f. In the **Default gateway** box, type the IP address of your partner's PartnerNet adapter, and then click **OK**. g. Click **OK** to close the **PartnerNet Properties** dialog box. h. Close Network and Dial-up Connections.
🛑 **Important:** Perform the following steps only on the computer with the higher student number.	
2. Configure Routing and Remote Access to function as a router.	a. Log on as administrator@*domain*.nwtraders.msft with a password of **password**. b. Open Routing and Remote Access from the **Administrative Tools** menu. c. In the console tree, right-click *server* (where *server* is the name of your computer), and then click **Configure and Enable Routing and Remote Access**. d. In the Routing and Remote Access Server Setup wizard, click **Next**. e. On the **Common Configurations** page, click **Network router**, and then click **Next**. f. On the **Routed Protocols** page, under **Protocols**, verify that **TCP/IP** displays, and then click **Next**.

(continued)

Tasks	Detailed Steps
2. *(continued)*	g. On the Demand-Dial Connections page, verify that No is selected, and then click Next. h. Click Finish to close the Routing and Remote Access Server Setup wizard. 💻 *The Routing and Remote Access service will now start.* i. Close Routing and Remote Access.
✋ Perform the following procedures on both student computers.	
3. Ping the instructor computer.	a. At a command prompt, type **ping 192.168.*z*.200** (where *z* is the number assigned to your classroom). 💻 *The **ping** should be successful from the student computer with the higher student number (the router), but unsuccessful from the student computer with the lower student number (the computer on the remote network).*
❓ Why didn't the **ping** work from the student computer on the remote network?	
	_____ _____ _____
❓ Would adding a default gateway to the instructor computer help solve this problem? Why or why not?	
	_____ _____ _____
3. *(continued*	b. Minimize the command prompt window.
✋ **Important:** Perform the following procedures only on the computer with the higher student number.	

(*continued*)

Tasks	Detailed Steps
4. Add a static route on the instructor computer for the network between your computer and your partner's computer. Use the following information to create the routing entry. Gateway: IP address of the PartnerNet adapter on the computer with the higher student number.	a. Click **Start**, point to **Programs**, point to **Administrative Tools**, right-click **Routing and Remote Access**, and then click **Run as**. b. In the **Run As Other User** dialog box, in the **User name** box, type **administrator@nwtraders.msft** c. In the **Password** box, type **password** d. Delete the contents of the **Domain** box, and then click **OK**. e. In the console tree, right-click **Routing and Remote Access**, and then click **Add Server**. f. In the **Add Server** box, click **The following computer**, type **London** and then click **OK**. g. In the console tree, expand **London**, expand **IP Routing**, and then click **Static Routes**. h. Right-click **Static Routes**, and then click **New Static Route**. i. In the **Static Route** dialog box, in the **Interface** box, verify that **Classroom** is selected. j. In the **Destination** box, type the first three octets of your PartnerNet connection, and then use 0 for the last octet. k. In the **Network mask** box, type **255.255.255.0** l. In the **Gateway** box, type **192.168.*z.x*** (where *z* is the number assigned to your classroom and *x* is your student number). m. Click **OK** to close the **Static Route** dialog box. n. In the console tree, right-click **London**, and then click **Delete**. o. Close Routing and Remote Access.
✋ Perform the following procedures on both student computers.	
5. Ping the instructor computer.	a. At a command prompt, type **ping 192.168.*z*.200** 🖥️ *The **ping** should be successful from both student computers.* b. Close the command prompt window.
6. Open Routing and Remote Access and connect to the computer with the higher student number. Examine the routing table.	a. Open Routing and Remote Access from the **Administrative Tools** menu. b. In the console tree, right-click **Routing and Remote Access**, and then click **Add Server**. c. In the **Add Server** box, click **The following computer**, type *partner_server* (where *partner_server* is the name of your partner's computer), and then click **OK**. d. In the console tree, expand *partner_server*, expand **IP Routing**, and then click **Static Routes**. e. Right-click **Static Routes**, and then click **Show IP Routing Table**. f. Examine all of the entries in the routing table.

(continued)

Tasks	Detailed Steps
❓	Your network has other internal partnernet networks connected to it. If you want to enable IP communication with the other networks, what static entries do you need to add to which routers? _____ _____
6. *(continued)*	g. Close the *server* - **IP Routing Table** window, and then close Routing and Remote Access.
✋ Perform the following procedure on both student computers.	
7. Close any open windows, and then log off.	a. Close any open windows, and then log off.

◆ Configuring a Routing Interface

- **Routing Interfaces in Routing and Remote Access**
- **Packet Filtering**
- **Configuring Filters on an IP Routing Interface**
- **Configuring Filter Settings on an IP Routing Interface**

When you enable network routing for your server, by default Routing and Remote Access adds all of the enabled network adapters that are installed as routing interfaces. The Windows 2000–based router uses the routing interfaces to forward packets to the network.

You can configure filters to allow or disallow the forwarding of specific types of IP traffic. Filters enable a network administrator to define what IP traffic is allowed to cross the router.

Routing Interfaces in Routing and Remote Access

- **LAN Interfaces**
- **Demand-Dial Interfaces**
- **IP-in-IP Tunnel Interfaces**

A routing interface is a physical or logical interface over which IP packets are forwarded. The Windows 2000–based router uses a routing interface to forward IP, IPX, or AppleTalk packets. To view installed and configured routing interfaces, in Routing and Remote Access, in the console tree, click **Routing Interfaces**.

There are three types of routing interfaces:

- *LAN interfaces*. Represent a local area connection that uses LAN technology such as Ethernet or Token Ring. A LAN interface is represented as an installed network adapter. LAN interfaces are always active and typically do not require an authentication process to become active.

- *Demand-dial interfaces*. Represent a point-to-point connection. The point-to-point connection is based on either a physical connection, such as two routers that use modems to connect over an analog telephone line, or a logical connection, such as two routers that use the Internet to connect over a VPN. Demand-dial connections are either *on-demand* (established only when needed) or *persistent* (established and then remain in a connected state). Demand-dial interfaces typically require an authentication process to become connected.

- *IP-in-IP tunnel interfaces*. Represent a tunneled point-to-point connection. IP-in-IP tunnel interfaces do not require an authentication process to become connected. A typical use for IP-in-IP interfaces is the forwarding of IP multicast traffic from one area of the intranet to another area of the intranet, across a portion of the intranet that does not support multicast forwarding or routing.

Packet Filtering

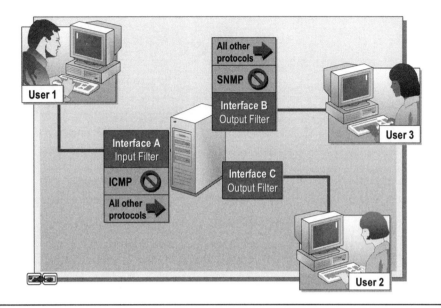

An IP router can provide the ability to allow or disallow the forwarding of specific types of IP traffic. This capability, called *IP packet filtering*, provides a way for the network administrator to precisely define what IP traffic is allowed to cross the router. IP packet filtering becomes important when you connect corporate intranets to public networks such as the Internet.

For example, user 1 attempts to ping user 2's computer. Because there is an input filter on interface A that is configured to block incoming Internet Control Message Protocol (ICMP) traffic, the ICMP packet is discarded at the router. When user 1 tries to communicate with user 2 by using other protocols, those packets are forwarded unmodified. By blocking ICMP traffic with an input filter, a network administrator can prevent users from causing unnecessary traffic to pass across the router.

When user 1 attempts to use Simple Network Management Protocol (SNMP) to manage user 3's computer, the attempt is unsuccessful because the router has an output filter on interface B that is configured to transmit all protocols except SNMP.

An output filter can also be configured to prevent SNMP traffic from entering certain networks. For example, if an organization has computers that are in an insecure location, such as a lab network, an administrator can configure a routing filter to block SNMP from that network. Blocking SNMP traffic prevents a user in that network from performing management functions on computers that are connected to the rest of the network.

Configuring Filters on an IP Routing Interface

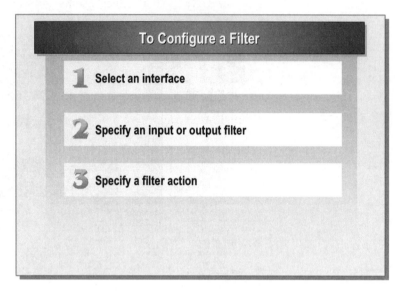

A network administrator can configure input and output filters on key fields in the IP, TCP, User Datagram Protocol (UDP), and ICMP headers in each interface.

To configure IP packet filtering in Routing and Remote Access, you create filters to allow or disallow certain types of traffic on a routing interface. An IP filter triggers a decision about what to do with the packet that is based on a match with the source, destination, and type of IP traffic. Configuring a filter involves selecting an interface, specifying an input or output filter, and specifying a filter action.

Selecting an Interface

Filters are defined on interfaces that you manage in Routing and Remote Access.

To select an interface:

1. Open Routing and Remote Access.

2. In the console tree, expand *server* (where *server* is the name of your computer), and then click **General**.

3. In the details pane, right-click the interface on which you want to add a filter, and then click **Properties**.

Specifying an Input or Output Filter

You can apply filters to either incoming or outgoing packets on an interface.

To specify an input or output filter, on the **General** tab, click either **Input Filters** or **Output Filters**.

Specifying a Filter Action

Filters are configured on an exception basis. You can configure the filter action to either receive all traffic except that which is specified, or drop all traffic except that which is specified. For example, you can configure a filter to allow all traffic except Telnet traffic (TCP port 23). Or, you can set up filters on a dedicated Web server to process only Web-based TCP traffic (TCP port 80) and HTTPS traffic (TCP port 443).

To specify a filter action, select one of the following options in the **IP Configuration** dialog box. You can select a filter action only after you have defined at least one filter.

- **Receive all packets except those that meet the criteria below**. Forwards all packets unless you specify to block them, which protects a network against specific threats. Use this setting when a high level of security is not required.

- **Drop all packets except those that meet the criteria below**. Forwards only packets that match specific criteria. Use this setting when a high level of security is required.

Configuring Filter Settings on an IP Routing Interface

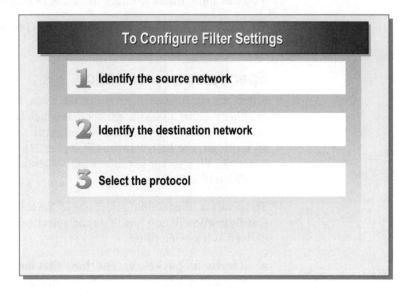

Configuring filter settings generally requires a thorough understanding of the protocols involved. After adding a filter, test your settings to make sure that the filters perform the action that you want and do not have any unintended side effects.

To add a filter, configure the following settings in the **Add IP Filter** or **Edit IP Filter** dialog boxes. Depending on the intended action, you only need to define some of these settings when you create a filter.

1. Identify the source network:

   - **IP Address**. Type the source IP network ID or a source IP address.

   - **Subnet Mask**. Type the subnet mask corresponding to the source network ID, or type 255.255.255.255 for a source IP address. The subnet mask bits must encompass all of the bits being used in the IP Address field. The IP address cannot be more specific than the subnet mask.

2. Identify the destination network:

   - **IP Address**. Type the destination IP network ID or a destination IP address.

   - **Subnet Mask**. Type the subnet mask corresponding to the destination network ID, or type 255.255.255.255 for a destination IP address. The subnet mask bits must encompass all of the bits being used in the IP Address field. The IP address cannot be more specific than the subnet mask.

3. Select the protocol:

- **TCP**. Select this option to specify a source TCP port and a destination TCP port. You can specify one or both. If you do not specify a port, the setting defaults to 0, meaning any port.

- **TCP (Established)**. Select this option to only include TCP packets that are part of a TCP connection that has been previously established.

- **UDP**. Select this option to specify a source UDP port and a destination UDP port. You can specify one or both. If you do not specify a port, the setting defaults to 0, meaning any port.

- **ICMP**. Select this option to specify ICMP code and an ICMP type. You can specify one or both. If you do not specify a port, the setting defaults to 255, meaning any code or any type.

- **Any**. Select this option to make *any* IP protocol value applicable.

- **Other**. Select this option to specify any IP protocol. You must specify the protocol by number.

    The file *systemroot*\system32\drivers\etc\protocol contains a list of protocols compatible with Windows 2000 and the number for each protocol. You can enable Windows 2000 to recognize additional protocols by editing this file.

Note To identify the ports that an application uses, see the documentation for that application. For a list of protocol numbers and well-known ports, see RFC 1700 under **Additional Reading** on the Student Materials compact disc. For a list of ports that Windows 2000 uses, see appendix C, "Port Assignments for Commonly Used Services,"under **Appendices** on the Web page on the Student Materials compact disc.

◆ Implementing Demand-Dial Routing

- Overview of Demand-Dial Routing

- Configuring Demand-Dial Connections

- Configuring IP Addressing for Inbound Demand-Dial Connections

- Restricting Demand-Dial Connections

- Configuring Static Routes for a Demand-Dial Interface

Some locations, such as branch offices, may only need occasional network connectivity to the main corporate network. To accommodate this need, you can configure a demand-dial connection that, when necessary, can use any remote access connection to connect to the main corporate network.

Overview of Demand-Dial Routing

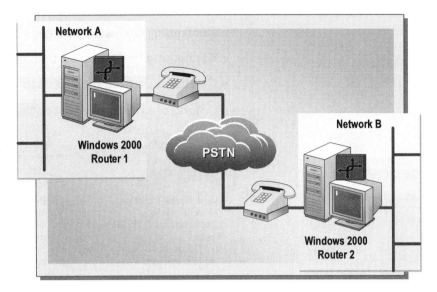

Routing and Remote Access can route packets across other communications networks, such as the public switched telephone network (PSTN). By using a demand-dial interface, a Windows 2000–based router can initiate a connection to a remote site when the router receives the packet to be routed. The connection is initiated only when data is sent to or from a remote site. When no data has been sent over the link for a specified amount of time, the link is disconnected. By making a demand-dial connection, you can use existing dial-up telephone lines, instead of leased lines, for low-traffic situations. Demand-dial routing can significantly reduce your connection costs.

The Windows 2000–based router includes support for:

- *Demand-dial filters*, which are used to specify the type of traffic that enables the router to establish the connection.

Note Demand-dial filters are separate from IP packet filters, which you configure to specify what traffic is allowed into and out of an interface after the connection is made.

- *Dial-out hours*, which are used to specify the hours that a router is allowed to dial out to make demand-dial connections.

Configuring Demand-Dial Connections

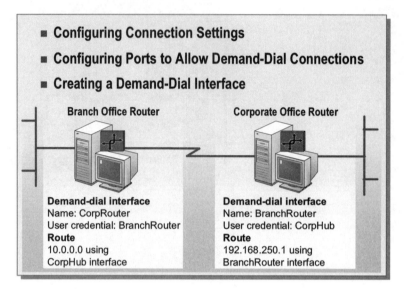

To implement a two-way, initiated demand-dial routing connection from a branch-office router to a corporate-office router, you must configure both the branch-office router and the corporate-office router to initiate and receive demand-dial connections.

To configure a corporate-office or branch-office router to support two-way initiated demand-dial connections:

- Configure connection settings to the corporate-office intranet.
- Configure ports to allow demand-dial connections.
- Configure demand-dial interfaces.

Configuring Connection Settings

After you install networking hardware and configure the relevant drivers, configure each of the dial-up adapters with:

- An IP address and a subnet mask that are valid for the network segment that connects the routers.
- The DNS and Windows Internet Name Service (WINS) servers that provide naming services for the corporate intranet.

Configuring Ports to Allow Demand-Dial Connections

For each dial-up port, you need to enable demand-dial connections in Routing and Remote Access.

To configure ports for demand-dial connections:

1. Open Routing and Remote Access.

2. In the console tree, expand *server* (where *server* is the name of your computer), right-click **Ports**, and then click **Properties**.

3. In the **Ports Properties** dialog box, click a device, and then click **Configure**.

Tip　If **Ports** does not appear in the console tree, you must first enable demand-dial routing in the **Properties** dialog box for your computer.

---

4. In the **Configure Device** dialog box for the device, select the **Demand-dial routing connections (inbound and outbound)** check box if necessary, and then click **OK** twice.

Creating a Demand-Dial Interface

You create a demand-dial interface by using the Demand-Dial Interface wizard in Routing and Remote Access.

To create a demand-dial interface:

1. Open Routing and Remote Access.

2. In the console tree, right-click **Routing Interface**, and then click **New Demand-dial Interface**.

3. In the Demand Dial Interface wizard, provide the following:

   - **Interface name**. Specify a name for the interface that represents the connection; for example, **CorpHub**.

   - **Connection type**. Click **Connect using a modem, ISDN adapter, or other physical device**.

   - **Select a device**. Click the device being used to create the connection. This page only appears when you have more that one device installed that is capable of making dial-up connections.

   - **Phone number or address**. Type the telephone number of the remote router. To specify alternate telephone numbers that Routing and Remote Access will dial when an initial connection attempt is unsuccessful, click **Alternates**, and then type additional telephone numbers.

- **Protocols and security**. Select the protocols to route and select the **Add a user account so a remote router can dial in** check box.

- **Dial-in credentials**. Type the user credentials for authenticating the local router to the remote router. The name of the account is the same as the demand-dial **Interface name**; for example, **CorpHub**.

- **Dial-out credentials**. Type the user credentials for authenticating the remote router to the local router. For example, for the branch-office router, the name of the account is **BranchRouter**.

Important   For two-way initiated demand-dial routing to work properly, the **Dial-out credentials** of the calling router must match the **Interface name** of the demand-dial interface on both sides of the connection.

Configuring IP Addressing for Inbound Demand-Dial Connections

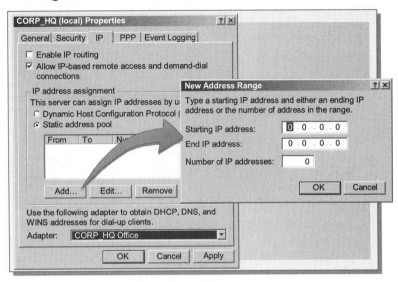

Each remote computer that connects to a remote access server running Windows 2000 on a TCP/IP network is automatically provided an IP address. The remote access server obtains the IP address that is allocated to the remote access client either from a DHCP server or from a static range of IP addresses that the Administrator assigns to the remote access server.

Using Static IP Address Pools

When the remote access server is configured to use a static pool of addresses, each range of IP addresses can be entered as either:

- A starting IP address and an ending IP address for the range

    -or-

- A starting IP address and the total number of IP addresses in the range

To configure IP address assignment for inbound demand-dial connections:

1. Open Routing and Remote Access.

2. In the console tree, right-click *server* (where *server* is the name of your computer), and then click **Properties**.

3. Click the **IP** tab, and then click **Static address pool**.

4. Click **Add**, and then configure the ranges of IP addresses that are dynamically allocated to demand-dial routers.

If the static IP address pool consists of ranges of IP addresses that are a subset of the range of IP addresses for the network to which the remote access server is attached, ensure that the ranges of IP addresses in the remote access IP address pool are not assigned to other hosts either statically or through DHCP.

Restricting Demand-Dial Connections

- **Configuring Demand-Dial Filtering**
- **Configuring Dial-Out Hours**

To prevent the calling router from making unnecessary on-demand dial-up connections, you can restrict connection activity by configuring demand-dial filtering and dial-out hours.

Configuring Demand-Dial Filtering

You can set demand-dial filters to permit or deny the type of IP traffic that can create a connection. For example, although ICMP traffic does not use much network bandwidth, a single ping can cause an expensive demand-dial connection to be connected. You can prevent ICMP traffic from initiating a demand-dial connection by creating a demand-dial filter to pass all traffic except ICMP.

To configure demand-dial filtering:

1. Open Routing and Remote Access.

2. In the console tree, expand *server* (where *server* is the name of your computer), and then click **Routing Interfaces**.

3. In the details pane, right-click the demand-dial interface that you want to configure, and then click **Set IP Demand dial Filters**.

4. In the **Set Demand-Dial Filters** dialog box, click one of the following options below **Initiate connection**. You can click an option only after you have defined at least one filter:

   - **Only for the following traffic**. This setting is used for connecting to a few networks or selected protocols. Use this setting when the dial-up connection is expensive and the connection is only used occasionally.

   - **For all traffic except**. This setting is used for allowing most traffic to initiate a dial-up connection, except for specific traffic. Use this setting to allow all packets to initiate the connection, with only a few specific exceptions.

5. Click **Add**.

6. In the **Add IP Filter** dialog box, specify the IP address, subnet mask, and protocol for the source and destination network.

7. Click **OK** to accept the changes, and then close all open dialog boxes.

   Although demand-dial rules perform a different role from routing filters, they both use the same format.

Important   To prevent the demand-dial connection from being established for traffic that the IP packet filters discard, configure the same set of filters for demand dialing that you configured for IP packet filtering.

Configuring Dial-Out Hours

You can set dial-out hours to permit or deny a day or time for creating a connection. For example, you can configure a demand-dial connection that is only to be used during off-peak hours.

To configure dial-out hours:

1. Open Routing and Remote Access.

2. In the console tree, expand *server* (where *server* is the name of your computer), and then click **Routing Interfaces**.

3. In the details pane, right-click the demand-dial interface that you want to configure, and then click **Dial-out Hours**.

4. In the **Dial-out Hours** dialog box, click either **Permitted** or **Denied**, click the appropriate day and time boxes, and then click **OK**.

Configuring Static Routes for a Demand-Dial Interface

- **Adding Static Routes**
- **Testing Static Routes**
  - Verifying the connection status
  - Using command-line utilities

For two-way communication to occur across a demand-dial link, you must establish static routes on both sides of the link. On each side of the link, you must create static routes for all networks to which you connect by using the demand-dial link. After configuring demand-dial connections, add static routes for demand-dial connections so that the routers can initiate the connection. After configuring the static routes, use the **ping** or **tracert** command to test the demand-dial connection.

Adding Static Routes

To add a static route:

1. Open Routing and Remote Access.

2. In the console tree, expand *server* (where *server* is the name of your computer), and then click **Static Routes**.

3. Right-click **Static Routes**, and then click **New Static route**.

4. In the **Static Route** dialog box, select the interface for the demand-dial connection, and then enter the destination, network mask, gateway, and metric.

Note   The gateway setting is unavailable for a demand-dial interface.

Testing Static Routes

After you configure static routes, you can send packets across the demand-dial interface to test the demand-dial connection.

Verifying the Connection Status

Before testing the connection, ensure that the demand-dial connection state is disconnected. To verify the status of a connection, in the console tree, click **Routing Interface**, and then in the details pane, view the **Connection Status** column for the demand-dial interface.

Using Command-Line Utilities

Use either the **ping** or **tracert** command to send ICMP packets across the demand-dial interface. With the **ping** command, use the **–t** option to ping the specified host continuously. If you do not use **–t**, the **ping** command only sends four packets and then stops. This is typically not long enough for the router to establish a connection and receive results.

To use **ping** to test a static route, type **ping –t** *IP_address* (where *IP_address* is the IP address of a host on the network to which you have configured a route).

To use **tracert** to test a static route, type **tracert** *IP_address* (where *IP_address* is the IP address of a host on the network to which you have configured a route).

Note   When using a utility to test a connection for the first time, the results are unsuccessful because the demand-dial interface is not active. However, after sending the first packet, the interface is activated. After the connection has been established, subsequent use of the testing utility should be successful.

◆ Configuring the Routing Information Protocol

- **Routing Protocols**
- **RIP Operation**
- **Adding the RIP Protocol**
- **Adding an Interface to Support RIP**
- **Configuring a RIP Interface**

After you configure your router to route packets between networks, you need a way to dynamically update the routing table if a change occurs on the network. On larger networks, it is not possible to configure all routing tables manually by changing static routes each time that a change occurs.

You can use routing protocols, such as the Routing Information Protocol (RIP), to automatically manage the routing table changes that become necessary because of network changes. RIP dynamically builds routing tables by announcing the contents of its routing table to its configured interfaces. Routers connected to those interfaces receive these announcements and use them to build the appropriate routing tables. Those routers then make announcements to build the routing tables for all routers in your network. Collectively, the RIP process prevents the management of the routing tables from becoming an administrative burden.

Routing Protocols

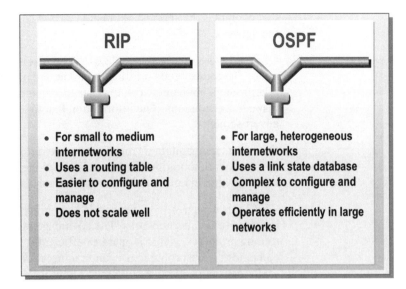

Routers use routing protocols to exchange information between routers to propagate network address and connection information. The two most common IP routing protocols that are used on intranets are RIP and Open Shortest Path First (OSPF).

RIP

RIP is designed for exchanging routing information within a small- to medium-sized internetwork. A RIP router maintains a routing table and periodically sends announcements to inform other RIP routers on the network about which networks it can reach and which it can no longer reach. RIP version 1 uses IP broadcast packets for its announcements, whereas RIP version 2 uses IP multicast packets for its announcements.

Compared with other protocols, RIP is simple to configure and deploy. However, as networks grow larger in size, the periodic announcements by each RIP router can cause excessive traffic on the network. RIP is typically used in networks with up to 50 servers.

Note   RIP is also the name of a similar but separate routing protocol for IPX networks.

OSPF

OSPF is a link-state protocol based on the Shortest Path First (SPF) algorithm that computes the shortest path between one source node and the other nodes in the network.

OSPF allows a router to calculate the shortest path for sending packets to each node. The router sends information about the nodes to which it is linked to other routers on the network in order to accumulate link-state information and make its calculations. The information that the router sends is called link-state advertisements.

OSPF routers maintain a "map" of the network that is updated after any change in the network topology. This map is called the link-state database. OSPF routers maintain both a link-state database and a routing table.

OSPF was designed in response to the inability of RIP to serve large, heterogeneous internetworks. The advantage of OSPF, compared with other routing protocols, is that it operates efficiently in large networks because it computes the best route to use, and requires fewer status messages. Unlike RIP, OSPF does not advertise all known routes to other routers, but only changes to its routes. The disadvantage of OSPF is its complexity: It is harder to configure and requires more management time than RIP.

Note   For more information about RIP, RIP version 2, and OSPF version 2, see RFC 1058, RFC 2328, and RFC 2453 under **Additional Reading** on the Student Materials compact disc.

RIP Operation

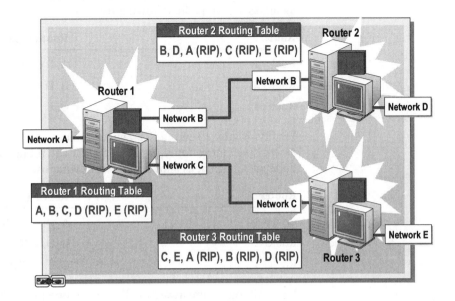

A router that uses RIP shares routing table information with the other routers in a network by announcing the contents of its routing table to all of its interfaces, and by receiving the same type of announcements from other routers. By using RIP, a router is constantly updating its routing table, until all networks are represented in a router's routing table.

For example, all routers begin with a default routing table that contains a routing entry for all of the networks to which the router is directly connected, as shown in the following list.

Router	Routing table entries
Router 1	A, B, C
Router 2	B, D
Router 3	C, E

Then, Router 2 sends a RIP announcement on all network interfaces, advertising that it has entries for networks B and D. The routing tables of the routers are updated, as shown in the following list.

Router	Routing table entries
Router 1	A, B, C, D (RIP)
Router 2	B, D
Router 3	C, E

Next, Router 3 sends a RIP announcement on all network interfaces, advertising that it has entries for C and E. The routing tables of the routers are updated again, as shown in the following list.

Router	Routing table entries
Router 1	A, B, C, D (RIP), E (RIP)
Router 2	B, D
Router 3	C, E

Finally, Router 1 sends a RIP announcement on all network interfaces, advertising entries for A, B, C, D, and E. The routing tables of the routers are updated yet again, as shown in the following list.

Router	Routing table entries
Router 1	A, B, C, D (RIP), E (RIP)
Router 2	B, D, A (RIP), C (RIP), E (RIP)
Router 3	C, E, A (RIP), B (RIP), D (RIP)

Now, all routers are aware of all of the networks to which they are connected. In RIP version 1, this announcement is always a broadcast. In RIP version 2, routers can instead use multicasts for these announcements, which reduces broadcast load on the network.

Adding the RIP Protocol

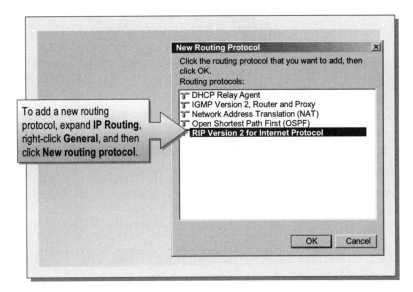

You use Routing and Remote Access to add the RIP protocol.

To add RIP for IP:

1. Open Routing and Remote Access.

2. In the console tree, expand *server* (where *server* is the name of your computer), expand **IP Routing**, right-click **General**, and then click **New routing protocol**.

3. From the list of routing protocols, click **RIP version 2 for Internet Protocol**, and then click **OK**.

Adding an Interface to Support RIP

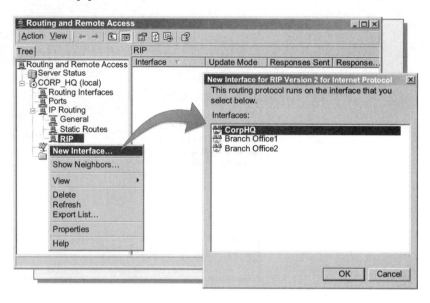

After adding the RIP protocol, you must add an interface that supports RIP from the list of interfaces that RIP uses on your computer. By default, interfaces do not support RIP until you add them.

To add an interface that supports RIP:

1. Open Routing and Remote Access.

2. Expand *server* (where *server* is the name of your computer), expand **IP Routing**, and then click **RIP**.

3. Right-click **RIP**, and then click **New Interface**.

4. In the **New Interface for RIP Version 2 for Internet Protocol** dialog box, click the interface that you want to add, and then click **OK**.

   Routing and Remote Access prompts you to configure RIP for the interface.

Configuring a RIP Interface

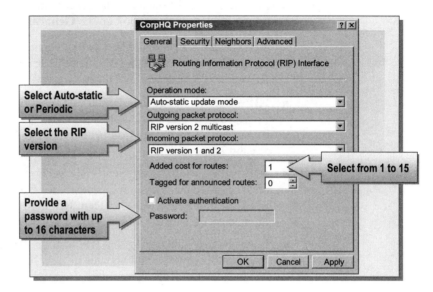

After adding an interface that supports RIP, you must configure settings for the update modes, versions, costs, and authentication.

Routing and Remote Access prompts you to configure RIP when you add an interface to RIP. You can also configure an interface that has been previously added.

To configure an interface for RIP:

1. Open Routing and Remote Access.

2. In the console tree, expand *server* (where *server* is the name of your computer), expand **IP Routing**, and then click **RIP**.

3. In the details pane, right-click the interface that you want to configure for RIP, and then click **Properties**.

Configuring Operation Mode

A RIP router periodically sends announcements that contain all of its routing table entries to inform other local RIP routers of the networks that it can contact. RIP routers can also communicate routing information through triggered updates. With triggered updates, the routing information is sent immediately instead of waiting for the next periodic announcement.

You can select the following operation mode settings in the **Operation mode** box on the **General** tab:

- **Auto-static update mode**. Sends RIP announcements only when other routers request an update. Routes learned over RIP are marked as static routes and remain in the routing table until manually deleted. Auto-static update is the default setting for a demand-dial interface.

- **Periodic update mode**. Sends RIP announcements periodically, as specified by the **Periodic announcement interval** setting on the **Advanced** tab. Periodic update is the default setting for a LAN interface.

Configuring Protocols for RIP Announcements

You can select the following protocols for outgoing RIP announcements in the **Outgoing packet protocol** box on the **General** tab:

- **RIP version 1 broadcast**. Sends RIP version 1 announcements as broadcasts. Use this setting if you are in an environment that contains only RIP version 1 routers.

- **RIP version 2 broadcast**. Sends RIP version 2 announcements as broadcasts. This is the default protocol for a LAN interface. Use this setting if you are in a mixed environment containing both RIP version 1 and RIP version 2.

- **RIP version 2 multicast**. Sends RIP version 2 announcements as multicasts. This is the default protocol for a demand dial-up interface. Use this setting only if the adjacent RIP network routers connected to this interface are also RIP version 2 routers.

- **Silent RIP**. Disables outgoing RIP announcements. The router listens to other announcements and updates its own routing table, but does not send announcements of its own routes.

You can select the following protocols for incoming RIP announcements in the **Incoming packet protocol** box on the **General** tab:

- **RIP version 1 and 2**. Accepts both RIP version 1 and RIP versions 2 announcements. This is the default selection.

- **RIP version 1**. Accepts only RIP version 1 announcements.

- **RIP version 2**. Accepts only RIP version 2 announcements.

Configuring the Cost of a RIP Interface

The cost setting specifies a numeric value that is associated with sending packets with the interface. Because RIP uses hops for interface cost, this number is added to the hop count as advertised in the RIP message. When a RIP router has multiple routes to a remote network in its routing table, the router always tries to use the route with the lowest cost. Setting a high cost for a routing interface ensures that the interface is only used when other lower-cost interfaces are not available.

You can select a value from 1 to 15. A high value indicates a slower route.

Activating Authentication

To require router authentication, on the **General** tab, select the **Activate authentication** check box, and then type a password in the **Password** box. RIP authentication requires that RIP advertisements include a password. For authentication, all incoming RIP version 2 packets must contain the same password, so you need to configure all routers that are connected to the interface with the same password. Because RIP uses clear-text passwords, this option is primarily used for identification and provides only minimal security.

Configuring Route Filtering

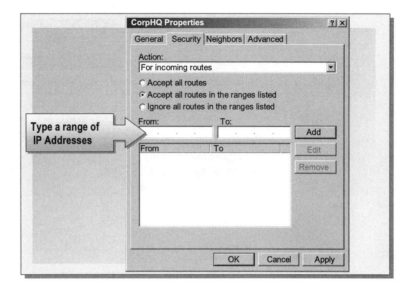

You set security to specify how a router accepts routes and how a router announces routes. You can use the security settings to prevent unauthorized routers from sending unauthorized route information. For example, you can prevent routers on the Internet from advertising routes to your router that are internal to your network You can also prevent routes from being advertised on an external interface to ensure confidentiality of your network topology.

To configure routes for a RIP interface:

1. Open Routing and Remote Access.

2. Expand *server* (where *server* is the name of your computer), expand **IP Routing**, and then click **RIP**.

3. In the details pane, right-click the interface that you want to configure, and then click **Properties**.

4. On the **Security** tab, on the **Action** list, click **For incoming routes** or **For outgoing routes**.

   Click one of the following options:

   - **Accept all routes**

   - **Accept all routes in the ranges listed**

   - **Do not announce all routes in the ranges listed**

5. Specify a range of IP address for the option, if necessary, and then click **OK**.

Configuring RIP for a Non-Broadcast Network

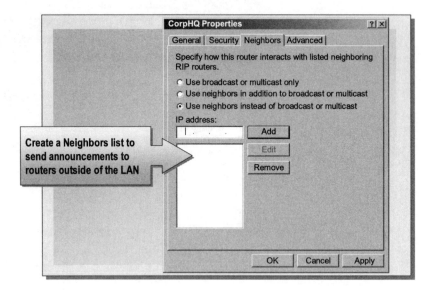

You use a neighbors list to send RIP messages between specific routers in non-broadcast networks. A neighbors list identifies a group of routers that are not on the same network segment as the router that you are configuring, but which may receive announcements. You create a neighbors list on the **Neighbors** tab in the **RIP Properties** dialog box.

To configure a neighbors list for a RIP interface:

1. Open Routing and Remote Access.

2. Expand *server* (where *server* is the name of your computer), expand **IP Routing**, and then click **RIP**.

3. In the details pane, right-click the interface that you want to configure, and then click **Properties**.

   On the **Neighbors** tab, click one of the following options:

   - **Use broadcast or multicast only**. Sends RIP announcements by using the outgoing packet protocol specified on the **General** tab. This is the default setting.

   - **Use neighbors in addition to broadcast or multicast**. Sends RIP announcements by unicast in addition to using the outgoing packet protocol specified on the **General** tab.

   - **Use neighbors instead of broadcast or multicast.** Sends RIP announcements by unicast only to the specified neighboring routers. Use this selection if you have non-broadcast networks, such as Frame Relay.

4. Specify one or more IP addresses, and then click **OK**.

Lab B: Configuring a Windows 2000–Based Router

Objectives

After completing this lab, you will be able to:

- Configure router interfaces.
- Configure filtering on router interfaces.
- Configure a demand-dial interface.
- Configure a router to use RIP.

Lab Setup

To complete this lab, you need the following:

- A computer running Windows 2000 Advanced Server that is configured as a domain controller in native mode
- A lab partner with a similarly configured computer
- IP addresses for the two network adapters in your computer
- IP addresses for the two network adapters in your partner's computer

If you are unsure about any of these values, please ask your instructor.

Adapter	Record IP address here
Your Classroom adapter	
Your PartnerNet adapter	
Your partner's Classroom adapter	
Your partner's PartnerNet adapter	

Scenario

Your company is expanding to more locations, and you need to connect these locations to the head-office network. Some branch-office locations do not yet have permanent connections available, so you will configure demand-dial connections for these offices. Also, now that your network is becoming large, you can no longer manually maintain the routing tables. To make routing more efficient, you will install RIP to build and maintain routing tables automatically.

Estimated time to complete this lab: 30 minutes

Exercise 1
Configuring a Router to Filter Protocols

Scenario

You have configured a router for your branch-office network so that you have connectivity to your head-office network, but for security and management reasons, you want to stop certain protocols from passing across the router to other networks.

Goal

In this exercise, you will work with your partner to configure the router interface for your branch-office router so that it will not route ICMP request traffic, as used by the **ping** command.

Tasks	Detailed Steps
✋ **Important:** Perform the following procedures only on the computer with the higher student number.	
1. Configure the Classroom router interface so that it will transmit all packets except ICMP packets with an **ICMP type** of **8** and an **ICMP code** of **0**.	a. Log on as administrator@*domain*.nwtraders.msft (where *domain* is the name of your domain) with a password of **password**.
	b. Open Routing and Remote Access from the **Administrative Tools** menu.
	c. In the console tree, expand *server* (where *server* is the name of your computer), expand **IP Routing**, and then click **General**.
	d. In the details pane, right-click **Classroom**, and then click **Properties**.
	e. In the **Classroom Properties** dialog box, click **Output Filters**.
	f. In the **Output Filters** dialog box, click **Add**.
	g. In the **Add IP Filter** dialog box, in the **Protocol** box, click **ICMP**.
	h. In the **ICMP type** box, type **8**
	i. In the **ICMP code** box, type **0** and then click **OK**.
	j. Click **OK** to close the **Output Filters** dialog box, and then click **OK** to close the **Classroom Properties** dialog box.
	k. Minimize Routing and Remote Access.
✋ **Important:** Perform the following procedure on both student computers. The student with the higher student number must have completed the previous procedure before continuing to this task.	

(continued)

Tasks	Detailed Steps
2. Ping the instructor computer (London), and then view the shared resources on London by typing **net view \\192.168.z.200**	**a.** At a command prompt, type **ping 192.168.z.200** (where *z* is the number assigned to your classroom), and then press ENTER. *You will receive a different error message on each computer. Ping will resolve London to the IP address for London on both, but you will receive a "Destination host unreachable" message on the computer with the higher student number and a "Request timed out" message from the computer with the lower student number. This indicates that the output filter is working and blocking ICMP packets from being transmitted from the Classroom interface.* **b.** Type **net view \\192.168.z.200** and then press ENTER. *On both computers, you will see the shared resources at \\london. This means that the filter is only filtering out ICMP packets.* **c.** Close the command prompt window.

Note: You have configured the Classroom adapter to filter ICMP traffic from being transmitted, but it will not block incoming ICMP traffic. If you ping your computer from the instructor computer, London, the ping will be successful.

Perform the following procedure only on the computer with the lower student number.

Tasks	Detailed Steps
3. In Routing and Remote Access, add your partner's computer as a server, and then configure an input filter for your partner's Classroom adapter that filters ICMP packets of type 8 and code 0.	**a.** Open Routing and Remote Access from the **Administrative Tools** menu. **b.** In the console tree, expand *partner_server* (where *partner_server* is the name of your partners computer), expand **IP Routing**, and then click **General**. **c.** In the details pane, right-click **Classroom**, and then click **Properties**. **d.** In the Classroom **Properties** dialog box, click **Input Filters**. **e.** In the Input **Filters** dialog box, click **Add**. **f.** In the **Add IP Filter** dialog box, in the **Protocol** box, click **ICMP**. **g.** In the **ICMP type** box, type **8** **h.** In the **ICMP code** box, type **0** and then click **OK**. **i.** Click **OK** to close the **Input Filters** dialog box, and then click **OK** to close the **Classroom Properties** dialog box. **j.** Minimize Routing and Remote Access.

Note: You have successfully filtered ICMP echo requests from being passed by your router. If you ping your computer from the instructor computer, London, Ping will reply "Request timed out."

Perform the following procedure only on the computer with the higher student number.

(continued)

Tasks	Detailed Steps
4. In Routing and Remote Access, remove the input and output filter.	a. Restore Routing and Remote Access.
	b. In the console tree, expand *server* (where *server* is the name of your computer), expand **IP Routing**, and then click **General**.
	c. In the console pane, right-click **Classroom**, and then click **Properties**.
	d. In the **Classroom Properties** dialog box, click **Input Filters**.
	e. In the **Input Filters** dialog box, verify that the routing filter is selected, click **Remove**, and then click **OK**.
	f. In the **Classroom Properties** dialog box, click **Output Filters**.
	g. In the **Output Filters** dialog box, verify that the routing filter is selected, click **Remove**, and then click **OK**.
	h. Click **OK** to close the **Classroom Properties** dialog box.
	i. Minimize Routing and Remote Access.

Exercise 2
Configuring Demand-Dial Connections

Scenario

You want your branch office to have connectivity to your head-office network via a secure, remote connection. The remote connection need not be permanent, but it needs to connect automatically whenever data from the branch office is destined for the head-office network.

Goal

In this exercise, you will configure a demand-dial VPN connection from one computer to the classroom network, through the branch office router. You will then test this connection by pinging the instructor computer to activate the connection.

Tasks	Detailed Steps
🖐 Perform the following procedure only on the computer with the higher student number.	
1. Create a user account for the demand-dial interface. Grant the user dial-in permissions. **User logon name: router***x*, (where *x* is your student number.) **Password: password** Grant this user dial-in permissions.	a. Open Active Directory Users and Computers from the **Administrative Tools** menu. b. In the console tree, expand domain.**nwtraders.msft** (where *domain* is the name of your domain), and then click **Users**. c. Right-click **Users**, point to **New**, and then click **User**. d. In the **New Object** – User dialog box, in the **First name** box, type **Router***x* (where *x* is your student number). e. In the **New Object** – User dialog box, under **User logon name**, type **router***x*, and then click **Next**. f. In the **Password** and **Confirm** password boxes, type **password** g. Click **Next**, and then click **Finish**. h. In the console tree, right-click **router***x*, and then click **Properties**. i. On the **Dial-in** tab, click **Allow access**, and then click **OK**. j. Close Active Directory Users and Computers.
2. Configure your computer to be a remote access server, and configure the router component to support LAN and demand-dial routing.	a. Restore Routing and Remote Access. b. In the console tree, right-click *server* (where *server* is the name of your computer), and then click **Properties**. c. On the **General** tab, click **LAN and demand-dial routing**, select the **Remote access server** check box, and then click **OK**. d. Click **Yes** to close the **Routing and Remote Access** message box. 🖥 *The Routing and Remote Access service is restarted to reflect the latest configuration changes.*

(continued)

Tasks	Detailed Steps
3. Configure both the Point-to-Point Tunneling Protocol (PPTP) and Layer Two Tunneling Protocol (L2TP) remote access ports to support both remote access connections and demand-dial routing connections.	a. In the console tree, right-click **Ports**, and then click **Properties**. b. In the **Ports Properties** dialog box, click **WAN Miniport (PPTP)**, and then click **Configure**. c. Verify that both the **Remote access connections (inbound only)** and **Demand-dial routing connections (inbound and outbound)** check boxes are selected, and then click **OK**. d. Repeat steps b and c to configure **WAN Miniport (L2TP)** to allow remote access and demand-dial routing connections. e. Minimize Routing and Remote Access.
✋ Perform the following procedure only on the computer with the lower student number.	
4. Configure your computer to be a remote access server, and configure the router component to support LAN and demand-dial routing.	a. Restore Routing and Remote Access from the **Administrative Tools** menu. b. In the console tree, right-click *server*, and then click **Configure and Enable Routing and Remote Access**. c. In the Routing and Remote Access Server Setup wizard, click **Next**. d. On the **Common Configurations** page, click **Network router**, and then click **Next**. e. On the **Routed Protocols** page, under **Protocols**, verify that **TCP/IP** displays, and then click **Next**. f. On the **Demand-Dial Connections** page, click **Yes**, and then click **Next**. g. On the **IP Address Assignment** page, verify that **Automatically** is selected, and then click **Next**. h. Click **Finish** to close the Routing and Remote Access Server Setup wizard. 🖥 *The Routing and Remote Access service will now start.*
5. Create a demand-dial interface called Head Office. The demand-dial interface must have the following properties: **Connection Type**: VPN **VPN Type**: Automatic **Destination Address**: IP address of your partner's PartnerNet adapter **User name**: **router***y*, where *y* is your partner's student number **Domain**: *domain* **Password**: **password**	a. In the console tree, expand *server*, right-click **Routing Interfaces**, and then click **New Demand-dial Interface**. b. In the Demand Dial Interface wizard, click **Next**. c. On the **Interface Name** page, in the Interface **name** box, type **head office** and then click **Next**. d. On the **Connection Type** page, click **Connect using** virtual **private networking (VPN)**, and then click **Next**. e. On the **VPN Type** page, verify that **Automatic selection** is selected, and then click **Next**. f. On the **Destination Address** page, type the IP address of your partner's PartnerNet adapter, and then click **Next**. g. On the **Protocols and Security** page, verify that **Route IP packets on this interface** is selected, and then click **Next**.

Tasks	Detailed Steps
5. (*continued*)	h. On the **Dial Out** Credentials page, in the **User name** box, type **router***y* (where *y* is your partner's student number). i. In the **Domain** box, type *domain* j. In the **Password** and **Confirm password** boxes, type **password** k. Click **Next**, and then click **Finish**.
6. Add a static route to initiate the demand-dial interface. Use the following information to create the route: **Interface**: Head Office **Destination**: 192.168.1.0 **Network mask**: 255.255.255.0 Select the **Use this route to initiate demand-dial connections** check box.	a. In the console tree, expand **IP Routing**, right-click **Static Routes**, and then click **New Static Route**. b. In the **Static Route** box, in the **Interface** box, verify that **head office** is selected. c. In the **Destination** box, type **192.168.1.0** d. In the **Network mask** box, type **255.255.255.0** e. Verify that the **Use this route to initiate demand-dial connections** check box is selected, and then click **OK**. f. Minimize Routing and Remote Access.

7. Ping the instructor computer by IP address, and then verify that the demand-dial connection has been initiated by checking in Routing and Remote Access.	a. At a command prompt, type **ping 192.168.***z***.200** (where *z* is the number assigned to your classroom), and then press ENTER.
	
	     The Ping will receive successful replies after initiating the demand-dial connection. If the connection has not yet been made, try step a again.
	
	b. Close the command prompt window, and then restore Routing and Remote Access.
	
	c. In the console tree, right-click **Routing Interfaces**, and then click **Refresh**.
	
	     The Head Office interface is now connected.
	
	d. Close Routing and Remote Access.

Exercise 3
Configuring Windows 2000 to use RIP

Scenario

Your network is expanding, and you want RIP to automatically update routing tables so that you do not need to enter additional static routes.

Goal

In this exercise, you will add RIP to your branch-office router and examine the routing tables that result to verify the correct operation.

You will work with a partner during this exercise to configure RIP on the computer with the higher student number. So that both partners get experience in configuring RIP, the lab instructions request that different parts of the configuration of RIP be performed on different computers.

Tasks	Detailed Steps
✋ Perform the following procedure only on the computer with the lower student number.	
1. Enable the Classroom network adapter, and clear the default gateway for the PartnerNet network adapter.	a. Right-click **My Network Places**, and then click **Properties**. b. In Network and Dial-up Connections, right-click **Classroom**, and then click **Enable**. c. In Network and Dial-up Connections, right-click **PartnerNet**, and then click **Properties**. d. In the **PartnerNet** Properties dialog box, click **Internet Protocol (TCP/IP)**, and then click **Properties**. e. In the **Default** gateway box, delete the IP address, and then click **OK**. f. Click **OK** to close the **PartnerNet Properties** dialog box. g. Close Network and Dial-up Connections.
✋ Perform the following procedure only on the computer with the higher student number.	
2. Add the RIP protocol and add the Classroom interface to support RIP.	a. Restore Routing and Remote Access. b. In the console tree, expand *server* (where *server* is the name of your computer), expand **IP Routing**, and then click **General**. c. In the console tree, right-click **General**, and then click **New Routing Protocol**. d. In the **New Routing Protocol** box, under **Routing Protocols**, click **RIP Version 2 for Internet Protocol**, and then click **OK**. 💻 *RIP is added to the console tree below **IP Routing**. Any routing protocols that you add will appear in the console tree under each network protocol that that they support.* e. In the console tree, **right**-click **RIP**, and then click **New Interface**. f. Under **Interfaces**, click **Classroom**, and then click **OK**. g. In the **RIP Properties – Classroom Properties** dialog box, verify that the **Added cost for routes** is **1**, and then click **OK**.

(*continued*)

Tasks	Detailed Steps
✋ Perform the following procedure only on the computer with the lower student number.	
3. Add the PartnerNet interface to support RIP. Configure the PartnerNet interface with an **Added cost for routes** of **2**.	a. Open Routing and Remote Access from the **Administrative Tools** menu.
	b. In the console tree, expand *partner_server* (where *partner_server* is the name of your partners computer), expand **IP Routing**, and then click **RIP**.
	c. In the console tree, right-click **RIP**, and then click **New Interface**.
	d. In the **New Interface for RIP Version 2 for Internet Protocol** dialog box, verify that **PartnerNet** is selected, and then click **OK**.
	e. In the **RIP Properties – PartnerNet Properties** dialog box, in the **Added cost for routes** box, type **2** and then click **OK**.
	🖥 *You have configured RIP on your branch-office router interfaces. After the other students in your class have added RIP to their computers, the routing tables for your computer will be updated by RIP.*
✋ Perform the following procedure on both student computers.	
4. In Routing and Remote Access, display the IP routing table for the computer with the higher student number.	a. In Routing and Remote Access, under *server*, under **IP Routing**, right-click **Static Routes**, and then click **Show IP Routing Table**.
	b. Drag the border of the window so that you can see all columns in the routing table.
	🖥 *Notice that after waiting a short time, entries for other networks will appear in your routing table. The entries that RIP added have **RIP** in the **Protocol** column.*
❓ In the IP Routing table, there will be several entries for the different networks in your classroom. If there are two entries for the same network, how will the router choose which route to use? _____ _____ _____ _____	
4. (*continued*)	c. Close the *server* – IP Routing Table window.

Exercise 4
Removing Routing and Remote Access

Goal

In this exercise, you will remove Routing and Remote Access.

Task	Detailed Steps
✋ Perform the following procedure on both student computers.	
1. Disable Routing and Remote Access on your computer, close all windows, and log off.	a. In Routing and Remote Access, in the console tree, right-click *server* (where *server* is the name of your computer), and then click **Disable Routing and Remote Access**.
	b. Click **Yes** to close the **Routing And Remote Access** dialog box.
	c. Close Routing and Remote Access, and then log off.

Review

- **Overview of Routers and Routing Tables**

- **Configuring Network Connections**

- **Enabling Routing by Using Routing and Remote Access**

- **Configuring Static Routes**

- **Configuring a Routing Interface**

- **Implementing Demand-Dial Routing**

- **Configuring the Routing Information Protocol**

1. You manage a large network with many computers that are connected to the same network by using hubs. Because of slowing network performance, you decide to segment the network by using routers. Describe two ways in which a router will help to increase available bandwidth to users.

2. What information does a router use to make decisions about where to forward IP packets?

3. You have installed three network adapters in your server, and you must configure each of them with a specific IP address. The adapters look identical. How can you identify each adapter in the Windows 2000 interface so that you can more easily assign the correct IP address to each adapter?

4. You are configuring the interface of a router that will be connected directly to the Internet. This router will be forwarding DNS queries to an ISP. What three settings must you configure?

5. You have a Windows 2000–based server that you are currently using as a remote access server and that you also want to use as a router. When you open Routing and Remote Access, the option to **Configure and Enable Routing and Remote Access** is not available. How do you enable routing?

6. You are testing network connectivity in your network after installing a Windows 2000–based router and enabling Routing and Remote Access. From the router, you can ping computers on networks that are connected to the router, but not computers on networks that are one or more routers away. What must you do to enable network communication?

7. You are testing connectivity from one network to another. You notice that you are not able to ping any hosts in a remote network, but you can view shared resources on those hosts. What is a likely cause of this symptom?

8. Your network has expanded, and you have added more routers. To make updating routing tables with static routes easier, you have installed RIP on all of the Windows 2000–based routers. After viewing the routing tables on the routers, you notice that there are no entries in the routing tables from RIP. What must you do so that RIP can update the routing tables?

Microsoft®
Training &
Certification

Module 11: Configuring Internet Access for a Network

Contents

Overview

- Options for Connecting a Network to the Internet
- Configuring Internet Access by Using a Router
- Configuring Internet Access by Using NAT

Microsoft® Windows® 2000 includes several technologies that you can use to connect your network to the Internet and to configure the connection to optimize network performance and security.

At the end of this module, you will be able to:

- Describe the options that are available for connecting a network to the Internet.

- Configure Internet access by using a router.

- Configure Internet access by using network address translation (NAT).

◆ Options for Connecting a Network to the Internet

- Connecting to the Internet by Using a Router

- Securing Internet Connections by Using a Firewall

- Connecting to the Internet by Using NAT

- Connecting to the Internet by Using Internet Connection Sharing

- Connecting to the Internet by Using a Proxy Server

- Comparing Internet Connectivity Options

Windows 2000 simplifies Internet access by including several technologies that you can use to connect to the Internet. You can configure permanent or part-time connectivity, connect your home or small office network to the Internet, and automate the process of connecting to the Internet. In addition, you can use a proxy server to optimize performance and reliability, or add a firewall to restrict Internet access.

Connecting to the Internet by Using a Router

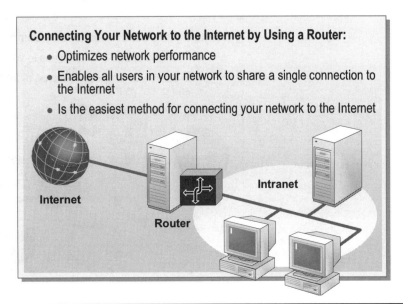

A router is a device that forwards packets of data from one local area network (LAN) or wide area network (WAN) to another. You can use routers to subdivide a LAN into subnets to balance traffic within your network. You can also place a router at the edge of your network to enable connections to remote offices and the Internet.

Routing Functionality

The router reads packet headers and selects the best path available for the packet based on the information contained in routing tables. The router then forwards the packet to its destination, or to another router. Routers optimize network performance because they do not perform any additional processing of packets.

Routing Services

Routers can be configured to enable all users in a network to share a single connection to the Internet. Routing and Remote Access in Windows 2000 provides built-in routing services that can be used to connect an organization to the Internet through a routed connection to an Internet service provider (ISP). For example, you can configure demand-dial routing to make a connection to an ISP only when packets are sent to or received from the Internet.

Routing Considerations

Using a router is the easiest method for connecting your network to the Internet, but it does not secure your network against unauthorized access through the Internet. In addition, you must ensure that you have public Internet Protocol (IP) addresses for each host that resides in your network.

Securing Internet Connections by Using a Firewall

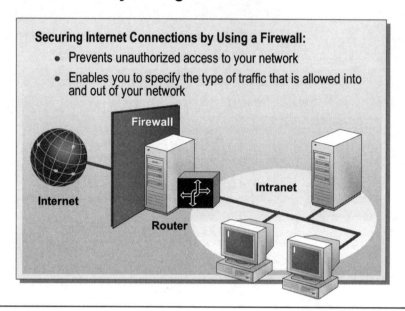

A firewall is a combination of hardware and software that provides a security system, usually to prevent unauthorized access from outside to an internal network or intranet.

A firewall can be configured to prevent unauthorized access to your internal network by enforcing a set of rules about which packets are allowed to pass from the external network to the internal network. Firewalls can be implemented by using hardware, software, or a combination of both. Many firewalls also include reporting features to alert an administrator when a security breach is attempted.

Configuring a Firewall

You can configure a firewall to specify the type of traffic that comes into and goes out from your network. A firewall routes all packets that comply with these specifications, or security rules, to the appropriate host. The firewall drops packets that do not comply with the security rules.

Establishing Security Rules

You can establish a simple security rule to forward selected incoming packets from the Internet. For example, you can create a rule to forward packets that are addressed to Transmission Control Protocol (TCP) port 80 (the default port that the Hypertext Transfer Protocol [HTTP] uses) to a Web server that resides inside the firewall, and to drop all other packets. This enables users who are outside the firewall to view Web pages on that Web server only, and prevents any other type of access into your internal network.

You can establish another common security rule to forward incoming packets from the Internet only when they are part of a communication that was initiated by a computer that resides on the internal network.

Note For information about installing and configuring a firewall, refer to the product information that is included with the particular firewall you are using.

Connecting to the Internet by Using NAT

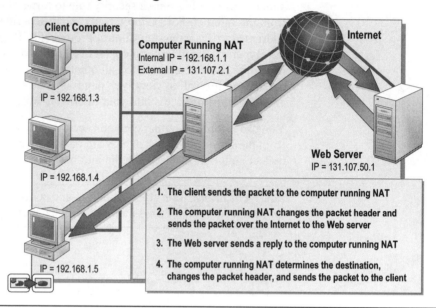

Network devices that are assigned private IP addresses cannot access Internet sites directly. Therefore, traffic must be routed through a NAT device, called a network address translator that has both an internal private IP address and a public IP address assigned to it.

Warning   NAT is not a recommended method to use for network connectivity without the inclusion of a firewall.

A network address translator is an IP router that can translate IP addresses and TCP or User Datagram Protocol (UDP) port numbers of packets as they are being forwarded. NAT translates private IP addresses to external, public IP addresses. This reduces IP address registration costs because you can use unregistered IP addresses internally and translate them to a small number of registered IP addresses that are used to communicate with external networks, such as the Internet. NAT also hides internal IP addresses from external networks, which protects against unauthorized access to your network. The only IP address that is visible to the Internet is the IP address of the computer running NAT.

Note   For more information on NAT, see RFC 1631 under **Additional Reading** on the Web page on the Student Materials compact disc.

How NAT Works

When a computer running NAT receives a packet from an internal client, it replaces the packet header and translates the client's port number and internal IP address to its own port number and external IP address. It then sends the packet to the destination host on the Internet, and keeps track of the mapping information in a table, so that it can route the reply to the appropriate client computer. When the computer running NAT receives a reply from the Internet host, it again replaces the packet header and sends the packet to the client. Both the client computer and the Internet host appear to be communicating directly with each other.

For example, a client computer with the IP address 192.168.1.5 wants to contact a Web server with the IP address 131.107.50.1. The client is configured to use 192.168.1.1 as the default gateway, which is the internal IP address of the computer running NAT. The external IP address of the computer running NAT is 131.107.2.1. In this example, the NAT process occurs as follows:

1. The client computer sends a packet to the computer running NAT. The packet header indicates that the packet originates from port 1074 on the computer with the IP address 192.168.1.5, and has a destination of port 80 on 131.107.50.1.

2. The computer running NAT changes the packet header to indicate that the packet originates from port 1563 on host 131.107.2.1, but does not change the destination. The computer running NAT then sends the packet to the Web server over the Internet.

3. The external Web server receives the packet and sends a reply. The packet header for the reply indicates that the packet originates from port 80 on 131.107.50.1, and has a destination of port 1563 on host 131.107.2.1.

4. The computer running NAT receives the packet and checks its mapping information to determine the destination client computer. The computer running NAT changes the packet header to indicate a destination of port 1074 on 192.168.1.5, and then sends the packet to the client. The source of the packet remains as port 80 on 131.107.50.1, which is the IP address of the Web server.

NAT Features and Benefits

The NAT routing protocol in Windows 2000 provides the following features and benefits:

-   NAT enables multiple users to use a single connection to access the Internet through dial-up networking and local networking media.

-   NAT can provide Dynamic Host Configuration Protocol (DHCP) and Domain Name System (DNS) services if no other servers on your network provide them.

-   NAT enables any IP-attached device on your intranet, including Windows-based and non-Windows–based clients, to communicate with computers on the Internet without requiring additional client software.

Connecting to the Internet by Using Internet Connection Sharing

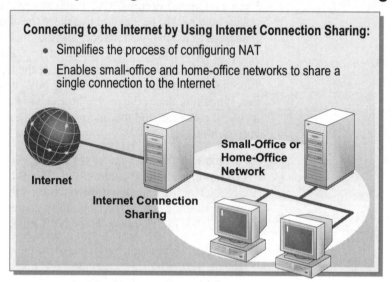

Connecting to the Internet by Using Internet Connection Sharing:
- Simplifies the process of configuring NAT
- Enables small-office and home-office networks to share a single connection to the Internet

Internet

Internet Connection Sharing

Small-Office or Home-Office Network

Internet Connection Sharing simplifies the configuration steps that are required to enable multiple computers to share a single connection to the Internet. Internet Connection Sharing performs the same function as NAT, but it allows very little configuration flexibility.

Warning   ICS is not a recommended method to use for network connectivity without the inclusion of a firewall.

Internet Connection Sharing is designed for a small office or home office network, and provides an easy-to-configure, but limited interface that connects clients to the Internet. Internet Connection Sharing configures NAT with preconfigured settings, which include a specific range of IP addresses for client computers, and the automatic assignment of IP addresses to client computers.

Note   Do not use Internet Connection Sharing in an existing network with Windows 2000 Server domain controllers, DNS servers, gateways, DHCP servers, or systems that are configured to use static IP addresses, because it may interfere with your existing network configuration. In an existing network, you must use NAT instead of Internet Connection Sharing.

To enable Internet Connection Sharing, select the **Enable Internet Connection Sharing for this connection** check box in the in the Network Connection wizard, or on the **Sharing** tab of the **Properties** dialog box for the connection.

Connecting to the Internet by Using a Proxy Server

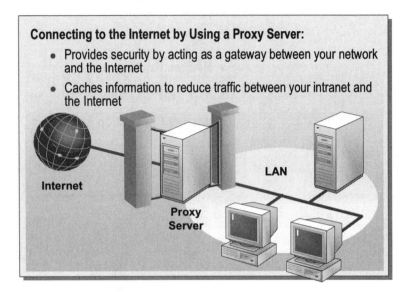

A proxy server manages traffic between your network and servers on the Internet, and determines whether network packets are allowed to pass through to the network. When a client computer makes a request, the proxy server translates the request and passes it on to the Internet. When a computer on the Internet responds, the proxy server passes the response back to the client computer.

Restricting Connections

You can configure a proxy server to block inbound connections in order to enable LAN clients to initiate connections to Internet servers, but also prevent Internet clients from initiating connections to LAN servers. You can also configure a proxy server to restrict outbound connections so that LAN clients are authenticated by using their standard security credentials. You can restrict outbound connections in several ways—by user, program, protocol, TCP/UDP port number, time of day, domain name, or IP address.

Caching Information

Proxy servers typically cache information from the Internet. For example, if multiple users view the same Web page on the Internet, a proxy server can retrieve that page only once from the Internet, keep a copy of the page in its cache, and then forward the copy to all users. This reduces traffic between your intranet and the Internet because the proxy does not have to retrieve the Web page from the Internet separately for each user.

Note Microsoft Internet Security and Acceleration Server 2000 (ISA Server) provides many advanced security features, and is a certified firewall. For more information, see the Microsoft ISA Server Web site at http://www.microsoft.com/ISAServer.

Comparing Internet Connectivity Options

- **NAT vs. Routing**
- **NAT vs. Proxy Server**
- **Internet Connection Sharing vs. NAT**

There are several options for connecting your network to the Internet, and each has different capabilities and advantages. Therefore, it is important to understand the differences between the various Internet connectivity options before you configure a connection between your intranet and the Internet.

NAT vs. Routing

NAT provides greater flexibility for designing your internal network, because it enables you to use unregistered IP addresses internally, and a small number of registered IP addresses externally. NAT provides network security that a router cannot provide, but it is more processor-intensive than routing and it does not support all protocols. In addition, NAT in Windows 2000 translates a computer's IP address in the packet header only, which prevents the use of Internet Protocol Security (IPSec).

NAT vs. Proxy Server

Both NAT and a proxy server allow connections to the Internet while restricting access to the internal network, and both provide address translation that enables clients on the intranet to use private IP addresses. Typically, all traffic on the Internet uses the IP address of the public network interface of the NAT or proxy server, whereas computers on the intranet use the IP address that is configured for the private network interface.

A proxy server must be configured to use the TCP or UDP ports that are used by all of the protocols for which it forwards packets to the Internet. This enables the proxy server to perform security checks. In addition, clients must be configured to use a proxy server. The client sends a request to the proxy server and the proxy server performs the necessary tasks to fulfill the request by supplying information from its cache or by sending a new packet to retrieve the information.

In contrast, NAT does not analyze the packets for security or caching purposes. Therefore, NAT only modifies IP addresses and port numbers in the IP and TCP/UDP headers, and is transparent to client and server.

Internet Connection Sharing vs. NAT

Internet Connection Sharing and NAT provide the same capabilities, but they differ in ease of use. You can enable Internet Connection Sharing by selecting a single check box, whereas enabling NAT requires more configuration tasks. In addition, Internet Connection Sharing must only be used in a small network because it:

- Requires a fixed IP address range for internal hosts.
- Is limited to a single public IP address for communicating with external networks.
- Only allows for a single internal network interface.

Note   It is strongly recommended that *any* connection to the Internet be secured by using a certified firewall such as ISA Server. For more information, see the Microsoft ISA Server Web site at http://www.microsoft.com/ISAServer.

Configuring Internet Access by Using a Router

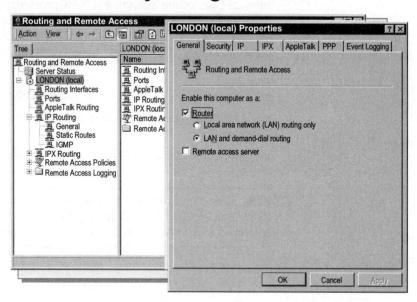

You can configure Routing and Remote Access to create a permanent connection from your network to the Internet, by using a dedicated, private, point-to-point connection. You can also configure Routing and Remote Access for demand-dial routing, which enables you to configure a connection that becomes active only when data is sent to the remote site. Demand-dial routing reduces connection costs because you can use existing dial-up telephone lines instead of leased lines.

To configure a routed connection to the Internet for a network, you must configure the Windows 2000–based router and the client computers in your internal network.

Configuring the Windows 2000–Based Router

To configure the Windows 2000–based router:

1. Confirm that the computer is configured with two network connections. One network interface must be connected to your internal network and represents a permanent connection. The other network connection can be a permanent connection or a dial-up connection.

2. Configure the network connection to your internal network with the IP address, subnet mask and gateway that you received from your ISP.

3. Install and enable Routing and Remote Access.

4. If you are using a demand-dial connection:

   a. Open Routing and Remote Access from the **Administrative Tools** menu.

   b. In the console tree, right-click the server that you want to configure, and then click **Properties**.

   c. In the **Properties** dialog box for the server, verify that **LAN and demand-dial routing** is selected, and then click **OK**.

   d. In the console tree, right-click **Ports**, and then click **Properties**.

   e. In the **Ports Properties** dialog box, click the dial-up connection that you want to enable for routing, and then click **Configure**.

   f. In the **Configure Device** dialog box, verify that **Demand-dial routing connections (inbound and outbound)** is selected, and then click **OK**.

   g. Click **OK** to close the **Properties** dialog box for the server.

5. Configure the default route to the IP address provided by your ISP:

   a. In the console tree, expand **IP Routing**, and then click **Static Routes**.

   b. Right-click **Static Routes**, and then click **New Static Route**.

   c. In the **Static Route** dialog box, type **0.0.0.0** in both the **Destination** and **Network mask** boxes.

   d. Type the IP address provided by your ISP in the **Gateway** box, and then select a metric, if required.

   e. If you use a dial-up connection, select the **Use this route to initiate demand-dial connections** check box, and then click **OK**.

6. If your internal network consists of multiple subnets, add routes for all of those subnets, and ensure that these routes use the internal network interface.

Configuring Client Computers On The Network

After you have configured the Windows 2000–based router, you must configure TCP/IP on the client computers in your network with the following settings:

- An IP address from the address range obtained from the ISP

- A subnet mask that corresponds to the address range obtained from the ISP

- A default gateway, which is the internal IP address of the Windows 2000–based router

- A DNS server (use a DNS server address that is assigned by the ISP or your own DNS server)

Note For IP packets to be properly routed from your ISP to your network, your ISP needs to configure its routers with routing information for the IP address ranges on your network so that the ISP routers forward IP packets from the Internet to destinations on your network.

◆ Configuring Internet Access by Using NAT

- **Installing NAT**
- **Configuring NAT**
- **Installing the Router Interface for NAT**

To configure the computer running NAT, you must first install and enable Routing and Remote Access on a computer that is connected both to your intranet and the Internet. You must then add and configure the NAT routing protocol on the router, by using Routing and Remote Access in Microsoft Management Console (MMC).

Installing NAT

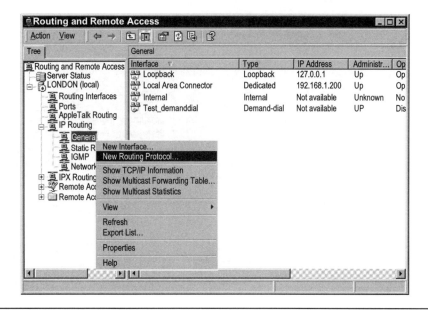

To install NAT, you must add the NAT routing protocol to the router.

To add the NAT routing protocol:

1. Open Routing and Remote Access.

2. In the console tree, double-click the name of the server that you want to configure, and then expand **IP Routing**.

3. Right-click **General**, and then click **New Routing Protocol**.

4. In the **New Routing Protocol** dialog box, click **Network Address Translation (NAT)**, and then click **OK**.

Configuring NAT

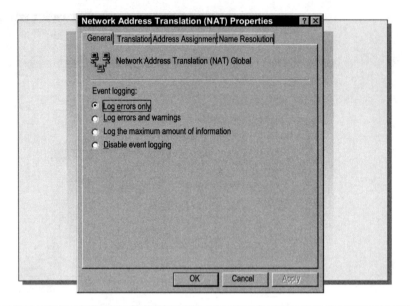

After you have installed the NAT routing protocol, you must configure the router to use NAT. You can configure NAT by using Routing and Remote Access. Double-click the name of the server that you want to configure, and then expand **IP Routing**. Right-click **Network Address Translation (NAT)**, and then click **Properties**.

The following table describes the options that you can configure in the **Network Address Translation (NAT) Properties** dialog box.

Tab	Description
General	Enables you to configure event logging, which specifies the type and amount of information that is logged in the system log in Event Viewer. The default setting is **Log errors only**.
Translation	Enables you to configure the following settings:
	• **Remove TCP mappings after**. Sets the number of minutes that a dynamic mapping for a TCP session remains in the translation table for the router. The default setting is 1,440 minutes (24 hours).
	• **Remove UDP mappings after**. Sets the number of minutes that a UDP message remains in the translation table for the router. The default setting is one minute.
	• **Reset Defaults**. Restores the default settings of the time-out values for dynamic mapping of TCP traffic and UDP traffic.
	Enables you to configure the following settings:
	• Click **Applications** to configure special applications on your private network that communicate with other applications that are running on computers on the Internet and that you want to make available to users on the Internet. These applications include those that send response traffic from a port other than the port used by the initial incoming traffic from the Internet client.

(continued)

Tab	Description
Address Assignment	Enables you to configure the computer running NAT to act as a DHCP server and assign IP addresses to clients.

- If your network does not contain a DHCP server, select the **Automatically assign IP addresses by using DHCP** check box, and then in the **IP address** and **Mask** boxes, configure the IP address range that the DHCP allocator will use to assign IP addresses. Click **Exclude** to exclude IP addresses from the range, such as the internal IP address of the computer or any static IP addresses that are assigned to computers in your network. The default network address range is based on the network 192.168.0.0 with a subnet mask of 255.255.255.0.

- If your network contains one or more DHCP servers, clear the **Automatically assign IP addresses by using DHCP** check box.

Tab	Description
Name Resolution	Enables you to configure the computer running NAT to appear as a DNS server to clients and to provide name resolution for these clients.

- If your network does not contain a DNS server, select the **Resolve IP addresses for clients using Domain Name System (DNS)** check box. Even though the computer running NAT is not a DNS server, it appears as a DNS server to clients. When the computer running NAT receives a DNS query, it forwards the query to a DNS server and forwards the reply that it receives from the DNS server to the client.

- To specify whether the NAT server makes a connection by using a demand-dial interface to resolve DNS names, select the **Connect to the public network when a name needs to be resolved** check box, and then, under **Demand-dial interface**, select an interface from the list.

Installing the Router Interface for NAT

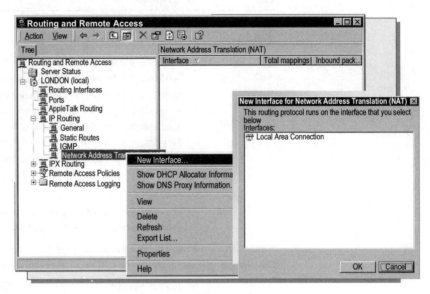

To enable NAT, you must add to the NAT routing protocol the interface on the Windows 2000–based router that connects to the Internet.

Note   Enable NAT translation only on interfaces that are connected to the Internet.

Adding the Router Interface

To add an interface to the NAT routing protocol:

1. Open Routing and Remote Access.

2. In the console tree, expand **IP Routing**, and then click **Network Address Translation (NAT)**.

3. Right-click **Network Address Translation (NAT)**, and then click **New Interface**.

4. In the **New Interface for Network Address Translation (NAT)** dialog box, click the interface you want to add, and then click **OK**.

5. On the **General** tab of the **Network Address Translation Properties** dialog box for the interface, select one of the following options:

    *   If this interface connects to the Internet, click **Public interface connected to the Internet**, and then select the **Translate TCP/UDP headers** check box.

    *   If this interface connects to the small-office or home network, click **Private interface connected to private network**.

6. Click **OK**.

Configuring the Router Interface

After you have added the interface, you must configure it by using the Routing and Remote Access administrative tool. In the console tree, click **Network Address Translation (NAT)**. In the details pane, right-click the connection that you want to configure, and then click **Properties**. The following table describes the tabs and associated options that you can configure in the **Properties** dialog box for the connection.

Tab	Description
General	Enables you to configure the following settings: • **Private interface connected to private network**. Specifies that the interface is a private interface that is connected to the private network. • **Public interface connected to the Internet**. Specifies that the interface is the public interface that is connected to the Internet. • **Translate TCP/UDP headers (recommended)**. Specifies whether the router performs TCP port and UDP port translation in addition to IP address translation. If you only have a single public IP address, you must select this check box. Otherwise, network traffic from hosts on the private network cannot be properly translated to Internet traffic.
Address Pool	Lists the configured ranges of public IP addresses that your ISP assigned to your network. • Click **Add** to add IP ranges to the address pool. In the **Add Address Pool** dialog box, type the start and end addresses of the address pool and the subnet mask of the subnet to which the range of addresses belongs. You can add multiple address ranges per interface. • Click **Reservations** to reserve public IP addresses for specific internal clients. Reservations enable computers to always use the same public IP address. In the **Add Reservations** dialog box, type the public IP address that you want to reserve, and the private IP address of the computer that will receive packets that are sent to the public IP address. Select the **Allow incoming sessions to this address** check box to make the internal computer accessible from the Internet.
Special Ports	Enables you to map incoming sessions to specific ports and addresses on your private network. In the **Protocol** box, select **TCP** or **UDP**, and then click **Add**. In the **Add Special Port** dialog box, under **Public address**, click: • **On this interface** to specify that the mapping applies to all addresses on this external interface. • **On this address pool entry** to specify that the mapping applies to a single address in the address pool. In the **Incoming port** box, type the number of the TCP or UDP port to which computers on the Internet connect. In the **Private address** box, type the IP address of the internal computer to which the NAT server will forward packets. In the **Outgoing port** box, type the TCP or UDP port on the internal computer to which the NAT server will forward packets.

Lab A: Configuring Internet Access by Using NAT

Objectives

After completing this lab, you will be able to:

- Configure a computer as a NAT client.
- Configure a computer as a NAT server.
- Configure NAT for incoming connections.

Prerequisites

Before working on this lab, you must have:

- Knowledge of how NAT enables shared network access.
- Experience configuring TCP/IP properties.

Lab Setup

To complete this lab, you need the following:

- A computer running Windows 2000 Advanced Server that is configured as a domain controller
- A partner with a similarly configured computer
- Microsoft Internet Explorer configured to use your local network connection

---

Important In this lab, you will work with a partner. One computer will be the NAT server and the other will be the NAT client. The computer of the student with the lower student number will act as the NAT server; the computer of the student with the higher student number will act as the NAT client. Before starting the lab, determine the role that your computer will play.

Important The lab does not reflect the real-world environment. It is recommended that you always use complex passwords for any administrator accounts, and never create accounts without a password.

Important Outside of the classroom environment, it is strongly advised that you use the most recent software updates that are necessary. Because this is a classroom environment, we may use software that does not include the latest updates.

Scenario

Your ISP has assigned a few IP addresses to your organization. You need to ensure that all of the users in your organization have access to the Internet. You also need to ensure that business partners can access information on select computers that are on your internal network.

Estimated time to complete this lab: 30 minutes

Exercise 1
Configuring a NAT Client

Scenario

Because your organization has a limited number of public IP addresses, you need to configure client computers to access the Internet by using NAT.

Goal

In this exercise, you will configure a NAT client.

Task	Detailed Steps
✊ Perform the following procedure only on the computer that will be the NAT client.	
1. Configure your computer to use your partner's PartnerNet network adapter as the default gateway, and then disable the Classroom network connection.	a. Log on as administrator@*domain*.nwtraders.msft (where *domain* is the name of your domain) with a password of **password**.
	b. Right-click **My Network Places**, and then click **Properties**.
	c. In Network and Dial-up Connections, right-click **PartnerNet**, and then click **Properties**.
	d. Click **Internet Protocol (TCP/IP)**, and then click **Properties**.
	e. In the **Default gateway** box, type the IP address of your partner's PartnerNet connection, and then click **OK**.
	f. Click **OK** to close the **PartnerNet Properties** dialog box.
	g. Right-click **Classroom**, and then click **Disable**.
	h. Minimize Network and Dial-up Connections.

Exercise 2
Configuring a NAT Server

Scenario

Because your company uses a private IP addressing scheme, and to control the security of your network, all access to the Internet from your organization must go through a NAT server.

Goal

In this exercise, you will configure a computer to become the NAT server for your organization.

Tasks	Detailed Steps
✋	Perform the following procedure only on the computer that will be the NAT server. If your computer will be the NAT client, observe while your partner configures the server.
1. Use Routing and Remote Access to configure your computer as NAT server. Configure the Classroom network connection as the Internet connection.	a. Log on as administrator@*domain*.nwtraders.msft (where *domain* is the name of your domain) with a password of **password**. b. Open Routing and Remote Access from the **Administrative Tools** menu. c. In the console tree, right-click *server* (where *server* is the name of your computer), and then click **Configure and Enable Routing and Remote Access**. d. In the Routing and Remote Access wizard, click **Next**. e. On the **Common Configurations** page, verify that **Internet connection server** is selected, and then click **Next**. f. On the **Internet Connection Server Setup** page, verify that **Set up a router with the Network Address Translation (NAT) routing protocol** is selected, and then click **Next**. g. On the **Internet Connection** page, verify that **Use the selected Internet connection** is selected, click **Classroom**, click **Next**, and then click **Finish**. h. In Routing and Remote Access, in the console tree, expand *server*, expand **IP Routing**, and then click **Network Address Translation (NAT)**.
✋	Perform the following procedure on the computer that is the NAT client only. Do not start this procedure until your partner has completed the preceding procedure.

(continued)

Tasks	Detailed Steps
2. Test network communications with the instructor's computer.	**a.** At a command prompt, type **ping london.nwtraders.msft** and then press ENTER.
	*You should see four replies to the **ping** command, even though your computer's connection to the Classroom network is disabled. Network traffic to the instructor's computer goes through the NAT server.*
	b. At the command prompt, type net view **london.nwtraders.msft** and then press ENTER.
	c. Confirm that you can see the shared folders on the instructor's computer, and then close the command prompt window.
	d. Open Internet Explorer.
	e. In the **Address** box, type **http://london.nwtraders.msft** and then click **Go**.
	If a Web site is configured on your partner's computer, a Web page is displayed. If no Web site is configured, a page titled Under Construction is displayed.
✋	Perform the following procedure on the computer that is the NAT server. Do not start this procedure until your partner has completed the preceding procedure.
3. Review NAT activity and port mappings on your computer.	**a.** In Routing and Remote Access, right-click **Network Address Translation (NAT)**, and then click **Refresh**.
	The Classroom network connection displays data for port mappings and packets that NAT translated as a result of your partner's actions. The PartnerNet network connection shows no activity.
	b. In the details pane, right-click **Classroom**, and then click **Show Mappings**.
	The Network Address Translation Session Mapping Table shows all client connections to the NAT server and the resulting external connections, including the IP addresses and the ports used.
	c. Close the *server* - **Network Address Translation Session Mapping Table** window.

Exercise 3
Configuring NAT Settings

Scenario

Users on your network use a network-based application that requires a server on the Internet to initiate a TCP connection with a client. Also, business partners need to access, from the Internet, information on a Web server that is located on your internal network.

Goal

In this exercise, you will configure the NAT server to allow external computers to establish TCP connections with a NAT client on TCP port 27960. You will also allow external users to access an internal Web server.

Tasks	Detailed Steps
✋ Perform the following procedures on the NAT server only.	
1. Configure NAT to allow an application called Seismic Activity Monitor to establish connections with a NAT client on port 27960.	a. In the console tree, right-click **Network Address Translation (NAT)**, and then click **Properties**.
	b. In the **Network Address Translation (NAT) Properties** dialog box, on the **Translation** tab, click **Applications**.
	c. In the **Network Application Settings** dialog box, click **Add**.
	d. In the **Internet Connection Sharing Application** dialog box, in the **Name of application** box, type **Seismic Activity Monitor**
	e. In the **Remote server port number** box, type **27960**
	f. Click **UDP**.
	g. In the **UDP** box, type **27960** and then click **OK**.
	h. Click **OK** to close the **Network Applications Settings** dialog box.
	i. In the **Network Address Translation (NAT) Properties** dialog box, on the **Address Assignment** tab, verify that the **Automatically assign IP addresses by using DHCP** check box is not selected.
	j. On the **Name Resolution** tab, verify that the **Clients using Domain Name System (DNS)** check box is not selected, and then click **OK**.

(continued)

Tasks	Detailed Steps
2. Configure NAT to allow external computers to connect to a Web server on your partner's computer, and then test the connection.	a. In the details pane, right-click **Classroom**, and then click **Properties**. b. In the **Classroom Properties** dialog box, on the **Special Ports** tab, in the **Protocol** box, ensure that **TCP** is selected, and then click **Add**. c. In the **Add Special Port** dialog box, in the **Incoming port** box, type **8080** d. In the **Private address** box, type the IP address of your partner's PartnerNet connection, and in the **Outgoing port** box, type **80** and then click **OK** twice. e. Ask the instructor or a student who is not your partner to open Internet Explorer and connect to **http://192.168.**z.x**:8080** (where z is the third octet of the Classroom connection and x is your student number). *If a Web site is configured on your partner's computer, a Web page is displayed. If no Web site is configured, a page Under Construction is displayed.*

Exercise 4
Removing NAT

Scenario

After you have tested NAT for your organization, you must remove all NAT configuration from your test network.

Goal

In this exercise, you will restore all settings on the NAT client and the NAT server.

Tasks	Detailed Steps
✋ Perform the following procedures only on the computer that is the NAT server.	
1. Disable Routing and Remote Access.	a. In Routing and Remote Access, in the console tree, right-click *server* (where *server* is the name of your computer), and then click **Disable Routing and Remote Access**.
	b. Click **Yes** to close the **Routing and Remote Access** dialog box.
	c. Close all open windows, and then log off.
✋ Perform the following procedure only on the computer that is the NAT client. Do not start this procedure until your partner has finished the preceding procedure.	
2. Restore your original TCP/IP configuration.	a. Restore Network and Dial-up Connections.
	b. Right-click **PartnerNet**, and then click **Properties**.
	c. Click **Internet Protocol (TCP/IP)**, and then click **Properties**.
	d. Clear the **Default Gateway** check box, and then click **OK**.
	e. Click **OK** to close the **PartnerNet Properties** dialog box.
	f. Right-click **Classroom**, and then click **Enable**.
	g. Close Network and Dial-up Connections.
	h. At a command prompt, type **ping london.nwtraders.msft** and then press ENTER.
	🖥️ *If you receive four replies, your network configuration has been correctly reconfigured. If you do not receive four replies after using the **ping** command several times, tell your instructor.*
	i. Close all open windows, and then log off.

If Time Permits
Configuring a Second NAT Server

Reverse roles with your partner and repeat all of the exercises in this lab so that the computer that you configured as a NAT client the first time that you completed the exercise is now configured as a NAT server.

Review

- Options for Connecting a Network to the Internet
- Configuring Internet Access by Using a Router
- Configuring Internet Access by Using NAT

1. How does NAT help to reduce IP address registration costs and protect against unauthorized access to your network?

2. What are the two connectivity options that are available for configuring Internet access by using a router?

3. What must you do to configure Internet access by using NAT?

Microsoft®
Training &
Certification

Module 12: Configuring a Web Server

Contents

Microsoft®

Overview

- **Overview of IIS**

- **Preparing for an IIS Installation**

- **Installing IIS**

- **Configuring a Web Site**

- **Administering IIS**

- **Troubleshooting IIS**

The Microsoft® Windows® 2000–based server products integrate Web publishing into the operating system with a built-in Web server, Microsoft Internet Information Services (IIS) 5.0. The integrated Web publishing environment that Windows 2000 provides makes it easy for an organization to publish and host Web content over a corporate intranet or the Internet.

At the end of this module, you will be able to:

- Describe the uses of IIS.

- Prepare for an IIS installation.

- Install IIS.

- Configure a Web site.

- Administer IIS.

- Troubleshoot IIS.

Overview of IIS

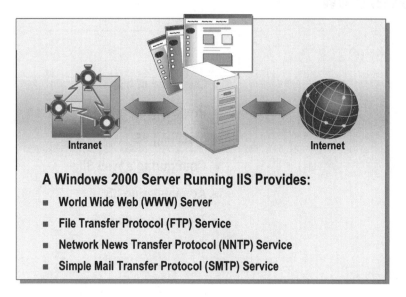

A Windows 2000 Server Running IIS Provides:

- World Wide Web (WWW) Server
- File Transfer Protocol (FTP) Service
- Network News Transfer Protocol (NNTP) Service
- Simple Mail Transfer Protocol (SMTP) Service

By default, IIS is installed automatically when you install Windows 2000. IIS is designed to support simple Web sites in addition to multiple Web sites on a single Web server. The Web publishing features of IIS integrate the latest Internet standards to provide high levels of security, better performance, and standards-based publishing protocols.

In addition to the World Wide Web (WWW) server, other Internet services that work in conjunction with IIS include:

- *File Transfer Protocol (FTP) service.* Enables you to set up FTP sites for uploading and downloading files.

- *Network News Transfer Protocol (NNTP) service.* Enables you to host electronic discussion groups, or newsgroups. Newsgroups contain threaded discussions, which consist of articles and follow-up messages that are related to a particular subject.

- *Simple Mail Transfer Protocol (SMTP) service.* Enables you to receive mail messages from a client application and send these mail messages to another server over the Internet. You can also configure domain controllers to use the SMTP service for replication over site links.

Important   It is recommended that you remove IIS if you do not plan on using the server as a Web server. To remove IIS from Windows 2000 Server, you can cancel the selection of IIS from the default installation.

Preparing for an IIS Installation

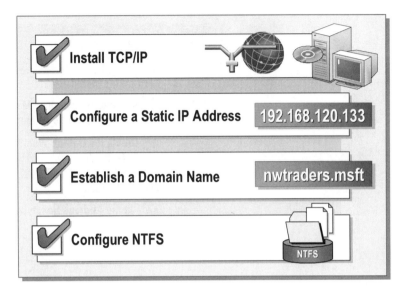

Before you install IIS, make sure you configure your server running Windows 2000 with the following network services and information:

- *Transmission Control Protocol/Internet Protocol (TCP/IP)*. IIS requires TCP/IP to provide the connectivity that is necessary for transmitting data.

- *Static IP address*. You must use a static IP address for your server if you intend to use IIS to publish content on the Internet.

- *Domain name*. To make your Web site accessible by a domain name, you need to have a Domain Name System (DNS) server available. Client computers use DNS to resolve the names of Web servers.

- *NTFS*. For Security purposes, it is recommended that you format all drives that contain Web content with the NTFS file system.

Installing IIS

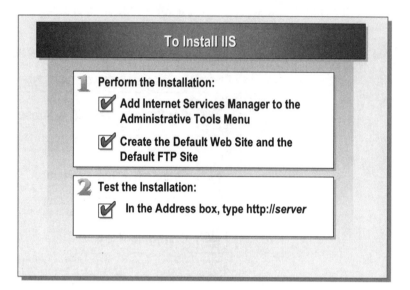

By default, IIS is installed automatically when you install Windows 2000, unless you choose not to install it. When you configure IIS during the installation of Windows 2000 Server, Setup adds Internet Services Manager to the **Administrative Tools** menu and creates the Default Web Site and Default File Transfer Protocol (FTP) Site. You can use Internet Services Manager to manage the Web server and to configure Web and FTP sites. After you install IIS, you can test the IIS installation by using a browser to view files over your intranet or the Internet.

Note   Setup will upgrade existing versions of IIS to IIS 5.0 when you install Windows 2000 Server.

Performing the Installation

If you choose not to install IIS during Windows 2000 Setup, you can install it later.

To install IIS:

1. In Control Panel, double-click **Add/Remove Programs**.

2. Click **Add/Remove Windows Components**, select the **Internet Information Services (IIS)** check box, and then follow the on-screen instructions in the Windows Components wizard to install IIS.

Note   To open Internet Services Manager, click **Start**, point to **Programs**, point to **Administrative Tools**, and then click **Internet Services Manager**.

Important   IIS requires continual management. To be informed of the latest security updates for IIS and Windows 2000, ensure that you subscribe to the security bulletin service at http://www.microsoft.com/technet/security/ bulletin/notify.asp.

Testing the Installation

After you install IIS, test your installation by using Microsoft Internet Explorer to view the files in your home directory. The *home directory* is the central location for your published pages. The location of the default home directory that IIS creates during Setup is C:\Inetpub\wwwroot.

To test your IIS installation:

1. Start Internet Explorer on a computer that has an active connection to your intranet or the Internet. This computer can be the computer that you are testing, although it is recommended that you use a different computer on the network.

2. In the **Address** box, type http://*server* (where *server* is the name of your computer), and then press ENTER.

   The home page for the default Web site installed during Setup appears in the browser. A *home page* is the initial page of information for a Web site. If you did not create a home page, Internet Explorer displays a message stating that the page is under construction.

Note   If the page cannot be displayed, open Internet Services Manager. In the console tree, click the name of the computer on which IIS is installed. In the details pane, verify that the Default Web Site, the Administration Web Site, and the Default SMTP Virtual Server are running.

◆ Configuring a Web Site

- **Configuring Web Site Identification**
- **Configuring the Home Directory**
- **Identifying Methods of Authentication**
- **Selecting a Method of Authentication**
- **Configuring Authentication**
- **Assigning a Default Document**

Before users can connect to your Web site, you must configure the IP address and domain name that users will use to connect to the Web site. You can also specify the type of authentication used to validate user logon information. IIS 5.0 provides four methods of authentication: Anonymous, Basic, Digest, and Integrated Windows authentication.

To publish Web content, you need to configure home and virtual directories to store that content. To help users browse your Web site, you can assign a default document. A *default document* is the page that appears if a user request to the Web server does not include a file name.

Configuring Web Site Identification

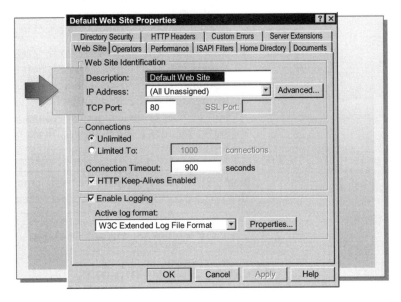

You must set identification parameters for your Web site to enable Web browsers to locate your Web server. To establish a Web site, you can configure the default Web site or use the Web Site Creation wizard to create a new site.

Configuring the Default Web Site

To configure the default Web site:

1. In Internet Services Manager, right-click the Web site, and then click **Properties**.

   You can specify the following identification settings on the **Web Site** tab.

   - **Description**. Determines the name of the Web site that appears in Internet Services Manager.

   - **IP Address**. The Web site's IP address. If your computer has multiple IP addresses, you can create a separate Web site for each of them.

- **TCP Port**. Determines the TCP port on which the Web service is running. The default is port 80. You can change the port to any unique TCP port number, but users must specifically request that port number or their requests will fail to connect to your server.

- **SSL Port**. Determines the port for connections that use Secure Sockets Layer (SSL) encryption. An SSL port number is required only when SSL encryption is used. The default is port 443. You can change the port to any unique TCP port number, but users must specifically request that port number or their requests will fail to connect to your server. A Web server requires a computer certificate or Web server certificate to enable SSL.

Note   SSL security is an increasingly common requirement for Web sites that provide e-commerce and access to sensitive business information.

---

2. Click **OK** to close the **Default Web Site Properties** dialog box.

Creating a New Web Site

To create a new Web site by using the Web Site Creation wizard, open Internet Services Manager, right-click the name of your computer point to **New**, and then click **Web Site**.

Follow the instructions in the Web Site Creation wizard to configure your new site. You must provide a description of the Web site, the IP address, port settings, and the path of the Web site home directory. You must also specify whether to allow anonymous connections to the Web site, and set Web access permissions.

Configuring the Home Directory

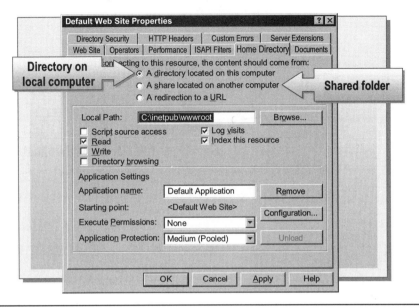

The home directory determines the location of the published content for a site. When you assign a home directory, you can specify either a local directory or a shared folder. A *local directory* stores published pages on the local computer. A *shared folder* stores published pages on another computer on the network, and appears to browsers as though it were located on the Web server.

You can assign the home directory for your site on the **Home Directory** tab in the **Properties** dialog box for the Web site.

Specifying a Local Directory

To specify a home directory that resides on the same computer as IIS, click **A directory located on this computer**. Specify the path to the home directory in the **Local Path** text box, or click **Browse** to locate the home directory.

Specifying a Shared Folder

To specify a home directory that resides on a different computer from IIS, click **A share located on another computer**.

Note When you specify a shared folder, most of the settings on the **Home Directory** tab remain the same as when you specify a local directory. However, the **Network Directory** text box replaces the **Local Path** text box, and the **Connect As** button replaces the **Browse** button.

Type the universal naming convention (UNC) name in the **Network Directory** text box, and click **Connect As** to specify the user name and password that IIS uses to connect to the shared folder.

Identifying Methods of Authentication

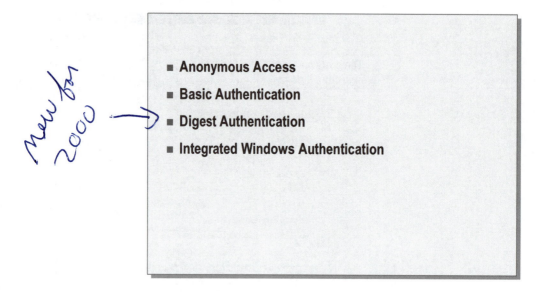

To prevent unauthorized access to your Web site, you must verify the identity of users. Configure your Web site so that no user can access the information on your Web site without providing a valid Windows user name and password. This identification process is called *authentication*. The authentication process determines whether a user has a valid Windows user account with appropriate permissions for accessing a particular Web site, folder, or file. Authentication can be set at the Web site, directory, or file level. IIS supports four methods of authentication for controlling access to content on your server.

Note   IIS also includes a method of authentication by using certificates. For more information about using certificates with IIS, see module 5, "Implementing Security on a Web Server," in course 2295A, *Implementing and Supporting Microsoft Internet Information Services 5.0*.

Anonymous Access

Anonymous access provides users access to the public areas of your Web site without prompting them for a user name or password. This authentication method is configured by default during the IIS installation process. When a user attempts to connect to your public Web site, your Web server assigns the user to the Windows user account called IUSR_*computername*, where *computernam*e is the name of the IIS server.

Note   The IUSR_*computername* account is included in the built-in Guests group. This group has security restrictions that determine the level of access.

Basic Authentication

Basic authentication prompts users for a user name and password before allowing access to a Web page. You can set Basic authentication at the Web site, folder, or file level. When the Web server verifies that the user name and password correspond to a valid Windows 2000 user account, it establishes a connection. You can configure IIS to use a specific domain when validating users' credentials because Basic authentication does not allow a user to specify a domain. If the server rejects the credentials, the Web browser repeatedly displays the **Logon** dialog box until the user either enters a valid user name and password or closes the dialog box.

Basic authentication is part of the Hypertext Transfer Protocol (HTTP) specification, and is supported by most browsers. However, Web browsers using Basic authentication transmit passwords in an unencrypted form. As a result, any hacker can intercept a user name and password. To secure user account information transmitted across the network, you must use Basic authentication with SSL security.

Digest Authentication

Digest authentication is a new feature of IIS 5.0. This method is similar to Basic authentication, but it involves a different way of transmitting the authentication credentials. The authentication credentials pass through a process called hashing. *Hashing* converts the password to a unique value, from which the server can verify the client's knowledge of the password without the client having to send the password.

Digest authentication works across proxy servers and other firewalls, unlike integrated Windows authentication. Digest authentication is only available for servers in a domain with Windows 2000 domain controllers. Also, Web browsers that support HTTP 1.1 can support Digest authentication.

Important All user accounts that use Digest authentication must be configured within the Active Directory™ directory service with the **Store password using reversible encryption** account option.

Internet Explorer 5.0 is the only browser that currently supports Digest authentication. The Digest authentication method proceeds as follows:

1. The Web server sends the browser certain information that will be used in the authentication process.

2. The browser encrypts the user name and password by adding the additional information sent by the server and then performing a hash on it.

3. The resulting hash is sent over the network to the server, along with the additional information in clear text.

4. The server then adds the additional information to a plain text copy of the client's password and hashes all of the information.

5. Finally, the server compares the hash value it received with the one it just made. Access is granted only if the two numbers are absolutely identical.

Note   A hash value consists of a small amount of binary data, no more than 160 bits. This value is produced by using a hashing algorithm.

Integrated Windows Authentication

Integrated Windows authentication is a secure form of authentication because in this method the user name and password are not sent across the network. The current Windows logon information on the client computer is used instead of the actual Windows user account and password information.

Note   Only Internet Explorer, version 2.0 or later, supports this authentication method. This method does not work over HTTP proxy connections.

Selecting a Method of Authentication

Authentication Method	Use When
Anonymous	You want users to access public areas of your Web site
Basic	You want to authenticate users who access your Web site through any browser or proxy server
Digest	You want to secure authentication for your Web sites and you must go through a proxy server
Integrated Windows	You are configuring an intranet site, where both the users and the Web server are in the same domain, or in domains with a trust relationship

You can select a method of authentication for your Web site depending on the type of information that you want to make available and the level of security that you want to assign to your site.

The following table describes which type of authentication method to select for different requirements.

Authentication Method	Use When
Anonymous access	You want users to access public areas of your Web site. This method does not offer any authentication at all.
Basic authentication	You want to authenticate users who access your Web site through any browser or proxy server. Use this method when you are sure that connections between the user and Web Server are secure, such as with a direct cable line or a leased line. To secure authentication data that is sent across the Internet, you must use Basic authentication with SSL.
Digest authentication	You want secure authentication for your Web sites and you must go through a proxy server. Also, Web browsers that support HTTP 1.1 can support Digest authentication.
Integrated Windows authentication	You are configuring an intranet site, where the users and the Web server are in the same domain or in domains with trust relationships between them. This method cannot authenticate users who access the Web site through a proxy server. This method works only with Internet Explorer version 2.0 or later.

Selecting Multiple Methods of Authentication

Based on your requirements, you can select more than one method of authentication. However, when you select multiple methods, one method takes precedence over others during authentication.

- When you use a combination of Anonymous access and any authentication method, Anonymous access takes precedence. If the anonymous user account does not have permission to access a specific resource, IIS and the Web browser negotiate an authentication method.

- When IIS and a Web browser negotiate an authentication method, The Web browser uses the most secure method that both can use. The order of preference is Integrated Windows authentication, Digest authentication, and Basic authentication. For example, if a web page is configured to use to use all three authentication methods, and a Web browser can use only Digest authentication and Basic authentication, the most secure authentication method that IIS and the Web browser can negotiate is Digest authentication.

Configuring Authentication

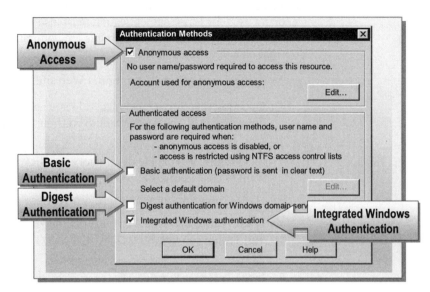

To use a method of authentication, you must configure authentication for a Web site, directory, or file on the Web server.

Configuring Anonymous Access

The anonymous account must have the user right to log on locally. If the account does not have the Log on locally user right, IIS cannot respond to any anonymous requests. By default, IUSR_*computername* accounts are granted this right, but you can change the security privileges. However, if the anonymous user account does not have permission to access a specific resource, your Web server refuses to establish an anonymous connection.

To change the account that is used for Anonymous access:

1. In Internet Services Manager, locate and right-click the Web site, directory, or file that you want to configure, and then click **Properties**.

2. In the **Properties** dialog box, click the **Directory Security** tab if you want to configure a Web site or directory, or click the **File Security** tab if you want to configure a file.

3. Under **Anonymous access and authentication control**, click **Edit**.

4. In the **Authentication Methods** dialog box, under **Anonymous access**, click **Edit**.

5. In the **Anonymous User Account** dialog box, type *useraccount* or click **Browse** to locate the valid Windows user account that you want to use for anonymous access.

6. If the user account is located on a different computer, clear the **Allow IIS to control password** check box and type the account password.

Configuring Basic Authentication

To authenticate users with Basic authentication, the Windows user accounts being used for Basic authentication must also have the Log on locally user right. By default, most user accounts are not granted the Log on locally user right on a domain controller.

To enable Basic authentication for a Web site:

1. Open Internet Services Manager, locate and right-click the Web site, directory, or file that you want to configure, and then click **Properties**.

2. In the **Properties** dialog box, click the **Directory Security** tab if you want to configure a Web site or directory, or click the **File Security** tab if you want to configure a file.

3. Under **Anonymous access and authentication control**, click **Edit**.

4. In the **Authentication Methods** dialog box, clear the **Integrated Windows authentication** check box, and then select the **Basic authentication** check box.

5. In the **Internet Service Manager** message box, click **Yes** to acknowledge that passwords will transmit without data encryption, and then click **OK** twice to close the **Authentication Methods** and **Properties** dialog boxes.

Configuring Digest Authentication

To enable Digest authentication for a Web site:

1. Open Internet Services Manager, locate and right-click the Web site, directory, or file that you want to configure, and then click **Properties**.

2. In the **Properties** dialog box, click the **Directory Security** tab if you want to configure a Web site or directory, or click the **File Security** tab if you want to configure a file.

3. Under **Anonymous access and authentication control**, click **Edit**.

4. In the **Authentication Methods** dialog box, select the **Digest authentication for Windows domain servers** check box.

5. In the **IIS WWW Configuration** message box, click **Yes** to acknowledge that the method works only with Windows 2000 domain controllers.

6. Click **OK** twice to close the **Authentication Methods** and **Properties** dialog boxes.

Configuring Integrated Windows Authentication

To enable Integrated Windows authentication:

1. Open Internet Services Manager, locate and right-click the Web site, directory, or file that you want to configure, and then click **Properties**.

2. In the **Properties** dialog box, click the **Directory Security** tab if you want to configure a Web site or directory, or click the **File Security** tab if you want to configure a file.

3. Under **Anonymous access and authentication control**, click **Edit**.

4. In the **Authentication Methods** dialog box, select the **Integrated Windows authentication** check box, and then click **OK** twice to close the **Authentication Methods** and **Properties** dialog boxes.

Assigning a Default Document

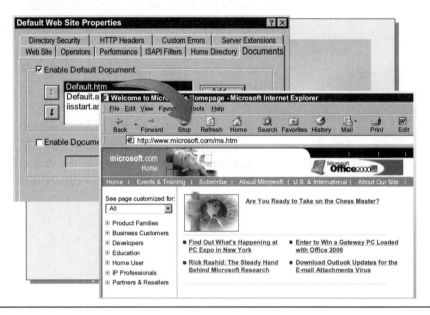

You can assign a default document so that Web page content appears to the user even when a browser request does not include a specific Hypertext Markup Language (HTML) file name. You can use a default document as:

- A home page that provides information for pages, Web sites, or section of a Web site.

- An index page that provides links to other content on the Web site.

To assign a default document:

1. Open the **Properties** dialog box for the Web site, and then click the **Documents** tab.

2. Select the **Enable Default Document** check box.

After you enable a default document, you can configure multiple default documents. To add a new default document, click **Add**.

When you assign multiple default documents, the Web server searches the list of default documents in the order in which the names appear. The server returns the first document it finds. To change the search order, select a document in the list of default documents, and then click the arrows to move the selected document up or down accordingly.

Administering IIS

- **Apply the Latest Security Updates**

- **Use Internet Services Manager to Manage Web Servers Remotely**

- **Use System Monitor to Monitor IIS Performance**

When administering IIS, it is important that you apply the most current security updates to ensure that your IIS server is up-to-date and secure. Also, Windows 2000 Administration Tools, which are included on the Windows 2000 Server compact disc, provide the administrative tools that enable you to manage a Web server remotely and monitor IIS performance.

Note   The file called adminpak.msi is located in the \i386 directory on the Windows 2000 Server compact disc, or in the systemroot\system32 directory on a computer running Windows 2000 Server. To install Windows 2000 Administration Tools, right-click **adminpak.msi**, and then click **Install**.

Applying the Latest Security Updates

To ensure that your Web server can take advantage of the most current security updates, you should verify that your Web server is running the most current software, including service packs, hot fixes, and security updates.

Important   To help you determine what software is needed on your Web server, to receive the most current security information, and to obtain information on the IIS lockdown tool, subscribe to the security bulletin service at http://www.microsoft.com/technet/security/bulletin/notify.asp.

Managing Web Servers Remotely

Use Internet Services Manager to connect to and manage Web servers remotely from any computer that is running Windows 2000.

To connect to another Web server by using Internet Services Manager:

1. Open Internet Services Manager from the **Administrative Tools** menu.

2. In the console tree, right-click **Internet Information Services**, and then click **Connect**.

3. In the **Connect To Computer** dialog box, type the name of the Web server to which you want to connect, and then click **OK**.

Note For more information about using Internet Services Manager to manage a Web server remotely, in Internet Services Manager, click the **Action** menu, and then click **Help**.

Monitoring Internet Information Services

Open System Monitor from the **Administrative Tools** menu to monitor IIS performance. When you install IIS, the following performance objects and counters for monitoring service activity are added to System Monitor:

- *Internet Information Services Global*. Contains counters that report on bandwidth throttling and on usage of the IIS Object Cache.

  Bandwidth throttling limits the bandwidth used by IIS services to a value that is set by an administrator. If the amount of bandwidth approaches or exceeds this limit, bandwidth throttling delays or rejects IIS service requests until more bandwidth becomes available.

  The IIS Object Cache stores frequently used objects and objects that can slow performance if they are retrieved repeatedly. The counters report on the size, content, and effectiveness of the IIS Object Cache.

- *Web Service*. Provides counters that show data about the anonymous and non-anonymous connections to the HTTP service application and HTTP requests that have been handled since the Web service was started.

- *Active Server Pages*. Monitors applications running on your Web server that use Active Server Pages. To monitor requests processed by calls to Common Gateway Interface (CGI) applications or Internet Server Application Programming Interface (ISAPI) extensions, use the counters on the Web Service object.

Note For more information about using System Monitor, see module 12, "Monitoring and Optimizing Performance in Windows 2000," in Course 2152, *Implementing Microsoft Windows 2000 Professional and Server*.

Troubleshooting IIS

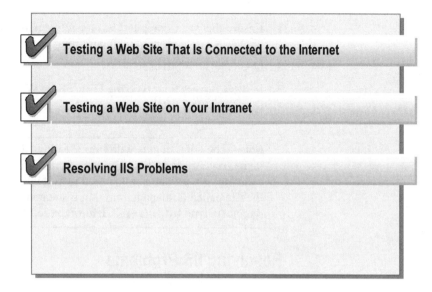

✓ Testing a Web Site That Is Connected to the Internet

✓ Testing a Web Site on Your Intranet

✓ Resolving IIS Problems

You can use your Web browser to test a Web site that is connected to the Internet, or to test a Web site on your intranet. If the Web page does not appear after using these testing methods, examine the error message to determine the cause of the problem.

Testing a Web Site that is Connected to the Internet

To test a Web site that is connected to the Internet:

1. Ensure that the home directory for your Web server contains all of the HTML files for the Web site.

2. Open the Web browser on a computer that has an active connection to the Internet. This computer can be the computer you are testing, although it is recommended that you use a different computer on the network.

3. In the **Address** box, type the Uniform Resource Locator (URL) for the Web site's home directory, and then press ENTER.

> **Note** The URL includes the name of your Web site and the path of the file that you want to view. For example, if your site is registered in DNS as examples.nwtraders.com and you want to view the file called homepage.htm that is located in the root of the home directory, type **http://examples.nwtraders.com/homepage.htm**

Testing a Web Site on Your Intranet

To test a Web site on your intranet:

1. Ensure that your computer has an active network connection and the DNS or WINS Server service is functioning properly.

2. Open the Web browser.

3. In the **Address** box, type the URL of the Web server's home directory, and then press ENTER.

Note   The URL begins with http:// followed by the Windows Networking name of your server and the path of the file that you want to view. For example, if your site is registered in WINS as Admin1 and you want to view the file called homepage.htm that is located in the root of the home directory, type **http://admin1/homepage.htm**

Resolving IIS Problems

When you are not able to display a Web page while testing a Web site, carefully examine the error message. The error message contains information that can help you to identify the cause of the problem. The following table lists common connectivity problems and their solutions.

Problem	Solution
The client cannot find the Web server.	Check name resolution and connectivity.
Access is forbidden.	Check the authentication method and file permissions.
File not found.	Check that the file exists and that its location is correct.
File does not display correctly.	Check the page design to ensure that all elements exist, such as graphics. Verify that the permissions are set correctly.

Tip   If your computer has IIS installed on it, you can use your Web browser to access the IIS online documentation, which contains many troubleshooting tips and procedures. To access the IIS online documentation, in the **Address** box, type **http://localhost/iishelp** and then press ENTER.

Lab A: Configuring a Web Server

Objectives

After completing this lab, you will be able to:

- Configure IIS.
- Create a Web site.
- Configure Web site security.
- Configure a default document for a Web site.

Prerequisites

Before working on this lab, you must have:

- Knowledge of the operations of IIS.
- Knowledge of the options for Web site security.

Lab Setup

To complete this lab, you need the following:

- A computer running Windows 2000 Advanced Server
- The files in the C:\MOC\Win2153\Labfiles\Module12\ folder

Important   The lab does not reflect the real-world environment. It is recommended that you always use complex passwords for any administrator accounts, and never create accounts without a password.

Important   Outside of the classroom environment, it is strongly advised that you use the most recent software updates that are necessary. Because this is a classroom environment, we may use software that does not include the latest updates.

Scenario

Northwind Traders is creating an intranet Web site to keep employees up-to-date about company initiatives and other news. All employees will access most of this Web site. However, parts of the Web site contain information to which only managers should have access. An important design objective for the Web site is that the information on the site be protected from unauthorized access.

Estimated time to complete this lab: 30 minutes

Exercise 1
Creating a Web Site

Scenario

As the network administrator for Northwind Traders, you have been given the responsibility to create an intranet Web site. Another company has designed the content of the Web site for Northwind Traders. You need to ensure that users in your company are able to access the content.

Goal

In this exercise, you will create a Web site by using IIS.

Tasks	Detailed Steps
1. Stop the Default Web Site.	a. Log on as administrator@*domain*.nwtraders.msft (where *domain* is the name of your domain) with a password of **password**.
	b. Open Internet Services Manager from the **Administrative Tools** menu.
	c. In the console tree, under **Internet Information Services**, expand *server* (where *server* is the name of your computer).
	d. Right-click **Default Web Site**, and then click **Stop**.
2. Create a new Web site with the name **NWTraders Web Site** and a Web site home directory of C:\MOC\ Win2153\Labfiles\ Module12\Web.	a. Right-click *server*, point to **New**, and then click **Web Site**.
	b. In the Web Site Creation wizard, click **Next**.
	c. On the **Web Site Description** page, in the **Description** box, type **NWTraders Web Site** and then click **Next**.
	d. On the **IP Address and Port Settings** page, verify that the Web site uses all unassigned IP addresses and TCP port 80, and then click **Next**.
	e. On the **Web Site Home Directory** page, in the **Path** box, type **C:\MOC\Win2153\Labfiles\Module12\Web**
	f. Verify that the **Allow anonymous access to this Web site** check box is selected, and then click **Next**.
	g. On the **Web Site Access Permissions** page, verify that the **Read** and **Run scripts** check boxes are selected, click **Next**, and then click **Finish**.
3. Set home.htm as the default home page for the Web site that you created.	a. In Internet Services Manager, in the console tree, right-click **NWTraders Web Site**, and then click **Properties**.
	b. Review the information on the **Web Site** and **Home Directory** tabs to verify that the information that you entered in the wizard appears.
	c. On the **Documents** tab, click **Add**.
	d. In the **Add Default Document** dialog box, in the **Default Document Name** box, type **home.htm** and then click **OK**.
	e. Click the arrow button to the left of the default document list until home.htm is at the top of the list.

Tasks	Detailed Steps
3. *(continued)*	f. On the **Operators** tab, verify that only the Administrators group is listed as operators.
	g. Click **OK** to close the **NWTraders Web Site Properties** dialog box.
	h. **Minimize** Internet Information Services.
4. View your Web site's home page.	a. Click **Start**, and then click **Run**.
	b. In the **Open** box, type **http://localhost** and then click **OK**.
	💻 *Internet Explorer displays the Northwind Traders home page.*
	c. Minimize Internet Explorer.

Exercise 2
Configuring Web Site Security

Scenario

Northwind Traders' intranet Web site is functional and employees are accessing it. Management has requested a secure area of the Web site where managers can place information that only other managers can access. After confidential portions of the Web site have been secured, all users need to continue to be able to access information on the Web site without having to enter user names and passwords.

Goal

In this exercise, you will configure Web site security by using several authentication methods.

Tasks	Detailed Steps
1. Assign the Log on locally right to Everyone.	a. Run the C:\MOC\Win2153\Labfiles\Module12\lab12.cmd command file to assign the Logon locally right to the Everyone group.
2. Configure the Web site for Basic Security, and then access your Web site as nwtraders.msft\Paul with a password of **password**.	a. Restore Internet Information Services.
	b. In the console tree, right-click **NWTraders Web Site**, and then click **Properties**.
	c. On the **Directory Security** tab, under **Anonymous access and authentication control**, click **Edit**.
	d. In the **Authentication Methods** dialog box, clear the **Anonymous access** and **Integrated Windows authentication** check boxes.
	e. Select the **Basic authentication** check box.
	f. In the **Internet Service Manager** message box, read the warning, and then click **Yes**.
	g. Click **OK** to close the **Authentication Methods** dialog box.
	h. Click **OK** to close the **NWTraders Web Site Properties** dialog box.
	i. Restore Internet Explorer.
	j. Click the **Refresh** button.
	Internet Explorer prompts you for your network credentials. When anonymous access is disabled, you must provide a valid user name and password to view any page on the Web site.
	k. In the **Enter Network Password** dialog box, in the **User Name** box, type **nwtraders.msft\Paul**
	l. In the **Password** box, type **password**
	m. Verify that the **Save this password in your password list** check box is not selected, and then click **OK**.
	n. Minimize Internet Explorer.

(continued)

Tasks	Detailed Steps
3. Set the permissions for managers.htm to only allow access for members of the Administrators group, and then test the permissions.	a. In Internet Information Services, right-click **Nwtraders Web Site**, and then click **Explore**.
	b. In Windows Explorer, right-click **managers.htm**, and then click **Properties**.
	c. In the **managers.htm Properties** dialog box, on the **Security** tab, clear the **Allow inheritable permissions from parent to propagate to this object** check box.
	d. In the **Security** dialog box, click **Remove**.
	e. Click **Add**.
	f. In the **Select Users, Computers, or Groups** dialog box, under **Name**, click **Administrators**, click **Add**, and then click **OK**.
	g. Allow the Administrators group the Full Control permission, and then click **OK**.
	h. Close Windows Explorer, and then restore Internet Explorer.
	i. On the Northwind Traders Intranet Web page, click **Click here for Public information about Northwind Traders**.
	j. Click **Back** to return to the home page.
	k. On the Northwind Traders Intranet Web Page, click **Click here for the Northwind Traders Management Web Page**.
	Internet Explorer prompts you for your network credentials. When the user account that you used to log on to a Web site does not have access to a file that you are attempting to access, you must provide a user name and password that does have access to the file.
	l. In the **Enter Network Password** dialog box, in the **User Name** box, type **Administrator**
	m. In the **Password** box, type **password**
	n. Verify that the **Save this password in your password list** check box is not selected, and then click **OK**.
	Internet Explorer displays the Northwind Traders Managers Only Web page.
	o. Close Internet Explorer.

(continued)

Tasks	Detailed Steps
4. Configure the Web site for Integrated Windows Authentication, and then test the authentication.	a. In Internet Services Manager, right-click **Nwtraders Web Site**, and then click **Properties**. b. On the **Directory Security** tab, under **Anonymous access and authentication control**, click **Edit**. c. In the **Authentication Methods** dialog box, select the **Integrated Windows authentication** check box. d. Clear the **Basic authentication** check box, and then click **OK**. e. Click **OK** to close the **NWTraders Web Site Properties** dialog box. f. Minimize Internet Information Services. g. Click **Start**, and then click **Run**. h. In the **Open** box, type **http://localhost** and then click **OK**. *Internet Explorer displays the Northwind Traders Web page without prompting you for your credentials.*

❓ Why were you not prompted for your credentials when you accessed the Northwind Traders Web site?

_____

_____

_____

_____

Tasks	Detailed Steps
4. *(continued)*	i. On the Northwind Traders Intranet Web Page, click **Click here for the Northwind Traders Management Web Page**. *Internet Explorer displays the secured Web page without prompting you for your credentials.*

❓ Why were you not prompted for your credentials when you accessed the secured Web page?

_____

_____

_____

_____

Tasks	Detailed Steps
4. *(continued)*	j. Close Internet Explorer.

Exercise 3
Restoring Your Configuration

Scenario

After you have tested the Web site for Northwind Traders, you must restore IIS to its original configuration.

Goal

In this exercise, you will restore the original Web site settings for your computer.

Task	Detailed Steps
1. Stop the NWTraders Web Site and start the Default Web Site.	a. Restore Internet Information Services. b. In the console tree, right-click **NWTraders Web Site**, and then click **Stop**. c. In the console tree, right-click **Default Web Site**, and then click **Start**. d. Close all open windows, and then log off.

Review

- **Overview of IIS**
- **Preparing for an IIS Installation**
- **Installing IIS**
- **Configuring a Web Site**
- **Administering IIS**
- **Troubleshooting IIS**

1. The computer running Windows 2000 Server in your department stores some product information and white papers that you want to share with other employees of your organization. Your organization has a network of computers running Windows 2000, Windows 98, and the Macintosh operating system. How do you publish the required information so that it is accessible to all of the users in your network?

2. You are about to host a new Web site for your company, and you want users to refer to the Web site by using a specific name. How do you enable users to connect to the Web site by using this name?

3. You are responsible for your company's intranet Web site that contains general information and white papers. Your network spans multiple domains, and you do not have a corporate standard for Web browsers. You must configure IIS to enable all employees of the company to have access to the information. Which access or authentication method do you use to achieve this?

    a. Anonymous access.

    b. Basic authentication.

    c. Digest authentication.

    d. Integrated Windows authentication.

4. Your Web page designer created Web pages for your company's Web site. The home page for the Web site is called nwtradershome.htm. You have been assigned the task of publishing the Web site. How do you ensure that users can access the home page without explicitly specifying the file name nwtradershome.htm?

5. You want to authenticate all of the users who access the official Web site of your organization through any Web browser. Which of the following methods of authentication is best suited for your requirements?

    a. Anonymous access.

    b. Basic authentication.

    c. Digest authentication.

    d. Integrated Windows authentication.

Microsoft®
Training &
Certification

Module 13: Deploying Windows 2000 Professional by Using RIS

Contents

Overview

- **RIS Overview**
- **Installing and Configuring RIS**
- **Configuring Remote Installation Options**
- **Deploying Images by Using RIS**
- **Creating an RIPrep Image**
- **Comparing CD-Based Images and RIPrep Images**
- **Identifying Solutions to RIS Problems**

Remote Installation Services (RIS) is the basis of the Microsoft® Windows® 2000 Remote OS Installation feature. RIS makes it easy to deploy Windows 2000 Professional throughout an organization without the need to physically visit each client computer.

The combination of RIS with other Microsoft IntelliMirror® management technologies—User Data Management, Software Installation and Maintenance, and User Settings Management—provides companies with the benefit of better disaster recovery through easier operating system and application management.

At the end of this module, you will be able to:

- Describe the purpose and benefits of RIS.
- Install and configure a RIS server by using the Remote Installation Services Setup wizard.
- Modify RIS configurations, including changing default options for client names and account locations, installation options, and diagnostic utilities.
- Deploy CD-based RIS images.
- Create Remote Installation Preparation (RIPrep) images.
- Compare CD-based images and RIPrep images.
- Provide solutions to potential RIS problems.

RIS Overview

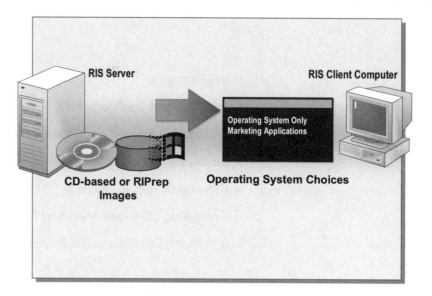

RIS enables client computers to connect to a server during the initial startup phase and remotely install Windows 2000 Professional. Unlike a standard network installation performed by running Winnt.exe, a remote installation does not require users to know where the installation source files are stored or what information to supply during the Setup program. The remote installation process includes three primary components:

- *RIS servers*. These servers host RIS and distribute Windows 2000 Professional to client computers that are enabled for remote startup. RIS servers can be either domain controllers or member servers in a Windows 2000 domain.

- *RIS client computers*. Upon startup, RIS client computers can connect to a RIS server to install Windows 2000 Professional remotely or run diagnostic and maintenance utilities.

- *Images*. These represent the operating system configurations that can be installed on client computers. RIS supports two types of images: CD-based images and RIPrep images.

You can use RIS to quickly and easily install Windows 2000 Professional on a replacement computer. When a user experiences computer problems, you can give the user a computer with an unformatted hard disk as a permanent or temporary replacement. When the user turns on the computer, he or she can use RIS to install the required operating system with the correct configuration, and then use IntelliMirror technologies to install all of the required applications and gain access to personal settings and documents.

Note   RIS only supports the remote installation of Windows 2000 Professional. In addition, RIS does not support images that are created by third-party imaging utilities.

◆ Installing and Configuring RIS

- ■ **Identifying RIS Requirements**
- ■ **Installing and Starting RIS**
- ■ **Configuring RIS Security Settings**

RIS requires that certain network services be installed and configured to ensure a successful RIS installation. You must also ensure that the server meets certain disk space requirements, and that clients meet specific hardware requirements, before installing RIS.

Identifying RIS Requirements

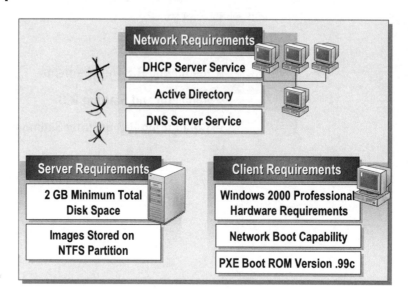

Certain services must be available on your network before RIS can be installed. In addition, the server on which RIS will be installed must meet certain disk space requirements, and client computers must meet specific hardware requirements and capabilities. It is important that these requirements be met to ensure successful RIS installation and operation.

Network Requirements

RIS requires that several services be running on the network. These services can run on the same computer as RIS, or they can be installed on other computers located on the network. RIS requires the following Windows 2000 services:

- *DHCP Server service*. Uses the Dynamic Host Configuration Protocol (DHCP) to assign Internet Protocol (IP) addresses to client computers.

- *Active Directory™directory service*. Locates client computer accounts and RIS servers and manages RIS configuration settings and client installation options.

- *DNS Server service*. Locates the Active Directory directory service. The DNS Server service must be configured to support SRV (service) resource records.

Server Requirements

A RIS server requires 2 gigabytes (GB) of disk space for the Windows 2000 Professional installation source files and the RIS support files. The hard disk must have at least two partitions (for a basic disk) or two volumes (for a dynamic disk). One partition or volume is used for the operating system and the other is used for images. The image partition or volume must be formatted with the NTFS file system.

RIS images cannot be installed on either the system or the boot partition. If the server uses a small system partition or volume and a larger boot partition or volume, a third NTFS partition or volume is required to support RIS images.

Important   Place the image files on a partition or volume on a separate hard disk or disk array. This increases performance when copying image files.

Client Requirements

Client computers that will receive remote installations must meet the hardware requirements for Windows 2000 Professional. In addition, the client computers must be able to boot from the network adapter, and the network adapter must support Pre-Boot Execution Environment (PXE) boot ROM version .99c or later.

Installing and Starting RIS

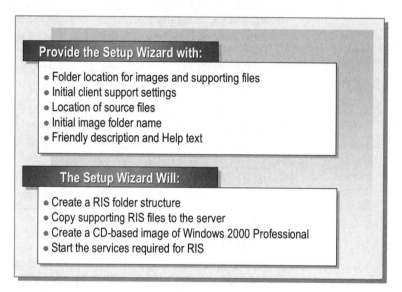

To install RIS, open Add/Remove Programs in Control Panel, and then click
Add/Remove Windows Components. Select the **Remote Installation
Services** check box, and then click **Next**. The Windows Components wizard
will guide you through the remainder of the installation process.

Important   Place the RIS servers in the same subnet as the client computers that
they will serve. This will provide better setup performance and limit the amount
of RIS-related network traffic that travels across slow network connections.

Running the Remote Installation Services Setup Wizard

After you install RIS, run the Remote Installation Services Setup wizard to
create the initial CD-based image and configure and start RIS.

To start the Remote Installation Services Setup wizard:

1. Click **Start**, and then click **Run**.

2. In the **Open** box, type **risetup** and then click **OK**.

3. Follow the on-screen instructions in the Remote Installation Services Setup wizard. When prompted, supply the information provided in the following table.

When prompted for	Do this
Remote Installation Folder Location	Specify the NTFS partition and folder on the RIS server where you want to install the supporting files and the first CD-based image. The location that you supply cannot be on a Distributed file system (Dfs) shared folder or a volume that is configured for encryption by using the Encrypting File System (EFS).
Initial Settings	Specify how the RIS server will respond to client computers. You can set the server so that it:
	• Does not respond to any client requests by clearing the **Respond to client computers requesting service** check box. This is the default setting.
	• Responds to all client requests by selecting the **Respond to client computers requesting service** check box.
	• Responds only to requests from clients that have prestaged computer accounts by selecting both the **Respond to client computers requesting service** and **Do not respond to unknown client computers** check boxes.
Installation Source Files Location	Specify the location of the Windows 2000 Professional source files that RIS uses to create the initial CD-based image. These files can be copied from either a compact disc or a shared folder on the network. You must create an initial CD-based image before you can start RIS, even if you plan to provide only RIPrep images to users.
Windows Installation Image Folder Name	Specify the name of the folder, within the RIS installation folder on the RIS server, in which the initial CD-based image will be created.
Friendly Description and Help Text	Specify the description and explanatory text for the initial CD-based image. This information will appear when the user logs on to the RIS server and selects this image from the list that appears in the Client Installation wizard.

Note Before running the Remote Installation Services Setup wizard, ensure that the latest service packs, hot fixes and security updates are applied to the server, or ensure that the installation files from a network source contain the latest service packs, hot fixes, and security updates.

Completing Post-Installation Tasks

After the Remote Installation Services Setup wizard is finished, Windows 2000 automatically:

- Creates the RIS folder structure.

- Copies the supporting files to the server.

- Creates the initial CD-based image of Windows 2000 Professional and the default answer file.

- Starts the required services on the RIS server.

Important   Do not activate client support until you are ready to use it. By default, client support is disabled when you run the Remote Installation Services Setup wizard. It is recommended that you leave this option disabled until you have fully configured the server and have set up all of the required images and answer files.

Configuring RIS Security Settings

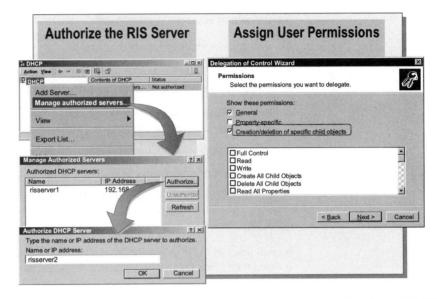

You must configure security settings to enable RIS to function properly before you can install Windows 2000 Professional by using RIS. A RIS server must be authorized within Active Directory before it can begin responding to client requests. In addition, users must have the right to create computer accounts in Active Directory to be able to install an image by using RIS.

Authorizing the RIS Server

You must authorize RIS servers in Active Directory. This prevents users from setting up an additional RIS server and installing unauthorized images on client computers, and then joining those computers to a domain.

You authorize the RIS server as you would authorize a DHCP server in the DHCP console. To authorize a RIS server in Active Directory:

1. Open DHCP from the **Administrative Tools** menu.

2. In the console tree, right-click **DHCP**, and then click **Manage authorized servers**.

3. In the **Manage Authorized Servers** dialog box, click **Authorize**. When prompted, type the name or IP address of the RIS server to be authorized, and then click **OK**.

When authorization is complete, the arrow on the server icon in the DHCP console changes from red to green.

Important   To authorize a DHCP or RIS server, a user must be a member of the Enterprise Admins group, which exists in the root domain of the forest.

Assigning User Permissions

You can assign users the permissions to create computer accounts anywhere in the domain or in a specified organizational unit (OU).

To assign users the permissions to create computer accounts in Active Directory:

1. Open Active Directory Users and Computers.

2. In the console tree, right-click the domain or OU in which you want to allow users to create computer accounts, and then click **Delegate Control**.

3. In the Delegation of Control wizard, click **Next**.

4. On the **Users or Groups** page, click **Add**.

5. In the **Select Users, Computers, or Groups** dialog box, click the name of the user or group that you want to add, click **Add**, click **OK**, and then click **Next**.

6. On the **Tasks to Delegate** page, click **Create a custom task to delegate**, and then click **Next**.

7. On the **Active Directory Object Type** page, under **Delegate control of**, verify that **This folder, existing objects in this folder, and creation of new objects in this folder** is selected, and then click **Next**.

8. On the **Permissions** page, under **Show these permissions**, select the **Creation/deletion of specific child objects** check box.

9. Under **Permissions**, select the **Create Computer Objects** check box, and then click **Next**.

10. On the **Completing the Delegation of Control Wizard** page, verify the delegation of control settings, and then click **Finish**.

Important   By default, each user account has the right to create up to 10 computer accounts in Active Directory. You must only give users permissions to create user accounts if you removed the default right, or if a user must create more than 10 computer accounts.

◆ Configuring Remote Installation Options

- **Configuring Client Computer Names and Locations**
- **Prestaging Client Computers**
- **Configuring Client Installation Options**
- **Configuring Maintenance and Troubleshooting Utilities**

After you install and start RIS, you can configure how the RIS server responds to client requests for service. You can customize how RIS operates by specifying a client computer naming format and the Active Directory location in which client computer accounts are created. Additional RIS configurations include prestaging client computer accounts, and specifying which installation options and third-party diagnostic utilities are available to users.

Configuring Client Computer Names and Locations

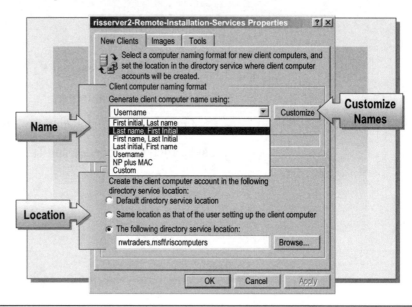

You can specify a standard naming convention and a computer account location for all client computers that are supported by a designated RIS server.

Client Computer Naming Format

The client computer naming format option provides a standard naming convention for computer accounts that RIS creates.

To configure client names:

1. In Active Directory Users and Computers, right-click the RIS server, and then click **Properties**.

2. In the **Properties** dialog box for the server, click the **Remote Install** tab, and then click **Advanced Settings**.

3. In the **Remote-Installation-Services Properties** dialog box for the server, click the **New Clients** tab, and click one of the predefined naming formats (for example, **First initial, Last name**) or click **Customize** to create a custom naming format.

   By default, RIS names computers after the user name of the user performing the remote installation. You can include any alphanumeric text as part of a custom naming format. You can also select from the following variables that are associated with user and computer properties stored in Active Directory. Any name that exceeds 64 characters is truncated.

Variable	Value used in computer name
%Username	User logon name
%First	User first name
%Last	User last name
%#	Incremental number
%MAC	MAC address of the network adapter

Client Computer Account Location

The client computer account location allows you to specify the Active Directory location where new computer accounts will be created. The following table describes the options available for setting computer account locations.

Option	Description
Default directory service location	Creates new computer accounts in the Computers container
Same location as that of the user setting up the computer	Creates new computer accounts in the same OU as the user account of the person who is performing the remote installation
The following directory service location	Creates new computer accounts in the OU that you specify

Prestaging Client Computers

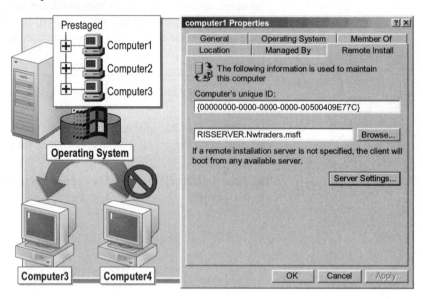

Prestaging a client computer involves preconfiguring a computer account for the client computer and assigning it to a designated RIS server. If you assign a client computer to a RIS server, only the designated server responds to service requests from that client computer.

You use prestaging primarily for security purposes. When used with the **Do not respond to unknown clients** client support option, prestaging prevents unknown RIS client computers from obtaining images, thereby preventing users from joining unauthorized computers to the domain.

Prestaging enables you to balance the load between RIS servers. You can ensure that a single server does not respond to a disproportionate number of installation requests by directing specific client computers to receive images from designated RIS servers.

Locating a GUID

Before you can prestage a client computer, you must know the globally unique identifier (GUID) of the computer. The manufacturer provides the GUID as part of the PXE specification. The information is generally located on a label on the side of the computer case, on a label within the computer case, or in the basic input/output system (BIOS) of the client computer.

For computers starting from a RIS Startup disk, the GUID is the media access control (MAC) address of the network adapter, with enough leading zeros added to ensure that the GUID is 32 characters in length.

For example: {921FB974-ED42-11BE-BACD-00AA0057B223}

Prestaging a Client Computer with a Known GUID

After you determine the GUID of a client computer, you can prestage the client computer.

To prestage a client computer with a known GUID:

1. In Active Directory Users and Computers, right-click the OU in which you want to create the computer account, point to **New**, and then click **Computer**.

2. In the **Create New Object – (Computer)** dialog box, type a name for the computer and a pre-Windows 2000 name for the computer, and then click **Next**.

3. Select the **This is a managed computer** check box, type the GUID of the computer without the dashes or brackets, and then click **Next**.

4. Under **Specify the remote installation server to support this client**, click **The following remote installation server**, and then type the fully qualified domain name (FQDN) of the designated RIS server—for example, london.nwtraders.msft.

5. Click **Next**, and then click **Finish**.

Prestaging a Client Computer with an Unknown GUID

If you do not know the GUID of a computer, you can prestage the computer by logging on to the RIS server.

To prestage a client computer with an unknown GUID:

1. Start the RIS client computer by using a network service startup, and then log on to the RIS server.

2. When prompted, use the arrow keys to select a setup option, and then press ENTER.

3. When prompted, use the arrow keys to select an image, and then press ENTER.

4. At the **Warning** screen, press ENTER.

   The GUID appears on the screen. The computer account is now prestaged. If you want to assign the client computer to a designed RIS server, you can do so in the **Properties** dialog box of the RIS client computer.

5. Turn off the computer to prevent it from receiving an image.

Configuring Client Installation Options

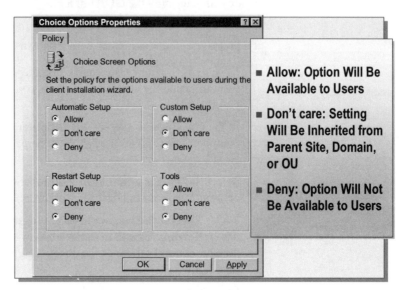

You can use Group Policy to configure the installation options that are presented to users in the Client Installation wizard. *Group Policy* is a collection of user-environment settings used to define configurations for groups of users and computers. You can create one Group Policy object (GPO) at the domain level to provide users with a minimal set of installation options, and you can create another GPO for users within a specific OU to provide the users with additional options. If Group Policy settings conflict, the GPO created at the OU level overrides the GPO created at the domain level.

Note   For more information on Group Policy, see course 2154, *Implementing and Administering Microsoft Windows 2000 Directory Services*.

To configure client installation options:

1. In Active Directory Users and Computers, right-click the name of the site, domain, or OU where you want to apply the policy, and then click **Properties**.

2. In the **Properties** dialog box, click the **Group Policy** tab, create a new GPO or click an existing GPO, and then click **Edit**.

3. In the **Group Policy** console, double-click **User Configuration**, double-click **Windows Settings**, and then click **Remote Installation Services**.

4. In the details pane, double-click **Choice Options**, select the appropriate client installation options, and then click **OK**.

The following table describes the client installation options.

Option	Description
Automatic setup	Installs Windows 2000 Professional by using the computer naming convention and computer account location predetermined for this RIS server.
Custom setup	Allows the user to override the automatic computer name assignment and computer account location. This option is useful if technical support personnel need to set up computers for other users.
Restart Setup	Allows you to restart a failed installation of Windows 2000 Professional from the beginning without requiring you to re-enter information previously entered in the Client Installation wizard.
Tools	Provides access to third-party maintenance and troubleshooting utilities. These options are typically intended for technical support personnel who need to perform maintenance or troubleshooting tasks.

The following table describes the options that you configure for each client installation option.

Option	Description
Allow	Makes the option available within the Client Installation wizard. Use this option if you want to offer the installation option to users for whom the policy applies.
Don't Care	Has no effect on whether the option is available in the Client Installation wizard. Instead, the policy settings for this option are inherited from a parent site, domain, or OU.
Deny	Prevents the option from being available within the Client Installation wizard. Use this option if you do not want the installation option to be available to users for whom the policy applies.

Note By default, only **Automatic Setup** is enabled when you install RIS. To provide users with access to any of the other options, you must specifically enable those options.

Configuring Maintenance and Troubleshooting Utilities

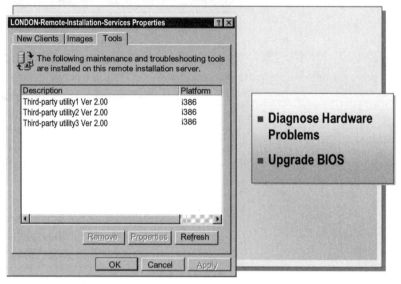

You can give users the option to use maintenance and troubleshooting utilities provided by independent software vendors (ISVs) and original equipment manufacturers (OEMs). These utilities can be used to troubleshoot hardware-related problems, and provide an easy way to update client computer systems. For example, a vendor may provide a way to upgrade a computer's BIOS by using the remote installation process.

Installing Maintenance and Troubleshooting Utilities

Maintenance and troubleshooting utilities are installed by using an external Setup program provided by the ISV or OEM. The Setup program copies the required files to the RIS server. In addition, it creates an answer file and copies it to the RIS server. When you open the **Remote-Installation-Services Properties** dialog box, the RIS server examines the answer file and displays the installed utilities on the **Tools** tab.

Enabling Access to Maintenance and Troubleshooting Utilities

Users can access third-party utilities by initiating a network service startup and then selecting the **Maintenance and Troubleshooting** option. However, these utilities are only available to users if you have used Group Policy to enable users to access them. You can also modify the NTFS permissions on the individual answer files to restrict access to any given utility. For example, you can ensure that a BIOS update utility is available only to users who have that particular BIOS by assigning the Read permission on the answer file for that utility only to those users.

◆ Deploying Images by Using RIS

- **Modifying the Installation of a CD-Based Image**
- **Associating an Answer File with an Image**
- **Restricting Images**
- **Creating a RIS Startup Disk**
- **Installing an Image on a RIS Client Computer**

The process for deploying images involves some or all of the following procedures. The steps you will need to take to actually deploy images depends on the types of images you are using, whether you would like to restrict images to designated groups, and the hardware that is available for the client computers. Deploying images may or may not involve modifying the installation of a CD-based image, associating an answer file with an image, restricting images to designated users, creating a RIS Startup disk for non-PXE network adapters, and installing an image on a RIS client computer.

Modifying the Installation of a CD-Based Image

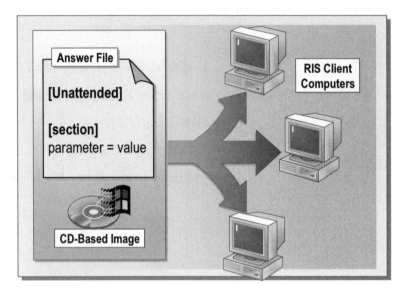

A CD-based image is an image of the operating system and its default settings. CD-based images are useful for deploying a basic Windows 2000 Professional installation that requires minimal configuration settings.

When you install RIS, a CD-based image and a standard answer file (called Ristndrd.sif) are created for you. After the CD-based image is created, you can configure the setup information file or .sif file, or you can create an additional answer file by using Setup Manager.

Note Setup Manager files are located on the Windows 2000 Server compact disc. To locate the files, open Windows Explorer and expand the CD-ROM drive. Expand the Support folder, and then click **Tools**. In the right pane, double-click **deploy.cab**, and copy the Setupmgr.exe and Setupmgx.dll files to an existing folder or a new folder on your hard disk. You can also copy the files Deptool.chm and Unattend.doc, which contain documentation for Setup Manager. To start Setup Manager, open the folder to which you copied the files and double-click **setupmgr.exe**.

Answer File

An answer file is a text file that contains the information that the user would usually have to supply during setup. It uses the same format as the unattend.txt files used for unattended installations in Windows 2000.

Note For more information about unattend.txt files, see the document *Microsoft Windows 2000 Guide to Unattended Setup*, under **Additional Reading** on the Web page on the Student Materials compact disc.

Configuring an Answer File

By using an answer file, you can:

- Deploy a partial or fully unattended setup of Windows 2000 Professional. You do this by configuring an answer file so that the image is installed with little or no user intervention.

- Deploy an image to a group of computers that require custom settings. For example, you can configure an answer file that sets the display resolution to 800x600 or sets regional settings such as the time zone.

Important The answer file supports a [RemoteInstall] section that contains the repartition parameter. If this value is not specified or set to **Yes**, a RIS installation deletes all partitions on the client computer and partitions and formats the hard drive with one NTFS partition. If this value is set to **No**, RIS uses the default parameters in the client answer file. The RIS formatting process does not affect partitions created for OEM power management.

Associating an Answer File with an Image

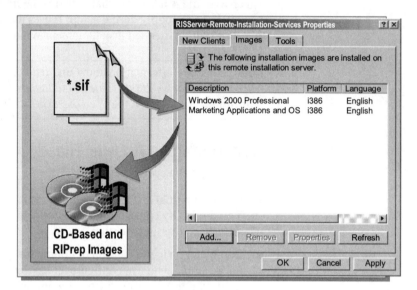

After you create an answer file, you must associate it with an existing image. You can associate multiple answer files with a single image. This is useful if you want to add a new configuration of an image to the RIS server without having to recopy all of the files for the image.

To associate an answer file with an image:

1. In Active Directory Users and Computers, right-click the RIS server, and then click **Properties**.

2. In the **Properties** dialog box for the server, click the **Remote Install** tab, and then click **Advanced Settings**.

3. In the **Remote-Installation-Services Properties** dialog box for the server, click the **Images** tab, and then click **Add**.

4. In the Add wizard, on the **New Answer File or Installation Image** page, click **Associate a new answer file to an existing image**, and then click **Next**.

5. On the **Unattended Setup Answer File Source** page, select the location of the answer file by clicking one of the options in the following table, and then click **Next**.

Click this option	To
Windows image sample files	Select from the sample image files that are installed with RIS.
Another remote installation server	Copy an answer file from another RIS server.
An alternate location	Specify a local or universal naming convention (UNC) path to an answer file.

6. Follow the on-screen instructions to finish associating the answer file with an existing image.

Restricting Images

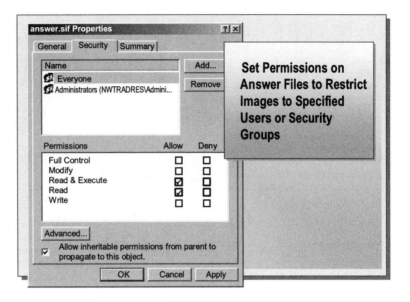

All images are available to all users by default. However, you can restrict the images that are available to users by setting NTFS permissions on an answer file. This allows you to determine which images a user can select and download.

Typically, you group users into security groups, and then permit selected security groups access to specific answer files. This allows you to create different menus of images that are customized for specific business units or departments within your organization.

To restrict operating system images:

1. In Windows Explorer, right-click the answer file that you want to restrict, and then click **Properties**.

2. In the **Properties** dialog box for the answer file, click the **Security** tab, click **Everyone**, and then click **Remove**.

   This removes access for all users to this image. If a user runs the Client Installation wizard, he or she does not have access to this image.

3. Click **Add**.

4. In the **Select Users, Computers, or Groups** dialog box, click the security group to whom you want to give access to this image, and then click **Add**.

   The default permissions (Read and Read & Execute) are the only permissions that a user needs to use the answer file to install the image.

Creating a RIS Startup Disk

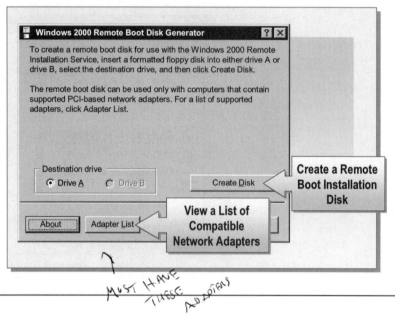

Before installing the images on client computers, you must verify that the network adapters of the client computers meet the PXE specification. If a client computer does not have a network adapter that meets the PXE specification, you can remotely install Windows 2000 Professional if the RIS Startup disk supports the network adapter.

The RIS Startup disk simulates the PXE startup process for computers with network adapters that do not support PXE. If the computer has a supported network adapter, you can start the computer from the RIS Startup disk and then initiate a RIS session by pressing F12 when prompted.

You can use the same RIS Startup disk on any client computer that has one of the supported network adapters installed. You do not need to create a separate Startup disk for each type of network adapter.

Use the Remote Boot Disk Generator utility (rbfg.exe) to create a RIS Startup disk. This utility is automatically installed when you install RIS.

To create a RIS Startup disk:

1. On any computer running Windows 2000, click **Start**, and then click **Run**.

2. In the **Open** box, type *RIS_server***reminst****admin****i386****rbfg.exe** (where *RIS_server* represents the name of the RIS server), and then click **OK**.

3. When the **Windows 2000 Remote Boot Disk Generator** dialog box appears, insert a blank disk into drive A, and then click **Create Disk**.

Note A RIS Startup disk may work with a network adapter that is not on the list of supported network adapters, because PXE compatibility is based on the chipset of the network adapter. You can also test the RIS Startup disk on a computer with an unsupported network adapter to determine whether the network adapter supports remote installation.

Installing an Image on a RIS Client Computer

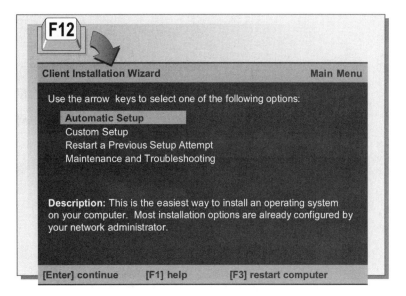

To perform a remote installation on a client computer, users must request a network service startup by pressing F12 after they turn on their computers, or by starting their computers with the RIS Startup disk. After the client computer establishes a connection with a RIS server, the user is prompted to press F12 again to download and start the Client Installation wizard. The Client Installation wizard prompts the user to log on to a domain, and then provides the user with a list of available installation options. The following table describes the installation options.

Option	Description
Automatic Setup	Users can choose which image to install. If only one image is available, the user is not prompted to press F12.
Custom Setup	Users can override the automatic computer naming process and the default location within Active Directory where client computer accounts will be created. Technical support personnel can use this option to install a client computer for someone else.
Restart a Previous Setup Attempt	Users can restart the operating system installation process. Select this option if the previous installation attempt failed. The option does not start copying files where the previous installation attempt failed; however, the user is not prompted to answer any questions within the Client Installation wizard from the previous setup attempt.
Maintenance and Troubleshooting	Users can gain access to third-party maintenance and troubleshooting utilities.

◆ Creating an RIPrep Image

- **Setting Up a Source Computer**

- **Modifying the Default User Profile**

- **Creating an Image by Using the Remote Installation Preparation Wizard**

If you want to deploy applications along with the operating system, or if you want to deploy the operating system by using the fastest method, use Remote Installation Preparation (RIPrep) images instead of CD-based images. Configuring an RIPrep image of Windows 2000 Professional requires a source computer and a RIS server. It is important for you to understand how to set up a source computer, modify the default user profile, and create the image by using the Remote Installation Preparation wizard.

Setting Up a Source Computer

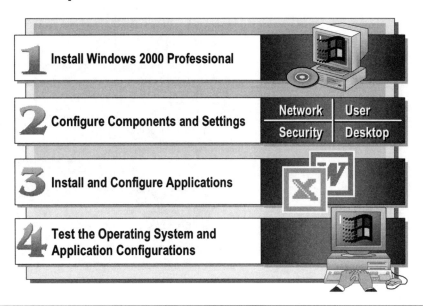

A *source computer* is a computer that is running Windows 2000 Professional and contains the components, settings, and applications that represent a standard client configuration. Configure a source computer with the exact configuration that you want deployed on other client computers.

When you designate a source computer, remember that the Remote Installation Preparation wizard can be used only to create an image of the contents of a single partition on a RIS server. Before you create and distribute an image, you must set up a source computer.

To set up a source computer:

1. Install Windows 2000 Professional.

2. Configure all components and settings that represent a standard client computer configuration. Always verify that any configuration settings that you make are appropriate for all users and computers that will install the image.

3. Install and configure applications. Install applications only if all users need them. Use Group Policy instead to install applications that are required only by specific individuals.

   Tip If you are planning to assign applications to computers, you can save time during installation by deploying the applications to the OU of the source computer before you create the image. Then, after you restart the source computer and create the image, the applications will already be installed.

4. Test the configuration of the operating system and all applications before you create an image. After the image is copied to the RIS server, you cannot alter the configuration. If you need to make any changes, you must create a new image.

Modifying the Default User Profile

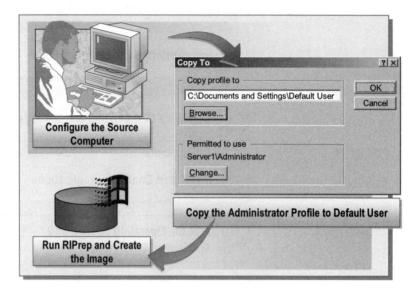

When you create an RIPrep image, any changes that you make are recorded in the Administrator profile. As a result, only users who log on as Administrator will receive your customized configuration. Users who log on by using their regular user accounts will receive the Default User profile.

To make your customized settings available to any user who logs on to a computer that has been configured from the RIPrep image, you must copy the Administrator profile to the Default User profile on the source computer before you run the Remote Installation Preparation wizard.

To copy the profile:

1. Make sure that you are logged on to the source computer as Administrator, and that you have completed all computer configuration tasks.

2. Right-click **My Computer**, and then click **Properties**.

3. In the **System Properties** dialog box, click the **User Profiles** tab, click the local Administrator profile from the **Profiles stored on this computer** list, and then click **Copy To**.

4. In the **Copy To** dialog box, in the **Copy profile to** text box, type the path to the Default User folder.

   This path is typically C:\Documents and Settings\Default User.

5. Click **Change** to display the **Choose User** dialog box.

6. In the **List Names From** box, click the local computer.

7. In the **Names** box, click **Everyone**, and then click **Add**.

8. Click **OK** twice to close the **Copy to** dialog box.

Creating an Image by Using the Remote Installation Preparation Wizard

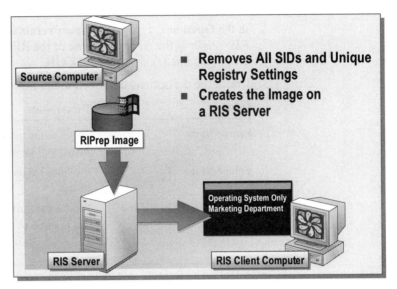

You use the Remote Installation Preparation wizard to create an image of the source computer on the RIS server. An image that has been created on a RIS server by using the wizard automatically appears as an installation option when the Client Installation wizard runs on a client computer. This happens because the Remote Installation Preparation wizard automatically creates the .sif file and places it in the appropriate folder.

Important Verify that the server still has a CD-based image stored on it before creating an RIPrep image on a RIS server. (A CD-based image is created by default when you first set up a RIS server.) You cannot create an RIPrep image on a RIS server unless that server has an existing CD-based image.

Remote Installation Preparation Wizard

After you finish configuring the source computer, create the image by running the Remote Installation Preparation wizard. The wizard:

- Configures the source computer to a generic state, removing all unique settings such as the unique security identifier (SID) of the computer, computer name, and any registry settings that are unique to that system.

- Creates the RIPrep image on the specified RIS server image partition.

- Creates an answer file and associates it with the newly created RIPrep image.

Creating an RIPrep Image

To create an RIPrep image:

1. On the source computer, click **Start**, and then click **Run**.

2. In the **Open** box, type *RIS_server***reminst\admin\i386\riprep.exe** (where *RIS_server* is the computer name of the RIS server on which you want to create this image), and then click **OK**.

3. Configure the options described in the following table.

Option	Description
Server Name	Provides the name of the RIS server where the image will be stored
Folder Name	Provides the name of the folder that will contain the image
Friendly Description and Help Text	Provides the information used to identify the name and purpose of the image

Important   The Remote Installation Preparation wizard creates an image on a single RIS server only. If you want to maintain an image on multiple RIS servers for load balancing or fault tolerance, you need to manually copy that image to each RIS server. Another solution is to use Microsoft Systems Management Server to manage the replication of images to multiple RIS servers.

Comparing CD-Based Images and RIPrep Images

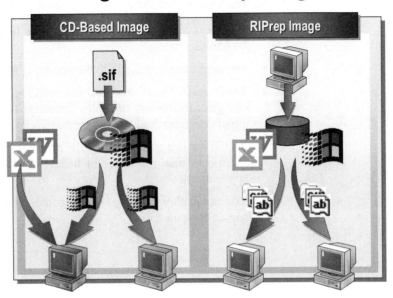

You can use a CD-based image or an RIPrep image to deploy Windows 2000 Professional on client computers. The following information compares CD-based images with RIPrep images.

CD-Based Images

CD-based images have the following characteristics:

- When you configure the RIS server, a default image is created automatically.

- A CD-based image can only contain the operating system. You can deploy applications separately by using Group Policy.

- The image is based on the default settings of the operating system. An answer file is required to customize the image.

- The image performs a full over-the-network setup by copying all of the files in the image to a temporary folder on the local hard disk before running the Setup program.

- You can deploy the image to any computer with a supported hardware abstraction layer (HAL).

RIPrep Images

RIPrep images have the following characteristics:

- You must create RIPrep images by using the Remote Installation Preparation wizard.

- The image can contain both the operating system and applications.

- The image is based on a preconfigured source computer. Making additional changes requires you to deploy the image to a client computer, configure the client computer, and then re-create the image.

- An RIPrep image copies only the necessary files and registry keys to the client computer, making it the fastest way to deploy an operating system and applications.

- You can deploy the image to any computer with the same HAL as the source computer.

Identifying Solutions to RIS Problems

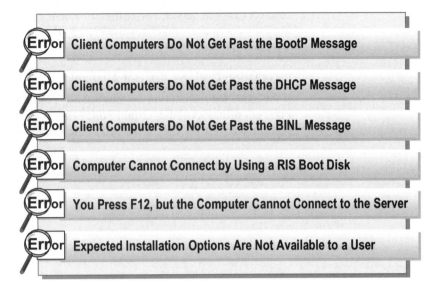

The following information provides possible solutions for problems that may occur when you set up a RIS server.

BootP Message

If client computers display a BootP message but do not display the DHCP message, determine whether non-RIS clients can obtain an IP address. If they cannot, make sure that the DHCP server is online, authorized, and has a defined and activated IP address scope. Make sure that DHCP packets are being routed.

DHCP Message

If client computers display the DHCP message but do not display the Boot Information Negotiation Layer (BINL) message, verify that the RIS server is online and authorized. In addition, you must ensure that DHCP packets are being routed.

BINL Message

If client computers display the BINL message but cannot connect to the RIS server, restart the Boot Information Negotiation Layer service (BINLSVC) on the RIS server.

RIS Boot Disk

If client computers cannot connect to a RIS server by using the RIS Startup disk, in the Remote Boot Disk Generator utility, click **Adapter List** to verify that the RIS Startup disk supports the client network adapter. To run the Remote Boot Disk Generator utility, click **Start**, click **Run**, type **rbfg.exe** and then press ENTER.

Computer Cannot Connect to the Server

If you press F12 to initiate the remote startup, but the client computer cannot connect to a RIS server, verify that the client PXE ROM is version .99c or later. Start the computer, and check the PXE ROM messages that appear on the screen.

Installation Options Are Not Available

If the expected installation options are not available to a user, check for Group Policy conflicts. Another Group Policy object (GPO) may have taken precedence over the GPO assigned to the installation options.

Lab A: Deploying Windows 2000 Professional by Using Remote Installation Services (Simulation)

Objectives

After completing this simulation, you will be able to:

- Install Remote Installation Services (RIS) on a computer running Microsoft Windows 2000 Advanced Server.

- Create a CD-based image of Windows 2000 Professional.

- Pre-stage a RIS Client Computer.

- Create an RIPrep image, including a modified profile and Microsoft Word.

- Deploy RIPrep images to select groups of users.

Lab Setup

This lab is an interactive exercise. To complete this lab, you need the following:

- A computer running Microsoft Windows 2000, Microsoft Windows NT version 4.0, Microsoft Windows 98, or Microsoft Windows 95.

- A minimum display resolution of 800 x 600 with 256 colors.

Important The lab does not reflect the real-world environment. It is recommended that you always use complex passwords for any administrator accounts, and never create accounts without a password.

Important Outside of the classroom environment, it is strongly advised that you use the most recent software updates that are necessary. Because this is a classroom environment, we may use software that does not include the latest updates.

▶ **To start the lab**

1. Insert the Student Materials compact disc into your CD-ROM drive.

2. At the root of the compact disc, double-click **Default.htm**.

3. On the Student Materials Web page, click **Lab Simulations**, and then click **Remote Installation Services**.

4. Read the introduction information, and then click the link to start the simulation.

Estimated time to complete this lab: 30 minutes

Review

- **RIS Overview**
- **Installing and Configuring RIS**
- **Configuring Remote Installation Options**
- **Deploying Images by Using RIS**
- **Creating an RIPrep Image**
- **Comparing CD-Based Images and RIPrep Images**
- **Identifying Solutions to RIS Problems**

1. What are the three network services that must be running before RIS can function?

2. What types of images does RIS support?

3. What are the four primary steps to set up a RIS server?

4. When is it necessary to create a RIS Startup disk for the client computer?

5. What can you do to distribute the network load among RIS servers that are servicing simultaneous requests for images?

6. How can you prevent users from performing remote installations on their own computers?

SYS PREP →

RI PREP →

COPY PROFILES / SYSTEM PROPERTIES / USER PROFILES / COPY TO.

RIS? needs DHCP, DNS, ACTIVE DIRECTORY.

Microsoft®
Training &
Certification

Module 14: Managing a Windows 2000 Network

Contents

SNMP

COMMUNITY NAME:
USUALLY PUBLIC

TRAPS → who send to
SECURITY → who ACCEPT FROM

Overview

- **Windows 2000 Administrative Strategies**
- **Performing Administrative Tasks Remotely by Using Terminal Services**
- **SNMP Operation**
- **Implementing the Windows 2000 SNMP Service**

As a network professional, you may be required to perform administrative tasks even when you are not physically present at the server that needs attention. Microsoft® Windows® 2000 provides solutions for your remote administrative needs. Using Terminal Services, you can control the server remotely to perform your administrative tasks. You can also use the Simple Network Management Protocol (SNMP) to manage network elements from a central location.

At the end of this module, you will be able to:

- Identify Windows 2000 administrative strategies
- Perform administrative tasks remotely using Terminal Services
- Explain how the SNMP protocol works
- Implement the Windows 2000 SNMP Service

SOLAR WINDS.NET.

SNMP → utilities for
gathering SNMP.

Windows 2000 Administrative Strategies

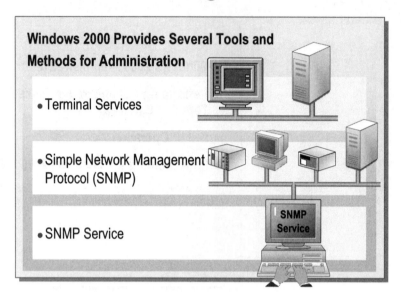

Windows 2000 Provides Several Tools and Methods for Administration

- Terminal Services

- Simple Network Management Protocol (SNMP)

- SNMP Service

Windows 2000 provides you with a great deal of flexibility when you administer your network. The tools and methods provided in Windows 2000 include:

- *Terminal Services.* From a client computer, you can run interactive sessions on a remote computer that is running Windows 2000 Server so that you can administer the server from the client computer as if you were using the server locally.

- *SNMP.* SNMP is a standard for retrieving information from a wide range of networking devices. It can also alert network administrators about events on these devices. You can manage computers running Windows 2000 by using an SNMP-based management application.

- *SNMP Service.* Windows 2000 supports SNMP with the SNMP service. The SNMP service provides Windows 2000 with the ability to use SNMP to query computers for data and communicate with the third-party management systems.

◆ Performing Administrative Tasks Remotely by Using Terminal Services

- **Using Terminal Services for Remote Administration**

- **Requirements for Terminal Services Remote Administration**

- **Installing Terminal Services for Remote Administration**

- **Configuring Terminal Services for Remote Administration**

You can use Terminal Services in Windows 2000 to remotely administer a network or a device on that network. Terminal Services allows you to open interactive sessions on a remote server and administer the server from a client computer as if you were using the server locally. The desktop of the server appears in a window on the desktop of your local computer. The Terminal Services client sends keystrokes and mouse movements to the Terminal server and receives screen updates from the server.

Using Terminal Services for Remote Administration

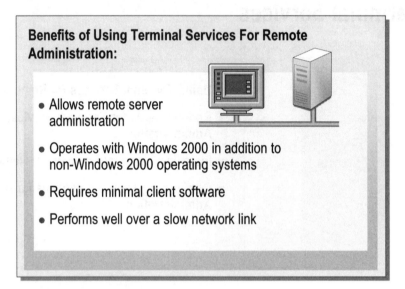

Benefits of Using Terminal Services For Remote Administration:

- Allows remote server administration
- Operates with Windows 2000 in addition to non-Windows 2000 operating systems
- Requires minimal client software
- Performs well over a slow network link

Using Terminal Services for remote administration provides the following benefits:

- You can perform all administrative tasks on a server from a remote computer, including software installation.

- You can connect to a server running Terminal Services from client computers running Windows 2000, Microsoft Windows NT®, Microsoft Windows 95, Microsoft Windows 98, Microsoft Windows 3.1, and Microsoft Windows CE.

- The Terminal Services client software requires minimal resources to run. The installation files for the client computer fit on two to four floppy disks.

- Terminal Services provides excellent performance, even over a slow network link. Because the Terminal Services client transmits only keystrokes and mouse movements, and Terminal Services only transmits screen updates, bandwidth requirements are low.

Requirements for Terminal Services Remote Administration

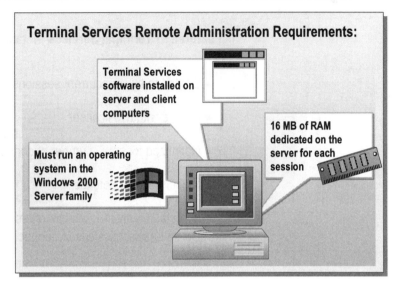

The computer on which you install Terminal Services must meet the following requirements to use Terminal Services for remote administration:

- The computer must be running one of the operating systems in the Windows 2000 Server family.

- You must install Terminal Services on the server and Terminal Services Client on the client computer.

- Each active session on the server requires approximately 16 megabytes (MB) of random access memory (RAM), in addition to memory requirements for the application in the Terminal Services session and other memory that the server is using. This amount of RAM is therefore unavailable for other use.

Note   For more information about Terminal Services, see module 15, "Installing and Configuring Terminal Services," in course 2152, *Implementing Microsoft Windows 2000 Professional and Server*.

Installing Terminal Services for Remote Administration

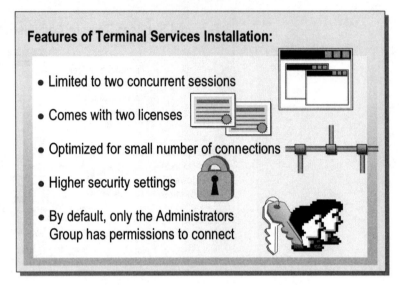

Features of Terminal Services Installation:

- Limited to two concurrent sessions

- Comes with two licenses

- Optimized for small number of connections

- Higher security settings

- By default, only the Administrators Group has permissions to connect

When you install Terminal Services on a computer running Windows 2000, you must decide whether to install it in application server mode or in remote administration mode. You must select the appropriate mode when you install Terminal Services. In order to use Terminal Services to administer your network, select remote administration mode when installing Terminal Services.

Characteristics of Remote Administration Mode

In remote administration mode:

- Terminal Services is limited to two concurrent connections.

- Two Terminal Services licenses are included. You do not need to purchase additional client licenses.

- Terminal Services performance is optimized for a small number of connections.

- Terminal Services security settings are configured to be higher than in application server mode.

- By default, only members of the Administrators group have permissions to connect to the remote computer by using Terminal Services.

Installing Terminal Services

To install Terminal Services:

1. Open Add/Remove Programs from Control Panel, and then click **Add/Remove Windows Components**.

2. In the Windows Components wizard, on the **Windows Components** page, select the **Terminal Services** check box, and then click **Next**.

3. On the **Terminal Services Setup** page, click **Remote administration mode**, click **Next** when prompted type the path to the setup files, and then click **Finish**.

4. When prompted, click **OK** to restart your computer.

Configuring Terminal Services for Remote Administration

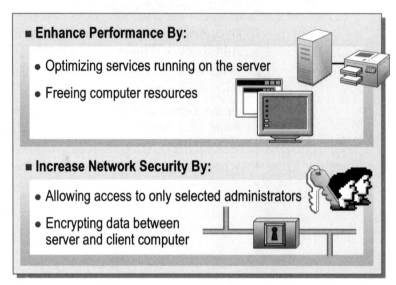

When you install Terminal Services for remote administration, Windows 2000 automatically optimizes many settings for a small number of client connections.

Windows 2000 also configures some security settings for a higher level because administrators may access confidential data while accessing the Terminal server from an insecure client computer. For example, only administrators have permissions to log on to a terminal server. Also, when you install Terminal Services in remote administration mode, Windows 2000 ensures that no data from a session can remain on the client computer's Clipboard. You can improve performance and security further by performing additional configuration steps.

Configuring Performance Parameters

You can configure two performance parameters to enhance the performance of the Terminal Services session.

Optimizing Services Running On The Server

Because performance for multiple Terminal Services sessions is not the primary purpose of the server that you are configuring, you must optimize the performance of background services, such as file and printer sharing.

To configure background services:

1. In Control Panel, double-click **System**.

2. In the **System Properties** dialog box, on the **Advanced** tab, click **Performance Options**.

3. For the **Optimize performance for** option, click **Background services**.

Freeing Computer Resources

You can configure Terminal Services to close inactive and disconnected Terminal Services client sessions after a designated amount of time. This is useful if you limit the number of concurrent sessions and an administrator forgets to end a session. These settings also enhance security.

To maximize resource availability, you should set the idle session limit to ten minutes and the time limit to end a disconnected session to five minutes.

To set the idle session limit and the time to end disconnected session limit:

1. Open Terminal Services Configuration from the **Administrative Tools** menu.

2. In the **RDP-Tcp Properties** dialog box, on the **Sessions** tab, ensure that **Override user settings** is selected.

3. In the **Idle session limit** list, click **10 minutes**.

4. In the **End a disconnection session** list, click **5 minutes**.

Configuring Security Parameters

You can configure two settings to enhance Terminal Services security. You configure all settings by using Terminal Services Configuration.

Controlling Administrator Access

You can control administrator access to the Terminal server to control which administrators can use Terminal Services for remote administration. To maintain a high level of security, you should allow only those administrators who are authorized to administer a specific server to connect from a Terminal Services client.

To configure administrator access:

1. Open Terminal Services Configuration from the **Administrative Tools** menu.

2. In Terminal Services Configuration, select **Connections**, and in the right pane, right-click the **RDP-Tcp** connection and then select **Properties**.

3. On the **Permissions** tab, assign the **Full Control** permission only to groups for selected administrators.

4. Remove all other user accounts and groups in the **Name** box, except for the System account.

Encrypting Terminal Services Data

You can encrypt the data between the Terminal Services server and client computer to prevent access to unauthorized people. Encrypting this data can decrease performance on slow client computers, but high encryption is recommended due to the often confidential nature of administrative tasks.

To encrypt data between Terminal Services clients and servers:

1. Open Terminal Services Configuration from the **Administrative Tools** menu.

2. In Terminal Services Configuration, select **Connections**, and in the right pane, right-click the **RDP-Tcp** connection and then select **Properties**.

3. On the **General** tab, click **High** to set the encryption level to high.

Note   To use high encryption, you must also install the Windows 2000 High Encryption Pack.

◆ SNMP Operation

- ■ Overview of SNMP

- ■ Management System and Agents

- ■ The Windows 2000 SNMP Service

- ■ The Management Information Base

- ■ The Hierarchical Name Tree

- ■ Defining SNMP Communities

SNMP is an industry-standard network management protocol that is used to manage network nodes (servers, workstations, routers, bridges, and hubs) from a centrally located host. SNMP is widely used with Transmission Control Protocol/Internet Protocol (TCP/IP) networks and, more recently, with Internetwork Packet Exchange/Sequenced Packet Exchange (IPX/SPX) networks. Windows 2000 supports SNMP through the SNMP service.

Understanding how to use SNMP helps you effectively implement SNMP to manage your network.

Overview of SNMP

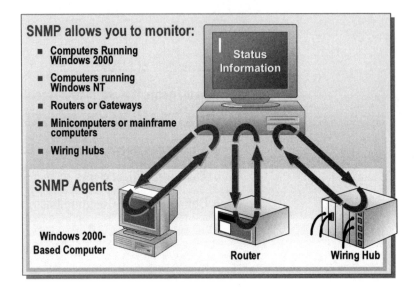

SNMP, a part of the TCP/IP protocol suite, was developed in the Internet community to monitor and troubleshoot routers and bridges. SNMP provides the ability to monitor and communicate status information between many different networking devices, such as:

- Computers running Windows 2000

- Computers running Windows NT

- Routers or gateways

- Minicomputers or mainframe computers

- Wiring hubs

The SNMP service sends status information to one or more hosts when the host requests the information, or when a significant event occurs—for instance, when a host runs out of hard disk space.

Note   For more information about SNMP, see RFC 1157 under **Additional Reading** on the Web page on the Student Materials compact disc. Many other RFCs update specific aspects of SNMP. For a more extensive listing of applicable RFCs, see the "Simple Network Management Protocol" section in the Windows 2000 Server Resource Kit.

Management System and Agents

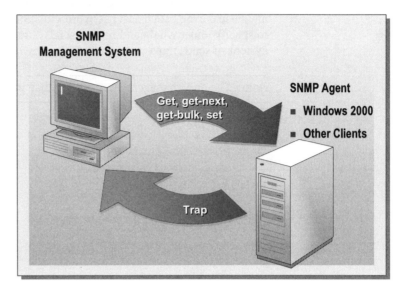

SNMP uses a distributed architecture. This architecture consists of two components: management systems and agents.

- *Management system.* A management system is any computer running SNMP management software. The primary function of any management system is to request information from an agent.

- *Agents.* An agent is any device running SNMP agent software, such as a server or router. The primary function of an agent is to send information that the management system requests.

SNMP Management System Information Request

A management system can request information through the **get**, **get-next**, **get-bulk**, and **set** operations.

- The **get** operation is a request for a specific value, such as the amount of hard disk space available.

- The **get-next** operation is a request for the "next" value. You use this operation to request data that follows the current data.

- The **get-bulk** operation is a request for a large amount of management data. You use this request to minimize the number of protocol exchanges.

- The **set** operation changes a value. You rarely use this operation, because most values have read-only access and cannot be set.

SNMP Agent Trap Messages

The notify operation, also called a trap message, alerts management systems to an unusual event, such as a password violation. You configure an SNMP agent to specify under what conditions it sends a trap, and to what management systems it sends traps.

Note   The only management operation that an agent can initiate is a trap.

The Windows 2000 SNMP Service

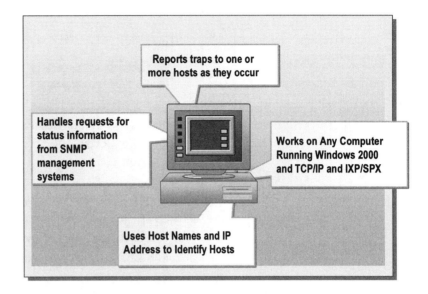

Computers running Windows 2000 can serve as SNMP agents by using the Windows 2000 SNMP service. Computers running Windows 2000 with the SNMP service installed can communicate with SNMP management systems.

The Windows 2000 SNMP service:

- Reports traps to one or more hosts as they occur.

- Handles requests for status information from SNMP management systems.

- Can be installed and used on any computer running Windows 2000 and TCP/IP or IPX/SPX.

- Uses host names and IP addresses to identify the hosts to which it reports information and from which it receives requests.

Note   SNMPUTIL, an SNMP management tool in the Windows 2000 Resource Kit, provides SNMP management features. In addition, there are many third-party products available to provide SNMP management features on a Windows 2000 network.

The Management Information Base

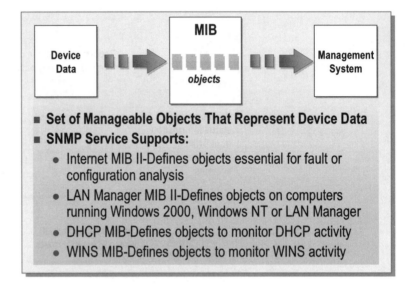

- **Set of Manageable Objects That Represent Device Data**
- **SNMP Service Supports:**
  - Internet MIB II-Defines objects essential for fault or configuration analysis
  - LAN Manager MIB II-Defines objects on computers running Windows 2000, Windows NT or LAN Manager
  - DHCP MIB-Defines objects to monitor DHCP activity
  - WINS MIB-Defines objects to monitor WINS activity

A management information base (MIB) defines what data a management system can request from an agent, how the management system must request the data, and how the agent formats the information that it returns. A MIB serves as a set of manageable objects that represent information about a network device, such as the number of active sessions or the version of network operating system software that runs on a host. SNMP management systems and agents must share a common understanding of MIB objects in order to operate.

A MIB combines similar objects. For example, the Internet MIB II defines 171 objects that are essential for either fault analysis or configuration analysis. The LAN Manager MIB defines objects to monitor computers running Windows 2000, Windows NT, or LAN Manager. Other MIBs cover components such as Dynamic Host Configuration Protocol (DHCP) or Windows Internet Name Service (WINS).

Typically, an SNMP management system removes the intricacies of understanding MIB definitions for manageable objects from an administrator. However, when selecting an SNMP management system, you must ensure that it supports all of the MIBs that Windows 2000 uses.

Note   For more information about Internet MIB II, see RFC 1213 under **Additional Reading** on the Web page on the Student Materials compact disc. For a complete list of the MIBs that Windows 2000 includes, see the appendix "MIB Object Types" in the Windows 2000 Server Resource Kit.

The Hierarchical Name Tree

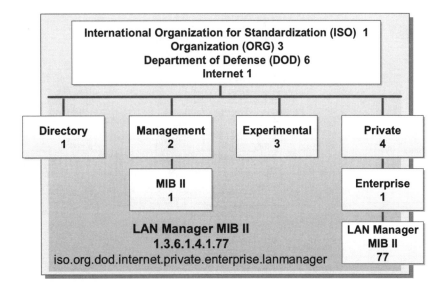

The MIB object namespace is hierarchical. It is structured so that each manageable object can be assigned a globally unique name. The International Organization for Standardization (ISO) has authority for the root of the namespace and assigns authority for parts of the namespace to individual organizations. This allows organizations to assign names without consulting an Internet authority for each assignment.

Object Identifier Format

The object identifier in the hierarchy is written as a sequence of labels beginning at the root and ending at the object. Labels are separated with periods. For example: 1.3.6.1.4.1.77.

Microsoft Object Identifier Namespace

Microsoft Corporation has been assigned object identifier namespace 1.3.6.1.4.1.311. All new MIBs for Microsoft are created under that branch. Microsoft has the authority to assign names to objects anywhere below that namespace.

For example, the object identifier for MIB II is iso.org.dod.internet.management.mibii, with an object number of 1.3.6.1.2.1. The object identifier for LAN Manager MIB II is iso.org.dod.internet.private.enterprise.lanmanager, with an object number of 1.3.6.1.4.1.77

Note   The namespace used to map object identifiers is distinct and separate from the hierarchical Domain Name System (DNS) namespace.

Defining SNMP Communities

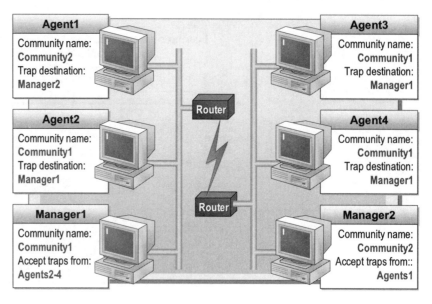

SNMP agents and management systems belong to groups called *communities*. Communities are identified by a community name. The use of a community name provides primitive security and context checking for agents and for management systems.

Only agents and managers that are members of the same community can communicate with each other. An agent will not accept a request from a management system outside the agent's configured community.

Note   The default community that most SNMP agents and management systems use is *public*. It is recommended that you change the default community name to a name other than public because public is the default, and keeping the default name can compromise security.

In the example in the previous slide, there are two defined communities: Community1 and Community2. An SNMP agent can be a member of multiple communities at the same time. This allows the SNMP agent to communicate with SNMP managers of the communities where the SNMP agent has membership.

- Agent1 can receive and send messages to Manager2 because they are both members of the Community2 community.

- Agent2, Agent3, and Agent4 can receive and send messages to Manager1 because they are all members of the Community1 community.

◆ Implementing the Windows 2000 SNMP Service

- ■ Installing the SNMP Service
- ■ Configuring SNMP Service Security
- ■ Configuring Windows 2000 SNMP Agent Properties
- ■ Configuring SNMP Traps
- ■ Using SNMPUTIL to Confirm the SNMP Configuration

Before a computer running Windows 2000 can function as an SNMP agent, you must install and configure the Windows 2000 SNMP service.

Installing the SNMP Service

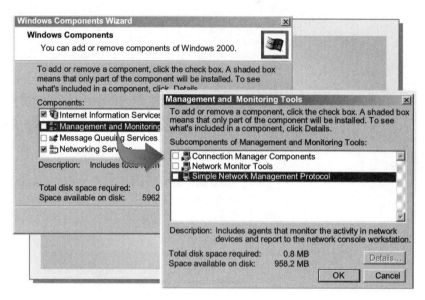

To install the SNMP service:

1. In Control Panel, double-click **Add/Remove Programs**.

2. In the **Add/Remove Programs** dialog box, click **Add/Remove Windows Components**.

3. In the Windows Components wizard, on the **Windows Components** page, click **Management and Monitoring Tools**, and then click **Details**.

4. In the **Management and Monitoring Tools** dialog box, select the **Simple Network Management Protocol** check box, and then click **OK**.

5. On the **Windows Components** page, click **Next**, and when Windows 2000 has configured all settings, click **Finish**.

Configuring SNMP Service Security

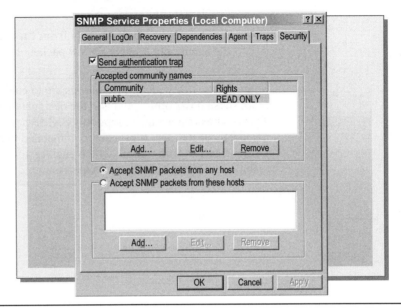

The SNMP service provides primitive security and context checking for Windows 2000–based agents and for management systems.

To configure SNMP security on a Windows 2000–based agent:

1. Open Computer Management from the **Administrative Tools** menu.

2. In Computer Management, expand **Services and Applications**, and then in the console tree, click **Services**.

3. In the details pane, right-click **SNMP Service**, and then click **Properties**.

4. In the **SNMP Service Properties** dialog box, click the **Security** tab.

5. Configure the following parameters:

   - **Send authentication trap**. If someone attempts to manage the system from an unauthorized SNMP management system, or a query is sent to the wrong community, the send authentication trap allows the SNMP agent to send an SNMP trap to the configured SNMP management station.

   - **Accepted community names**. A host must belong to a community that appears on this list for the SNMP service to accept requests from that host. Typically, all hosts belong to public, which is the standard name for the common community of all hosts. Add or remove community names and select the rights for a management system. The default right is Read-Only.

- **Accept SNMP packets from any host**. If you click this option, the agent accepts all SNMP packets regardless of which host they originated from.

- **Only accept SNMP packets from these hosts**. If you click this option, the agent only accepts SNMP packets from the hosts listed.

Note   The security recommendations are to enable the **Accept SNMP packets from these hosts** option and add the designated SNMP management stations. This ensures that agents accept only SNMP packets from authorized SNMP management stations. It is also recommended that you enable the **Send authentication trap** option, which enables authentication traps to log when an unauthorized host tries to access the system.

Configuring Windows 2000 SNMP Agent Properties

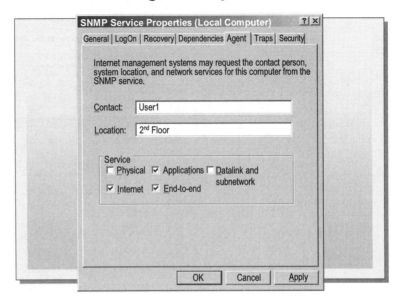

The SNMP service can provide an SNMP management system with information about itself. You enter information about a contact, a location, and the layer of the TCP/IP protocol suite at which the computer operates.

To configure SNMP agent properties:

1. In the **SNMP Service Properties** dialog box, click the **Agent** tab.

2. In the **Contact** box, type a contact name, such as an administrator, and in the **Location** box, type a description for the location of the computer.

3. Under **Service**, select the check boxes for the types of services that the computer on which SNMP is running provides.

Service	Select this option if
Physical	This host manages any physical devices, such as repeaters.
Applications	This host uses any applications that use TCP/IP. This option should always be selected.
Datalink and subnetwork	This host manages a bridge.
Internet	This host acts as an IP gateway (router).
End-to-end	This host is an IP host. This option should always be selected.

Note The Applications, Internet, and End-to-end services are enabled by default.

4. Click **OK**.

Configuring SNMP Traps

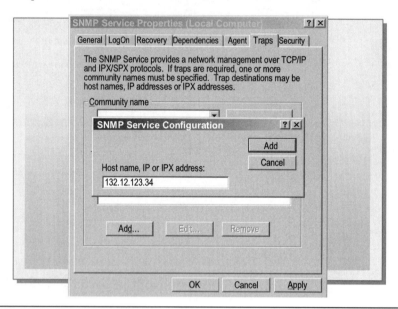

You can configure the SNMP service to send notification messages to a management system that collects these notification messages for a particular community name.

You must select the **Send authentication trap** box on the **Security** tab before Windows 2000 can generate traps. With this option selected, Windows 2000 generates traps when:

■ A management system makes an attempt to connect to an agent by using an invalid community name.

■ A management system makes an attempt to connect to an agent from an unauthorized host.

To set destinations for traps:

1. On the **Traps** tab, in the **Community name** box, type a valid community name, and then click **Add to list**.

2. In the **Community name** box, click a community name, and then in the **Trap destinations** box, add one or more computer names or IP addresses of management systems that collect traps for that community.

Using SNMPUTIL to Confirm the SNMP Configuration

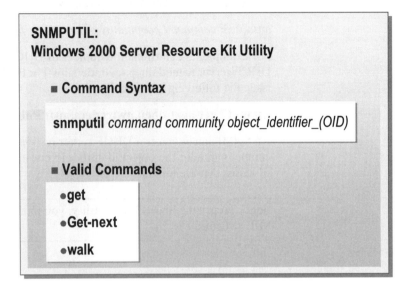

Microsoft provides a utility that you can use to test your SNMP installation. The Windows 2000 Server Resource Kit includes the SNMPUTIL utility, which you can use to send simple commands to an SNMP agent to verify whether the SNMP service has been correctly configured to communicate with SNMP management systems. SNMPUTIL sends the same SNMP commands as an SNMP management system.

SNMPUTIL Commands

There are three SNMPUTIL commands:

- **Get**. Gets the value of the requested object identifier.

- **Get-next**. Gets the value of the next object following the specified object identifier.

- **Walk**. Steps through the MIB branch specified by the object identifier. An SNMP management system uses this command to retrieve a large number of objects by using a single command.

Note The SNMP management tool, SNMPUTIL, in the Windows 2000 Resource Kit provides SNMP management features.

SNMPUTIL Syntax

The syntax of SNMPUTIL is as follows:

snmputil *command community object_identifier_(OID)*

For example, to determine the number of DHCP server addresses leased by a DHCP server named dhcp.nwtraders.msft in the Public community, you would issue the following command:

snmputil get-next dhcp.nwtraders.msft Public .1.3.6.1.4.1.311.1.3.2.1.1.1

An SNMP agent that is a DHCP server responds with the object identifier and counter value for the object identifier in question—in this case, the number of IP leases that are issued.

Note   To use the SNMPUTIL utility, you must know the relevant MIB structure.

Lab A: Managing a Windows 2000 Network

Objectives

After completing this lab, you will be able to:

- Configure Terminal Services for remote administration.
- Use Terminal Services to remotely administer a computer.
- Install the SNMP service.
- Configure SNMP.
- View the configuration of a remote computer by using SNMP.

Prerequisites

Before working on this lab, you must have:

- Knowledge of how Terminal Services works.
- Knowledge of the role of SNMP in a Windows 2000 network.

Lab Setup

To complete this lab, you need the following:

- A computer running Windows 2000 Advanced Server

- A partner with a similarly configured computer

- The files in the C:\Moc\Win2153\Labfiles\Module14\ folder

Important   The lab does not reflect the real-world environment. It is recommended that you always use complex passwords for any administrator accounts, and never create accounts without a password.

Important   Outside of the classroom environment, it is strongly advised that you use the most recent software updates that are necessary. Because this is a classroom environment, we may use software that does not include the latest updates.

Scenario

You need to administer a large number of servers that are located in several locations. Because of time and budget restrictions, you cannot travel to the remote locations when problems arise. To do your job, you must implement methods of remotely administering and monitoring all servers.

Estimated time to complete this lab: 60 minutes

Exercise 1
Using Terminal Services to Administer a Remote Computer

Scenario

You want to install software on remote computers without physically being at those computers. You have found that you cannot use a Microsoft Management Console (MMC) console running on another computer for this purpose. You decide to install Terminal Services on your servers so that you can accomplish all administrative tasks on these servers, including the installation of software.

Goal

In this exercise, you will install Terminal Services, optimize Terminal Services security for remote administration, optimize Terminal Services performance for remote administration, log on to a remote computer by using Terminal Services, and install the Windows 2000 Support Tools by using Terminal Services.

Tasks	Detailed Steps
1. Add Terminal Services in remote administration mode.	**a.** Log on as administrator@*domain*.nwtraders.msft (where *domain* is the name of your domain) with a password of **password**.
	b. In Control Panel, double-click **Add/Remove Programs**.
	c. In Add/Remove Programs, click **Add/Remove Windows Components**.
	d. On the **Windows Components** page, select the **Terminal Services** check box, and then click **Next**.
	e. On the **Terminal Services Setup** page, verify that **Remote administration mode** is selected, and then click **Next**.
	f. In the **Files Needed** dialog box, type **\\London\Setup\Winsrc** and then click **OK**.
	g. When the configuration process is complete, click **Finish**.
	h. In the **System Settings Change** dialog box, click **Yes** to restart your computer.
ⓘ **Tip:** When changing Terminal Services configuration settings, refer to the tables in this module for an explanation of each setting.	
2. Optimize Terminal Services for remote administration by optimizing performance for background services. Configure Terminal Services to end disconnected sessions after 5 minutes, and end idle sessions after 10 minutes.	**a.** Log on as administrator@*domain*.nwtraders.msft (where *domain* is the name of your domain) with a password of **password**.
	b. Minimize Control Panel.
	c. Right-click **My Computer**, and then click **Properties**.
	d. In the **System Properties** dialog box, on the **Advanced** tab, click **Performance Options**.
	e. In the **Performance Options** dialog box, under **Optimize performance for**, verify that **Background services** is selected, and then click **OK**.
	f. Click **OK** to close the **System Properties** dialog box.
	g. Open Terminal Services Configuration from the **Administrative Tools** menu.

Tasks	Detailed Steps
2. *(continued)*	**h.** In Terminal Services Configuration, in the details pane, right-click **RDP-Tcp**, and then click **Properties**.
	*Changing the **RDP-Tcp** properties alters the configuration for all Terminal Services connections that use the Remote Desktop Protocol (RDP) over TCP/IP.*
	i. In the **RDP-Tcp Properties** dialog box, on the **Sessions** tab, select the first **Override user settings** check box.
	j. In the **End a disconnected session** box, click **5 minutes**.
	k. In the **Idle session limit** box, click **10 minutes**.
3. Increase Terminal Services security by removing permissions to use Terminal Services from all users except those from the Administrators group, and by setting the encryption level to high.	**a.** On the **General** tab, in the **Encryption level** box, click **High**.
	b. On the **Permissions** tab, remove the Administrators group, add the Administrator user account from your domain, and allow Full Control for the Administrator account.
	c. Click **OK** to close the **RDP-Tcp Properties** dialog box.
	d. Close Terminal Services Configuration.
4. Install the Terminal Services client software from the C:\winnt\system32\clients\ts client folder.	**a.** Click **Start**, and then click **Run**.
	b. In the **Open** box, type **C:\winnt\system32\clients\tsclient\net\win32\Setup.exe** and then click **OK**.
	c. In the **Terminal Services Client Setup** dialog box, click **Continue**.
	d. In the **Name and Organization** dialog box, type your name and organization, and then click **OK**.
	e. In the **Confirm Name and Organization Information** dialog box, confirm that the information is correct, and then click **OK**.
	f. In the **License Agreement** dialog box, review the license agreement, and then click **I Agree**.
	g. In the **Terminal Services Client Setup** dialog box, click the large button.
	h. In the **Terminal Services Client Setup** dialog box, click **Yes** to apply the same configuration to all users.
	i. After Terminal Services Client Setup copies all required files, click **OK** to close the **Terminal Services Client Setup** message box.

Before starting the following procedure, verify that your partner has completed the preceding procedure.

(continued)

Tasks	Detailed Steps
5. Log on to your partner's computer as Administrator by using Terminal Services.	a. Click **Start**, point to **Programs**, point to **Terminal Services Client**, and then click **Terminal Services Client**. b. In the **Terminal Services Client** dialog box, in the **Server** box, type the name of your partner's computer. c. In the **Screen area** box, verify that **640x480** is selected. d. Verify that the **Enable data compression** check box is selected, select the **Cache bitmaps to disk** check box, and then click **Connect**.
ℹ **Note:** Configuring Terminal Services for low-speed connections by enabling data compression and caching bitmaps reduces network traffic and provides faster responses. These settings are particularly useful if you use Terminal Services over a dial-up connection.	
5. *(continued)*	e. In the **Log On to Windows** dialog box, use the following information: User Name: **administrator@***domain***.nwtraders.msft** (where *domain* is your domain) Password: **password** f. Click **OK**.
✋ Perform the following procedures entirely inside the Terminal Services window.	
6. Use Add/Remove Programs to install the Windows 2000 Support Tools on your partner's computer from the \Support\Tools folder on the Windows 2000 compact disc Installation Type: Typical	a. In Control Panel, double-click **Add/Remove Programs**, click **Add New Programs**, and then click **CD or Floppy**. b. In the Install Program From Floppy Disk or CD-ROM wizard, click **Next**. c. On the **Run Installation Program** page, in the **Open** box, type **\\london\support\setup.exe** and then click **Finish**. d. On the **Welcome to the Windows 2000 Support Tools Setup Wizard** page, click **Next**. e. On the **User Information** page, in the **Name** box, type **Student**x (where *x* is your student number) if necessary, and then click **Next**. f. On the **Select An Installation Type** page, verify that **Typical** is selected, and then click **Next**. g. On the **Begin Installation** page, click **Next**. h. On the **Completing the Windows 2000 Support Tools Setup Wizard** page, click **Finish**. i. Close **Add/Remove Programs**.
7. Verify that the Windows 2000 Support Tools are available.	a. On the **Programs** menu, verify that **Windows 2000 Support Tools** is available, and then log off the Terminal session. b. Close the Terminal Services Client window.

Exercise 2
Installing and Using SNMP

Scenario

Your organization has purchased an SNMP management system to monitor and control most devices in your network centrally. You need to configure the computers that are running Windows 2000 so that they can be monitored by using SNMP.

Goal

In this exercise, you will install the SNMP service and then confirm that it works by using the Snmputil.exe program.

Tasks	Detailed Steps
1. Install SNMP.	**a.** In Control Panel, double-click **Add/Remove Programs**.
	b. In Add/Remove Programs, click **Add/Remove Windows Components**.
ℹ **Note:** In the next detailed step, click the text **Management and Monitoring Tools** rather than the check box to avoid selecting all options under **Management and Monitoring Tools**.	
1. *(continued)*	**c.** On the Windows Components page, click **Management and Monitoring Tools**, and then click **Details**.
	d. In the **Management and Monitoring Tools** dialog box, select the **Simple Network Management Protocol** check box, click **OK**, and then click **Next**.
	e. On the **Terminal Services Setup** page, click **Next**.
	f. In the **Files Needed** dialog box, type **London\Setup\Winsrc** and then click **OK**.
	g. When the configuration process is complete, click **Finish**, and then close all open windows.
⚠ **Important:** In the following three procedures, type community names in lowercase. SNMP community names are case sensitive.	
2. Configure SNMP with your contact information and a community name of **private**, and configure it to accept packets only from your computer.	**a.** Open Computer Management from the **Administrative Tools** menu.
	b. In the console tree, expand **Services and Applications**, and then click **Services**.
	c. In the details pane, right-click **SNMP Service**, and then click **Properties**.
	d. In the **SNMP Service Properties (Local Computer)** dialog box, on the **Agent** tab, in the **Contact** box, type your name.
	e. In the **Location** box, type the location of your classroom.
	f. On the **Security** tab, verify that the **Send authentication trap** check box is selected.

Tasks	Detailed Steps
2. *(continued)*	**g.** Under **Accepted community names**, click **public**, and then click **Edit**.
	h. In the **SNMP Service Configuration** dialog box, in the **Community rights** box, verify that **READ ONLY** is selected.
	i. In the **Community Name** box, type **private** and then click **OK**.
	j. Click **Accept SNMP packets from these hosts**, and then click **Add**.
	k. In the **SNMP Service Configuration** dialog box, type the IP address of your Classroom connection, and then click **Add**.
	l. Repeat the preceding step for your PartnerNet connection.
	m. Click **OK** to close the **SNMP Service Properties (Local Computer)** dialog box.
	n. Close Computer Management.
3. Use Snmputil.exe to retrieve the description of your computer.	**a.** At a command prompt, change to the C:\MOC\Win2153\Labfiles\Module14 directory.
	b. Type **snmputil getnext** *ip_address* **public .1.3.6.1.2.1** (where *ip_address* is the IP address of your Classroom connection), and then press ENTER.
	After approximately one minute, an error message appears.

Why did Snmputil display an error message when you specified **public** as the community name?

_____

_____

_____

_____

3. *(continued)*	**c.** Type **snmputil getnext** *ip_address* **private .1.3.6.1.2.1** (where *ip_address* is the IP address of your Classroom connection), and then press ENTER.
	Snmputil displays the system description for your computer.
	d. Close the command prompt window.

Exercise 3
Restoring Your Configuration

Scenario

After you have tested remote administration and configuration features in Windows 2000, you must restore your original configuration.

Goal

In this exercise, you will restore the original computer configuration.

Tasks	Detailed Steps
✋ Before starting the following procedure, verify that your partner has completed the preceding procedure.	
1. Use Add/Remove Programs to remove Terminal Services Client and Windows 2000 Support Tools from your computer.	a. In Control Panel, double-click **Add/Remove Programs**. b. Verify that **Terminal Services Client** is selected, and then click **Change/Remove**. c. In the **Terminal Services Client Setup** dialog box, click **Remove All**. d. In the **Setup Message** dialog box, click **Yes**. 🖳 *Terminal Services Client is removed from your computer.* e. In the **Terminal Services Client – Restart Windows** dialog box, click **Exit Setup** to postpone restarting Windows 2000. f. In the **Terminal Services Client – Restart Failed** message box, click **OK**. g. In the **Terminal Services Client Setup** message box, click **OK**. h. In Add/Remove Programs, click **Windows 2000 Support Tools**, and then click **Remove**. i. In the **Add/Remove Programs** dialog box, click **Yes**. 🖳 *Windows 2000 Support Tools is removed from your computer.*
2. Use the Windows Components wizard to remove Terminal Services and SNMP from your computer, and then restart your computer.	a. In Add/Remove Programs, click **Add/Remove Windows Components**.
ℹ **Note:** In the next detailed step, click the text **Management and Monitoring Tools** rather than the check box to avoid selecting all options under **Management and Monitoring Tools**.	

Tasks	Detailed Steps
2. *(continued)*	b. On the **Windows Components** page, click **Management and Monitoring Tools**, and then click **Details**.
	c. In the **Management and Monitoring Tools** dialog box, clear the **Simple Network Management Protocol** check box, and then click **OK**.
	d. On the **Windows Components** page, clear the **Terminal Services** check box.
	e. Click **Next**.
	f. When the configuration process is complete, click **Finish**.
	g. In the **System Settings Change** dialog box, click **No** to postpone restarting your computer.
	h. Close all open windows, and then restart your computer.

Review

- Windows 2000 Administrative Strategies
- Performing Administrative Tasks Remotely by Using Terminal Services
- SNMP Operation
- Implementing The Windows 2000 SNMP Service

1. You need to administer a server remotely from several locations, including over a dial-up connection. Which is the best method to use?

2. Which SNMP operations are initiated by a management system? Which SNMP operation does an agent initiate?

3. What is the purpose of a community name?

Course Evaluation

Your evaluation of this course will help Microsoft understand the quality of your learning experience.

At a convenient time between now and the end of the course, please complete a course evaluation, which is available at http://www.metricsthatmatter.com/survey.

Microsoft will keep your evaluation strictly confidential and will use your responses to improve your future learning experience.

Microsoft®
Training &
Certification

Module 15:
Troubleshooting
Windows 2000 Network
Services

Contents

Overview

- ■ **Troubleshooting Network Problems**

- ■ **Identifying the Symptoms and Causes of Network Problems**

- ■ **Resolving TCP/IP Problems**

- ■ **Resolving Name Resolution Problems**

- ■ **Troubleshooting Network Services**

- ■ **Monitoring the Network**

Microsoft® Windows® 2000 includes many protocols and services that you can use to build your network, and each of these technologies has specific requirements and dependencies. Therefore, it is important to understand how these network components function and how they interact to be able to effectively and efficiently troubleshoot network problems that may occur.

At the end of this module, you will be able to:

- ■ Troubleshoot network connectivity problems.

- ■ Identify the symptoms and causes of network problems.

- ■ Resolve Transmission Control Protocol/Internet Protocol (TCP/IP) problems.

- ■ Resolve name resolution problems.

- ■ Troubleshoot network services.

- ■ Monitor the network data stream.

Troubleshooting Network Problems

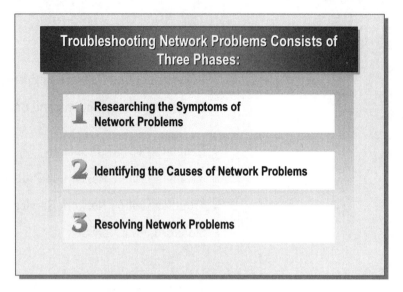

The Windows 2000 network infrastructure consists of many different components and connections, and network problems can occur in any of them. This complicates the network troubleshooting process, because a problem can have more than one probable cause. For example, if a user cannot access a shared folder, the problem could be the result of a faulty network cable or incorrect user permissions. Therefore, you must be able to identify the symptoms and causes of network problems to isolate and correct the problem.

Effective network troubleshooting consists of three phases:

■ *Researching the symptoms of network problems.* Gather specific information that is related to a network problem, such as the error message that a user received when the problem occurred.

■ *Identifying the causes of network problems.* Identify all possible causes for the problem, based on the symptoms. This phase often requires additional research. After you have identified all possible causes, you must isolate the specific cause of the problem. This is the most challenging part of the network troubleshooting process.

■ *Resolving network problems.* Apply your knowledge of Windows 2000 and its networking technologies to resolve the problem. This phase is often the easiest of the network troubleshooting process, because you have already identified the cause of the problem.

Identifying the Symptoms and Causes of Network Problems

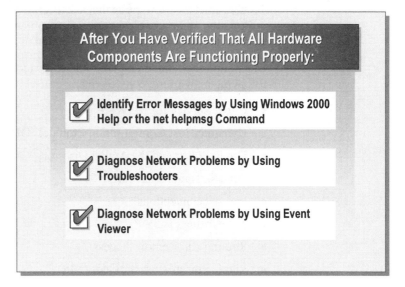

Verify that hardware components, such as cables and network adapters, are working properly before you begin to research the symptoms and causes of network problems. If a network problem is hardware related, checking these components first can reduce the amount of time spent researching software-related network problems. If the problem is not hardware-related, you must investigate further to identify its symptoms and causes.

Identifying Error Messages

Windows 2000 often displays error messages when a network operation fails. These error messages include a brief description of the problem that has occurred. Windows 2000 also provides troubleshooting information for common system errors, which can assist you in diagnosing the problem.

Click **Help** in an error message to receive a detailed description of the error, suggestions about how to resolve the error, and a list of related tools and Help topics that may help to prevent the error from occurring in the future.

You can also use the **net helpmsg** command to locate troubleshooting information for a specific error message. The **net helpmsg** command explains why an error occurred and how to resolve the problem. To view an explanation of an error message that a core component of Windows 2000 generated, at a command prompt, type **net helpmsg** *number* (where *number* is the number that is associated with the error message).

Note   For more information about error messages, see the "Error and Event Messages Help" section in the Windows 2000 Support Tools.

Diagnosing Network Problems by Using Troubleshooters

Windows 2000 Help includes troubleshooters, which you can use to quickly solve common network configuration or interoperability problems. Troubleshooters are wizards that ask a series of questions and provide detailed information about troubleshooting the problem. There are several different troubleshooters, each of which is designed to solve a different type of problem.

Use troubleshooters to diagnose and solve technical problems with the following networking components:

- Client Service for NetWare
- Dynamic Host Configuration Protocol (DHCP)
- Group Policy and the Active Directory™ directory service
- Domain Name System (DNS)
- Internet connections
- Networking (TCP/IP)
- Routing and Remote Access
- Remote Installation Services (RIS)
- Server Management
- Windows Internet Name Service (WINS)

Diagnosing Network Problems by Using Event Viewer

Event Viewer is a monitoring and diagnostic Windows 2000 administrative tool that allows you to view logs about program, security, and system events on your computer. You can use Event Viewer to view and manage event logs, and to gather system information to identify when a particular service has been started, stopped, or failed to start because of an error. By using Event Viewer, you can monitor event logs to predict and identify the sources of system problems.

Note For information about using Event Viewer, see Windows 2000 Help, or course 2151, *Microsoft Windows 2000 Network and Operating System Essentials*.

◆ Resolving TCP/IP Problems

- ■ Verifying TCP/IP Configuration
- ■ Testing IP Configuration
- ■ Testing IP-to-MAC Resolution
- ■ Troubleshooting IP Routing

To determine whether a network problem occurred as a result of a TCP/IP failure, you must be able to verify TCP/IP configuration and connectivity, test IP configuration and IP-to-media access control (MAC) resolution, and check IP security configuration and the IP routing process.

The TCP/IP process that enables computers to communicate over a network can be divided into four distinct steps. Before it sends a packet from a sending host, the TCP/IP protocol:

1. Resolves the host name or network basic input/output system (NetBIOS) name to an IP address.

2. Determines the interface to use and the forwarding IP address by using the destination IP address and the IP routing table.

3. Uses the Address Resolution Protocol (ARP) to resolve the forwarding IP address to a MAC address. This occurs for unicast IP traffic on shared access technologies such as Ethernet, Token Ring, and Fiber Distributed Data Interface (FDDI).

    For multicast IP traffic on Ethernet and FDDI, the destination multicast IP address is mapped to the appropriate multicast MAC address. Multicast IP traffic on Token Ring uses the functional address of 0xC0-00-00-04-00-00. For broadcast traffic on shared access technologies, the MAC address is mapped to OxFF-FF-FF-FF-FF-FF.

4. Sends the packet to the MAC address that is resolved by using ARP or multicast mapping.

The TCP/IP stack follows this sequence when it determines how to send a packet from point-to-point. If the destination to be reached by an application is in the form of a NetBIOS name or host name, name resolution is required before IP can send the first packet.

Verifying TCP/IP Configuration

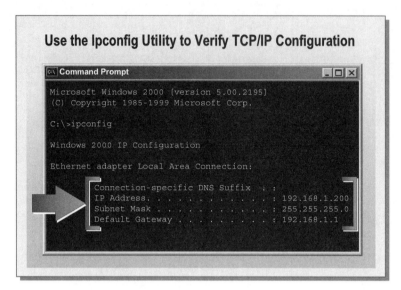

When troubleshooting a TCP/IP networking problem, begin by checking the TCP/IP configuration on the computer on which the problem occurs. The Ipconfig utility is a command-line tool that displays current TCP/IP network configuration values, including the:

- IP address
- Subnet mask
- Default gateway

This information helps to determine whether the configuration is initialized, or whether a duplicate IP address exists on a network. To view TCP/IP configuration information, at a command prompt, type **ipconfig**

Note   If the local address is returned as 169.254.*x.x*, the Automatic Private IP Addressing feature of Windows 2000 has assigned the IP address. This local address of 169.254.*x.x*. indicates that the local DHCP server is not configured properly or cannot be reached from your computer, and an IP address has been assigned automatically with a subnet mask of 255.255.0.0. Enable or correct the DHCP server, and restart the local computer.

Displaying TCP/IP Configuration Details

You can use the **/all** switch to produce a detailed configuration report for all interfaces, including any configured remote access adapters. At a command prompt, type **ipconfig /all** to verify configuration information.

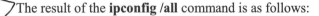

The result of the **ipconfig /all** command is as follows:

- If a network connection was initialized, the Ipconfig utility displays the IP address and subnet mask. The default gateway also appears, if it has been assigned.

- If a duplicate IP address exists, the Ipconfig utility indicates that the IP address is configured; however, the subnet mask is 0.0.0.0.

- If the computer is unable to obtain an IP address from a DHCP server on the network, the Ipconfig utility displays the IP address provided by Automatic Private IP Addressing.

- If the computer obtained its address from a DHCP server, the Ipconfig utility displays the IP address of the DHCP server.

The output of the **ipconfig /all** command also includes additional configuration information, such as the addresses of DNS and WINS servers that you configured or that a DHCP server assigned.

Saving Ipconfig Output

Ipconfig output may be redirected to a file and pasted into other documents. To save Ipconfig output, at a command prompt, type **ipconfig >** *folder name\file name* (where *folder name* is the name of a folder that already exists, and *file name* is the name that you want to assign to the file when it is created). A file that contains the Ipconfig output is created with the specified file name, in the specified folder.

You can review the Ipconfig output to identify problems in the computer network configuration. For example, if a computer has been configured with a duplicate IP address, the subnet mask appears as 0.0.0.0. If no problems appear in the TCP/IP configuration, the next step is to test TCP/IP connectivity to other host computers on the network.

Testing IP Configuration

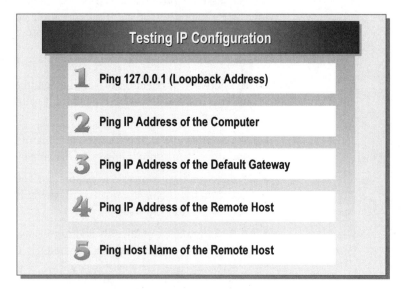

The Ping utility is a diagnostic tool that you can use to test TCP/IP configuration and diagnose connection failures by sending an Internet Control Message Protocol (ICMP) Echo Request to a target host name or IP address. Use the Ping utility to determine whether a particular TCP/IP host is available and functional.

Testing Network Connections

To verify that a route exists between the local computer and a network host, at a command prompt, type **ping** *IP address* (where *IP address* is the IP address of the network host to which you want to connect). By default, the following message appears four times after a successful **ping** command:

```
Reply from IP_address
```

Testing TCP/IP Configuration and Connections

Perform the following tasks to test TCP/IP configuration and connections:

1. Use the **ping** command with the loopback address (**ping 127.0.0.1**) to verify that TCP/IP is correctly installed and bound to your network adapter.

   If this step fails, the IP stack is not responding. Possible causes for this include:

   - The TCP drivers are damaged or missing.

   - The network adapter is not working.

   - Another service is interfering with IP.

2. Use the **ping** command with the IP address of the local computer to verify that the computer was added to the network correctly and does not have a duplicate IP address. If the routing table is correct, this simply forwards the packet to the loopback address of 127.0.0.1.

3. Use the **ping** command with the IP address of the default gateway to verify that the default gateway is operational and that your computer can communicate with a host on the local network.

4. Use the **ping** command with the IP address of a remote host to verify that the computer can communicate through a router.

   If the **ping** command is successful after this step, steps 1 through 3 are successful by default. If the **ping** command is not successful, **ping** the IP address of another remote host because the current host might be turned off.

5. Use the **ping** command with the host name of a remote host to verify that the computer can resolve a remote host name.

   Ping uses host name resolution to resolve a computer name to an IP address, so if pinging by IP address succeeds, but fails by host name, the problem is with host name resolution, not network connectivity.

Verifying TCP/IP Properties

If you cannot use Ping successfully at any point, verify that the local computer's IP address is valid and appears correctly on the **IP Address** tab of the **Internet Protocol (TCP/IP) Properties** dialog box. You can also use the Ipconfig utility to verify the IP address of the local computer.

Verifying Valid IPSec Connections

You can use the Ping utility to determine whether Internet Protocol Security (IPSec) communication can occur when a predefined policy is assigned to a computer. Using the Ping utility will allow you to separate network problems from IPSec issues.

If using the **ping** command results in a "Destination Host Unreachable" error message, the other computer cannot be contacted at all. If the result is a "Request Timed Out" error message, the computer can be contacted, but it may have an IPSec policy applied to it that is blocking communication.

Testing IP-to-MAC Resolution

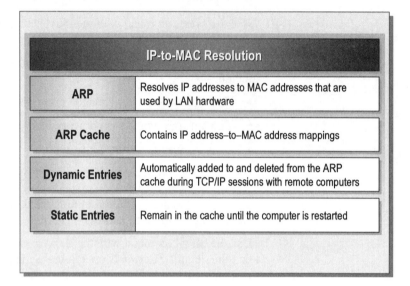

IP-to-MAC Resolution	
ARP	Resolves IP addresses to MAC addresses that are used by LAN hardware
ARP Cache	Contains IP address–to–MAC address mappings
Dynamic Entries	Automatically added to and deleted from the ARP cache during TCP/IP sessions with remote computers
Static Entries	Remain in the cache until the computer is restarted

Windows 2000 TCP/IP allows an application to communicate over a network with another computer by using an IP address, a host name, or a NetBIOS name. The destination must be resolved to a MAC address for shared access media, such as Ethernet and Token Ring, regardless of the naming convention that is used.

Address Resolution Protocol

The Address Resolution Protocol (ARP) is a protocol in the TCP/IP suite that provides IP address–to–MAC address resolution for IP packets. ARP resolves IP addresses to MAC addresses that are used by local area network (LAN) hardware. When given the node's IP address, ARP enables a host to find the MAC address of a node with an IP address on the same physical network.

ARP Cache

When an ARP request is answered, both the sender of the ARP reply and the original ARP requester record each other's IP address and MAC address in a local table called the ARP cache, which contains both dynamic and static entries. By using the Arp utility, you can view and modify the ARP cache. At a command prompt, type **arp -a** to view ARP cache entries on the local computer.

Note   Each network adapter has a separate ARP cache on a computer running Windows 2000.

[handwritten margin notes:] MAC ADDRESS ON (SWITCHES) FRAMES / IP ADDRESS ON (ROUTERS) PACKETS. / ARP IP TO MAC ADDRESS

Dynamic Entries

Dynamic entries are automatically added to and deleted from the ARP cache during the normal use of TCP/IP sessions with remote computers. Dynamic entries age and expire from the cache if they are not reused within two minutes. If a dynamic entry is reused within two minutes, it may remain in the cache and age up to a maximum cache life of ten minutes before it is removed or requires cache renewal through the ARP broadcast process.

Static Entries

Static entries remain in the cache until the computer is restarted, and can help minimize ARP broadcast traffic on your network. You can use the Arp utility to add static entries to the ARP cache. To add a static entry, at a command prompt, type **arp -s** *IP_address MAC_address* (where *IP address* is the IP address of a local TCP/IP node, and *MAC address* is the MAC address for a network adapter that is installed and used on the local TCP/IP node).

Detecting Invalid Entries in the ARP Cache

Invalid entries in the ARP cache can be the result of two computers that are using the same IP address on the network. The main source of these conflicts is most likely to be an incorrect static IP addresses, because DHCP-assigned addresses do not cause address conflicts.

Verifying Static Addresses

As a best practice, maintain a list of static addresses (and corresponding MAC addresses) as they are assigned. You can then compare the IP and MAC address pairs in the ARP cache with the recorded values to determine whether the static entries in the ARP cache were entered correctly.

If you do not have a record of all IP and MAC address pairs on your network, but you have a record of the network adapters that each computer uses, you can often deduce which adapter has a given MAC address by examining the manufacturer bytes of the MAC addresses of the network adapters. These three-byte numbers are called Organizationally Unique Identifiers (OUIs). You can compare the OUIs with the MAC addresses in the ARP cache to determine whether a static address was entered in error. You can obtain a list of OUIs from the Institute of Electrical and Electronic Engineers, Inc. (IEEE) at http://standards.ieee.org/regauth/oui/index.html.

Deleting Invalid Entries

Delete invalid static entries from the ARP cache by using the Arp utility. At a command prompt, type **arp -d** *IP_address* (where *IP address* is the IP address of the invalid entry). To add the correct address, use the **arp -s** command.

Troubleshooting IP Routing

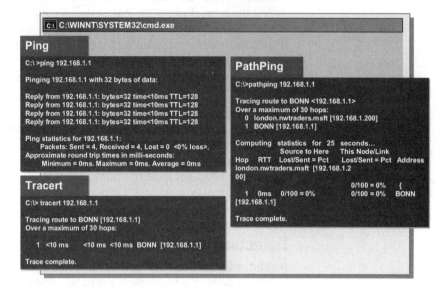

The first step for troubleshooting IP routing is to verify that a default gateway is configured and that the link between the host and the default gateway is operational. Make sure that only one default gateway is configured. Although it is possible to configure more than one default gateway, additional gateways are only used if the IP stack determines that the original gateway is not functioning. To determine the status of the first configured gateway, delete all other gateways to simplify the troubleshooting process.

Verifying the Default Gateway

If the gateway address is not on the same network as the local host, messages from the host computer cannot be forwarded to any location that is outside the local network. Therefore, you must verify that the default gateway address is correct. Next, check to see that the default gateway is configured as a router, and that it is enabled to forward IP datagrams.

Verifying Communications Between Networks

If the default gateway is configured correctly, use the **ping** command with the IP address of a remote host to ensure that network-to-network communications are functioning properly. The **ping** command may return the following error messages if a routing problem exists:

- *TTL Expired in Transit.* Indicates that the number of hops required to reach the destination exceeds the Time to Live (TTL) value that the sending host sets for forwarding packets. The default TTL value is 32, which may not be enough time for a packet to travel the required number of links to a destination. Use the **ping -i** command to increase the TTL value, up to a maximum of 255.

Note Some routers will drop packets with an expired TTL. This is known as a silent discard.

- *Destination Host Unreachable.* Indicates that the local system has no route to the desired destination, or a remote router reports that it has no route to the destination. If the "Destination Host Unreachable" message appears, no route from the local system exists, and the packets to be sent were never forwarded. If the "Reply From *IP address*: Destination Host Unreachable" message appears, the routing problem occurred at the remote router that is associated with the specified IP address.

- *Request Timed Out.* Indicates that no "Echo Reply" messages were received within the default time of one second. This message may be the result of network congestion, failure of the ARP request, packet filtering, a routing error, or a silent discard. Most often, it indicates that a route back to the sending host has failed, because the destination host, one of the intermediary routers, or the default gateway of the destination host does not recognize the route back to the sending host.

  Check the routing table of the destination host to determine whether it has a route to the sending host before checking the routing tables of the individual routers. If the remote routing tables are correct and contain a valid route back to the sending host, use the **arp -a** command to determine whether the correct address is listed in the ARP cache. In addition, check the subnet mask to ensure that a remote address has not been interpreted as a local address.

- *Unknown Host.* Indicates that the requested host name cannot be resolved to its IP address. Verify that the name is entered correctly and that the DNS servers can resolve it.

Tracert Utility

The Tracert utility is a command-line tool that you can use to check the path to the destination IP address that you want to reach. The **tracert** command displays a list of IP routers that are used to deliver packets from your computer to the destination, and the amount of time that the packet remained at each hop. If the packets are unable to be delivered to the destination, you can use the **tracert** command to identify the last router that successfully forwarded the packets.

Note   Some routers silently drop packets with expired TTLs. These routers do not appear in the Tracert display.

PathPing Utility

The PathPing utility is a command-line tool that detects packet loss over multiple-hop trips. The **pathping** command sends packets to each router on the route to a final destination, and computes the results based on the packets that are returned from each hop. You can use the **pathping** command to identify the degree of packet loss at any given router or link and determine whether a particular router or link is causing network problems.

To verify that the routers on the route to the destination are operating correctly, at a command prompt, type **pathping** *IP address* (where *IP address* is the IP address of the remote host).

◆ Resolving Name Resolution Problems

- **Resolving Host Name Resolution Problems**
- **Resolving NetBIOS Name Resolution Problems**

TCP/IP for Windows 2000 allows an application to communicate over a network with another computer by using an IP address, or either of the following types of destination designations:

- Host name
- NetBIOS name

If you are unable to access a system by host name or NetBIOS name, a problem with name resolution could exist on your network. You must determine whether it is a host or domain name or a NetBIOS name resolution problem. The first step in distinguishing host name resolution problems from NetBIOS name resolution problems is to determine whether the failing application uses NetBIOS or host names. If the application uses host names, the problem is the result of incorrect host name resolution.

Resolving Host Name Resolution Problems

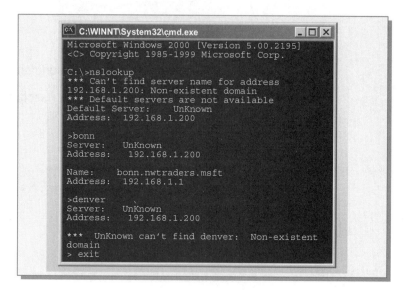

Problems with host name resolution can be the result of an incorrectly configured Hosts file or DNS server, an incorrect Hosts file entry or IP address, or multiple entries for a single host in a Hosts file.

Verifying Host Name Resolution Configuration

To verify host name resolution configuration:

1. Open Network and Dial-up Connections, right-click **Local Area Connections**, and then click **Properties**.

2. In the **Local Area Connection Properties** dialog box, click **Internet Protocol (TCP/IP)**, and then click **Properties**.

3. In the **Internet Protocol (TCP/IP) Properties** dialog box, click **Advanced**.

4. On the **DNS** tab of the **Advanced TCP/IP Settings** dialog box, confirm that DNS is configured properly. If the DNS server IP address is missing, add it to the list of DNS server addresses.

Note This procedure does not take DHCP clients into account, because DNS servers are not listed for DHCP clients.

Checking the Hosts File

The Hosts file or a DNS server resolves host names to IP addresses whenever you use TCP/IP utilities such as the Ping utility. Verify that the name of the remote computer is spelled correctly in the Hosts file, and in the application that uses it for name resolution.

Note The Hosts file is located in the *systemroot*\System32\Drivers\Etc folder.

Nslookup Utility

Nslookup is a command-line utility that you can use to make DNS queries to test and troubleshoot your DNS installation. Name resolution errors can occur if DNS server or client entries are not configured correctly, the DNS server is not running, or there is a problem with network connectivity. At a command prompt, type **nslookup** to view the host name and IP address of the DNS server that is configured for the local system.

If the DNS server is offline, the DNS service is not enabled on the host computer, or if a hardware or routing problem exists, the following message appears:

```
C:\nslookup
*** Can't find server name for address <IP_Address>: No
response from server
*** Default servers are not available.
```

To look up a host's IP address by using DNS, type the host name and press ENTER. By default, Nslookup uses the DNS server configured for the computer on which it is running. If the DNS server cannot resolve the host name, the following message appears:

```
C:\nslookup <Destination_host>
Server: <fully_qualified_domain_name>
Address: <server_IP_address>
***   <fully_qualified_domain_name> can't find
<Destination_host>: Non-existent domain
```

If a query fails as a result of connectivity issues or network congestion, or if the DNS server is overloaded with requests, the following message appears:

```
C:\nslookup Valid_Host
Server: [IP_Address]
Address: w.x.y.z
DNS request timed out.
  timeout was 2 seconds.
```

NetDiag Support Tool

NetDiag is a command-line, diagnostic tool that helps isolate networking and connectivity problems by performing a series of tests to determine the state of the network client. NetDiag diagnoses network problems by checking all aspects of a host computer's network configuration and connections. In addition to troubleshooting TCP/IP issues, it examines a host computer's Internetwork Packet Exchange (IPX) and NetWare configurations. NetDiag is included in the Windows 2000 Support Tools.

Note For more information about NetDiag, see Windows 2000 Support Tools Help. For information about installing and using the Windows 2000 Support Tools and Support Tools Help, see the file Sreadme.doc in the \Support\Tools folder on the Windows 2000 Server compact disc.

Resolving NetBIOS Name Resolution Problems

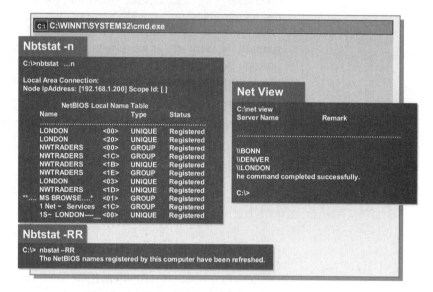

When a network is functioning normally, NetBIOS over TCP/IP (NetBT) resolves NetBIOS names to IP addresses by using several options for NetBIOS name resolution. These options include local cache lookup, WINS server query, broadcast, Lmhosts lookup, Hosts file query, and DNS server query.

NetBIOS Name Resolution Process

Windows 2000 first checks the host computer's internal NetBIOS name cache to resolve a NetBIOS name to an IP address. If this fails to provide an IP address, the NetBIOS name can be resolved to an IP address by using a broadcast, checking the Lmhosts file, or querying a WINS server. The order in which Windows 2000 uses these mechanisms depends on the node type of the client.

The default node type is hybrid or H-node, which queries a WINS server, and then attempts a local broadcast to resolve the name. If these mechanisms are unsuccessful, the client queries its Hosts file. If the Hosts file does not contain the IP address, the client queries its DNS server if it is configured to use one.

Note If the only problem is NetBIOS name resolution, the computer should still be able to reach the remote resource by IP address.

Diagnosing NetBIOS Name Resolution Problems

You can use the **nbtstat** or **net view** command to diagnose NetBIOS name resolution problems.

NETBIOS STATISTICS.

Nbtstat

You use the Nbtstat utility to view and register NetBIOS names on a computer running Windows 2000. Nbtstat displays protocol statistics and name information used by NetBT connections, which can help with troubleshooting NetBIOS name resolution problems. For example, to identify the NetBIOS names that a computer has registered by using NetBT, type **nbtstat -n** at a command prompt.

In Windows 2000, you can re-register NetBIOS names with the name server after a computer has already been started. Type **nbtstat -R** at a command prompt to re-register NetBIOS names.

Note For more information on the parameters that you can use with the Nbtstat utility, type **nbtstat** at a command prompt.

Net View Command

You can use the **net view** command to display a list of domains, a list of computers, or the resources that the specified computer shares. At a command prompt, type **net view** to display a list of computers in your current domain.

The following table describes the parameters that you can use with the **net view** command to troubleshoot NetBIOS name resolution problems.

Parameter	Description
\\computer name	Specifies the computer whose shared resources you want to view.
/domain:domain name	Specifies the domain for which you want to view the available computers. If domain name is omitted, all domains in the network will be displayed.

Resolving Common NetBIOS Name Resolution Errors

The most common symptom of a problem in NetBIOS name resolution is when the Ping utility returns a Network Path Not Found (Error 53) error message. This message is generally returned when name resolution fails for a particular computer name. This type of error can also occur when there is a problem establishing a NetBIOS session.

Determining the Cause of the Error

To determine the cause of a Network Path Not Found error message, at a command prompt, type **net view** *hostname* (where *hostname* is an active network resource). If this command is successful, name resolution is probably not the source of the problem. Use the **ping** command with the host name to confirm that name resolution is working properly. If the **ping** command returns an Unknown Host error message, name resolution has failed and you must check the status of your NetBIOS session.

Checking the Status of a NetBIOS Session

To check the status of your NetBIOS session, at a command prompt, type **net view** *IP address* (where *IP address* is the IP address of the network resource that you specified when determining the cause of the error).

If the computer is on the local subnet, confirm that the name is spelled correctly and that the target computer is running TCP/IP. If the computer is not on the local subnet, be sure that its name and IP address mapping are available in the DNS database, the Hosts or Lmhosts file, or the WINS database. If all TCP/IP elements appear to be installed properly, use the **ping** command with the remote computer to ensure that the TCP/IP protocol is working.

Lab A: Troubleshooting Routing (Simulation)

Objectives

After completing this lab, you will be able to:

■ Troubleshoot router connectivity problems.

■ Troubleshoot a demand-dial connection.

Prerequisites

Before working on this lab, you must have:

■ Knowledge about the differences between a workgroup and a domain.

■ Experience logging on and off Windows 2000.

■ The knowledge and skills to create user accounts by using User Manager for Domains.

Lab Setup

This lab is a simulation. To complete this lab, you need the following:

- A computer running Windows 2000, Microsoft Windows NT® version 4.0, Microsoft Windows 98, or Windows 95.

- A minimum display resolution of 800 x 600 with 256 colors.

Important The lab does not reflect the real-world environment. It is recommended that you always use complex passwords for any administrator accounts, and never create accounts without a password.

Important Outside of the classroom environment, it is strongly advised that you use the most recent software updates that are necessary. Because this is a classroom environment, we may use software that does not include the latest updates.

▶ **To start the lab**

1. Insert the Student Materials compact disc into your CD-ROM drive.

2. At the root of the compact disc, double-click **Default.htm**.

3. On the Student Materials Web page, expand Lab Simulations and then click **Troubleshooting Routing**.

4. Read the introduction, and then click the link to start the lab.

Scenario

You are responsible for configuring and maintaining the routers for your company, Contoso Ltd. Contoso has two buildings in its headquarters office, and a branch office that is connected by a demand-dial virtual private network (VPN) connection. The diagram below shows the routers and connections that are used in the Contoso Ltd. network. If a problem occurs with the routers at any time, you are responsible for determining the cause of the error and fixing it.

Contoso

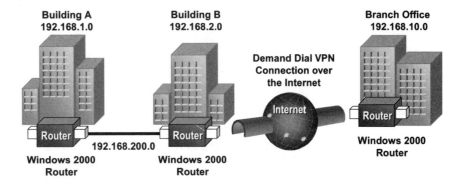

Estimated time to complete this lab: 45 minutes

◆ Troubleshooting Network Services

- Viewing Service Information
- Modifying Service Properties

To troubleshoot and resolve problems with network services, use Services, which you can access from the **Administrative Tools** menu or from Computer Management. For example, you can use Services to start, stop, pause, or resume services on remote and local computers, and configure startup and recovery options.

Some services are configured to start automatically in Windows 2000, depending on the computer configuration and the network services and protocols that are in use. You can use Services to determine which services are configured to start automatically and which services are not starting.

Viewing Service Information

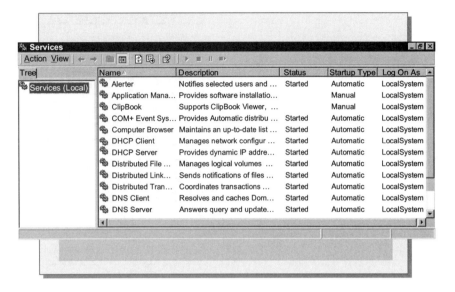

Open Services from the **Administrative Tools** menu, or from Computer Management. The details pane of Services contains network service information, such as the service name and description, whether the service has started, how it is configured to start, and the logon account that the service uses. The information in the details pane of the Services window is organized into the following columns:

- **Name**. Displays the names of the network services that are installed on the computer.

- **Description**. Provides a brief description of the services that are installed on the computer. The description is not available when connecting to a remote computer running earlier versions of Windows.

- **Status**. Shows the status of the services that are installed on the computer.

- **Startup Type**. Identifies the startup type for the services that are installed on the computer, as follows:

  - *Automatic*. Specifies that the service is designed to start automatically when the system starts.

  - *Manual*. Specifies that a user or a dependent service can start the service. Services with manual startup do not start automatically when the system starts.

  - *Disabled*. Prevents the service from being started by the system, a user, or any dependent service.

- **Log On As**. Specifies the logon account that is used by the services that are installed on the computer. Most services log on as the system account, but some services can be configured to log on as other user accounts. This enables the service to access resources, such as files and folders, by using the access permissions of the user account that you specify.

Modifying Service Properties

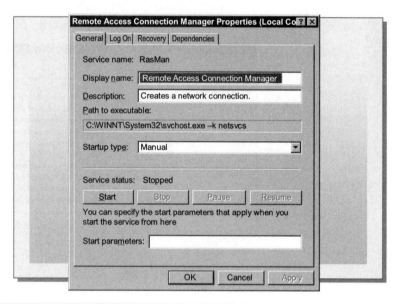

To modify the properties of a service, open Services. In the details pane, right-click the name of the service that you want to modify, and then click **Properties**.

General Tab

To modify the information that appears in the details pane of the Services window, configure the options on the **General** tab of the **Properties** dialog box for a service. After you have modified the service properties, click **OK**. You can use the **General** tab to:

- Change the name of the service that appears in the **Name** column.
- Modify the description that appears in the **Description** column.
- Change the startup type that appears in the **Startup Type** column.

You can also view the service's status, and start, stop, pause, or resume the service by clicking the appropriate button under **Service status**. Before you start a service by clicking the **Start** button under **Service status**, you can specify the start parameters that apply when the service starts in the **Start parameters** box.

Note   You can view the path and file name of the service on the **General** tab, under **Path to executable**. This information cannot be changed.

Log On Tab

To modify the information that appears in the **Log On As** column of the Services window, configure the options on the **Log On** tab of the **Properties** dialog box for a service. You can use the **Log On** tab to:

- Select one of the following options to specify the account that the service uses to log on.

  - *Local System account*. Specifies that the service will log on by using the system account, rather than a user account. Most services log on as the local system account.

  - *This account*. Assigns a logon account to the service. Although most services log on as the system account, some services can be configured to log on to special user accounts so that the service can access resources, such as files and folders, by using the access permissions of the user account that you specify.

Note   Select the **Allow service to interact with desktop** check box to enable the service to provide a user interface on the desktop when the service is started. This option is available only if the service is running as the Local System account.

- Enable or disable the service for a specific hardware profile.

Recovery Tab

Use the **Recovery** tab to specify the recovery actions that you want to occur if a service fails, such as restarting the service automatically or restarting the computer. You can set a different recovery action for the first failure, the second failure, and for all subsequent failures of a service. Set recovery actions to configure Windows 2000 to take no action, restart the service, run a file, or restart the computer if a service fails.

If you select **Run a File**, specify the file name under **Run file**. Do not specify programs or scripts that require user input. If you select **Reboot the Computer**, click **Restart Computer Options** to specify the amount of time that Windows 2000 will wait before restarting the computer. You can also create a message to send to computers on the network before the computer restarts.

Dependencies Tab

The **Dependencies** tab lists other services that depend on the service, or that the service depends on. When you open the **Properties** dialog box for a particular service, the **Dependencies** tab:

- Lists the other network services that the service requires to run properly.

- Lists the other network services that require the service to run properly.

This information is useful when troubleshooting network services, because a network service failure may be the result of a problem with a dependent service.

◆ Monitoring the Network

- **Installing Network Monitor**
- **The Network Monitor Interface**
- **Capturing Data by Using Network Monitor**
- **Displaying Data by Using Network Monitor**

You can use a network packet analyzer to compile information about network functionality. A network packet analyzer is a tool that captures, filters, and analyzes network traffic. Network packet analyzers can be software based, or a combination of specialized hardware and software. By using network packet analyzers, you can:

- Monitor real-time network utilization or bandwidth.

- Troubleshoot network errors by diagnosing cable connections, bandwidth or protocol issues, or defective network cards.

- Use monitoring information to determine how you can optimize the network by dividing it into subnets.

- Use monitoring information to plan the purchase of additional devices for your network.

Microsoft Network Monitor

Microsoft Network Monitor is a software-based traffic analysis tool that enables you to capture and display network packets that a computer running Windows 2000 Server sends to and receives from a LAN. By using Network Monitor, you can:

- Capture packets directly from the network.

- Display and filter packets immediately after a capture, or save the captured data for later analysis.

- Edit captured packets and transmit them back onto the network.

- Capture packets from a remote computer.

Important   To install or use Network Monitor, you must be a member of the Administrators group.

Troubleshooting Network Problems

You can use Network Monitor to detect and troubleshoot networking problems on a local computer. For example, use Network Monitor to diagnose hardware and software problems when a server cannot communicate with other computers. In addition, you can save to a file the packets that Network Monitor captures, and then send the file to professional network analysts or support organizations for analysis.

Simple Version vs. Full Version

Network Monitor is included with Windows 2000 Server (simple version), and with Microsoft Systems Management Server (full version). The following table describes the differences between the simple and full versions of Network Monitor.

Function	Network Monitor (simple)	Network Monitor (full)
Local capturing	To and from the computer running Network Monitor only	All devices on the entire subnet
Remote capturing	Not available	Available
Determining the top user of network bandwidth	Not available	Available
Determining which protocol consumed the most bandwidth	Not available	Available
Determining which devices are routers	Not available	Available
Resolving a device name into a MAC address	Not available	Available
Editing and retransmitting network traffic	Not available	Available

Installing Network Monitor

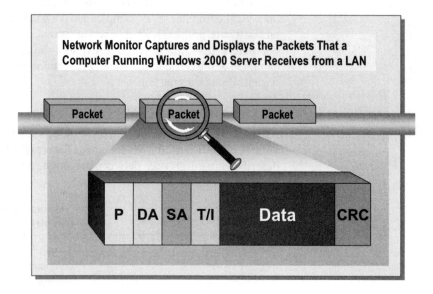

Network Monitor captures and displays the packets that a computer running Windows 2000 Server receives from a LAN. Install Network Monitor on the computer from which data will be captured. When you install Network Monitor, the Network Monitor Driver is installed automatically on the same computer. The Network Monitor Driver appears as a network service in the **Properties** dialog box for local area connections.

Note Network Monitor can be installed only on computers running Windows 2000 Server.

To install Network Monitor:

1. Open Control Panel, and then double-click **Add/Remove Programs**.

2. In the **Add/Remove Programs** dialog box, click **Add/Remove Windows Components**.

3. In the Windows Components wizard, click **Management and Monitoring Tools**, and then click **Details**.

4. In the **Management and Monitoring Tools** dialog box, select the **Network Monitor Tools** check box, click **OK**, and then click **Next**.

5. If you are prompted for additional files, insert your Windows 2000 Server compact disc, or type a path to the location of the files on the network, and then click **OK**.

6. Click **Next**, and then click **Finish**.

The Network Monitor Interface

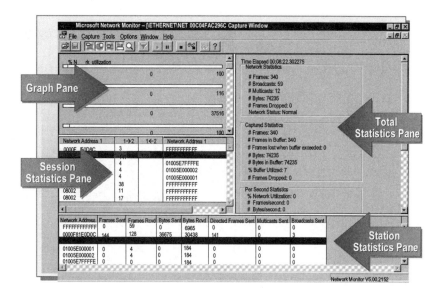

Open Network Monitor from the **Administrative Tools** menu. The first window to appear in Network Monitor is the Capture window, which is the basic Network Monitor interface. The Capture window provides different types of statistical data that is useful in analyzing overall network performance.

The Capture window is divided into the four major areas, as described in the following table.

Pane	Description
Graph	Displays the current activity as a set of bar charts that indicate the percentage of network utilization, frames per second, bytes per second, broadcasts per second, and multicasts per second during the capture process.
Session Statistics	Provides a summary of the conversations between two hosts, and indicates which host is initiating broadcasts and multicasts.
Total Statistics	Displays statistics for the traffic that is detected on the network, statistics for the frames captured, per-second utilization statistics, and network adapter card statistics.
Station Statistics	Provides a summary of the total number of frames that a host initiates, the number of frames and bytes sent and received, and the number of initiated broadcast and multicast frames.

Capturing Data by Using Network Monitor

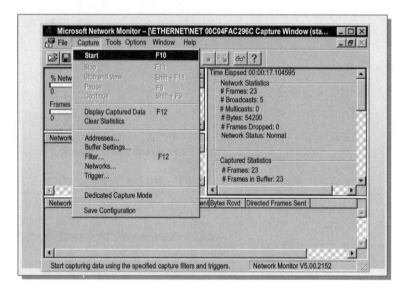

Network Monitor performs much of the data analysis for you by translating captured data into its logical frame structure. After data has been captured, it can be analyzed immediately or saved to a capture file (.cap) for later analysis.

Capturing Network Traffic

To capture network traffic:

1. Open Network Monitor.

2. If you are prompted for a default network on which to capture frames, select the local network from which you want to capture data.

3. Click **Capture**, and then click **Start**.

   As data is being captured, information will appear in each of the four sections of the Capture window. This includes current network statistics, in addition to statistics for the captured data.

4. To stop the capture, click **Capture**, and then click **Stop**.

Saving Captured Data

You can save captured data to a capture file (.cap) for later analysis. You can view these files in Network Monitor at a later time, or you can send the file to professional network analysts or support organizations for analysis. To save captured data to a file, on the **File** menu, click **Save As**. In the **Save As** dialog box, specify the folder in which you want to save the file.

Important   You must use the .cap file extension if you want to be able to view the file in Network Monitor at a later time.

Capture Filters

A common method for controlling the amount of data that is captured is to set a capture filter. A capture filter describes the frames that are to be captured, buffered, displayed, and saved. Before any frame can be buffered, it must pass through the filter. Filters are commonly configured for specific types of traffic (protocols), such as IP and IPX, or on source or destination addresses. These addresses can be MAC addresses, or protocol addresses (IP or IPX).

Capture Triggers

You can also specify a set of conditions that trigger an event in a Network Monitor capture filter. By using triggers, Network Monitor can respond to events on your network. For example, you can start an executable file when Network Monitor detects a particular set of conditions on the network.

Note For more information about capture filters and triggers, open Network Monitor, and then click **Help**.

Displaying Data by Using Network Monitor

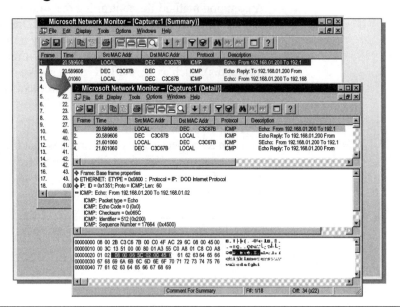

Network Monitor simplifies data analysis by interpreting raw data collected during the capture and displaying it in the Capture Summary window. To view captured data, start a capture. When you want to stop the capture, click **Capture**, and then click **Stop and View**.

Displaying Frames

The Capture Summary window displays a summary of all captured frames, and includes three panes—the Summary pane, the Detail pane, and the Hexadecimal pane. If you want to focus on a particular pane, you can change the appearance of the Capture Summary window so that one pane fills the entire window.

To view only one pane in the Capture Summary window, click anywhere inside the pane that you want to view, click **Window**, and then click **Zoom**. To view all three panes, perform the same procedure and verify that **Zoom** is not selected on the **Window** menu.

Summary Pane (Top)

This pane lists all frames that are included in the current view of the captured data. When a frame is selected in the Summary pane, Network Monitor displays the frame's contents in the Detail and Hexadecimal panes. The columns in the Summary pane include the following.

Column	Description
Frame	Displays the frame number. All frames captured during one capture session are numbered in the order of capture time.
Time	Displays the frame's capture time relative to the beginning of the capture process. It can be configured to display the time of day when the frame was captured, or the time that has elapsed since the previous frame capture.

(continued)

Column	Description
Src MAC Addr (Source MAC Address)	Displays the hardware address of the computer that sent the frame.
Dst MAC Addr (Destination MAC Address)	Displays the hardware address of the target computer.
Protocol	Lists the protocol that was used to transmit the frame.
Description	Displays a summary of the frame's contents. The summary information can include the first protocol used in that frame, the last protocol used in that frame, or an automatic selection.
Src Other Addr (Source Other Address)	Provides an additional identifying address for the originator of the frame, other than the MAC address. This can be an IP or IPX address.
Dst Other Addr (Destination Other Address)	Provides an additional identifying address for the destination of the frame.
Type Other Addr (Type Other Address)	Specifies which type of address is displayed in the previous two columns.

Detail Pane (Middle)

The Detail pane displays protocol information for the frame that is selected in the Summary pane. When a frame contains several protocol layers, the Detail pane displays the outermost level first.

When you select a protocol in the Detail pane, the associated hexadecimal strings for the current frame are in the Hexadecimal pane. When you expand the protocol information, a line of data appears for each property associated with that frame.

Hexadecimal Pane (Bottom)

The Hexadecimal pane displays the content of the selected frame in hexadecimal format. When you select information in the Detail pane, the corresponding hexadecimal data is selected in the Hexadecimal pane. This information is often the focus of data analysis, especially when determining the appropriate application programming interface (API) call that is used in a transaction.

Filtering Data

You can set display filters to filter frames of interest, such as those from a particular host, or those using a particular protocol. You can configure display filters for a specific protocol or a specific MAC or protocol address, or for a unique property of a frame, such as a specific source or destination port.

Note   For more information about display filters, see Network Monitor Help.

Lab B: Troubleshooting Network Problems by Using Network Monitor

Objectives

After completing this lab, you will be able to:

- Install Network Monitor.
- Use Network Monitor to capture and display network traffic.

Prerequisite

Before working on this lab, you must be familiar with Network Monitor concepts, utilities, and operations.

Lab Setup

To complete this lab, you need a computer running Windows 2000 Advanced Server.

Scenario

Your production department has 25 new employees. You have installed 25 new computers on your network. As the new employees begin using these computers, you notice problems on the subnet in which users are periodically losing their connections to the network. You want the ability to monitor the network so that you can prevent connectivity issues, keep track of performance, and prevent future problems.

Estimated time to complete this lab: 30 minutes

Exercise 1
Installing Network Monitor

Scenario

You are the administrator for Northwind Traders. You have connected new computers to the network for newly hired employees. After installing these new computers, you notice problems with network performance.

Goal

In this exercise, you will install Network Monitor.

Task	Detailed Steps
1. Install Network Monitor.	**a.** Log on as administrator@*domain*.nwtraders.msft (where *domain* is the name of your domain) with a password of **password**.
	b. In Control Panel, double-click **Add/Remove Programs**, and then click **Add/Remove Windows Components**.
ⓘ Note: In the next detailed step, click the text **Management and Monitoring Tools** rather than the check box to avoid selecting all options under **Management and Monitoring Tools**.	
1. *(continued)*	**c.** In the Windows Components wizard on the **Windows Components** page, under **Components**, select **Management and Monitoring Tools**, and then click **Details**.
	d. In the **Management and Monitoring Tools** window, select the **Network Monitor Tools** check box, click **OK**, and then click **Next**.
	e. If the **Insert Disk** dialog box appears, click **OK**. In the **Files Needed** dialog box, type **\\London\Setup\Winsrc** and then click **OK**.
	f. When the configuration process is complete, click **Finish**, and then close all open windows.

Exercise 2
Capturing Data with Network Monitor

Scenario

You have installed Network Monitor. You want to discover why your network is having performance problems.

Goal

In this exercise, you will use Network Monitor to collect data about your network.

Tasks	Detailed Steps
1. Determine the media access control address of the network card associated with the Classroom connection.	a. At a command prompt, type **ipconfig /all** and then press ENTER.
❓ What is the physical address of the network card associated with the Classroom connection? The physical address will be in the following format: XX-XX-XX-XX-XX-XX. _____ _____ _____ _____	
1. *(continued)*	b. Minimize the command prompt window.
2. Set a Network Monitor trigger.	a. Open Network Monitor from the **Administrative Tools** menu. b. Click **OK** to close the **Network Monitor – Select Default Network** dialog box.
ℹ **Note:** You must select a default network because the computer has more than one network card.	
2. *(continued)*	c. In the **Select a network** dialog box, expand **Local Computer**. d. Click the Ethernet adapter that is associated with the physical address of the Classroom network connection, and then click **OK**. 🖥 *The Network Monitor Capture window appears.* e. On the **Capture** menu, click **Trigger**. 🖥 *The Capture Trigger dialog box appears.* f. Under **Trigger on**, click **Buffer space**. g. Under **Buffer space**, click **50%**. h. Under **Trigger Action**, click **Stop Capture**, and then click **OK**.

(continued)

Tasks	Detailed Steps
3. Capture network data and generate network traffic.	a. On the **Capture** menu, click **Start**. b. Click **Start**, and then click **Run**. c. In the **Open** dialog box, type **London** and then click **OK**. *A list of resources on \\London appears.* d. In the London window, double-click **Setup**.
4. View network data statistics.	a. Restore Network Monitor. b. On the **Capture** menu, click **Stop**. c. On the **Capture** menu, click **Display Captured Data**. d. Scroll through the list of captured frames, and view the addresses that are listed in the **Src MAC Addr** and **Dst MAC Addr** columns. View the protocols that are listed in the **Protocol** column. *Notice the London server name is in the **Src and Dst MAC Addr** columns. TCP, SMB and RIP are protocols that you will see in the **Protocol** column.* e. Close Network Monitor. f. Close all windows, and then log off.

Review

- **Troubleshooting Network Problems**
- **Identifying the Symptoms and Causes of Network Problems**
- **Resolving TCP/IP Problems**
- **Resolving Name Resolution Problems**
- **Troubleshooting Network Services**
- **Monitoring the Network**

1. What are the three phases of effective network troubleshooting?

2. Which of the Windows 2000 administrative tools can you use to diagnose network problems, and what does it allow you to do?

3. What are the four main areas in which TCP/IP problems can occur?

4. What is the easiest way to distinguish host name problems from NetBIOS name resolution problems?

5. You have added five TCP/IP clients to your network. You now notice that the subnet to which you added the clients periodically disconnects some of them from the network. What tool can you use to troubleshoot this problem?

6. Your network uses TCP/IP and is connected to the Internet. You are unable to access a particular host on the Internet. You have verified that the gateway is functional, because you can access other sites on the Internet. Which TCP/IP utility can you use to troubleshoot this problem?

TCP/IP   → APPLICATRATION

LAYERS   → TRANSPORT (END TO END)   (TCP/UDP)

                    PORT NUMBER (APPL) IDENTIFIES AN

                                   APPL)

                       65,000 PORT #'S AVAILABLE.

         → INTERNET

        → NETWORK INTERFACE (ACCESS)

IPCONFIG /FLUSHDNS → Clears DNS CACHE ON LOCAL COMPUTER.

PING HOST NAME.

PING IP ADDRESS

PING ROUTER.

Microsoft®
Training &
Certification

Module 16: Configuring Network Connectivity Between Operating Systems

Contents

Overview

- **Configuring Access to NetWare Resources**

- **Providing Macintosh Users Access to Windows 2000 Resources**

- **Connecting to SNA Hosts by Using Host Integration Server 2000**

- **Connecting to UNIX Resources**

Microsoft® Windows® 2000 Server supports interoperability with Novell NetWare, Macintosh, IBM hosts, and UNIX, enabling you to integrate Windows 2000 into an existing environment. You can introduce Windows 2000 incrementally into a network environment because it provides migration paths from any number of existing systems, devices, and applications.

At the end of this module, you will be able to:

- Configure access to NetWare resources.

- Provide Macintosh users with access to Windows 2000 resources.

- Connect to Systems Network Architecture (SNA) hosts by using Microsoft Host Integration Server 2000.

- Connect to UNIX resources.

◆ Configuring Access to NetWare Resources

- ■ Overview of Gateway Service for NetWare
- ■ Installing Gateway Service for NetWare
- ■ Configuring Gateway Service for NetWare
- ■ Services for NetWare

Windows 2000 provides several features and services that enable computers running Windows 2000 Server to interoperate with Novell NetWare servers. You can use these features to support a heterogeneous environment composed of both Windows 2000–based servers and NetWare servers.

Windows 2000 Server includes Gateway Service for NetWare, which enables a computer running Windows 2000 Server to connect to computers running NetWare 3.*x* or 4.*x* server software. You can also use Gateway Service for NetWare to enable computers running any type of Microsoft client software to gain access to NetWare resources.

Services for NetWare is a separate product that you can use to enable a computer running Windows 2000 Server to interoperate with NetWare and NetWare-compatible computers.

Overview of Gateway Service for NetWare

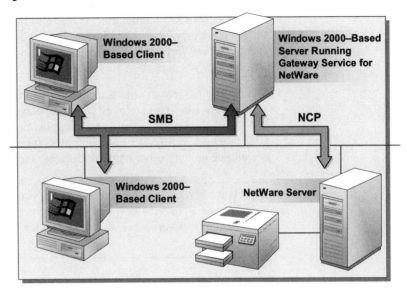

Gateway Service for NetWare enables a computer running Windows 2000 Server to access the resources on a NetWare server. The Windows 2000–based server can then provide client computers with access to the NetWare resources.

Accessing NetWare Resources

Gateway Service for NetWare acts as a gateway between the server message block (SMB) or Common Internet File System (CIFS) protocol used on Windows networks, and the NetWare Core Protocol (NCP) used on NetWare networks. When you enable this gateway, Windows 2000–based network clients can access resources on NetWare servers through the gateway located on the computer running Windows 2000 Server. You can use Gateway Service for NetWare to provide users with occasional access to NetWare-based resources.

Install NetWare client software on client computers that use NetWare servers frequently, because all access to NetWare servers must go through the computer on which Gateway Service for NetWare is installed.

The NWLink Protocol

Gateway Service for NetWare depends on and works with the NWLink IPX/SPX/NetBIOS Compatible Transport Protocol (NWLink). Internetwork Packet Exchange/Sequenced Packet Exchange (IPX/SPX) is the protocol used in Novell NetWare networks. NWLink is the Microsoft implementation of the IPX/SPX protocol used in Novell networks.

Windows 2000–based clients can use NWLink to access client and server applications running on Novell NetWare servers. NetWare clients can use NWLink to access client and server applications running on Windows 2000–based servers. With NWLink, computers running Windows 2000 can communicate with other network devices, such as printers, that use IPX/SPX.

Important NWLink alone does not allow you to access file and printer resources on a Novell NetWare server. To access these resources, you must install client software, such as Client Service for NetWare or Gateway Service for NetWare.

Installing Gateway Service for NetWare

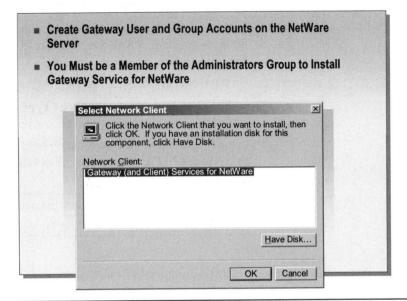

You can use Gateway Service for NetWare in a mixed NetWare and Windows 2000 network to provide users with access to resources on NetWare servers. Users of computers running Windows 2000 can access resources on a NetWare server through the computer running Gateway Service for NetWare. Client computers do not require NetWare client software when accessing resources through Gateway Service for NetWare.

Note The NWLink protocol is installed during the Gateway Service for NetWare installation process, if it is not already on the server.

Preparing to Install Gateway Service for NetWare

You must create gateway user and group accounts on the NetWare server before you install Gateway Service for NetWare on the Windows 2000–based server. You must meet the following requirements to prepare to install Gateway Service for NetWare:

- Set up a user account on the NetWare server, with the same name and password as the user account that you configure as the gateway account, on the computer running Windows 2000. Assign to the gateway user account the NetWare rights for files that users will access. You can restrict a user's level of access for shared folders on the computer running Gateway Service for NetWare, but the gateway user account must have sufficient rights to access files on the NetWare server. These rights are required because the gateway account accesses all files on the NetWare server.

- Create a group account named NTGateway on the NetWare server. Add the user account that was set up previously to this group account.

Performing the Installation

To install Gateway Service for NetWare:

1. In Network and Dial-up Connections, right-click the local area connection for the network on which the NetWare server resides, and then click **Properties**.

2. On the **General** tab, click **Install**.

3. In the **Select Network Component Type** dialog box, click **Client**, and then click **Add**.

4. In the **Select Network Client** dialog box, click **Gateway (and Client) Services for NetWare**, and then click **OK**.

Note   You must be a member of the Administrators group to install Gateway Service for Netware.

Configuring Gateway Service for NetWare

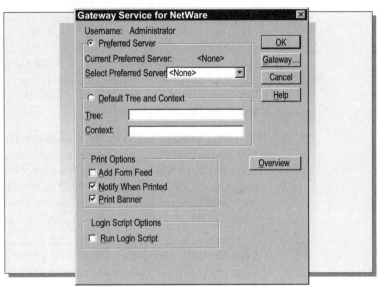

After you have installed Gateway Service for NetWare, you must configure it to enable the gateway. Then, on the Windows 2000–based server, establish a connection and create a shared resource for the Microsoft clients. This provides network clients running Microsoft client software with access to NetWare files and printers without having to run NetWare client software locally.

Configuring the Windows 2000–Based Server Gateway

To configure Gateway Service for NetWare, open the **Gateway Service for NetWare** dialog box by double-clicking **GSNW** in Control Panel.

To enable the Windows 2000–based server gateway:

1. In the **Gateway Service for NetWare** dialog box, click **Gateway**.

2. In the **Configure Gateway** dialog box, select the **Enable Gateway** check box.

3. Type the gateway account name that you want to use for this gateway connection, type the password, and then click **OK**.

   The password must be identical to the password for the user account that you created on the NetWare server. You need to do this only once for each server that acts as a gateway.

Establishing Shared Folders and Permissions

After you install Gateway Service for NetWare and configure the gateway, you can establish shared folders and permissions. To user of computers running Windows 2000, the shared folder appears as a typical shared folder on the server running Gateway Service for NetWare. When a user accesses a file in the shared folder, Gateway Service for NetWare retrieves the file from a NetWare server by using the gateway account. The server running Gateway Service for NetWare then makes the file available to the user as if it were located on the server itself.

To create a shared folder, in the **Configure Gateway** dialog box, click **Add**. In the appropriate text boxes, type the share name of the shared folder that users will see, the network path of the Novell volume and directory that you are mapping the shared folder to, a drive mapping, and the user limit for that particular folder. To complete the configuration, set user permissions on the shared folder for an appropriate access level to NetWare resources.

Important   All users have access to all of the NetWare files that you have assigned to the gateway account, unless you configure permissions.

Activating a Gateway to a NetWare Printer

You can configure and establish a connection to a NetWare-based printer through Gateway Service for NetWare. However, you can only do this after you establish the appropriate user and group accounts, set the necessary rights on the NetWare servers, and install and configure Gateway Service for NetWare on the Windows 2000–based server.

Note   For more information about setting up a gateway printer share, in the **Gateway Service for NetWare** dialog box, click the **Overview** button.

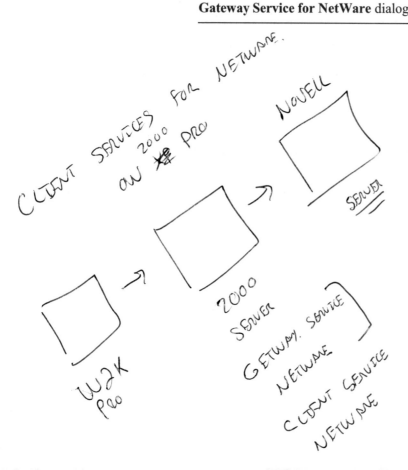

Services for NetWare

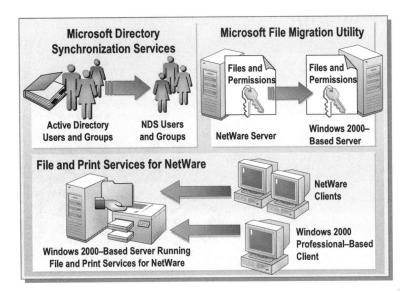

Services for NetWare is separate product that includes interoperability services and tools that you can use to integrate an existing NetWare environment into a Windows 2000 network.

Services for NetWare includes the following utilities:

- *Microsoft Directory Synchronization Services*. Provides two-way synchronization of directory information stored in the Active Directory™ directory service and NDS. This helps to reduce costs and simplifies network management because it eliminates the need to replace existing directories or manage separate directories.

- *File Migration Utility*. Enables you to migrate files from NetWare servers to a computer running Windows 2000 Server, while preserving directory structures and security permissions. This helps you to quickly and securely migrate to Windows 2000 from a NetWare environment.

- *File and Print Services for NetWare*. Enables a computer running Windows 2000 to provide file and print services to NetWare clients. The Windows 2000–based server appears as a NetWare server to the NetWare clients, and the clients can access volumes, files, and printers through the server. No changes or additions to the NetWare client software are necessary. This simplifies network management and eases the transition to Windows 2000 from a NetWare environment.

Note For more information about Services for NetWare, see the white paper *Services for Netware Version 5 Overview*, under **Additional Reading** on the Web page on the Student Materials compact disc.

Lab A: Configuring Gateway Service for NetWare (Simulation)

Objectives

After completing this lab, you will be able to:

- Install and configure Gateway Service for NetWare.

- Access resources by using Gateway Service for NetWare.

Prerequisites

Before working on this lab, you must have an understanding of Gateway Service for NetWare, the NWLink protocol, shared folders, and permissions.

Lab Setup

This lab is a simulation. To complete this lab, you need the following:

- A computer running Windows 2000, Microsoft Windows NT® version 4.0, Microsoft Windows 98, or Microsoft Windows 95.

- A minimum display resolution of 800 x 600 with 256 colors.

Important   The lab does not reflect the real-world environment. It is recommended that you always use complex passwords for any administrator accounts, and never create accounts without a password.

Important   Outside of the classroom environment, it is strongly advised that you use the most recent software updates that are necessary. Because this is a classroom environment, we may use software that does not include the latest updates.

▶ **To start the lab**

1. Insert the Student Materials compact disc into your CD-ROM drive.

2. At the root of the compact disc, double-click **Default.htm**.

3. On the Student Materials Web page, click **Lab Simulations**, and then click **Configuring Services for NetWare**.

4. Read the introduction information, and then click the link to start the lab.

Estimated time to complete this lab: 15 minutes

◆ Providing Macintosh Users Access to Windows 2000 Resources

- **Overview of AppleTalk Network Integration Services**

- **Identifying Connectivity Options**

- **Installing File Services and Print Services for Macintosh**

- **Configuring File Services and Print Services for Macintosh**

Windows 2000 includes AppleTalk network integration (formerly known as Services for Macintosh); this enables Microsoft and Macintosh clients to share files and printers.

Overview of AppleTalk Network Integration Services

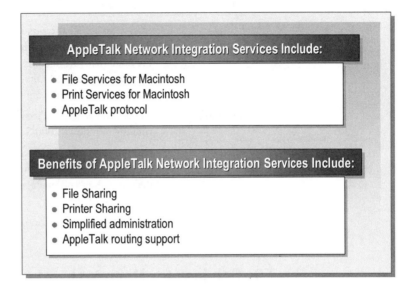

With AppleTalk network integration services, you can create accessible volumes that provide a central location from which clients running Microsoft operating systems and Macintosh clients can access file and print resources. The three components of AppleTalk network integration are:

- File Services for Macintosh

- Print Services for Macintosh

- The AppleTalk protocol

Note File Services for Macintosh and Print Services for Macintosh, combined, were formerly known as Services for Macintosh.

The following table describes the benefits of AppleTalk network integration.

Function	Description
File sharing	Users can access the same documents, even if some users access the documents from Macintosh computers and other users access the documents from computers running Windows or MS-DOS®. For these users to edit the same file, applications must also be able to open the same document format.
Printer sharing	Clients can send print jobs either to a printer on a computer running Windows 2000 Server or to a Macintosh-based printer.
Simplified administration	Resources in mixed networks with both Windows 2000–based or MS-DOS–based computers and Macintosh clients can be maintained on and managed from a computer running Windows 2000 Server.
AppleTalk routing support	Macintosh networks can be connected to create an AppleTalk internetwork.

File Services for Macintosh

File Services for Macintosh is an AppleTalk network integration service that enables Macintosh clients and Microsoft clients to share files on a computer running Windows 2000 Server.

Print Services for Macintosh

Print Services for Macintosh enables Macintosh clients to send and spool documents to printers attached to a computer running Windows 2000 Server. Print Services for Macintosh also enables Macintosh and Windows clients to send documents to printers anywhere on an AppleTalk network.

AppleTalk Protocol

The AppleTalk protocol is the set of network protocols on which the AppleTalk network architecture is based. The AppleTalk protocol stack must be installed on a computer running Windows 2000 Server to enable Macintosh clients to connect to it.

Note   Windows 2000 automatically installs the AppleTalk protocol when you install File Services for Macintosh or Print Services for Macintosh.

Identifying Connectivity Options

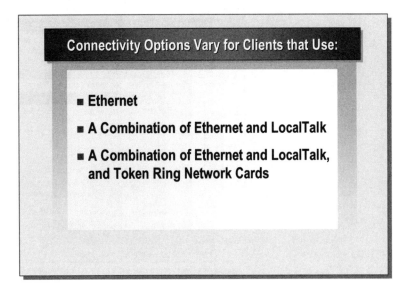

There are various options available for connecting to a Macintosh network. The option that you choose depends on the local area network (LAN) technology that is used on your network and is used by the Macintosh clients.

The following table describes the different connectivity options for a Windows 2000–based server that uses Ethernet.

Macintosh Clients Use	Connectivity Options
Ethernet	• Install File Services for Macintosh on the server. This creates a central storage location from which clients can access files.
Combination of Ethernet and LocalTalk	• Install a LocalTalk card on the server to communicate with the Macintosh computers that use LocalTalk.
	- Or -
	• Install Ethernet cards on all of the Macintosh computers.
	- Or -
	• Use an Ethernet/LocalTalk router.
Combination of Ethernet and LocalTalk, and token ring network cards	• Install a token ring network card on the server to communicate with the clients that have token ring network cards.
	- And -
	• Install Ethernet cards on all of the Macintosh computers, or use an Ethernet/LocalTalk router.

Installing File Services and Print Services for Macintosh

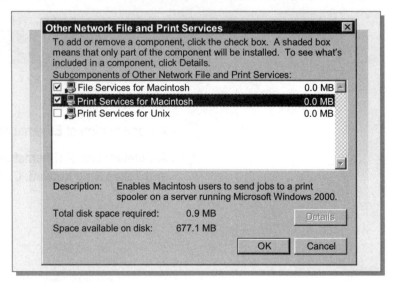

You can install File Services for Macintosh or Print Services for Macintosh from **Add/Remove Programs** in Control Panel. Before installing File Services for Macintosh, you must ensure that there is an NTFS file system partition for each computer on which you will install File Services for Macintosh or Print Services for Macintosh.

To install File Services for Macintosh or Print Services for Macintosh (or both):

1. In Control Panel, open Add/Remove Programs, and then click **Add/Remove Windows Components**.

2. On the **Windows Components** page of the Windows Components wizard, click **Other Network File and Print Services** (but do not select or clear the check box), and then click **Details**.

3. In the **Other Network File and Print Services** dialog box, select the **Print Services for Macintosh** check box or the **File Services for Macintosh** check box (or both), and then click **OK**.

4. On the **Windows Components** page, click **Next**, and then click **Finish**.

Configuring File Services and Print Services for Macintosh

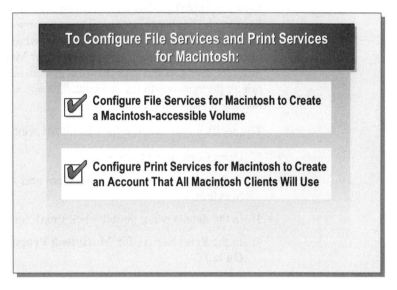

After you install File Services for Macintosh or Print Services for Macintosh, you must configure them to enable Macintosh clients to access resources on a computer running Windows 2000 Server.

Configuring File Services for Macintosh

After installing File Services for Macintosh, you must create and share a Macintosh-accessible volume. A Macintosh-accessible volume is a folder on a computer running Windows 2000 Server that is made available to Macintosh clients.

To create a Macintosh-accessible volume:

1. Open Computer Management.

2. In the console tree, double-click **Shared Folders**, right-click **Shares**, and then click **New File Share**.

3. In the **Create Shared Folder** dialog box, in the **Folder to share** box, type the drive and path to the folder that you want to make available to Macintosh clients, or click **Browse** to locate the folder.

4. In the **Share name** box, type the name of the shared folder as it will appear to users who access the shared folder from a Windows-based computer. You can also type a description of the shared folder in the **Share description** box.

5. Under **Accessible from the following clients**, verify that the **Microsoft Windows** check box is selected, select the **Apple Macintosh** check box, and then click **Next**.

6. In the **Macintosh share name** box, type the name of the shared folder as it will appear to users who access the shared folder from a Macintosh computer.

7. Select the appropriate share permission, and then click **Finish**.

Configuring Print Services for Macintosh

Because AppleTalk has no mechanism for enforcing printer security, by default, Macintosh clients can access all printers on a computer that has Print Services for Macintosh installed. You can restrict which printers Macintosh clients can print to by configuring the Print Server for Macintosh service to log on as a different user account than the local system account. You can then assign printer permissions to this account. The account that you specify must also have the Log on as a service user right.

To specify a user account for Macintosh print jobs:

1. Open Computer Management.

2. In the console tree, expand **Services and Applications**, and then click **Services**.

3. In the details pane, double-click **Print Server For Macintosh**.

4. In the **Print Server for Macintosh Properties** dialog box, click the **Log On** tab.

5. Click **This account**, and then type the name of the user account, or click **Browse** to locate the user account.

6. Type the password of the user account in the **Password** and **Confirm password** boxes, and then click **OK**.

Lab B: Configuring File Services and Print Services for Macintosh (Simulation)

Objectives

After completing this lab, you will be able to install and configure File Services and Print Services for Macintosh.

Prerequisites

Before working on this lab, you must have:

- An understanding of the AppleTalk protocol.
- An understanding of File Services and Print Services for Macintosh.
- An understanding of shared folders and permissions.

Lab Setup

This lab is a simulation. To complete this lab, you need the following:

- A computer running Windows 2000, Windows NT 4.0, Windows 98, or Windows 95.
- A minimum display resolution of 800 x 600 with 256 colors.

▶ **To start the lab**

1. Insert the Student Materials compact disc into your CD-ROM drive.

2. At the root of the compact disc, double-click **Default.htm**.

3. On the Student Materials Web page, click **Lab Simulations**, and then click **Configuring File Services and Print Services for Macintosh**.

4. Read the introduction information, and then click the link to start the lab.

Estimated time to complete this lab: 15 minutes

Connecting to SNA Hosts by Using Host Integration Server 2000

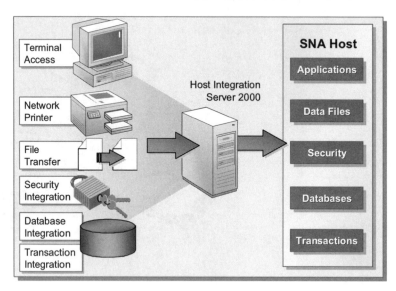

Many large organizations run applications on IBM mainframe systems that use the SNA networking protocol. Host Integration Server 2000 (formerly known as SNA Server) is a separate product in the Microsoft BackOffice® family of products that enables Window 2000–based clients and servers to connect to IBM host systems (also known as SNA hosts) over standard networking protocols.

Connection Types

Host Integration Server 2000 is a set of server processes that run on Windows 2000 Server. Host Integration Server 2000 acts as an SNA gateway and integrates systems on a LAN or a wide area network (WAN) with IBM mainframe systems and AS/400 systems by using two types of connections:

- The physical connections and logical connections into the Host Integration Server 2000 environment

- The client/server network connections to the non-SNA systems on the LAN or WAN, such as personal computers or server applications, which need access to Host Integration Server 2000 applications

Host Integration Server 2000 completes the network connection to the mainframe or AS/400 system by using standard IBM SNA protocols, such as Data Link Control (DLC) or Transmission Control Protocol/Internet Protocol (TCP/IP).

Note   Heterogeneous clients can connect to Host Integration Server 2000 through other networking protocols, such as IPX/SPX, NetBIOS Enhanced User Interface (NetBEUI), Banyan VINES IP, AppleTalk, and Windows 2000 Routing and Remote Access.

The DLC Protocol

Token ring, Ethernet, and Fiber Distributed Data Interface (FDDI) connections use the IEEE 802.2 protocol. With a mainframe, an 802.2 DLC connection goes to a 37*xx* FEP or a 3174 communications controller (or, rarely, to an adapter in the mainframe). With an AS/400 system, an 802.2 DLC connection goes directly to the AS/400. These connections are generally faster than most other connections, except for channel connections.

Type of 802.2 connection	Common speeds
Token ring	4 or 16 megabits per second (Mbps)
Ethernet	10/100 Mbps
FDDI	100 Mbps (or faster)

Connecting to UNIX Resources

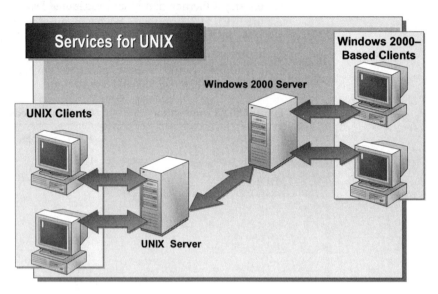

UNIX and Windows 2000 do not have a common mechanism for sharing files. UNIX uses Network File System (NFS) and Windows 2000 uses CIFS. To share files, one system must be modified to communicate with the file-sharing protocol of the other.

To integrate Windows 2000 with UNIX, use Windows Services for UNIX version 2.0, which is an add-on utility that provides core network interoperability with existing UNIX environments and synchronizes user passwords between Windows 2000–based systems and UNIX. Services for UNIX enables users of Windows 2000–based computers to access UNIX resources just as they would access any Windows-based resources.

Windows Services for UNIX 2.0:

- Enables you to share network resources among Windows NT, Windows 2000, and UNIX-based systems.

- Provides a subset of UNIX utilities to give UNIX users and administrators their familiar set of tools.

- Simplifies both local and remote network administration, and supports either graphical or character-based administration.

- Provides the ability to consolidate UNIX accounts and Windows accounts in Windows 2000, to centralize and synchronize account management.

Note   For more information about Services for UNIX, see the white paper *Services for UNIX version 2.0*, under **Additional Reading** on the Web page on the Student Materials compact disc, and the Services for UNIX Web site at http://www.microsoft.com/windows2000/sfu.

Review

- **Configuring Access to NetWare Resources**

- **Providing Macintosh Users Access to Windows 2000 Resources**

- **Connecting to SNA Hosts by Using Host Integration Server 2000**

- **Connecting to UNIX Resources**

1. The Accounting department in your company is running a Novell NetWare 4.11 server on a network that is separate from the rest of the company. The rest of the company has recently upgraded to a Windows 2000 domain environment. You must configure a connection between the Accounting department and the rest of the company to enable the Sales department to share data with the accounting department. After you have configured a connection between the two networks, what solutions can you implement that will allow the two departments to share data, and why?

2. What are the different options for connecting Macintosh clients to a Windows 2000 network?

3. Describe the connection types that Host Integration Server 2000 uses.

4. The Engineering department in your company uses UNIX workstations for mathematical three-dimensional modeling. You must create a solution to enable Windows 2000–based computers in your company to share data with the UNIX systems. What product would you use to accomplish this?

Course Evaluation

Your evaluation of this course will help Microsoft understand the quality of your learning experience.

To complete a course evaluation, go to http://www.metricsthatmatter.com/survey.

Microsoft will keep your evaluation strictly confidential and will use your responses to improve your future learning experience.

⇒ POSIX 1.1   FILES FOR UNIX ON MS

PRINT {
LPR → LINE PRINTER REQUEST (CLIENT)
LPD → LINE " DAEMON ⇒ FULLFILLS PRINT REQUEST (SERVER)
LPQ ⇒
}

INSTALL OTHER FILE & PRINT
                    SERVICE

VIEWS PRINTER QUEUE.

INSTALL LPR REQST.
⇒ PRINT SERVICES FOR MACINTOSH.
            → NTFS PARTITION .NEEDED.

Microsoft®
Training &
Certification

Appendix A: Computer Browser Service

Contents

Overview

- **Browse List**
- **Browser Roles**
- **The Browser Process**
- **Browser Election**
- **Configuring Browsers**
- **Browsing an IP Internetwork**
- **Browsing by Using the Lmhosts File**
- **Browsing by Using WINS**

To use resources across a network efficiently, users must be able to determine the availability of resources on the network. The Active Directory™ directory service in Microsoft® Windows® 2000 enables users to find this information.

Windows 2000 also uses the Computer Browser service to display a list of currently available network basic input/output system (NetBIOS)–based resources. The Computer Browser service maintains an up-to-date list of computers and provides the list to applications as requested. This enables users to locate resources on servers that are not running Windows 2000. It also enables users using client computers that are not running Windows 2000 to locate resources on servers that are running Windows 2000.

At the end of this module, you will be able to:

- Identify the different roles that a computer running Windows 2000 can perform in the browser process.
- Explain how the Computer Browser service locates available resources on the network.
- Describe how the browser election process ensures that the Computer Browser service is functioning properly.
- Configure a computer as a browser.
- Describe the problems involved with browsing in an Internet Protocol (IP) internetwork, and describe solutions to those problems.

Note For this appendix, a *server* is defined as any computer that provides resources to the network. For example, in the context of the Computer Browser service, a computer running Windows 2000 Professional is a server if it shares file or print resources with other computers on the network.

Browse List

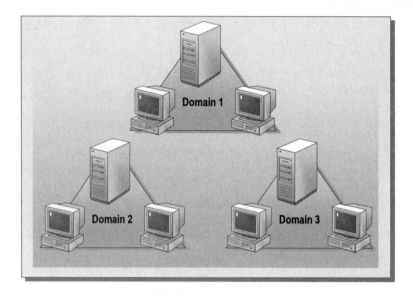

The Computer Browser service maintains a centralized list of available network resources, called the *browse list*. The browse list is distributed to specially assigned computers that perform browsing services along with their standard services. Browser computers eliminate the need for all computers to maintain a list of all shared resources on the network. By assigning the browser role to specific computers, the Computer Browser service reduces the amount of network traffic required to build and maintain a list of all shared resources on the network. This improves performance, because only the computers that are assigned the browser role need to create a network resource list.

To view the browse list in Windows 2000:

1. In My Network Places, double-click **Entire Network**.

2. Click **entire contents**.

3. Double-click **Microsoft Windows Network**.

Note   On computers running Microsoft Windows NT® version 4.0, Microsoft Windows 98, or Microsoft Windows 95, open Network Neighborhood to view the browse list. On computers running Microsoft Windows for Workgroups, use File Manager.

Browser Roles

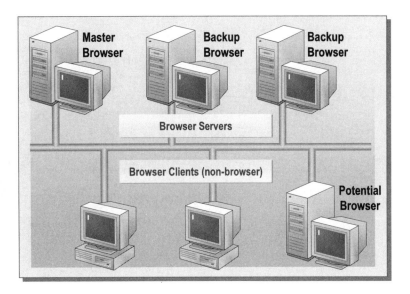

The task of providing a list of servers to clients is distributed among multiple computers on a network. You can assign different roles to computers that use the Computer Browser service. These roles include master browser, backup browser, potential browser, and browser clients (non-browsers). You can configure computers running Windows 2000 to perform any of the Computer Browser service roles.

The following table identifies the browsing roles that you can assign to a computer running Windows 2000:

Browser type	Description
Domain master browser	Collects and maintains the master list of available network servers, and the names of other domains and workgroups. It distributes this list to the master browser of each subnet in the Windows 2000 domain. There is only one domain master browser in a Windows 2000 domain, and it is the domain controller that holds the primary domain controller (PDC) emulator role.
Master browser	Collects and maintains the master list of available network servers in its workgroup or subnet, and shares this list with the domain master browser. The master browser receives information about other workgroups, domains, and subnets from the domain master browser, and incorporates this information into its list of available resources. The master browser distributes this list to the backup browsers. There is one master browser for each workgroup or subnet in a domain.
Backup browser	Receives a copy of the browse list from the master browser. It then distributes the list to the browser clients upon request.
Potential browser	Has the ability to become either a backup or a master browser if instructed to do so by a master browser or in the absence of other browser servers. A potential browser is not a browser server.
Non-browser	Does not maintain a browse list. Peer-to-peer networking computers are commonly non-browsers, even though they have server services.

The Browser Process

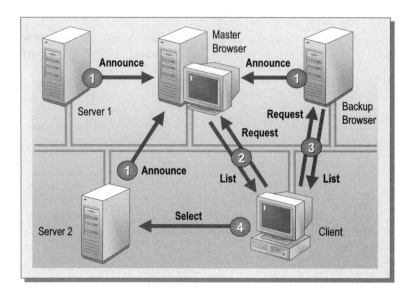

The following process describes how the Windows 2000 Computer Browser service operates:

1. After startup, all computers that are running the Server service announce their presence to the master browser in their workgroup or domain subnet. This occurs regardless of whether they contain shared resources.

2. The first time that a client tries to locate available network resources, it contacts the master browser of the domain subnet or workgroup for a list of backup browsers.

3. The client then requests the network server list from a backup browser. The backup browser responds to the client request with a list of domains and workgroups, and a list of servers that are local to the client's domain or workgroup.

4. The user at the client selects a server, searches for the appropriate resource, and then contacts the appropriate server to establish a session to use that resource.

Browser Election

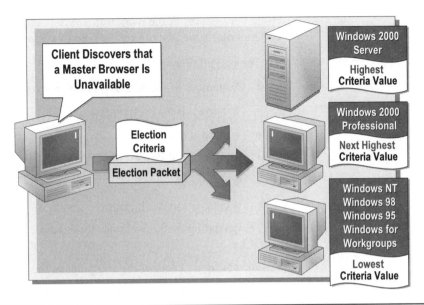

A new master browser must be elected if a client cannot locate a master browser, or if a backup browser attempts to update its network resource list but cannot locate the master browser. The election process ensures that there is only one master browser per workgroup or segment in a domain.

Election Process

Network computers initiate an election by broadcasting a special message called an *election packet*. The election packet contains the criteria value of the computer that initiated the request. All browsers process the election packet.

When a browser receives an election packet, it examines the packet and compares the criteria of the requesting computer with its own election criteria. If the receiving browser has higher election criteria than the computer that issued the election packet, the browser issues its own election packet, and then enters an *election-in-progress* state. This process continues until a master browser is elected based on the highest criteria value.

Browser Criteria

Browser criteria determine the hierarchical order of the different types of computer systems in the workgroup or domain. Each browser computer has certain criteria, depending on the type of system. The criteria include:

- The operating system.
  - A member of the Windows 2000 Server family of products
  - Windows 2000 Professional
  - Windows NT Server
  - Windows NT Workstation
  - Windows 95
  - Windows for Workgroups
- The operating system version: for example Windows NT 4.0, 3.51, 3.5, or 3.1.
- The configured role of the computer in the browsing environment.
  - Browser—either master browser or backup browser
  - Potential browser
  - Non-browser

During an election, the criteria ranking is used to determine which computer should be the master browser if the current master browser is unavailable.

Note For more information about browser criteria and election, see the chapter "Windows 2000 Browser Service" in the Windows 2000 Server Resource Kit.

Configuring Browsers

- **Windows 2000–Based Computers Can Be Configured To:**
  - Attempt to become a browser server
  - Never participate as a browser server
  - Possibly become a browser server
- **Registry Value Entry Options Include:**
  - Yes
  - No
  - Auto

Computers running Windows 2000 can be configured to:

- Attempt to become a browser server.
- Never participate as a browser server.
- Possibly become a browser server.

Use Registry Editor to make these configurations, and follow the registry path:
\HKEY_LOCAL_MACHINE\SYSTEM\CurrentControlSet\Services \Browser\Parameters\MaintainServerList

The following table describes the **MaintainServerList** values.

Value	Use this value to configure the computer to
Yes	Attempt to become a browser server. **Yes** is the default value for Windows 2000 Server domain controllers.
No	Never participate as a browser server. Use this value entry to prevent computers that are frequently taken off line, such as mobile or test computers, from becoming browser servers.
Auto	Possibly become a browser server, depending on the number of currently active browsers. A potential browser is notified by the master browser as to whether it should become a backup browser. **Auto** is the default value for computers running Windows 2000 Server (non-domain controllers) and Windows 2000 Professional.

To determine whether a computer running Windows 2000 will become a browser, when the computer initializes, the Computer Browser service looks in the registry for the value that has been configured for the computer.

Browsing an IP Internetwork

> - **IP Routers Do Not Propagate Broadcast Traffic**
> - **There Must Be Mechanisms For:**
>   - Collecting, distributing, and servicing client requests
> - **IP Router Solution**
>   - Not recommended
> - **Windows 2000 Solutions**
>   - Lmhosts File
>   - WINS

The Computer Browser service relies on a series of broadcast packets; as a result, browsing across IP routers that do not forward broadcasts can create certain problems. To facilitate client browsing of all network resources in an IP internetwork, there must be mechanisms for the collection, distribution, and servicing of client requests for browse lists.

The IP Router Solution

Some routers can be configured to forward broadcasts from one IP subnet to another. If the IP router is configured to forward these NetBIOS broadcasts, the browsing service works the same way—as if all of the domains or workgroups were located on the same subnet. All master browsers are aware of all servers in their own and other domains or workgroups, and all client browsing requests can be satisfied.

Unless these settings are enabled on all IP routers in the internetwork, this solution is not recommended because it propagates all NetBIOS over Transmission Control Protocol/Internet Protocol (TCP/IP) broadcast traffic across an internetwork, which decreases performance of all nodes on the internetwork. Enabling broadcast forwarding can cause browser election conflicts that report errors in the system log.

Windows 2000 Solutions

If the IP routers are not configured to forward NetBIOS broadcasts (which is typical), browsing collection and distribution and the servicing of client requests must take place over *directed* IP traffic rather than broadcast IP traffic. There are two ways to facilitate this in Windows 2000:

- *Lmhosts file entries*. Special entries in the Lmhosts file help facilitate the distribution of browsing information and the servicing of client requests.

- *WINS*. Windows Internet Name Service (WINS) is used to collect browse lists and to service client requests.

Browsing by Using the Lmhosts File

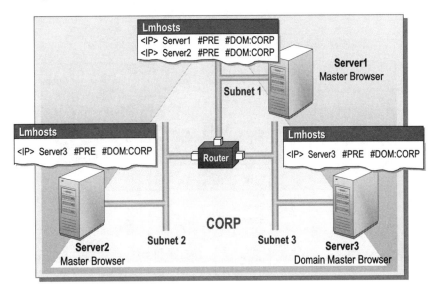

To implement direct communication between master browsers on remote subnets and the domain master browser, the Lmhosts file must be configured with the NetBIOS names and IP addresses of the browser computers.

Master Browsers

For computers running Windows 2000, the Lmhosts file on each subnet's master browser should contain the following information:

- The IP Address and computer name of the domain master browser
- The domain name, preceded by the **#PRE** and **#DOM:** keywords

For example:

```
130.20.7.80 <domain master_browser> #PRE #DOM:<domain_name>
```

Domain Master Browsers

At the domain master browser, the Lmhosts file must be configured with entries for each of the master browsers on remote subnets.

It is recommended that each master browser have a **#DOM** entry for all of the other master browsers in the domain. Therefore, if one master browser is promoted to the domain master browser, the Lmhosts files do not need to be changed on the other master browsers.

When multiple Lmhosts file entries exist for the same domain name, the master browser sends a query to the IP address for each entry to determine which of the entries corresponds to the domain master browser. Only the domain master browser will respond to the query. The master browser then contacts the domain master browser to exchange browse lists.

Browsing by Using WINS

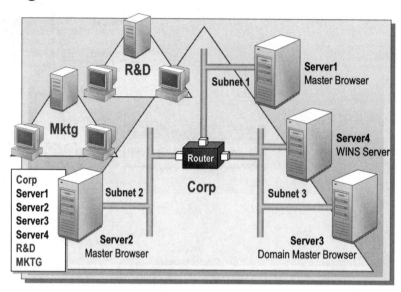

WINS resolves NetBIOS name broadcast problems by dynamically registering a computer's NetBIOS name and IP address and storing them in the WINS database. When WINS clients communicate with TCP/IP hosts across subnets, the destination host's IP address is retrieved from the database rather than by using a broadcast.

WINS improves the mechanism of collecting domain or workgroup names, because a domain master browser running as a WINS client periodically queries the WINS server for a list of all of the domains listed in the WINS database.

Note The list of domains that is obtained by using a WINS query contains only the domain names and their corresponding IP addresses. It does not include the names of the master browsers from which the WINS records originated.

The main benefit of this process is that the domain master browser for a given domain now has a compete list of all master browsers for all domains, including all master browsers for other domains that are on remote subnets. To build a complete list without using WINS, there must be a master browser that belongs to the same domain as the domain master browser on every subnet.

Microsoft®
Training &
Certification

Appendix B: IP Addressing Basics

Contents

Overview

- **What Is an IP Address?**
- **Network ID and Host ID**
- **Converting IP Addresses from Binary to Decimal**
- **Address Classes**
- **Address Class Summary**
- **Addressing Guidelines**
- **Assigning Network IDs**
- **Assigning Host IDs**
- **What Is a Subnet Mask?**

Using Transmission Control Protocol/Internet Protocol (TCP/IP) requires that an IP address be provided for each computer, either automatically by Microsoft® Windows® 2000, dynamically through the Dynamic Host Configuration Protocol (DHCP) service, or statically by using an IP address that you have obtained from your Internet service provider (ISP).

Objectives

At the end of this module, you will be able to:

- Identify the network identifier (ID) and host ID in a class A, B, or C IP address.

- Distinguish between a valid and invalid class A, B, or C IP address.

- Identify the network components that require an IP address.

- Describe subnetting.

What Is an IP Address?

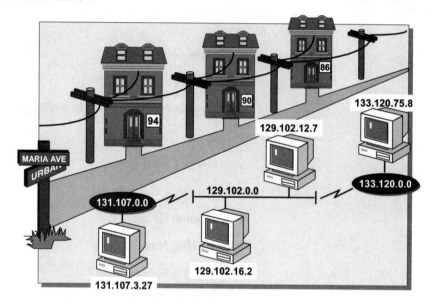

Each TCP/IP host is identified by a logical IP address. A unique IP address is required for each host and network component that communicates by using TCP/IP.

The IP address identifies a system's location on the network in the same way that a street address identifies a house on a city block. Just as a street address must identify a unique residence, an IP address must be globally unique and have a uniform format.

Network ID

Each IP address defines the network ID and host ID. The network ID identifies the systems that are located on the same physical segment. All systems on the same physical segment must have the same network ID. The network ID must be unique to the internetwork.

Host ID

The host ID identifies a workstation, server, router, or other TCP/IP host within a segment. The address for each host must be unique to the network ID.

Network ID and Host ID

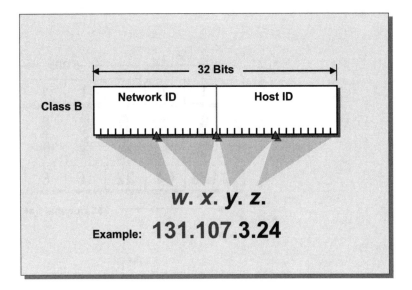

Each IP address is 32 bits long and is composed of four 8-bit fields, called *octets*. Octets are separated by periods. The octet represents a decimal number in the range 0–255. This format is called *dotted decimal notation*. The following is an example of an IP address in binary and dotted decimal formats.

Binary format	Dotted decimal notation
10000011 01101011 00000011 00011000	131.107.3.24

Converting IP Addresses from Binary to Decimal

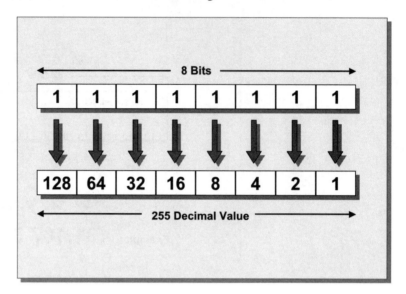

Each bit position in an octet has an assigned decimal value. A bit that is set to 0 always has a zero value.

A bit that is set to 1 can be converted to a decimal value. The low-order bit represents a decimal value of one. The high-order bit represents a decimal value of 128. The highest decimal value of an octet is 255—that is, when all bits are set to 1.

Converting Bits From Binary to Decimal

The following table shows how the bits in one octet are converted from binary code to a decimal value.

Binary code	Bit values	Decimal value
00000000	0	0
00000001	1	1
00000011	1+2	3
00000111	1+2+4	7
00001111	1+2+4+8	15
00011111	1+2+4+8+16	31
00111111	1+2+4+8+16+32	63
01111111	1+2+4+8+16+32+64	127
11111111	1+2+4+8+16+32+64+128	255

Practice

1. Convert the following binary numbers to decimal format.

Binary value	Decimal value
10001011	

2. Convert the following decimal values to binary format.

Decimal value	Binary value
250	

Tip Use the calculator (scientific view) in the **Accessories** group to convert decimal format to binary format, and vice versa.

Address Classes

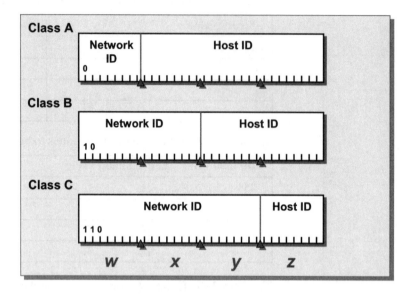

The Internet community has defined five IP address classes to accommodate networks of varying sizes. TCP/IP in Windows 2000 supports class A, B, and C addresses assigned to hosts. The class of address defines which bits are used for the network ID and which bits are used for the host ID. It also defines the possible number of networks and the number of hosts per network.

The following chart shows the network and host ID fields for class A, B, and C IP addressing:

Class	IP address	Network ID	Host ID
A	*w.x.y.z*	*w*	*x.y.z*
B	*w.x.y.z*	*w.x*	*y.z*
C	*w.x.y.z*	*w.x.y*	*z*

Class A

Class A addresses are assigned to networks with a very large number of hosts. The high-order bit in a class A address is always set to zero. The next seven bits (completing the first octet) complete the network ID. The remaining 24 bits (the last three octets) represent the host ID. This allows for 126 networks and approximately 17 million hosts per network.

Class B

Class B addresses are assigned to medium-sized to large-sized networks. The two high-order bits in a class B address are always set to binary 1 0. The next 14 bits (completing the first two octets) complete the network ID. The remaining 16 bits (last two octets) represent the host ID. This allows for 16,384 networks and approximately 65,000 hosts per network.

Class C

Class C addresses are used for small local area networks (LANs). The three high-order bits in a class C address are always set to binary 1 1 0. The next 21 bits (completing the first three octets) complete the network ID. The remaining 8 bits (last octet) represent the host ID. This allows for approximately 2 million networks and 254 hosts per network.

Class D

Class D addresses are used for multicast group usage. A multicast group may contain one or more hosts, or none at all. The four high-order bits in a class D address are always set to binary 1 1 1 0. The remaining bits designate the specific group in which the client participates. There are no network or host bits in the multicast operations. Packets are passed to a selected subset of hosts on a network. Only those hosts registered for the multicast address accept the packet. Microsoft uses class D addresses for applications to multicast data to hosts on an internetwork, including Windows Internet Name Service (WINS) and Microsoft NetShow®.

Class E

Class E is an experimental address that is not available for general use; it is reserved for future use. The high-order bits in a class E address are set to 1 1 1 1.

Note   For more information about multicasting, see the white paper *Multicasting* under **Additional Reading** on the Web page on the Student Materials compact disc.

Address Class Summary

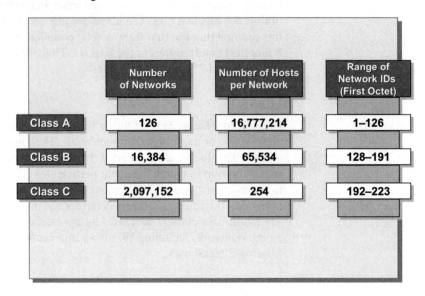

	Number of Networks	Number of Hosts per Network	Range of Network IDs (First Octet)
Class A	126	16,777,214	1–126
Class B	16,384	65,534	128–191
Class C	2,097,152	254	192–223

The graphic in the previous slide summarizes the number of networks and number of hosts per network, and the range of network IDs in class A, B, and C IP addresses. The 32-bit IP addressing scheme presented in the graphic supports a total of 3,720,314,628 hosts.

Addressing Guidelines

- **Network ID Cannot Be 127**
    - 127 is reserved for loopback functions
- **Network ID and Host ID Cannot Be 255 (All Bits Set to 1)**
    - 255 is a broadcast address
- **Network ID and Host ID Cannot Be 0 (All Bits Set to 0)**
    - 0 means "this network only"
- **Host ID Must Be Unique to the Network**

Follow these guidelines when assigning network IDs and host IDs:

- The network ID cannot be 127. This ID is reserved for loopback functions.

- The network ID and host ID cannot be 255 (all bits set to 1). If all bits are set to 1, the address is interpreted as a broadcast rather than a host ID.

- The network ID and host ID bits cannot all be set to 0. If all bits are set to 0, the address is interpreted to mean "this network only."

- The host ID must be unique to the local network ID.

Assigning Network IDs

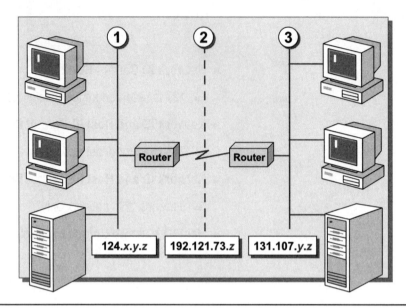

The network ID identifies the TCP/IP hosts that are located on the same physical network. All hosts on the same physical network must be assigned the same network ID to communicate with each other.

If your networks are connected by routers, a unique network ID is required for each wide area connection. For example, in the graphic:

- Networks 1 and 3 represent two routed networks.

- Network 2 represents the wide area network (WAN) connection between the routers. Network 2 requires a network ID so that the interfaces between the two routers can be assigned unique host IDs.

Notes If you plan to connect your network to the Internet, you must obtain the network ID portion of the IP address to guarantee IP network ID uniqueness. For domain name registration and IP network number assignment, see your ISP.

For more information about IP address allocation for private networks, see RFC 1918 under **Additional Reading** on the Web page on the Student Materials compact disc.

Assigning Host IDs

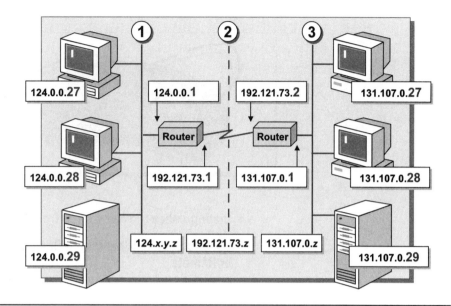

The host ID identifies a TCP/IP host within a network and must be unique to the network ID. All TCP/IP hosts, including interfaces to routers, require unique host IDs.

The host ID of the router interface is the IP address configured as a default gateway to the workstation when TCP/IP is installed. For example, for the host on subnet 1 with an IP address of 124.0.0.27, the IP address of the default gateway is 124.0.0.1.

Valid Host IDs

The following table lists the valid ranges of host IDs for a private internetwork.

Address class	Beginning range	Ending range
Class A	w.0.0.1	w.255.255.254
Class B	$w.x$.0.1	$w.x$.255.254
Class C	$w.x.y$.1	$w.x.y$.254

Suggestions for Assigning Host IDs

There are no rules for assigning valid IP addresses. You can number all TCP/IP hosts consecutively, or you can number them so they can easily be identified—for example:

- Assign host IDs in groups based on host or server type.
- Designate routers by their IP address.

What Is a Subnet Mask?

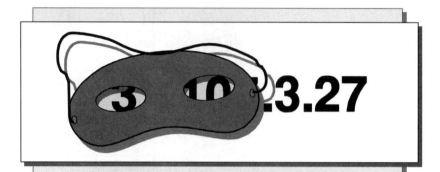

- ■ **Distinguishes the Network ID from the Host ID**
- ■ **Used to Specify Whether the Destination Host Is Local or Remote**

A subnet mask is a 32-bit address used to:

- ■ Block out a portion of the IP address to distinguish the network ID from the host ID.
- ■ Specify whether the destination host's IP address is located on a local network or a remote network.

Each host on a TCP/IP network requires a subnet mask—either a default subnet mask, which is used when a network is not divided into subnets, or a custom subnet mask, which is used when a network is divided into subnets.

Default Subnet Masks

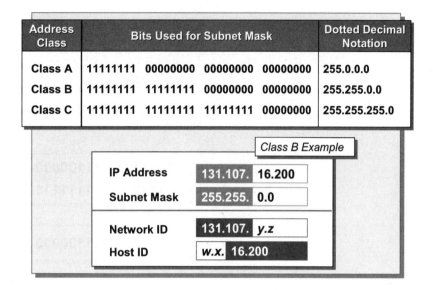

Address Class	Bits Used for Subnet Mask				Dotted Decimal Notation
Class A	11111111	00000000	00000000	00000000	255.0.0.0
Class B	11111111	11111111	00000000	00000000	255.255.0.0
Class C	11111111	11111111	11111111	00000000	255.255.255.0

Class B Example

IP Address	131.107. 16.200
Subnet Mask	255.255. 0.0
Network ID	131.107. *y.z*
Host ID	*w.x.* 16.200

A default subnet mask is used on TCP/IP networks that are not divided into subnets. All TCP/IP hosts require a subnet mask, even on a single-segment network. The default subnet mask that you will use depends on the address class.

All bits that correspond to the network ID are set to 1. The decimal value in each octet is 255.

All bits that correspond to the host ID are set to 0.

Determining the Destination of a Packet

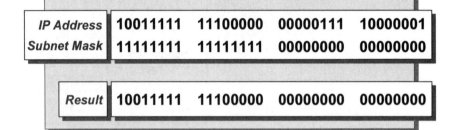

ANDing is the internal process that TCP/IP uses to determine whether a packet is destined for a host on a local network or a remote network.

When TCP/IP is initialized, the host's IP address is ANDed with its subnet mask. Before a packet is sent, the destination IP address is ANDed with the same subnet mask. If both results match, IP knows that the packet belongs to a host on the local network. If the results do not match, the packet is sent to the IP address of an IP router.

To AND the IP address to a subnet mask, TCP/IP compares each bit in the IP address to the corresponding bit in the subnet mask. If both bits are set to 1, the resulting bit is 1. If there is any other combination, the resulting bit is 0.

Bit combination	Result
1 AND 1	1
1 AND 0	0
0 AND 0	0
0 AND 1	0

Practice

AND the following IP addresses to determine whether the destination IP address belongs to a host on a local network or a remote network.

Source (host) IP address	10011001 10101010 00100101 10100011
Subnet mask	<u>11111111 11111111 00000000 00000000</u>
Result	

Destination IP address	11011001 10101010 10101100 11101001
Subnet mask	<u>11111111 11111111 00000000 00000000</u>
Result	

1. Do the results match?

2. Is the destination IP address located on a local or remote network?

Note ANDing is a process that IP uses internally and is not a process that a user would typically do.

◆ Understanding Subnetting

- ■ What Is a Subnet?
- ■ Implementing Subnetting
- ■ What Are Subnet Mask Bits?
- ■ Defining a Subnet Mask
- ■ Subnetting More than One Octet
- ■ Defining Subnet Ids
- ■ Shortcut to Defining Subnet IDs
- ■ Defining Host IDs for a Subnet
- ■ Supernetting

Network IDs and host IDs within an IP address are distinguished by using a subnet mask. Each subnet mask is a 32-bit number that uses consecutive bit groups for identification. The network ID is identified by bit groups that are all set to 1, and the host ID portions of an IP address are identified by bit groups that are all set to 0.

What Is a Subnet?

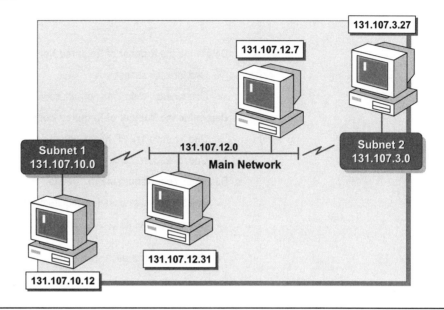

A subnet is a physical segment in a TCP/IP environment that uses IP addresses derived from a single network ID. Typically, an organization acquires one network ID from its ISP.

Dividing the network into subnets requires that each segment use a different network ID or subnet ID. A unique subnet ID is created for each segment by partitioning the bits in the host ID into two parts. One part is used to identify the segment as a unique network, and the other part is used to identify the hosts. This is referred to as *subnetting* or *subnetworking*.

Subnetting Benefits

Organizations use subnetting to apply one network across multiple physical segments. Therefore, you can:

- Mix different technologies, such as Ethernet and token ring.

- Overcome limitations of current technologies, such as exceeding the maximum number of hosts per segment.

- Reduce network congestion by redirecting traffic and reducing broadcasts.

Note   For more information about subnetting, see RFC 950 under **Additional Reading** on the Web page on the Student Materials compact disc.

Implementing Subnetting

- **Determine the Number of Required Network IDs**
  - One for each subnet
  - One for each wide-area network connection
- **Determine the Number of Required Host IDs per Subnet**
  - One for each TCP/IP host
  - One for each router interface
- **Based on Your Requirements, Define**
  - One subnet mask based on requirements
  - A unique subnet ID for each physical segment based on the subnet mask
  - Valid host IDs for each subnet based on the subnet ID

Before you implement subnetting, you need to determine your current requirements and plan for future requirements. Follow these guidelines:

- Determine the number of required network IDs. You require:
  - One network ID for each subnet.
  - One network ID for each wide-area connection.
- Determine the number of required host Ids per subnet.
  - Each TCP/IP host requires at least one IP address.
  - Each router interface requires at least one IP address.
- Based on your requirements, define:
  - One subnet mask for your entire network based on your requirements.
  - A unique subnet ID for each physical segment based on the subnet mask.
  - A range of valid host IDs for each subnet based on the subnet ID.

What Are Subnet Mask Bits?

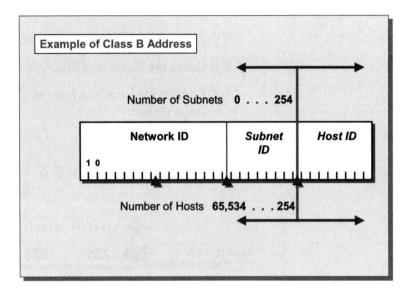

Before you define a subnet mask, you should determine the number of segments and hosts per segment that you will require in the future.

As the graphic in the previous slide illustrates, when more bits are used for the subnet mask, more subnets are available, but fewer hosts are available per subnet. Using more bits than needed will allow for growth in the number of subnets, but will limit the growth in the number of hosts. Using fewer bits than needed will allow for growth in the number of hosts, but will limit the growth in the number of subnets.

Defining a Subnet Mask

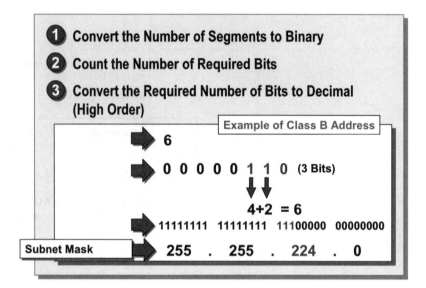

Defining a subnet mask is required if you are dividing your network into subnets. Follow these steps to define a subnet mask:

1. Once you have determined the number of physical segments in your network environment, convert this number to binary format.

2. Count the number of bits required to represent the number of physical segments in binary. For example, if you need six subnets, the binary value is 110. Representing six in binary requires three bits.

3. Convert the required number of bits to decimal format in high order (from left to right). For example, if three bits are required, configure the first three bits of the host ID as the subnet ID. The decimal value for binary 11100000 is 224. The subnet mask is 255.255.224.0 (for a class B address).

Contiguous Mask Bits

Because subnets are defined by the subnet mask, there is nothing to prevent an administrator from using low-order or unordered bits to determine the subnet ID. When subnetting was initially defined in RFC 950, it was recommended that subnet IDs be derived from high-order bits. Today, however, few router vendors support the use of low-order or non-order bits in subnet IDs. Furthermore, it is now a requirement that the subnet ID make use of contiguous, high-order bits of the local address portion of the subnet mask.

Conversion Tables

The following table lists the subnet masks already converted using one octet for class A networks.

Number of subnets	Required number of bits	Subnet mask	Number of hosts per subnet
0	1	Invalid	Invalid
2	2	255.192.0.0	4,194,302
6	3	255.224.0.0	2,097,150
14	4	255.240.0.0	1,048,574
30	5	255.248.0.0	524,286
62	6	255.252.0.0	262,142
126	7	255.254.0.0	131,070
254	8	255.255.0.0	65,534

The following table lists the subnet masks already converted using one octet for class B networks.

Number of subnets	Required number of bits	Subnet mask	Number of hosts per subnet
0	1	Invalid	Invalid
2	2	255.255.192.0	16,382
6	3	255.255.224.0	8,190
14	4	255.255.240.0	4,094
30	5	255.255.248.0	2,046
62	6	255.255.252.0	1,022
126	7	255.255.254.0	510
254	8	255.255.255.0	254

The following table lists the subnet masks already converted using one octet for class C networks.

Required Number of subnets	Required number of bits	Subnet mask	Number of hosts per subnet
Invalid	1	Invalid	Invalid
1–2	2	255.255.255.192	62
3–6	3	255.255.255.224	30
7–14	4	255.255.255.240	14
15–30	5	255.255.255.248	6
31–62	6	255.255.255.252	2
Invalid	7	Invalid	Invalid
Invalid	8	Invalid	Invalid

Subnetting More than One Octet

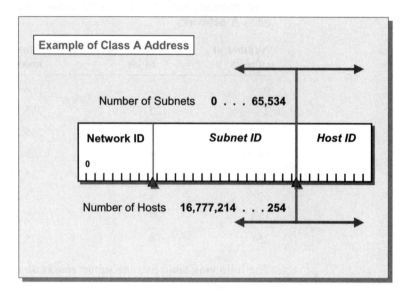

Example of Class A Address

Number of Subnets   0 . . . 65,534

| Network ID | Subnet ID | Host ID |

Number of Hosts   16,777,214 . . . 254

Until this point, we have worked within one octet to define a subnet mask. At times, it may be advantageous to subnet using more than one octet, or more than eight bits.

For example, suppose you are on a team responsible for configuring an intranet for a large corporation. The corporation plans to internally connect its sites that are distributed across Europe, North America, and Asia. This totals approximately 30 geographical locations with almost 1,000 subnets and an average of 750 hosts per subnet.

It is possible to use several class B network IDs and further subnet them. To meet our host requirements per subnet with a class B network address, we will need to use a subnet mask of 255.255.252.0. Further adding our requirement of subnets, we will need at least 16 class B addresses.

However, there is an easier way. Because we are on an intranet, we can use a private network. If we choose to allocate a class A network ID of 10.0.0.0, we can plan for growth and meet our requirements at the same time. Obviously, subnetting only the second octet will not meet our requirements of 1,000 subnets. However, if we subnet both the second octet and a portion of the third octet, we can meet all of our requirements with one network ID.

Network ID	Subnet mask	Subnet mask (binary)
10.0.0.0	255.255.248.0	1111111111 11111111 11111000 00000000

Using 13 bits for the subnet ID in a class A address, we have allocated 8,190 subnets, each with up to 2,046 hosts. We have met our requirements with flexibility for growth.

Defining Subnet IDs

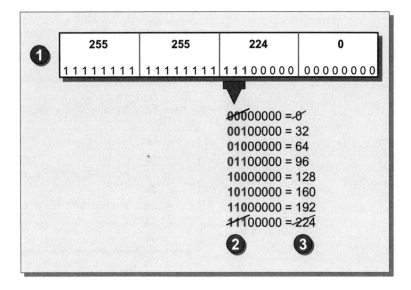

The subnet ID for a physical segment is defined using the same number of host bits as used for the subnet mask. The possible bit combinations are evaluated and then converted to a decimal format. Follow these steps to define a range of subnet IDs for an internetwork:

1. Using the same number of bits as used for the subnet mask, list all possible bit combinations.

2. Cross out values that use all 0s or 1s. All 0s and 1s are invalid IP addresses and network IDs, because all 0s indicate "this network only" and all 1s match the subnet mask.

3. Convert to decimal the subnet ID bits for each subnet. Each decimal value represents a single subnet. This value is used to define the range of host IDs for a subnet.

Special Case Subnet Addresses

Subnet IDs comprising all 0s or all 1s are called *special-case subnet addresses.* A subnet ID of all 1s indicates a subnet broadcast, and a subnet ID of all 0s indicates "this subnet." When subnetting, it is recommended that you do not use these subnet IDs. However, it is possible to use these special-case subnet addresses if they are supported by all routers and hardware on your network. RFC 950 discusses the limitations imposed when using special-case addresses.

Shortcut to Defining Subnet IDs

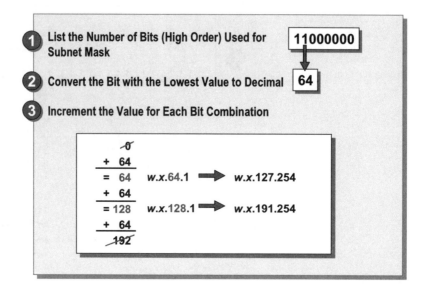

Using the previous method is impractical when you are using more than four bits for your subnet mask because it requires listing and converting many bit combinations. Follow these steps to define a range of subnet IDs:

1. List the number of bits (in high order) used for the subnet ID. For example, if two bits are used for the subnet mask, the binary octet is 11000000.

2. Convert the bit with the lowest value to decimal format. This is the increment value to determine each subnet. For example, if you use two bits, the lowest value is 64.

3. Starting with zero, increment the value for each bit combination until the next increment is 256.

Tip If you know the number of bits you need, you can raise two to the power of the bit, and then subtract two to determine the possible bit combinations.

Determining the Number of Valid Subnets

To determine the number of valid subnets:

1. Convert the number of bits used for the subnet ID to low order.

2. Convert the low order binary number to decimal format.

3. Subtract one.

Defining Host IDs for a Subnet

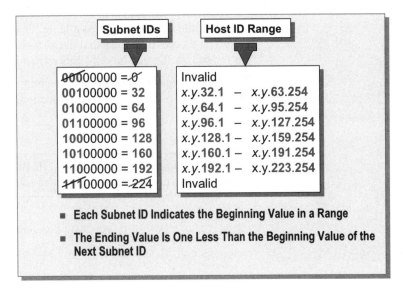

- **Each Subnet ID Indicates the Beginning Value in a Range**
- **The Ending Value Is One Less Than the Beginning Value of the Next Subnet ID**

The result of each incremented value indicates the beginning of a range of host IDs for a subnet. If you increment the value one additional time, you can determine the end of the range (one less than the subnet mask).

The following table shows the valid range of host IDs on a class B subnet using three bits for the subnet mask.

Bit values	Decimal value	Beginning range value	Ending range value
00000000	0	Invalid	Invalid
00100000	32	x.y.32.1	x.y.63.254
01000000	64	x.y.64.1	x.y.95.254
01100000	96	x.y.96.1	x.y.127.254
10000000	128	x.y.128.1	x.y.159.254
10100000	160	x.y.160.1	x.y.191.254
11000000	192	x.y.192.1	x.y.223.254
11100000	224	Invalid	Invalid

Determining the Number of Host per Subnet

To determine the number of hosts per subnet:

1. Calculate the number of bits available for the host ID. For example, if you are given a class B address that uses 16 bits for the network ID and two bits for the subnet ID, you have 14 bits remaining for the host ID.

2. Convert the binary host ID bits to decimal. For example, 11111111111111 in binary is converted to 16,383 in decimal format.

3. Subtract one.

Tip   If you know the number of host ID bits that you need, you can raise two to the power of the number of host ID bits, and then subtract two.

Supernetting

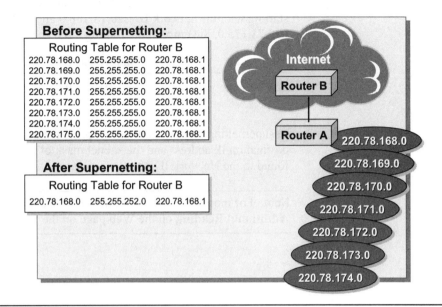

Before Supernetting:

Routing Table for Router B		
220.78.168.0	255.255.255.0	220.78.168.1
220.78.169.0	255.255.255.0	220.78.168.1
220.78.170.0	255.255.255.0	220.78.168.1
220.78.171.0	255.255.255.0	220.78.168.1
220.78.172.0	255.255.255.0	220.78.168.1
220.78.173.0	255.255.255.0	220.78.168.1
220.78.174.0	255.255.255.0	220.78.168.1
220.78.175.0	255.255.255.0	220.78.168.1

After Supernetting:

Routing Table for Router B		
220.78.168.0	255.255.252.0	220.78.168.1

To prevent the depletion of network IDs, Internet authorities devised a scheme called *supernetting*. In opposition to subnetting, supernetting borrows bits from the network ID and masks them as the host ID for more efficient routing. For example, rather than allocating a Class B network ID to an organization that has 2,000 hosts, the American Registry for Internet Numbers (ARIN) allocates a range of eight Class C network IDs. Each class C network ID accommodates 254 hosts for a total of 2,032 host IDs.

Classless Inter-Domain Routing

While this technique helps conserve Class B network IDs, it creates a new problem. Using conventional routing techniques, the routers on the Internet now must have an additional seven entries in their routing tables to route IP packets to the organization. To prevent overwhelming the Internet routers, a technique called *Classless Inter-Domain Routing* (CIDR) is used to collapse the eight entries used in the above graphic to a single entry corresponding to all of the class C network IDs used by that organization.

Allocating Network IDs

To express the situation in which eight class C network IDs are allocated starting with the network ID 220.78.168.0 and ending with network ID 220.78.175.0, the entry in the routing table becomes:

Network ID	Subnet mask	Subnet mask (binary)
220.78.168.0	255.255.248.0	1111111111 11111111 11111000 00000000

In supernetting, the destination of a packet is determined by ANDing the destination IP address and the subnet mask of the routing entry. If a match is found to the Network ID, the route is used.

Note For more information about CIDR, see RFC 1518 and RFC 1519 under **Additional Reading** on the Web page on the Student Materials compact disc.

Microsoft®
Training &
Certification

Appendix C: Commonly Used Port Numbers

Contents

Port Assignments for Commonly Used Services

There are many services associated with the Microsoft® Windows® 2000 operating system. These services may require more than one Transmission Control Protocol (TCP) or User Datagram Protocol (UDP) port for the service to be functional. The following table shows the default ports that each service uses.

Service Name	UDP	TCP
Browsing datagram responses of NetBIOS over TCP/IP (NetBT)	138	
Browsing requests of NetBT	137	
Client/Server Communication		135
Common Internet File System (CIFS)	445	139, 445
Content Replication Service		560
Cybercash Administration		8001
Cybercash Coin Gateway		8002
Cybercash Credit Gateway		8000
Distributed Component Object Model (DCOM) (SCM uses UDP/TCP to dynamically assign ports for DCOM)	135	135
Domain Name System (DNS) client to server lookup (varies)	53	53
DNS Administration		139
Dynamic Host Configuration Protocol (DHCP) client		67
DHCP Manager		135
DHCP server		68
Exchange Administrator		135
Exchange Server 5.0		
File shares name lookup	137	
File shares session		139
File Transfer Protocol (FTP)		21
FTP-data		20
Hypertext Transfer Protocol (HTTP)		80
HTTP-Secure Sockets Layer (SSL)		443
Internet Information Services (IIS)		80
Internet Key Exchange (IKE)	500	
Internet Message Access Protocol (IMAP)		143
IMAP (SSL)		993
Internet Protocol Security (IPSec) Authentication Header (AH)		
IPSec Encapsulating Security Payload (ESP)		
Internet Relay Chat (IRC)		531
ISPMOD (SBS 2nd tier DNS registration wizard)		1234
Kerberos de-multiplexer		2053
Kerberos klogin		543
Kerberos kpasswd (v5)	464	464

(continued)

Service Name	UDP	TCP
Kerberos krb5	88	88
Kerberos kshell		544
Layer Two Tunneling Protocol (L2TP)	1701	
Lightweight Directory Access Protocol (LDAP)		389
LDAP (SSL)		636
Login Sequence	137, 138	139
Macintosh, File Services (AFP/IP)		548
Membership DPA		568
Membership MSN		569
Message transfer agent (MTA) - X.400 over TCP/IP		102
Microsoft Chat client to server		6667
Microsoft Chat server to server		6665
Microsoft Message Queue Server	1801	1801
Microsoft Message Queue Server	3527	135, 2101
Microsoft Message Queue Server		2103, 2105
NetBT datagrams	138	
NetBT name lookups	137	
NetBT service sessions		139
NetLogon	138	
NetMeeting Audio Call Control		1731
NetMeeting H.323 call setup		1720
NetMeeting H.323 streaming RTP over UDP	Dynamic	
NetMeeting Internet Locator Server (ILS)		389
NetMeeting RTP audio stream	Dynamic	
NetMeeting T.120		1503
NetMeeting User Location Service		522
Network Load Balancing	2504	
Network News Transport Protocol (NNTP)		119
NNTP (SSL)		563
Outlook (see for ports)		
Pass Through Verification	137, 138	139
Point-to-Point Tunneling Protocol (PPTP) control		1723
PPTP data		
Post Office Protocol version 3 (POP3)		110
POP3 (SSL)		995
Printer sharing name lookup	137	
Printer sharing session		139

(continued)

Service Name	UDP	TCP
Remote Authentication Dial-In User Service (RADIUS) authentication (Routing and Remote Access)	1645 or 1812	
RADIUS accounting (Routing and Remote Access)	1646 or 1813	
Remote Install TFTP		69
Remote procedure call (RPC)		135
RPC client fixed port session queries		1500
RPC client using a fixed port session replication		2500
RPC session ports		Dynamic
RPC user manager, service manager, port mapper		135
Service Control Manager (SCM) used by DCOM	135	135
Simple Mail Transfer Protocol (SMTP)		25
Simple Network Management Protocol (SNMP)	161	
SNMP Trap	162	
SQL Named Pipes encryption over other protocols name lookup	137	
SQL RPC encryption over other protocols name lookup	137	
SQL session		139
SQL session		1433
SQL session		1024 - 5000
SQL session mapper		135
SQL TCP client name lookup	53	53
Telnet		23
Terminal Services		3389
UNIX Printing		515
Windows Internet Name Service (WINS) Manager		135
WINS NetBT name service	137	
WINS Proxy	137	
WINS Registration		137
WINS Replication		42
X400		102

Notes

Notes

Notes

Notes

Notes

Notes

Notes

Notes

Notes

Notes

Notes

Notes

MSM2153BCPCW/C90-02016